HS

The
COWKEEPER'S WISH
A GENEALOGICAL JOURNEY

TRACY KASABOSKI &
KRISTEN DEN HARTOG

Douglas & McIntyre

Douglas and McIntyre (2013) Ltd.
P.O. Box 219, Madeira Park, BC, VON 2HO
www.douglas-mcintyre.com

Photos courtesy of the authors' family collection except where otherwise noted.
Edited by Derek Fairbridge
Text design by Carleton Wilson
Jacket design by Anna Comfort O'Keeffe
Printed in Canada

Canada

Canada Council   Conseil des Arts
for the Arts   du Canada

BRITISH COLUMBIA
ARTS COUNCIL
An agency of the Province of British Columbia

Douglas and McIntyre (2013) Ltd. acknowledges the support of the Canada Council for the Arts,
which last year invested $153 million to bring the arts to Canadians throughout the country. We also
gratefully acknowledge financial support from the Government of Canada and from the Province
of British Columbia through the BC Arts Council and the Book Publishing Tax Credit.

LIBRARY AND ARCHIVES CANADA CATALOGUING IN PUBLICATION

Kasaboski, Tracy, author
    The cowkeeper's wish : a genealogical journey / by Tracy
Kasaboski and Kristen den Hartog.

Includes bibliographical references.
Issued in print and electronic formats.
ISBN 978-1-77162-202-8 (hardcover).--ISBN 978-1-77162-203-5
(HTML)

    1. Kasaboski, Tracy--Family. 2. Den Hartog, Kristen,
1965- --Family. 3. Deverill family. 4. Canada--Genealogy.
I. Den Hartog, Kristen, 1965-, author II. Title.

CS89.K38 2018   929.20971   C2018-902184-5
                                     C2018-902185-3

*For Mom, for inspiring our curiosity,
and in memory of Bill and Doris.*

"Don't forget to remember."
Joe Deverill, April 1923.

CONTENTS

St. Saviour, Southwark, depicted in Charles Booth Poverty Map, Sheet 9.
Adapted from map detail courtesy of Charles Booth's London, LSE Library.

THE STREETS ARE COLOURED ACCORDING TO THE GENERAL CONDITION OF THE INHABITANTS, AS UNDER:—

Lowest class. Vicious, semi-criminal. | Very poor, casual. Chronic want. | Poor. 18s. to 21s. a week for a moderate family. | Mixed. Some comfortable, others poor. | Fairly comfortable. Good ordinary earnings. | Middle class. Well-to-do. | NIL Upper-middle and Upper classes. Wealthy.

Whitechapel depicted in Charles Booth Poverty Map, Sheet 5.

Adapted from map detail courtesy of Charles Booth's London, LSE Library.

PROLOGUE

There's never a beginning to any family story, but it's tempting, scrolling through census documents and church registers and adding names and dates to a chart, to continue backward in pursuit of one, as if it might be found. Each discovery – an entry on a census that reveals a missing sibling, a marriage certificate that records the maiden name of a wife – is like a small light illuminating an otherwise dark pathway, and the searcher is beckoned on, rarely stopping to peer into the gloaming where the real treasure lies.

As the searcher makes her journey into the past, tracing yet another generation or growing her tree by a branch, it may occur to her that what she has gathered are clues, and that the part that matters, the story, has yet to be told. For even the most ordinary family has its story, with twists and turns unapparent on the surface, and if she looks hard enough, and probes simple facts, forgotten lives emerge, becoming more vibrant with each new detail. When the broader scope of world history is allowed to permeate the tale, the backdrop gains colour and texture, until the searcher can almost smell the dank odour, taste the bitter brew, or feel the chill air of the past. Then she can claim to know something of the story, and can perhaps see the path that led from there to where she is now.

What follows is the result of a similar journey. This tale picks up its thread more than a century and a half ago when a cowkeeper from Wales tries to better his lot. It wends its way forward through work-houses and asylums and war, accompanied by brass-band musicians, suffragettes and philanthropists, coming at last to the cowkeeper's great-granddaughter, an ocean and an era away.

PART ONE

In Darkest London
1840s–1913

These formal portraits of cowkeeper Benjamin Jones and his wife, Margaret Davies, likely taken in the 1860s when photography became affordable for the working class, disguise the fact that the couple lived amid grinding poverty. Most people owned "Sunday best" with threadbare sleeves and mending invisible to the camera's eye.

Jones Family Tree

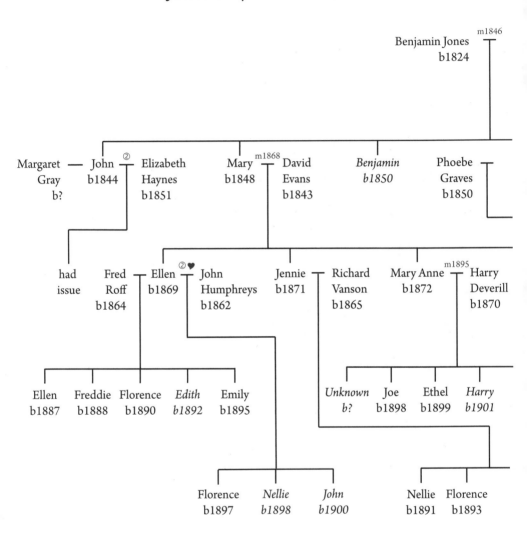

Benjamin Jones ^m1846
b1824

Margaret — John ② Elizabeth | Mary ^m1868 David | *Benjamin* | Phoebe
Gray b1844 Haynes | b1848 Evans | *b1850* | Graves
b? b1851 | b1843 | | b1850

had | Fred — Ellen ②♥ John | Jennie — Richard | Mary Anne ^m1895 Harry
issue | Roff b1869 Humphreys | b1871 Vanson | b1872 Deverill
| b1864 b1862 | b1865 | b1870

Ellen | Freddie | Florence | *Edith* | Emily | *Unknown* | Joe | Ethel | *Harry*
b1887 | b1888 | b1890 | *b1892* | b1895 | *b?* | b1898 | b1899 | *b1901*

Florence | *Nellie* | *John* | Nellie | Florence
b1897 | *b1898* | *b1900* | b1891 | b1893

Margaret Davies
b1821

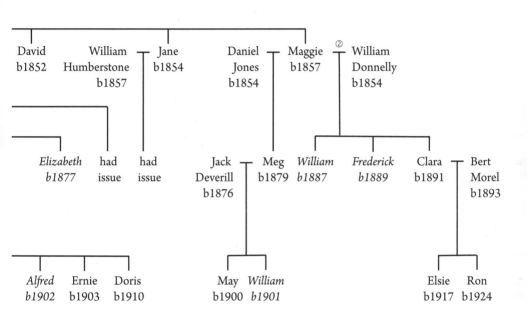

David
b1852

William
Humberstone
b1857

Jane
b1854

Daniel
Jones
b1854

Maggie
b1857

② William
Donnelly
b1854

Elizabeth
b1877

had
issue

had
issue

Jack
Deverill
b1876

Meg
b1879

William
b1887

Frederick
b1889

Clara
b1891

Bert
Morel
b1893

Alfred
b1902

Ernie
b1903

Doris
b1910

May
b1900

William
b1901

Elsie
b1917

Ron
b1924

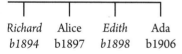

Richard
b1894

Alice
b1897

Edith
b1898

Ada
b1906

Italics denote infant and child deaths

♥ denotes informal union

② denotes second relationship

b indicates born

m indicates marriage

Bits of Ragged Laundry and Wide-Eyed Dossers

Sometime in the early 1840s, a young, as yet unmarried couple left coastal Wales with their dairy cows and set out for London, climbing into the Welsh hills and following pebbled paths and muddied cart tracks. It was a journey of some weeks, made to the tinny clank of cow bells and with the dust of the road thick on their boots. Benjamin Jones was twenty or so and Margaret Davies two years older. Each night they slept beneath the cart that carried their few possessions, and each morning they resumed the trek that surely seemed endless, but with every step they put distance between themselves and the hard rural existence they sought to escape. Ahead was London, with its promise of opportunity.

They settled on Red Cross Street in the Borough of Southwark. Directly to the north was the murky water of the Thames and beautiful St. Paul's Cathedral on the opposite side; to the west, where the Thames curved and changed direction, was the bridge that led to Westminster Abbey and Buckingham Palace, newly renovated as the home for a young Queen Victoria. While physically close to these places, Benjamin and Margaret's new neighbourhood, known simply as the Borough then, was a world away, and a startling change from Wales, too. But though the new life could not have felt less like the old, Red Cross Street housed many other Welsh migrants, all living in grinding poverty. Benjamin's cows were kept in the yard, and later – so the crumbling land tax ledgers tell us – in sheds he rented in alleys that branched off Red Cross. Faraway Aberaeron, their village in Wales, had green open spaces, animals in their pastures, fishing boats on sparkling water, lush vegetation. In the Borough, if you touched a leaf, your finger came away dirty. Benjamin and Margaret had left Wales to escape poverty, but as countless newcomers to the city discovered, it was as much an urban as a rural disease. Here in the Borough, it was endemic.

The home on Red Cross Street sat on the dividing line between the parishes of St. Saviour's and St. George the Martyr, in the heart of Charles Dickens's London. As a child, Dickens himself had lived just steps south for a time, on Lant Street, so he knew the area first-hand. His Little Dorrit was married at St. George the Martyr Church, however fictitiously, and the infamous St. George's Workhouse was said to be the model he'd used while writing *Oliver Twist* in the 1830s – though other workhouses made that same claim, as if it was something to boast about. Commonly referred to as the Mint Street workhouse, St. George's sat near the bottom of Red Cross, its walls hugging the street, its rooms full of people who depended on England's Poor Law system for their basic needs. Reformed in 1834, the system was structured so that each area, or union, was responsible for its own poor and was funded by taxes paid by members of the middle and upper classes, many of whom resented having to support people who couldn't look after themselves. A few years before Benjamin and Margaret's arrival in London, the laws were amended so that people in need couldn't get direct handouts from the parish, but had to enter the local workhouse and perform manual labour in exchange for food, clothing and shelter. And there were plenty of people down and out in the Borough.

In dairyman Benjamin's time, the area was still known as one of the city's "black holes" – among the most ragged places in all of "Ragged London," the nickname coined by contemporary journalist John Hollingshead. "It has scores of streets that are rank and steaming with vice; streets where unwashed, drunken, fishy-eyed women hang by dozens out of the windows, beckoning to the passers-by. It has scores of streets filled with nothing but thieves, brown, unwholesome tramps' lodging-houses, and smoky receptacles for stolen goods…The whole district is far below the level of high-water mark in the river, and the sewage in many places bubbles up through the floors. The courts and alleys branch off on either side at every step, leading into endless mazes of low, sooty passages, squares, and 'rents.'"

The Borough brimmed with the dead as well as the living. It held disused plague pits that had long ago been filled in and built on, as well as overstuffed hospital graveyards and church cemeteries. Just north of the Joneses' house, the Cross Bones graveyard served as St. Saviour's "poor ground," where the cost of burials was a pittance or was entirely covered by the parish. Not even the poor wanted the shame of having their dead buried here, but frequently there was no alternative. For more than two hundred years, the spot had been a regular dumping ground for bodies no one claimed, or for the most destitute members of the parish who could afford nothing more. Long before that, the ground had been used for "low women who frequented the neighbourhood." Cadavers were buried in layers until no more than eighteen inches of earth hid them from the surface. In time it was estimated that the small plot of land held some fifteen thousand bodies, though the cemetery was unconsecrated and there are no definitive records of who lies there. A high brick wall surrounded the graveyard, topped with shards of glass, but it didn't deter the resurrection men. Unscrupulous sorts who visited at night, they quickly unearthed the newly buried corpses, carted them to hospitals close by and sold them for medical research. Eventually Cross Bones was closed to further burials, like many of London's overcharged grounds. The final report on the subject stated that Cross Bones was "crowded with dead, and many fragments of undecayed bones, some even entire, are mixed up with the earth of the mounds over the graves." While it was "a convenient place for getting rid of the dead, ... it bears no mark of ever having been set apart as a place of Christian sepulture." And yet it meant something to the people of the Borough, whose friends and relatives were buried there.

With the closing of Cross Bones and churchyard cemeteries, death, or at least its by-product, moved out of Benjamin and Margaret's neighbourhood to cemeteries at the city's edges, where there was still space to accommodate the growing number of bodies. The spectre of death would always hover, but life in the street carried on. The dairy couple had children who would go on to marry other Welsh migrants, and soon there were relatives up and down Red Cross Street, in one parish or the other, in pockets that seemed like tiny, transplanted Welsh villages, if not for the mayhem and the grime.

When the local "inspector of nuisances," John Errington, did his rounds on Red Cross Street in autumn of 1855, he declared a number of houses north of Benjamin and Margaret's unfit for human habitation. They were in a "foul and filthy state," London's *Morning Post* reported. "The cess pool was full, and the soil was running about." The local doctor supported Errington's charges and said that, inside and out, the houses were "deplorable...The stench was so great as to be injurious to the health of the inhabitants." Farther south, Benjamin's cowsheds did not escape Inspector Errington's critical eye. "Mr. Jones, cowkeeper of Red Cross Street, was also summoned under the same act," the paper stated, "for allowing a quantity of dung and filthy matter to accumulate on his premises."

The cows Benjamin kept lived in cramped quarters, and as far as the local Medical Officer of Health was concerned, they did not belong in the city. The sheds throughout the area were makeshift and unclean, and Benjamin's were obviously no exception. Though sanitary regulations grew stricter as the years went on, the cowkeepers were typically slow to improve – not just careless, the officer claimed, but often "thoroughly ignorant." In many of his annual reports, he longed for the day that cows would no longer be kept in the city. "Sure I am that the existence of many thousands of feet of almost stagnant foul liquid, slowly running from cow-sheds and piggeries, cannot be right in close neighbourhoods... The first dairy authority agrees that 'Hot, close cow-houses are disgraceful affairs.'"

But Benjamin carried on with his trade all of his working life. He knew the secret of milking quickly and thoroughly, and taught his sons to do the same, hoping in time to pass the business down, despite the public-health controversy. His family helped deliver the milk through the streets, carrying shoulder-yokes that held barrels, and later using horse and cart.

Like all cowkeepers, he did constant battle with chronic illnesses that affected his stock, pleuropneumonia and foot-and-mouth disease, as well as the dreaded rinderpest, an infectious disease that brought fever, sores, diarrhea and finally death to the animals on which he depended. In 1865, when Benjamin and Margaret's children were beginning to make families of their own, this insidious affliction rushed so quickly through the whole of Britain that panic spread alongside the virus. Ten, then twenty, then fifty thousand cows perished. In the end, roughly 80 percent of the cattle in London alone died or were slaughtered due to rinderpest, though it was difficult to come up with an accurate figure because cowkeepers were reluctant to report problems among their herds, and were also swift to be rid of an animal that showed any sign of illness. While unscrupulous sorts had always diluted their milk, the practice became more common as supply dwindled, though the filth of the water brought with it the danger of cholera, dysentery and typhoid fever. Before long, and with somewhat dark humour, the water pump was nicknamed "the cow with the iron tail." The Medical Officer of Health seethed about the rinderpest outbreak, but pointed out that it shouldn't have surprised anyone. The cowsheds were surrounded by dung heaps, he said, and the cattle drank from ponds contaminated by the dung. Calves and cows were kept in a "highly artificial state of existence," which left them weak and unable to resist disease. If cowkeeping was outlawed in the city, he said, there would be no need for slaughterhouses either, and he lamented the sight of droves of cattle moving toward these places through the busy streets. The animals were "foot sore and weary," he said, "exhibiting symptoms of suffering painful to behold."

Many of London's cowkeepers never recovered from the tragedy; Benjamin did. Was he shrewd, or lucky? Or did the workhouse looming down the street motivate him? Scores in the neighbourhood entered that stable for human beings once they became desperate enough. Just that September, *The Lancet* medical journal had reported on the "mischievous state of things" in the Mint Street workhouse, which served as both home for the needy and infirmary for the ill. It was well known that if you didn't enter the Mint Street workhouse with an illness of some kind, you'd probably catch one during your stay. There were fourteen sick wards scattered throughout the building, and lately there'd been one outbreak after another inside this "manufactory of fever," just as the cows were dying outside. The "pauper nurses," despite their brown checked uniforms, were not trained in nursing and worked for a trifling wage that included tea, meat and beer. In condemning the place, *The Lancet* wrote:

> The tramp ward for the women is a miserable room, foul and dirty, with imperfect light and ventilation, the floor being simply bedded with straw. Into this open sty the women are passed in, often with little or no clothing; and there, in considerable numbers, they pass the night. There being no watercloset attached, a large can or tub is placed in the room. This is the sole accommodation which the apartment possesses. The master informed us that there is no matron to look after the women, and that the place was really "a den of horrors"... After a very limited term of occupancy of this place, the women were struck down with fever, the place proving a perfect "fever bed"... It is our duty to condemn this workhouse, which ought to be removed, and one built better adapted to fulfill its duties to the poor and sick of the neighbourhood.

But there it stood, year after year, a place of last resort for Benjamin and Margaret, and so, in that sense, an inspiration too. If a family entered, the mother and father were separated, and the children were sent on to a pauper school. Admission ledgers were full of harsh notations that never told the full story of families broken this way: "Father in house," "deserted by Mother," "foundling left in the... public house, Boro Road." If he wanted to keep his clan from getting pulled into that Poor Law spiral, Benjamin needed to earn enough to support them. Whatever came, he and Margaret must defeat it. And against all odds, he seems to have withstood the industry's challenges, for alongside Benjamin's name on the scant family documents that surface – the birth and marriage records of his children, the cyclical census reports and finally his death certificate – are the words *cowkeeper* or *dairyman* or *milkman*.

In an 1860s photograph, Benjamin is burly and bearded, with dark, somewhat unkempt hair. He's plumper than you'd imagine a poor man to be, and his face looks friendly enough as he gazes straight at the camera. He looks uncomfortable in his good clothes: a tight, shiny vest with straining buttons, an open frock coat that can't possibly close around his stout body but may once have done so nicely, as on the day he married Margaret. Seated, he holds a cane between his legs, and a top hat rests, brim up, on the table beside him. In the companion photo, his wife looks similarly constrained by her outfit, a plain gown that spills to the floor. Her glossy hair is parted in the centre and pulled back from her broad face so that not a tendril escapes to soften her expression. She averts her eyes from the photographer's lens and gives little more for posterity than her signature does: "x" for the mark of Margaret Jones nee Davies, conveying only that she couldn't read or write. However elusive, she is the one who passed down Welsh lullabies carried from her own childhood.

Not long after the rinderpest disaster and the sumptuous Windsor Castle wedding of Queen Victoria's son Crown Prince Edward to Alexandra of Denmark, Benjamin and Margaret's daughter Mary wed David Evans in a rather more humble ceremony. The marriage occurred in September 1868 in the crumbling "St. Saviour's folly," an ancient, once-glorious church so badly restored that prominent architect Augustus Pugin had deemed it "as vile a preaching place…as ever disgraced the 19th century." Yet many important family events took place there, from Margaret and Benjamin's wedding in September 1846 on down. If they were like many of their class in the Borough and wider London, though, they didn't attend regular services. An 1851 ecclesiastical census examining British worship habits had found the labouring classes to be by far the largest group that stayed away. Horace Mann, who undertook the study, mused that the poor, relegated to the "free seats" at the back of the church, "cannot enter our religious structures without having pressed upon their notice some memento of their inferiority." Edward Miall, writing around the same time in the weekly newspaper *The Nonconformist*, said of churches like St. Saviour's, "Here in Great Britain we carry our class distinctions into the house of God…The poor man is made to feel that he is a poor man, the rich reminded that he is rich." St. Saviour's loomed on the skyline of the Borough just as it dominated the community in its shadow, running soup kitchens, Sunday schools and missions, and distributing bread, coal and blankets for the poor at Christmas. But despite the church's efforts at philanthropy, few of the working poor like Margaret and Benjamin were tempted out to Sunday morning service on the one day of the week they were able to sleep past dawn. If they'd been at the pub the night before, they were even less inclined to attend. Nor would they want to spend any part of the day in the poor seats when Sunday was the day to visit the barber and relax after a proper family meal. For dairymen like Benjamin, Sunday was little different from any other day, with cows to be fed and milked, and manure to be shovelled, the same tasks he likely performed on the day of daughter Mary's wedding to David Evans.

Like his new in-laws, David had come from a farming family near Aberaeron and now found himself in the thick of the Borough. He arrived sometime around 1865, when London's cows were dying, and worked as a brewer's labourer rather than with Benjamin in the troubled, predominantly Welsh milk industry. The Barclay Perkins Brewery was a few blocks north of the family's Red Cross home, facing the River Thames, between the Borough Market and the road to Southwark Bridge. It was a massive complex that filled the Borough with the smell of hops and steaming grains. Firms the size of Barclay Perkins employed a handful of educated, handsomely paid men who were the brewers, and hundreds of others like David who were the worker bees: the bottle washers and fillers, the dray men and coopers and cellarmen. The grounds were necessarily sprawling and included a wharf, where the beer was shipped for export, and a range of storehouses. There were water reservoirs, a cooperage, buildings where the casks were cleaned and inspected, and sheds to hold the empty casks. There were also brewhouses, and stables for the dray horses that delivered the beer. Sturdy porters hauled goods from a barge at the riverside to the malt warehouse. The men followed each other closely, carrying the sacks up several flights of stairs to the warehouse, and then dumping the contents into bins that were big enough to contain a house, chimney and all. David worked long hours, starting at dawn and continuing until the work was done, usually at least twelve hours later. On Saturdays, he put in a few hours in the afternoon. The work was physical rather than skilled labour, and the men doing it were brawny types whose pay included five or six pints of beer each day.

The aches and pains that came with the job were made bearable by the fact that, year in, year out, there was work at the brewery. Few other manufacturing industries offered such steady employment, but there was always a call for beer. Heading home each night, David passed the pubs that proved this very point, and he likely stopped in for some refreshment himself, the threadbare sleeves of his jacket rubbing a shine on the wood of the bar. These public houses were the centres of their communities, with colourful names like The Moulders Arms, Three Jolly Gardeners, and The World Turned Upside Down. Depending on each publican's efforts, some were dingy, with sawdust on the floors and frosted windows. In others, flowers brightened the bar, and paper doilies danced from the rafters. The glow of these pubs spilled into the street like an invitation, and inside, on a cold night, the rooms were warm with the press of bodies. They were homes away from home, where women shelled peas into their aprons and men argued about the issues of the day. They'd gossip about each other, too, and the goings-on up and down Red Cross Street – the eccentric old lady with the evil black cat; the daft girl who'd married her uncle; and Benjamin Jones, charged for watering down his milk in the middle of a second rinderpest outbreak in the summer of 1877.

Once again, Inspector Errington caught him out. The heading in *The Sanitary Record: A Journal of Public Health* reads "Flagrant Milk Adulteration," and the short piece that follows says that Errington received "great complaints" about the quality of Benjamin's milk from the employees of Welch, Margetson & Co., a menswear factory he regularly supplied. Inspector Errington dutifully went to the establishment and lurked in the office until Benjamin arrived with his can of milk. Errington asked a workman to purchase some milk on his behalf, and once the deed was done he emerged from his hiding place, declared himself and told Benjamin that the sample would be taken to St. Thomas' Hospital for testing. It was found to be 53 percent water. At the hearing, Benjamin denied responsibility. "The defendant said that owing to the market being closed to beasts," the *London Daily News* reported, "he was unable to purchase cows, and being short of milk on the day in question, he purchased three quarts off a man in the street, and believed it to be all right." It was certainly the case that no cattle were being brought in while the rinderpest still flourished, but what involvement Benjamin had in watering the milk, no one can say. The powers that be did not believe him, laid on a hefty fine and declared it "a very bad case."

And yet on he went. By 1881, Benjamin Jones had been in the milk business in Southwark for close to forty years, and together he and his son-in-law David were the breadwinners of this burgeoning family. Covered with climbing hydrangea and Virginia creeper, their cramped, rickety house was like so many others in these old streets, a crooked cobbling of damp brick and clapboard, the windows soot stained and the chimney crumbling. In this residence were housed three generations: Benjamin and Margaret, Mary and David, their daughters Ellen, Jennie, Mary Anne and Elizabeth, and Mary's newly widowed sister Maggie and her baby daughter Meg. David had developed chronic bronchitis, and sometimes his hacking cough kept them all awake at night. There was little privacy for anyone. But it was the same up and down Red Cross Street, where people spilled out of their close quarters on summer evenings to escape the heat and the sticky closeness.

And there was the fog, so thick that people stumbled over curbs, conveyances crashed, and boats ran aground in the river. By Victorian times, burning coal and the smoke of industry that permeated the Borough had turned ordinary fog into a toxic mixture of soot, sulphur and other airborne pollutants, prevalent enough that a pamphlet called *London Fogs* became a curious bestseller. Its author, the meteorologist Francis Albert Rollo Russell, described the fog in painstaking detail and warned of the long-term health effects of such a "removable evil" were it not eradicated. "A London fog is brown, reddish-yellow, or greenish... and produces, when thick, a choking sensation. Instead of diminishing while the sun rises higher, it often increases in density, and some of the most lowering London fogs occur about midday or late in the afternoon. Sometimes the brown masses rise and interpose a thick curtain at a considerable elevation between earth and sky. A white cloth spread out on the ground rapidly turns dirty, and particles of soot attach themselves to every exposed object."

None of this was news to Benjamin and his ilk in the Borough. They sat on their front steps, or in the tiny enclosures between brick wall and garden fence, and in the yards behind their houses laundry formed an endless line from neighbour to neighbour, hanging in the dirty air. The smell was now of hops and cow dung, now of vinegar or the acrid burn of a foundry. This part of the city was home to numerous industries making everything from hats, soap and lead to tallow, beer and stove black. From across the River Thames, one couldn't fail to notice the plethora of smoking chimneys. Some said Southwark was as distinguishable at a distance for these chimneys as London proper was for its church spires.

Of course Southwark had its own spires too. The four pinnacles of St. Saviour's Church had been a Borough landmark for centuries, and when a bolt of lightning struck one of the pinnacles in 1870 and sent it hurtling down, *The Graphic* reported "a terrible crash, and the fall of a ton or two of masonry through the roof, while splinters of stone varying from a pound to a hundredweight were scattered among the stalls of the marketplace below." The once-grand church that had already undergone a botched renovation now looked less dignified than ever. Stained with soot from passing trains, it was increasingly hemmed in by its surroundings – industrial warehouses, Borough Market and the railway lines, and the busy approach to London Bridge. But soon plans for a magnificent transformation began to take shape, spearheaded by an appeal to the community for donations. "Were the church thrown open daily for public inspection," one man wrote in *The Morning Post*, "sympathy would be invited and perhaps stimulated of a material kind." The efforts paid off. Rich and poor responded, with collections taken at Sunday services, and contributions made by Barclay Perkins Brewery and other area businesses. Perhaps even Benjamin was caught up in the spirit of renewal and contributed some of his milk money, feeling a twinge of pride knowing that the church's "sad and yet exquisite beauty" would be restored.

The surrounding streets would wait much longer for significant change. In broader London, though, this was the beginning of a period of enormous transformation, a growth so substantial that the city buzzed with an energy all its own. By the early 1880s, the population had soared past five million, making London the largest city in the world by far – so large that even Londoners didn't know it well, and mostly kept to their own neighbourhoods. Still, there was an awareness of the masses in all corners, and of a rumbling that hinted at social, political and technological change beyond imagining. As the city grew, so did the urge to define it; yet it was in constant flux, and so that much more difficult to characterize. In 1878, the raconteur Augustus Hare roamed the streets with his notebook to create *Walks in London*, which he claimed aimed at "nothing original" but offered a charming account of the city's landmarks interspersed with amusing historical tidbits. "It is very easy to live with eyes open," Hare wrote, "but it is more usual, and a great deal more fashionable, to live with them shut. Scarcely any man in what is usually called 'society' has the slightest idea of what there is to be seen in his own great metropolis, because he never looks, or still more perhaps, because he never inquires."

George Robert Sims's perambulations cut deeper. Sims, who dabbled in all sorts of writing, had a dramatist's interest in crime and abject poverty, and the flair for describing it. In "How the Poor Live," a series of articles published in the paper *The Pictorial World* in 1881, he gave many upper- and middle-class Londoners their first shocking glimpse of the city's slums. He took with him on this "painful journey" the illustrator Frederick Barnard, who sketched sensational images of fat landlords wearing top hats and heavy gold chains, waifs in dark rooms strung with bits of ragged laundry, and wide-eyed "dossers" caught in a policeman's torch beam. Of the Joneses' and Evanses' home turf, Sims wrote: "Scene after scene is the same. Rags, dirt, filth, wretchedness, the same figures, the same faces, the same old story of one room unfit for habitation yet inhabited by eight or nine people, the same complaint of ruinous rent absorbing three-fourths of the toiler's weekly wage, the same shameful neglect by the owner of the property of all sanitary precautions, rotten floors, oozing walls, broken windows, crazy staircases, tileless roofs, and in and around the dwelling-place of hundreds of honest citizens the nameless abominations which could only be set forth were we contributing to the *Lancet* instead of *The Pictorial World*."

Sims's horror aside, the streets he describes must have seemed ordinary to the families who lived there. Benjamin and Margaret were longtime residents of the Borough now, and David Evans had lived with them in Red Cross Street for two decades. His wife Mary and their daughters – Ellen, Jennie, Mary Anne and little Elizabeth – knew the Borough as home rather than a place "awful enough" to be worthy of Sims's inquiries and Barnard's sketches. There were highs and lows. Now and again, when someone important passed through in a flower-laden carriage, people flocked and sang and waved flags as the church bells pealed. When the dignitaries went back across the Thames, the Borough settled again, a city within a city. If you knew nothing different, it had everything you needed: St. George the Martyr and the looming St. Saviour's Church, whose tower got lost in the fog; the High Street and its pharmacy full of coloured liquids in bottles of all sizes; the bustling Borough Market, where Mary and her girls shopped for fruit and vegetables and flowers. In and around Red Cross Street they could visit the butcher and the baker and the shoemaker, the fishmonger, the egg merchant, the rag merchant, the coffeehouse, the greengrocer, and the railway office, if they had anywhere to go. But they didn't. Their whole life was here. And it was a busy life, with a house full of people, clothes to scrub, meals to prepare and cook, and always the water to heat and the dishes to wash, the mattresses to turn, the rugs to beat, the floor to sweep. The house had so many people that it took each of them, working in their various ways, to keep all of them going. But just a year after the 1881 census, which listed eleven people in one small house, the numbers began to dwindle.

It was distressing but not unusual that in a home containing three generations, a young one went first, seemingly setting off a chain of deaths over a few years. In March of 1882, when four-year-old Elizabeth came down with a severe case of whooping cough, her mother Mary might have tried a popular folk remedy: snipping a lock of Elizabeth's hair, tucking it into a slice of bread and feeding it to a passing dog. People still set store by superstition and old wives' tales, even with the

Evelina Hospital for Sick Children right around the corner. It had been built more than a decade earlier by a rich man who'd lost his wife in childbirth. With its spacious wards and out-patient care, it was a godsend for such a poor community. In Elizabeth's case, though, neither old nor new methods saved her. Records show she was admitted to the Evelina, and that Mary was there with her when she died.

Then in 1884, the matriarch, Margaret, died at home, and because she was alone at the time, a coroner's visit was required. The inquest was little more than a meeting held at the pub, with simple questions asked of family and neighbours to determine that there'd been no foul play. In Margaret's case, no evidence of the sort was found. Her death certificate states that she died suddenly, of heart disease, at the age of sixty-three years. A year later, in the gloom of March when the rains seemed endless, David Evans died at just forty-two. "Widow of the deceased" – Mary – "present at death." Cause of death was again heart disease, and the bronchitis that had bothered him for years. Just like Elizabeth, he and Margaret had succumbed to ailments the purported cure-alls could not assuage, despite the claims on the important-looking tins and boxes displayed in the pharmacy: Clarke's World Famed Blood Mixture cleansed the blood from "scrofula, scurvy, and sores of all kinds … Its effects are marvelous." Holloway's Pills "purify the blood, act powerfully yet soothingly on the liver and stomach, giving tone, energy, and vigour to these great main springs of life." Whelpton's Vegetable Purifying Pills cured disorders of the head, chest, liver, bowel, and kidneys, and should therefore "be kept always at hand." And without Eno's Fruit Salt for the prevention of diarrhea – so common in the deaths of children – "the jeopardy of life is immensely increased." The family that had split the seams of this house was rapidly shrinking, but in a time and place of such unrelenting hardship, it was nothing unusual.

A month after David died, one April Friday at two in the morning, a fire broke out at an oil and colourman's shop just north of their house, on Union Street. Such shops specialized in mixing paints, so the gunpowder and casks of oil kept onsite for that purpose quickly ignited and the fire spread rapidly. The shopman and his family, sleeping in the rooms above, were soon woken and trapped by the flames. Neighbours gathered in the street, blankets wrapped around their nightclothes. If Mary and her daughters were there, they'd have seen the horse-drawn fire engine arrive in short order, carrying firefighters with their Spartan helmets, axes holstered at their waists. But it was already too late to lean the ladders against the bricks – flames lashed out of the windows, and heat from the burning oil emanated from the building. When a woman appeared in a third-storey window, neighbours called to her to jump, but she disappeared from view. The smoke curled in the crisp spring air, and the crowd grew thicker, faces lighted by the glow of the fire. And then the woman reappeared. She pushed a feather mattress through the window to the ground, and the crowd called again to her to jump, but instead she lifted a small, startled girl, about five years old, up to the window ledge and dropped her to the mattress below. She slipped away and returned to the window with another girl, this one smaller than the last, crying and clinging to her, refusing to be dropped. But the woman threw the child out and someone held up their arms and caught her. Once more she returned, with the smallest girl yet, and dropped her to the mattress. The voices in the crowd were ragged now, screaming to the woman to save herself. They could see that she was losing strength and having trouble breathing. She tried to push herself from the window, but fell from the frame, and on the way down she struck her head on the shop sign below. She landed head-down, cracking her spine, and though she was rushed to hospital and did regain consciousness, she died soon after.

The woman's name was Alice Ayres. She was sister-in-law to the oil and colourman who owned the shop, and nursemaid to the little girls she had released through the window one by one. Once the blaze was put out, the remains of Alice's sister, the girls' mother, were found inside, along with a son and the oil and colourman himself, holding a locked box of cash, terrified of losing everything he owned. The obvious horror of the family's last moments affected the neighbourhood deeply, and captured the imagination of the larger population as well, fuelling a rumour that as Alice had lain in hospital, Queen Victoria had sent a lady-in-waiting to inquire about her worsening condition.

The event was a tragedy, but also appealed to the Victorian love of melodrama and sentiment. *Reynolds's Weekly Newspaper* called Alice

Ayres "a humble heroine," and asserted that "Such a woman, although only a poor domestic, deserves to be placed among the small but noble army of martyrs to duty." Mourners flocked to the memorial service at St. Saviour's, so many that there was not even standing room left in the church. Those in the back strained to hear the words of the minister, who preached a sermon about heroism. Nearly a thousand coins were raised, and it was said that the money would go toward a memorial window for Alice Ayres when the church was restored to its original splendour. Overnight, she had gone from anonymity to working-class heroine, and in the years to come, White Cross Street, running parallel to Red Cross Street, would be renamed Ayres in her honour. She'd undergone a near canonization, with gilded poems and stories written about her selfless duty and devotion. To the growing number of social reformers, Alice Ayres was an irresistible example of what every woman of the lower class should strive to be: hard-working, loyal and self-sacrificing.

Hers was the kind of tale George Sims would tell, or the type you'd see dramatized at a magic lantern show, where projected images appeared by some mysterious combination of quicklime and flame. The beautiful pictures borne from a shaft of light were set to odes about righteousness. There were whole studios dedicated to producing these spectacles: models photographed on sets with elaborate backdrops, ladies who hand-painted the glass slides with tiny brushes and translucent colours, drawing angels floating beside a dying child's bed, or Jesus in his robes, gazing mournfully upon a group of drunkards. Audiences sat rapt as they watched these illuminations, which seemed a marvel of technology: food for thought and a feast for the eyes all at once. Sometimes there were stunning special effects, such as day fading to night, or a train passing by in the background. The slides were popular with Sunday school children, who saw their favourite nursery rhymes or bible stories set to pictures. But they were big events for adults too. People crowded their church and community halls, sitting shoulder to shoulder and whispering among themselves that the lime and the gases combined could explode if the projectionist wasn't careful. And then the gaslights were dimmed, and the show began.

The story I'm going to tell you
Is truth from beginning to end.
It didn't come under my notice,
It was told me by a friend,
A relation, the wife of my brother,
And the saddest part that's true
Appeared in the Daily Papers,
As dozens such stories do.

The biggest story played out on a much grander stage. In 1887, all England and the British dominion celebrated the Golden Jubilee of Queen Victoria. The accompanying revelry boosted the popularity of a queen who'd become reclusive with widowhood nearly 30 years earlier. In the days preceding the celebration, the papers published all sorts of articles about Victoria, chronicling her childhood, the zigzag of royal deaths that had led to her unexpected coronation at just eighteen, her marriage to her beloved German prince, Albert, their passel of children, and then Albert's death – the queen's "crushing sorrow." In her astonishingly lengthy period of bereavement, the black-cloaked queen was fortunate to have "so willing, affable and indefatigable a deputy at hand as the Prince of Wales," one paper reported, calling Edward the most popular man in England. In reality he was a self-indulgent charmer, a philanderer and a gambler, and a longtime source of worry for the queen. But his frivolous side was only one aspect of his character. While most among the elite regarded the poor as "beings of a totally different order from themselves," Edward held more progressive convictions. In an 1883 speech opening the Royal College of Music, he asserted that music speaks "in different tones, perhaps, but with equal force to the cultivated and the ignorant, to the peer and peasant ... The time has come," he insisted, "when class can no longer stand aloof from class; and that man does his duty best who works most earnestly in bridging over the gulf between different classes which it is the tendency of increased wealth and increased civilisation to widen." What would Benjamin, mucking out the cow stalls, have made of such a statement? Or of the fact that a few years before the jubilee, Edward had joined the Royal Commission on Housing of the Working Class? Removing his gentlemanly garb, he'd pulled on the disguise of a working man, and travelled with a couple of others to some of the city's worst slums. The squalor he'd seen had stunned him. The conditions of the dwellings were "perfectly disgraceful," he later told Parliament, urging "measures of a drastic and thorough character." After decades of Victorian rule, with the queen approaching seventy years of age, people grew increasingly curious about what Edward's reign might bring.

Foreign royalty and leaders came to join in the jubilee festivities, among them Victoria's erratic grandson Prince Wilhelm, who would soon be the German Kaiser, as well as the King of Denmark and "Willy of Greece," as Victoria called him. In her diary, she wrote that Willy was seated next to her at the sumptuous banquet held at Buckingham Palace – "a large family dinner" she called it, and in truth the genealogical maze was dizzying. Willy was the son of the Danish king, whose daughter Alexandra was married to Victoria's son Edward; Alexandra's sister had wed the Russian tsar, and their daughter had married another of Victoria's sons. And on it went. The Supper Room at Buckingham Palace gleamed with gold plate as the gourmet delights emerged: turtle soup, chicken garnished with cocks' combs and cocks' kidneys, sliced *foies gras* with truffles, duckling with peas, haunch of venison, cream rice with cherry juice, and iced puffed pastries. The large table was covered with candles, and the jewels, silverware and crystal glittered at this private celebration for those with an immediate connection to the queen.

Outside, the decorated streets lay waiting for the grand procession, which would take Victoria from Buckingham Palace to Westminster Abbey for the official ceremony. People wandered up and down the route in the twilight, taking in the sights, and knowing that the following day, the crush would be relentless. By morning the multitudes came from every part of the city, and from the towns and villages beyond. Mary Evans and her daughters, along with others from the Borough, may have made the trek across the Thames to the opulent surroundings of Westminster, where miles of terraced scaffolding had been laid out for the spectators, though it wasn't enough to hold the thousands who came. They lined the streets behind neat rows of guards in red jackets;

they gathered on balconies and rooftops. Some shimmied up statues to get a look at the queen rolling by in her open landau. In England's long history, few monarchs had reached the fifty-year mark of their reign, and none in such prosperous times. Six cream-coloured horses pulled the grand lady's carriage along, while her son Edward followed, riding a chestnut horse amid a princely retinue. Though she wore no crown, the queen's lacy bonnet sparkled with diamonds. She dressed in black, as she had done since the day her husband died. The people roared and cheered as she turned from one side to the other to acknowledge them, and the evening closed with fireworks filling the sky. If the day was all you saw of London, you would scarcely guess at what lurked in its darker corners.

Benjamin Jones died later that year, at home, at the age of sixty-four. He'd been a young man when he'd come from Aberaeron, one of a preponderance of Welsh dairymen with rural skills that could be put to use in the city. A study by the social reformer Charles Booth was only just underway around the time of Benjamin's death, but it would later claim that Welsh dairymen were the only inhabitants of the United Kingdom who could make a living keeping cows in London; "or rather," he wrote,

> perhaps they alone are content to accept the conditions under which the cow-keeper is forced to work in order to make a living. Without exception, these men seem to be the sons or near relations of small Welsh farmers; they are, for the most part, poorly educated; they speak English very imperfectly, and come to London unfit for any other occupation than that to which they have been brought up in their own country. They are thrifty and self-denying; prepared to live in rough surroundings; and content to work exceedingly hard, and for abnormally long hours, with a very small return. Even accepting these conditions, most of them now have a hard struggle for existence.

But Benjamin's struggle was over. A photograph, washed out now, and brittle, has survived more than a century. Benjamin and Margaret are

gray-haired, seated in chairs before an ivy-covered wall, potted gera-
niums on the ground behind them. Margaret has a plump cushion behind her head and eyes the camera, while a bearded Benjamin holds a
cat in his lap and watches his wife. Oddly casual, the photo hints that
this was a couple content with the life they'd made, but whether in the
end the move from Wales seemed wise to them – if they contemplat-
ed such things – is impossible to say. In any case they kept their brood
together for all those years, ensconced at number 64 Red Cross Street.
And it was there, with the death of Benjamin Jones, that the family
began to splinter.

A casual and candid shot of cowkeeper Benjamin Jones and wife Margaret, taken around 1880. The thick cushion behind Margaret's head, the cat on Benjamin's lap, and the potted plants suggest leisure time that was surely hard-earned.

Maggie Jones Donnelly, right, appears here with a woman we believe is Mary Jones Evans, aka Lazy Mary, who loathed tying her own bootlaces. If so, the buttons on her jacket must have been daunting. (Photo circa 1890)

CHAPTER 2

When the Horse Is Down

One might think that with her father, mother and husband gone, Mary Jones Evans would have become the matriarch of the family on Red Cross Street. But according to family lore she seems not to have been capable of the task, and the job fell to her youngest sister, Maggie, who'd been widowed just after New Year 1880, at the tender age of twenty-three. Her man, Daniel, had died of "intestinal obstruction," so perhaps gallstones, a horribly painful demise, and Maggie had come home to Red Cross Street with her three-month-old daughter Meg. In 1885 she married William Donnelly, a Yorkshireman whose accent must have seemed strange beside the Welsh chimes she was accustomed to. They took a house at number 79, across the street from her family, and a clue to how they met can be found in the birth record for their son, named for his father, where William gives his occupation as milk carrier.

Mary's teenage girls went to live with the couple, packing their things and crossing the street, but before long the eldest, Ellen, married a young potter named Frederick Roff and moved to the nearby parish of Lambeth, an area chock full of artisans. Fred was a moulder for Doulton Pottery Works, his days spent with his hands in clay, breathing fumes from toxic glazes and dust that collected in the lungs. He was from a large family, and some of his brothers worked at Doulton as well, along the Albert Embankment overlooking the Thames. Another was a "perfumer" at a soapworks, though the stench that emanated from there was of boiled animal bones, rancid and lingering. At just seventeen, Ellen was already pregnant when she left the Borough to marry Fred, and her condition made unpleasant smells more acute.

Middle sister Jennie had found a beau as well – a young bootmaker named Richard Vanson who'd set up shop in Red Cross Street – but Jennie was still too young to marry, and she and Mary Anne stayed on with Aunt Maggie, who became more like a mother to the sisters than Mary had been. With Ellen gone to Lambeth, the girls' cousin Meg, a few years younger than Mary Anne, rounded out a new threesome. Aunt Maggie and Uncle William had taken over Benjamin's dairy work, though William was a carpenter by trade. Family stories suggest he was a boozer too, and that an already difficult life only grew more trying for Maggie as the years of their marriage went on, with Maggie shouldering much of the burden of earning a living and keeping a home.

William's local was the Prince of Wales pub just steps from his door, near Richard Vanson's place, but he could have ventured north on the street for his respite, too – in recent years a travelling showman had set up a lucrative carnival on the disused Cross Bones Burial Ground, and *Reynolds's Weekly* reported that foul-mouthed crowds regularly gathered in the street waiting for the show to open. Locals moving through the throng had to walk in the road to get by, suffering catcalls and rude jokes as they passed. Once the fairgoers were inside the grounds and the show had begun, the pandemonium continued. There was music and dancing as well as merry-go-rounds, and festival games like coconut shies, where you threw a ball at a row of exotic coconuts in hopes of winning one. There were rifle galleries and a rideable "razzle-dazzle" carnival ship that imitated the rolling motions of being at sea. Spookiest of all, given the venue, was a ghost show that set the crowd screaming and further annoyed the people who lived within earshot of old Cross Bones, such as Jennie and Mary Anne.

If their mother Mary was ever with them at Aunt Maggie's, she didn't stay long. This was the beginning of a long decline for Mary Evans. Little is known of her life in the years after her husband David's death, but family lore is harsh and says she was so lazy that David had always done up her boots for her. Life without him was wearying, and at some point in the 1880s she entered the Mint Street workhouse, likely around the time her daughters crossed the street to live with Maggie. Although no definitive record of her original admission has been found, other entries indicate that Mary lived at the workhouse for many years, a "pauper charwoman" born in "Red X Street."

The longtime master at Mint Street was one William Tompson, his wife Edith the matron. They lived onsite with their children and oversaw the employees, the admission of people like Mary, termed pauper inmates, and the day-to-day matters that cropped up among inmates and staff. Tompson also met regularly with the local Board of Guardians, the body elected by ratepayers to manage Poor Law matters; it was up to him to satisfy them that all was well within workhouse walls and that money was being wisely spent. And yet, frequently, all was not well. Workhouse scandals were common topics in the newspapers – though sometimes exaggerated too. One widely reported story told of a brother and sister admitted to Mint Street when their father was destitute. When he went to retrieve them, he was shocked to find the children in a dreadfully filthy state. The girl's hair – long and golden upon admission – had been hacked short, the tresses sold to a wax-doll maker working in the Borough. Tompson had little to say for himself when questioned by the magistrate, and claimed he and his wife had been unaware of the goings-on. "That is no answer to these serious allegations," the magistrate scolded. But it would not be the last time Tompson appeared in an unsavoury story about the workhouse.

Why would Mary enter such a place, with so much family all around her? Surely laziness was not the true reason. As an institution, the workhouse had improved since the scathing *Lancet* report in Benjamin's day, but it remained a last resort for the old or sick or utterly bereft; most of its residents had suffered hard times long before they ever knocked on workhouse doors. Even the admission procedures were degrading: Mary would have been asked who in her family could care for her, and if she divulged that she had daughters, sisters, and brothers nearby, she would then be asked why they were not looking after her. Relatives could be tracked down and questioned to ascertain the truth of the pauper's statement that she was indeed "destitute for admission," as entry after entry claims. Aside from financial particulars, Mary would have been interviewed by a Relieving Officer appointed by the Board, or might even have appeared before the guardians themselves to determine her right to receive relief from the area's Poor Law union, surely an intimidating experience.

Residing in the union's jurisdiction for a minimum of one year was a stipulation for entering the workhouse, and Mary easily met it. An applicant could stay if she belonged elsewhere, but her home parish had to cover the cost. Officials from the various unions that oversaw the workhouses sent picayune letters back and forth to one another, arguing in formal language about who was responsible for whom, and tallying the costs of maintenance. The details of their detective work are filed away with the reams of forms filled in for each person. Some of these old books still exist, the pages rippled and dry, cracking with each turn, but nevertheless like peepholes into troubled private lives.

Once the initial paperwork was done, Mary was stripped and bathed. She was given a workhouse uniform, and her own clothes were scoured and stored away, along with anything else she'd brought with her. These items were noted in the master's "Inventory of Inmates' Effects" and held for safekeeping. A glance through the pages shows how little most people had: pawn tickets, a pair of earrings, small amounts of cash. A notation beside each item confirmed whether or not it was to be returned on discharge. While at the workhouse, Mary had nothing more than her narrow bed in a row of beds, and the uniform she wore. Did she think, that first day, that her time in the workhouse would be fleeting? If so, she was greatly mistaken. The routines she was learning now more or less summed up her future. She and her fellow inmates were put to work in the kitchen or laundry, or given some other domestic chore that kept the institution functioning. When the women did their scrubbing in the basement, clad identically in drab workhouse issue – striped cotton skirts, flannel petticoats, rough woolen shawls – they could be glimpsed through the grating in the street. Mary's daughters must have regularly walked by and spotted her, but for whatever reason they didn't take her into their own homes.

Grim as it was, the workhouse offered some security for Mary, a widow in her forties. North of the Borough, on the other side of the Thames in the impoverished East End, a woman her age was found in a pool of blood on the first-floor landing of a Whitechapel lodging house. Martha Tabram was a Southwark lass, born and bred a little south of Red Cross Street. She had fallen out with her husband years earlier, and in Whitechapel she'd worked as a prostitute and sometimes sold cheap trinkets as a way of earning enough money for liquor. Whoever killed her that August night had stabbed her thirty-nine times and left her bleeding in her black bonnet, dark green skirt and worn boots. *The Times* reported it as "one of the most dreadful murders any one could imagine." And yet imagining was soon widespread, since just three weeks later another body was found a block from where Martha had been killed, but outdoors this time, lying on the pavement in Buck's Row with her skirts lifted. Polly Nichols was a prostitute too, mid-forties and a drinker. Over the years she'd been in and out of the Lambeth Workhouse, as her petticoats attested. One wool, one flannel, each had the workhouse name stenciled on it. Another inmate of the workhouse eventually identified her body. And when a string of killings with startling similarities followed these two into the fall, a subtext began to emerge, and another of London's grubby little warrens – a match for the Borough – was illuminated for all to see.

Figuratively speaking, that is, for in reality the streets were oppressively dark. Reverend Samuel Barnett, whose church, St. Jude's, was close to the crime scenes, claimed the so-called Whitechapel murders were "bound to come," and that "dark passages lead to evil deeds." In a lengthy letter to *The Times*, he asserted that "Whitechapel horrors will not be in vain if at last the public conscience awakes to consider the life which these horrors reveal." He insisted there were practical solutions, such as increased police supervision, responsible landlords and clean, well-lit streets. A correspondent for the *Daily News* agreed. On walking the streets to see the situation for himself, he decided that "whole masses of crime would die out like toadstools under sunlight" if the neighbourhood was flooded with the electric light that brightened the West End.

The evil deeds Samuel Barnett referred to kept coming, with two more murders occurring minutes apart in the wee hours on the morning of a Sunday in September 1888. The "double event," it was called. Again the women were Mary's age: mid-forties, down on their luck and no strangers to the workhouse world. One of them, Catherine Eddowes, had lived in the Borough, had frequented nearby Newington Workhouse and had had a child at the Mint Street workhouse. Described by friends as a good-natured, intelligent woman, Catherine was from Wolverhampton, the daughter of a tinsmith whose parents, like Mary's, had walked to London in search of a better life. Catherine had taken up with Thomas Conway, an Irishman who travelled about, writing and selling "gallows ballads" that described local hangings. She had the initials "T.C." tattooed on her left forearm, but eventually her drinking, or Tom's violence, or both, caused them to separate. Although they had never married, they'd had several children together, and their daughter Annie still lived in the Borough with her husband, Louis Phillips.

A bit of snooping through birth and marriage records reveals a connection to the Evans family, through Jennie's beau, Richard Vanson. Annie and Louis were friends with Richard's brother Stephen and his wife, Emmie, and Stephen and Louis both worked as lampblack packers, handling the carbon soot used as a pigment in printing inks and shoe polish. The Vansons were witnesses at the Phillipses' wedding, and for a time the four lived together at Emmie's parents' home in the Bermondsey area, next to the Borough, growing their families in step with each other. By the time Annie's third child was born, the two couples had moved together to King Street, a twenty-minute walk from Red Cross, and Catherine Eddowes came to help with the birth. According to Annie's later testimony, once Catherine's work was done, in un-grandmotherly fashion she extended her hand for payment. That had been just over two years before her murder, and it was the last time Annie had seen her.

Lately, Catherine had been living with a fellow named John Kelly at Cooney's Lodging House in Flower and Dean Street, across the river in Whitechapel, and the two made money by going hop picking in season, or by pawning possessions or taking odd jobs. Catherine also worked as a casual prostitute, and although some sources say she was not a habitual drinker, on the night of September 29, 1888, a policeman found her lying on a footpath in Aldgate High Street, very drunk and barely able to stand. When she'd parted ways with John Kelly earlier in the day, she'd supposedly been going in search of Annie to beg some money, but she hadn't found her. She was tossed into jail to sober up and released soon after midnight once she'd slept off some of the effects of the liquor. The constable on duty asked her to pull the door closed on her way out, to which she replied, "All right, old cock," and then she left the station. Less than an hour later her body was discovered in Mitre Square, her throat slit, her intestines pulled from her abdomen, and her face badly mutilated. Catherine Eddowes – "otherwise Conway, otherwise Kelly" – had found notoriety as one of two women brutalized and murdered within hours of each other in the dark alleys of Whitechapel. After Catherine's death a kidney supposedly extracted from her body was mailed to the Whitechapel Vigilance Committee, and notes signed "Jack the Ripper" were sent to the press and the police, promising more killings.

When Annie testified at the inquest in October, the family's sordid history was laid bare. She and Louis moved frequently to avoid Annie's mother, who often sought Annie looking for money. Records show that the Vansons usually went with them – if not sharing a residence, then living nearby. Catherine had not found her daughter that day precisely because she didn't want to be found. Nor did Tom Conway, who'd begun using a different last name to make himself more difficult to track down. His sons had also evaded her, though one was still frequently in the Borough, and in Mint Street workhouse when the inquest began.

"Were your addresses purposely kept from her?" Annie was asked.

"Yes. To prevent her applying for money."

Gossip about Annie's mother's death, and her pitiful life, must have been rife on Red Cross Street. But though the murders were shocking, the stories behind them were familiar to descendants of Benjamin Jones and the many others who inhabited this world: lives shattered by misfortune, families ground down by poverty, the cycles repeating, just like the given names. Stephen and Richard Vanson's family was a case in point. Their father, another Stephen who was the son of a Stephen, hailed from a long line of Kentish gardeners, but something had set him roaming for a different life. Before coming to the Borough, he and his wife had bounced around Wales and southwest England, trying to carve out an existence for themselves. Eventually Stephen resorted to burglary but was caught, with two other men, trying to rob a jeweller's shop. The press called it an extraordinary story, since the men insisted that they'd been "weary of a vagabond life" and that "their object in attempting the burglary was to obtain sufficient property to enable them to set up in a respectable way of business, and hereafter lead a life of honesty and good conduct!" One writer claimed that Stephen told him, "This was the first job that I ever did," and that he'd confided to his wife before the attempted robbery that he was afraid he would be caught. In the end he said he was glad it had not come off, since the shop owner turned out to be an elderly widow. But in his own defense he told the court, "I was in a destitute state." His health was poor, he said, and he was unable to do hard, physical work. "I seized the opportunity, with these two young men, thinking it might probably bring me out of my poverty and set me up in the world in a respectable manner." He and his friends were imprisoned for twelve months with hard labour, health concerns aside, and when his sentence was done, the Vansons' wandering continued. Eventually he and his wife made their way to the Borough, where Stephen had relatives, hoping their luck would improve.

St. Saviour's Church was still in the throes of its most recent renovation when Jennie married Richard Vanson there on Christmas Day in 1890. The ongoing work made the normally large church tiny, and the only place in use at the time of Jennie and Richard's wedding was the ancient and intimate Lady Chapel, a portion of St. Saviour's that had not been spoiled in earlier years. Experts considered it a perfect example of thirteenth-century ecclesiastical architecture, and while work went on in the rest of the building, this part served as the beautiful but necessarily shrunken parish church. Mary Anne signed as witness, along with Ellen's husband, potter Fred. If Ellen attended the gathering with her two small children – a boy and a girl she and Fred had named after themselves – she may already have been feeling labour pains; her third child, a daughter named Florence, was born the following day.

It was cold that December, a chill, bleak month almost completely without sunshine, which would hold the record as London's coldest for the next 120 years. The south of England was thrashed with storms that brought sleet and fierce, biting winds. In the countryside, sheep and cattle were smothered by snow, and trains were buried on their tracks. Even in London the drifts climbed to twice the height of a man. But spring came, just as it always had, and when the census was taken in April 1891, it listed Jennie with Richard a few doors south of Aunt Maggie on Red Cross Street, between the Prince of Wales pub and some cowsheds. There were fewer and fewer city cows now, and the regulations that governed their keep were more stringently applied, so Maggie must have struggled to keep Benjamin's legacy going.

Next door to the cows, Jennie began her new life with Richard, moving toward a future that hopefully held more for them than their parents' had. Not long after Richard's parents came to the Borough, his father, the would-be burglar, had died at just forty-two, of tuberculosis. A few years later, one January day when Richard was nine, his deathly ill mother entered Newington Workhouse with the same condition, bringing Richard and his three younger siblings with her. The three eldest boys, though barely in their teens, fended for themselves, earning coins as market porters, perhaps, or chimney sweeps, or even by stealing. Their mother had been sick for quite some time and died the following day of the "lingering malady" that brought on fever and night sweats and coughs that produced blood. Within a week, Richard and the others – a brother and two sisters – were transferred to Hanwell School, formally the Central London District School at Hanwell, a large institution outside London built to house the parish's orphans and so-called destitute children. Set atop Cuckoo Hill on old farmland, it was also known as Cuckoo Schools.

An 1874 report that looked into the education offered in pauper schools said that impoverished charges could be classified into three groups: there were the true orphans, like the Vansons, whom the schools had the best chance of transforming into decent little humans; then there were those who'd been deserted by their parents and who also stood a fair chance of transformation, provided the parents didn't turn up sometime later to retrieve them; and finally there were the casuals, who came and went depending on whether their parents were in the workhouse or otherwise incarcerated. These were viewed as the most challenging cases, the report said, since they brought the evils of their world into the school with them, returning each time "more and more versed in sin."

No one can say what sins Richard brought at the ripe age of nine, but he was destined for a long stay. He was grouped with the older boys, aged nine to fourteen, while his brother Robert, just four, lived with the little ones. Their sisters were housed on the girls' side, and for the remainder of their years at Hanwell, the siblings ceased to live as a family.

The goal at Hanwell was to lift children out of the "gutter population," as a *London City Press* article put it, and steer them toward "proper paths." The paper reported on a yearly celebration that showed off the school's progress toward this end, and noted that boys and girls, looking "extremely clean" and "remarkably well," sang songs and played musical instruments in the decorated dining hall. Afterward they were entertained by Chinese jugglers and Italian acrobats, and given cake and oranges. In closing, speeches by school board managers underscored the wonderful work they'd done with the children and asked what would have become of their charges had they not been "rescued" in this way. The children were directly addressed as well, and encouraged to continue learning so as to better fight "the battle of the world" and "never again become a burden on the poor rates."

Richard was given a rudimentary education and groomed for a trade, a process that culminated in a typically lengthy apprenticeship. By fifteen he was sent from the school to a bootmaker in the parish of Camberwell, south of the Borough, to be apprenticed there until the age of twenty-one. His apprenticeship record, filed among hundreds like it in the Poor Law books, implies that he fulfilled his duties, though boy after boy did not. The file is thick with letters from frustrated employers whose boys have "absconded" for the second, third and even fourth time. One employer wrote, "It is from no want of kindness on my part" that the boy ran away, while another letter in support of a different boy claimed, "I have heard of great unkindnesses toward him by those you have trusted, and I have encouraged the lad to bear patiently his trials in the hope that they would cease." There were frequent mentions in the newspapers about "Master and Apprentice" difficulties. One article told of a Hanwell boy who'd had his ears boxed once too often two years into his apprenticeship, and subsequently ran away – perhaps in search of family he'd long ago lost track of, for Hanwell children also appeared in the "Long-Lost Relatives" column of *Lloyd's Weekly Newspaper*. "George William Rapley would like to trace his parents, whom he has never seen or heard of. He was put in a school at Hanwell called the 'Cuckoo school.'" "James Boneer, who 22 years ago left St. Pancras Workhouse for Hanwell, wishes to hear of his relatives." "Matthew (Henry), who was put…at Hanwell with his sister Emily, ran away to sea…She can gain no tidings since."

The pull of family brought Richard back to the Borough once his apprenticeship was complete in the mid-1880s. His brother Stephen, the lampblack packer, wasn't far away, and his younger siblings would emerge from Hanwell and make their way "home" too, though officially they had none. By 1891 the apprenticeship had served Richard well. Bootmaking was a poorly paid occupation, especially when one's customers were poor, yet he was listed on the census as a man in his own employ. In his workshop he was surrounded by his tools – bits of leather, adjustable tin patterns, a collection of lasts, dyes, threads and waxes – but his was another waning specialty, increasingly given over to factory work. For now, though, he was getting by, and he and Jennie lived in two rooms of a four-room house, taking in lodgers to help them pay the rent.

Just south of them, the Mint Street workhouse held 391 "pauper inmates" and "vagrants," many of them elderly, plus Master and Matron Tompson and their staff. For more than a century the building had housed the desperately poor, with poverty apparent outside its walls too, in every damp brick and dark alley of the neighbourhood. Behind Richard and Jennie was a cluster of rundown lodging houses so full with people that their names filled three pages of the census schedule.

On the evening of April 5, 1891, one of the census enumerators for the Borough walked the streets collecting the forms residents had completed. Spring was finally taking hold after a long, strange winter. The buds pushed their way open, covering soot-blackened walls with flowers and greenery, and that fact and the census papers the man carried were evidence of how things cycled onward. Every ten years, people like him assisted in documenting the world around them, recording who lived where, with whom and in how many rooms. What did they do for a living? How old were they, and were they married, widowed, single; deaf, dumb, blind; lunatic, imbecile, idiot? The task of collecting such information was serious and important, but it's doubtful that even enumerators understood how thoroughly the details would be pored over by tenacious descendants greedy for names and numbers, and hopeful for clues to stories, doors to the past.

This particular year marked the first time that some of these census takers were women, wearing long dresses with small, neat bustles, jackets with cinched waists and high collars, and hats that covered their pinned-up hair. Men wore their good clothes: toppers, if they had them, frock coats and silk puff ties. They carried their books and pencils, and a list of instructions to follow when things went awry, as things will when so many questions are asked about private matters. Just days before, the *Illustrated London News* had run a cartoon that showed an enumerator holding his hat on, grasping his bag and umbrella, and racing away from a roughly clad man shaking his fist in the air.

By law, those refusing to co-operate with enumerators could be fined, and any who'd read the papers knew it was

> the duty of the enumerator to open and examine to see that it has been correctly and intelligibly filled in, and he may ask any question which may be necessary to satisfy himself on this point. Errors are to be rectified by him upon the spot, and if, from ignorance, or any other cause the schedule has not been filled up, the enumerator must enter upon it himself all the particulars he can ascertain from the occupier or other competent member of the family. Should the schedule be lost, or mislaid, he will supply a fresh one. The strictest precautions will be taken to preserve as secret and confidential the information given in the schedules.

The enumerator's shoes clicked on the cobblestones as they took him briskly along, past the Prince of Wales pub and Richard's bootmaking shop, past the fried-fish shops and the coffee houses. Sometimes he put pencil to paper himself when he encountered someone who couldn't read or write, and therefore had been unable to fill in the form. It happened often enough in the densely populated Borough, with building after building packed with transient lodgers. One place was called the Farm House, though there couldn't have been a less apt name. Inside were housed dock labourers, hawkers, market porters, bricklayers and clerks like the enumerator collecting their forms. Some of the worst places in the area were the passages that snaked off Red Cross Street, with pretty names like Bird Cage Alley and Falcon Court, where Benjamin's cowsheds had been. Sometimes reached by an archway that emphasized their isolation, these passages were airless and dark and plagued by rats, but also by gamblers, prostitutes and the pimps – known as bullies – who lived off their earnings. The bulk of the crimes tried at the Southwark Police Courts were committed in these few blocks, but Red Cross Street itself was of mixed flavour, with pockets of lively pubs and busy greengrocers, and a tight-knit, neighbourly character. The census taker made note of the "fairground" at Cross Bones cemetery, listing the travelling showman, his fellow performers and their wives and children. Between the graveyard and the Farm House there was now mostly shoddy tenement housing, but also a lush country garden and a row of cottages so charming they seemed to belong elsewhere.

The Red Cross Cottages had been built just a few years earlier, part of social reformer Octavia Hill's effort to improve the lot of the working class, and to bring some dignified living space to an otherwise bleak area. As a child, Hill had experienced her father's bankruptcy, as well as her mother's resilience and resourcefulness in supporting the family. Octavia, her mother and her sisters all worked for a living, and were regularly surrounded by intellectuals, socially conscious thinkers and their ideas, which eventually led Octavia to activism. With the help of philanthropist John Ruskin, a family friend, she acquired her first properties in 1864 and became a landlord, intent on improving the buildings she bought and meeting personally with her tenants to encourage self-reliance and inspire them to improve their lives. She believed in "the healing gift of space," both inside a dwelling and outside, and wrote of her frustration visiting cramped lodgings that were meant to be homes. "When I am in [these] rooms, I feel often how much even a foot or two would be worth, if the room were only large enough to let the wife open the window without climbing on the bed, or if she could get further away from the hot fire on a June day, or if everyone who came in wasn't forced to brush against the wall so that a great black mark quickly showed itself." She held firm to the belief that people should and could have "four things: places to sit in, places to play in, places to stroll in, and places to spend a day in." Now around fifty, Hill had been working in the field of social housing for decades and made a strong moral distinction between what she saw as the deserving poor – those who accepted a little aid and improved their lot – and the undeserving – the drunkards and thieves who took what was given readily enough and came back again for more, none the better for what they'd received.

When Hill went to work on the Red Cross site, it was a desolate piece of property owned by the Ecclesiastical Commissioners, the group that managed the Church of England's holdings, and which had also owned the stables Benjamin rented. They had approached Hill to take on development of the site, part of it containing an abandoned warehouse, the rest the remains of a burnt-out paper factory. There were still heaps of blackened paper littering the space, stinking and soaked with rain, and the neglected spot had become a kind of dump site, with rubbish tossed in by careless passersby. Hill and her workers spent weeks burning the refuse, lighting bonfires that blazed day and night. They tore down the warehouse, too, so that the sun could reach the spot, and a bigger patch of sky could be seen by the other tenants neighbouring the site.

When the gabled cottages went up, each was a little different from the next, with bright red doors and intricately patterned brickwork, and gardens laid out in front, complete with fountain, mosaic tile, and rambling flower beds. Red Cross Hall was built next to the cottages for parties, concerts, classes and evening performances like *The Pilgrim's Progress*, which attracted a less raucous group than the fairgoers at Cross Bones. On a beautiful moonlit night, the hall was full for that show, and the audience followed the Pilgrim's journey from the City of Destruction to the Celestial City. Large gatherings of local people joined Hill for Sunday afternoon concerts – Mary Anne with Aunt Maggie and Meg perhaps, or Richard and Jennie Vanson arm in arm. The hall served as a reading room, too, stocked with books and illustrated papers. Eventually its walls were decorated by the artist Walter Crane, who was heavily involved with the Socialist movement and committed to art as a tool for change. For Red Cross Hall he designed scenes of ordinary people who'd done heroic deeds, including Alice Ayres, whose tragic story Borough residents knew well. It was a bright change indeed from Benjamin's day.

But bettering lives here was challenging work, and it was not possible to house all of the poor in quaint cottages. Even Hill believed such accommodation was not suitable for the lowest of the low, with their ruinous habits and rough lives: "Transplant them tomorrow to healthy and commodious homes, and they would pollute and destroy them," she maintained. Aside from running the cottages, she'd been hired to manage two large groups of warehouse-style buildings on Red Cross Street that offered basic rooms at "reasonable rents." These so-called model dwellings were part of a London-wide housing scheme that purported to provide sanitary and comfortable housing for the labouring classes, and yet the ones on Red Cross Street – the Mowbray Buildings and the Stanhope – were among the worst spots in the area. Five storeys high, with a single front entrance and built in already narrow streets, they dwarfed the houses around them and added to the confined atmosphere. While the fronts of the structures looked tidy enough, rotting garbage piled up at the backs, and inside, the halls were "so dark that even by day you could not see the numbers on the doors." At odds with the communal character of the rest of the street, the residents here were transient types, the population for the most part "anonymous." The vicar at St. George the Martyr made an effort to visit every tenement and get to know his flock, but seven months later he found that half of his acquaintances had moved on.

So there were the transients, the long-time residents and the newcomers. The 1891 census tells us that eighteen-year-old Mary Anne Evans, the youngest of Lazy Mary's daughters, was still with Aunt Maggie and Uncle William that year, living next door to the Mowbray.

Maggie had a new baby girl, Clara, and Mary Anne surely held her now and again, and helped care for her, imagining being a mother one day. Across the street, a young man named Harry Deverill had moved in next to the Red Cross Gardens and the cottages. Pictures show him as slender and dark-haired, with an intense expression. He'd come to the Borough from nearby Deptford and was learning the trade of oil and colourman, mixing pigments and oils and paints as Alice Ayres's brother-in-law had done before the fire. Twenty-year-old Harry had plans to branch out and open a grocer's shop of his own; grocer had been his father's trade, so it was a business he knew well, though running a shop was not without its dangers. Street gangs were a constant worry to shopkeepers throughout the city: the Monkey Parade gang roamed in Whitechapel, the New-Cut gang haunted Lambeth, and the Black gang, with their faces painted black, terrorized the Borough. "They prowl about the streets armed with belts and sticks, they fight, and when they get a chance, most of them steal," wrote the *Pall Mall Gazette*. Sometimes they did worse. One wonders if Harry had heard of the "savage assault" made on the grocer a couple of doors down by members of that group of ruffians. Late one night, while the grocer was putting up his shutters, an encounter with one of the gang members brought others out of the shadows. According to the *Morning Post*, the gang's leader beat and bit the man so severely that he ended up in hospital.

If thieves and hooligans weren't worry enough, Harry's early days on Red Cross were marred by the infamous fairground at Cross Bones. The fair was open Monday to Friday evenings from seven to ten, and a large organ fitted with trumpets churned out a steady blare of music. It opened on Saturday afternoons, as well, and did business late into Saturday night, just as Harry did, providing long hours for the convenience of his customers, even if it meant stuffing his ears with cotton to drown out the noise. After years of complaints from locals on both moral and nuisance grounds, the issue had finally got the attention of the current nuisance inspector, Arthur Grist, who resolved to take legal proceedings against the fair's owners and urged them to move on. Soon the "razzle-dazzle" fair had vacated Cross Bones.

Was Harry even slightly sorry to see it go? All evidence points to the fact that he loved music and hailed from a family that valued it. He played the euphonium, and his younger brother Jack played the piccolo; their sister Nell was a piano teacher. Perhaps it was this musical streak that drew Harry to the Salvation Army, a charitable organization whose war against crime, poverty and sin had been waging for some twenty-five years now, but which was still often criticized by the mainstream because of its unusual, garish methods: parades and brass bands and even women preaching in public, all led by rangy William Booth with his long white beard and feverish eyes. A letter to the editor of the *Daily Mail* opined that the Army's "discordant row with drum, lung, and other instruments" was liable to "disgust those they aim to attract," especially on Sunday afternoons, when the working classes were looking for a little peace and quiet. Likewise, workhouse officials complained that Salvation Army bands serenaded outside infirmary walls, "to the great annoyance of the seriously ill or dying inmates."

But Booth's clamorous approach was constant. He called himself "the General," and there were captains, officers and soldiers beneath him, as well as the indefatigable "hallelujah lasses" who roamed the darkest streets in their capes and poke bonnets, handing out the Army's *War Cry* magazine to all who would take it. The lasses sang, too, and banged their tambourines, and squeezed accordions. Early on, Booth (egged on by his wife Catherine) had decreed that there'd be no difference between men and women as to rank, authority and duties within the Army. The highest positions were open to all.

Harry Deverill was a bandsman for the Army's Borough division – a place rich with sinners – and could be seen marching through the streets in his uniform, dwarfed by his shining tuba. The band's repertoire was not limited to traditional hymns; they plucked songs from pubs and music halls and put new words to them to bring God's message to the streets – to the vagrants and the prostitutes, the poor who had lost their way. They gathered in the most notorious places and let the music pour forth, and if the outing was successful, new recruits would follow them back to the hall for food, sleep and, of course, the praising of Jesus. Unlike Octavia Hill, Booth did not draw a line between the deserving and the undeserving poor, but aimed to herd all of them Godward. While the average slum clergyman despaired that so few entered his church, General Booth went out to find his audience, convinced that poverty stood like a roadblock between people and God. Who could think about his soul when his basic physical needs were wanting? Maverick Booth was a hero to men like Harry, who believed that if secular music indeed belonged to the devil, then they would gladly join Booth in plundering him for it. As the General put it, "He has no right to a single note of the whole seven…Every note, and every strain, and every harmony is divine, and belongs to us."

Yet often the Army met with resistance, and not only because it made too much noise. The Army's crusades against alcohol and rough living inspired a group of publicans and beer-sellers to rise up against Booth and his followers in order to protect their livelihood. The reform of their customers was bad for business, and they began to enlist members for a "Skeleton Army" that mocked everything the Salvation Army stood for. Instead of "Soup, Soap and Salvation," the Skeletons championed "Beef, Beer and Bacca." As one army grew, so did the other. When the Salvationists marched, the Skeletons threw rocks, dead rats and rotten eggs; when the Salvationists played their instruments, the Skeletons trailed after them, "beating a drum and burlesquing their songs." The altercations often descended into riots and mass arrests, but according to the *War Cry*, "the skeletons did all the shouting and we had only the opportunity of blessing them by showing unruffled love in answer to the disturbance in our proceedings."

By 1891 Booth had made considerable progress in his war. The Skeleton Army was waning, but the Salvationists continued to grow in number, and Harry Deverill was proudly among them. Who had drawn him into that world, and what condition had he been in prior to that? Had his soul needed saving when he'd taken his place at the "mercy seat" and committed to joining the battle? Like other new recruits he'd given his testimony upon joining, articulating to the best of his ability how his life had been changed by God. These were the kinds of powerful stories Booth loved so much that he often printed them in issues of the *War Cry*. He'd learned early that, even when poorly spoken, "ordinary

60

working men in their corduroys and bowler hats could command attention from their own class which was refused point-blank to me with my
theological terms and superior knowledge." The silence that came over
an audience at such times was astounding. Nothing could move a thief
or a drunkard quite so much as an ex-thief or an ex-drunkard telling the
tale of his climb from the abyss.

When the enumerator called at 68 Red Cross Street to collect
Harry's census form, there was nothing on it to indicate the details of
his testimony or his new religious leanings or his love of music or the
fact that the pretty girl across the street had caught his notice. Mary
Anne had wide-set eyes and a candid expression, and though the census recorded her as a domestic servant for Aunt Maggie and Uncle
William, another future was taking shape now that Harry Deverill
had arrived in the street that had always been her home. He himself
had come from a family of non-conformers – meaning not Church of
England – and his Methodist background (like the General's) merged
well with the Salvation Army. Popular opinion continued to shift in
the Army's favour, so Mary Anne was probably not put off by Harry's
involvement.

The General's wife had succumbed to breast cancer that past
autumn – had been "promoted to glory," the Army called it – and more
than thirty thousand people had turned out for her funeral. Booth's
book *In Darkest England and the Way Out*, completed as his wife lay
dying, had been an instant and controversial bestseller. It outlined his
rescue plan for the poor, and opened with a colourful illustration that
gave what Booth called "a bird's-eye view of the Scheme described in
this book, and the results expected from its realization." In the foreground, Salvation Army workers kneel on the shore of a choppy sea,
struggling to save "the sinking classes" – desperate people drowning in
vice and poverty. A trail of the rescued can be seen climbing the hill to
the "city colony," where they'll be fed, clothed, and trained for decent
work. Some of these move farther afield, to a verdant colony of villages,
mills, co-operative farms and factories "far away from the neighbourhood of the public house." From here, steamers take a contingent of the
fully reformed across a calm sea, to settlements in a new land.

Booth conceded that it was good for men to "climb unaided out of the whirlpool," but insisted that for many such a feat was impossible. He likened "poor broken-down humanity" to an overworked, underfed cab horse falling in the streets of London. "If you put him on his feet without altering his conditions, it would only be to give him another dose of agony...These are the two points of the Cab Horse's Charter. When he is down he is helped up, and while he lives he has food, shelter and work. That, although a humble standard, is at present absolutely unattainable by millions – literally by millions – of our fellow-men and women in this country. Can the Cab Horse Charter be gained for human beings? I answer, yes."

Regardless of the various strains of philanthropy running through the Borough, the area's age-old spirit persisted – dank and depressing, with bursts of wild revelry. The infamous pea-soup fog hung over all of London at times, but here in the Borough it seemed greasier, yellower, more cloying. Those bent on social reform – and there were more and more of them since the recent Whitechapel murders across the Thames – had differing opinions on how to achieve it. George Sims with his powerful pen; Octavia Hill with her cottages and gatherings; General William Booth with his brass bands and colonies; and also Charles Booth, who had undertaken a massive study he called *Inquiry into the Life and Labour of the People in London.*

A businessman who dabbled in politics, Charles Booth travelled in the same circles as Octavia Hill and Samuel Barnett but took an analytical rather than emotional approach to social reform. Back in 1884, a newly formed political party called the Social Democratic Federation had claimed its studies showed 25 percent of Londoners lived in extreme poverty. Booth believed the number was exaggerated and set about gathering facts and figures that could provide a clearer picture of the scale and scope of London's problems. The census did little to determine poverty statistics, he claimed, and without specifics on how people lived, not much could be done to improve their situation. He set up his headquarters in Whitechapel, and together with his team of "social investigators" – his own salvation army, in a sense, though he was unrelated to Booth the preacher – he roamed the streets of the city, skeptical, at first, but open to whatever the data might show him. The real slums lay hidden, he said, "behind a curtain on which were painted terrible pictures: starving children, suffering women, overworked men; horrors of drunkenness and vice; monsters and demons of inhumanity; giants of disease and despair." His goal was to lift the curtain through serious and careful research, and thereby find out whether the melodramatic pictures offered a true likeness or not.

The team's copious notes, embellished with sketched maps, included a colourful cast from the Borough, such as "one middle-aged woman pulling fur at her open window, air full of fluff and herself covered with it. Spoke in shaky husky voice, 'Must do it to live you know!'" There were "undergrown men: women slouching with draggled skirts, hatless but hidden under long shawls: a deformed boy with a naked half formed leg turned in the wrong direction." Another entry describes "a notorious women's lodging house at the N.E. end … hardly a whole pane of glass in any window on the S side: a row of stables … runs down the centre … tenanted by one scarecrow horse." The stable yard was full of manure, bones and rotting oranges. The investigator – in this case the aristocrat George Duckworth, who worked for Booth for ten years without pay – was cautioned by a policeman not to venture into the area; police themselves rarely went, and never singly. The chances were good, the officer warned, of "brickbats or slops upon [his] head," like the brutal attack Harry's grocer neighbour had endured. But Duckworth went anyway, making a special note in his journal that "this danger overrated: have been down twice since at night, between 11 and 12 p.m." Still, there was no question in his mind that the area formed a "serious blot" on the map. Though the Borough was home for so many, it was also "a set of courts and small streets which for number, viciousness, poverty and crowding, is unrivalled in anything I have hitherto seen in London."

The project lasted nearly twenty years, and eventually the information Charles Booth collected was published in a seventeen-volume work and an excruciatingly detailed, colour-coded map that showed where there was money and where there was none. Black areas held the lowest class, designated "vicious" and "semi-criminal," whose only luxury, according to Booth, was drink. Dark blue, like the Mowbray

Buildings, stood for "chronic want." Light blue was poor. Pink, like the Red Cross Cottages, was reserved for "fairly comfortable." On it went up to red for well-to-do, and yellow for wealthy, colours that were rare in the black-and-blue Borough, where prostitutes sometimes worked for a pot of beer.

But there was this too: as part of his research, Booth roomed anonymously with families like Mary Anne's for weeks at a time, and saw first-hand how they lived. Provided they were not destitute, he found much to admire, and the plain food agreed with his digestion. Of the children, he wrote:

> I certainly think their lives are happier, free from the paraphernalia of servants, nurses and governesses, always provided they have decent parents. They are more likely to suffer from spoiling than from harshness, for they are made much of, being commonly the pride of their mother, who will sacrifice much to see them prettily dressed, and the delight of their father's heart. This makes the home, and the happiness of the parents; but it is not this, it is the constant occupation, which makes the children's lives so happy. They have their regular school hours, and when at home, as soon as they are old enough, there is "mother" to help, and they have numbers of little friends … Let it not be supposed, however, that on this I propose to base any argument against the desire of this class to better its position. Very far from it … The uncertainty of their lot, whether or not felt as an anxiety, is ever present as a danger.

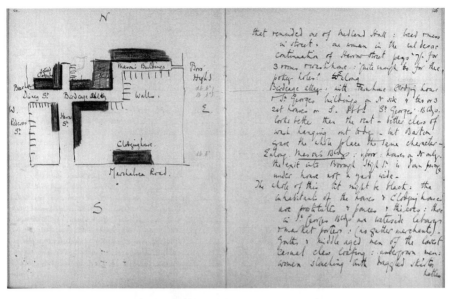

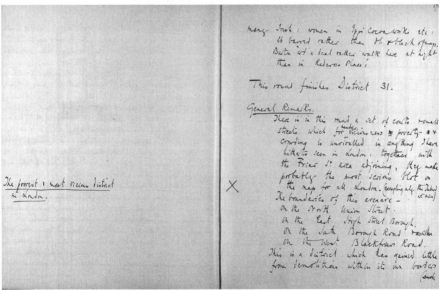

Many of the notebooks of Charles Booth and his social investigators have been digitized by the Booth archives at the London School of Economics. These old pages, sometimes embellished with little maps and sketches, provide extraordinary glimpses into troubled neighbourhoods. Red Cross Street was in District 31, "the poorest and most vicious district in London." Courtesy Charles Booth's London, LSE Library.

This "cabinet card" portrait of Mary Anne Evans was likely taken around 1893, celebrating her engagement to Harry Deverill. Her hand is placed to show off her ring, which was typical of photographs of this kind. The reverse of the card, featuring a seated lady preparing for a portrait, was a popular design in the early 1890s.

Potter's Rot

The earliest known photograph of Mary Anne Evans can be dated to around 1893, judging by the front and back of the cabinet card and the many clues each gives. It was taken by "Artist & Photographer H. Bown," whose name appears in a flourish on both sides. He had three Southwark studios at the time and, like most of his contemporaries, advertised his services on the backs of the pictures he took. This one features an illustration of a woman with flowers in her hair and butterflies dancing around her. She's seated, and posing for the camera draped in cloth on a tripod in front of her. A naked cherub with wings is poised to take the picture, of which "copies can be had at any time."

The actual photograph is less ornate. Mary Anne's hair is pulled back, but not tightly, and her expression is gentle and somewhat timid, unlike the pictures that come later and suggest a strong woman who meets challenges head-on. Tiny buttons travel up the bodice of her dress to a lace flounce pinned to a high collar. The skirt is gathered at the hips, and the fabric falls in neat, successive curves that extend from one side of the dress to the other. She is about twenty years old and newly engaged, as the ring on her finger attests. Her hand rests on a stack of books, positioned to show the ring prominently, which is typical of both engagement and wedding portraits in Victorian times. There is no photo of Harry in a dapper suit; not even a casual shot of him with sleeves rolled up, plying his trade, but the music hall song "He's Going to Marry Mary Ann" seemed written for the pair as they anticipated Mary Anne's move across the street.

He'd bought a bed, and a table too
A big tin dish for making stew
A large flat iron, to iron his shirt
And a flannel, and a scrubbing brush to wash away the dirt
And he's bought a pail and basins three
A coffee pot, a kettle, and a tea-pot for the tea
And a soup bowl and a ladle
And a grid-iron and a cradle
And he's going to marry Mary Ann, that's me
He's going to marry Mary Ann.

On Sunday, June 2, 1895, after a relatively long engagement, Mary Anne and Harry entered into their marriage contract as defined by the times: his role was to provide support for the household they'd establish; hers to run the household with the money he earned – an understanding, and a constant, delicate balance. Being a Salvationist, Harry would have taken particular notice of General Booth's advice regarding "the pearl of kindness... A man may not be able to give the partner of his joys and sorrows much money for her housekeeping, or place her in any high position in Society," the General wrote in the *War Cry*, "...but he can constantly give her those gentle and untiring attentions which spring from a heart of kindness." It was his duty, too, to watch over her health and see that she avoided "the danger of hurry and scurry" once children arrived, "with their teething and other troubles, endless in number and wonderful in variety."

Harry and Mary Anne likely had some sort of celebration with their Salvation Army friends, but theirs was a Church of England wedding, aligning with Mary Anne's background. Like Richard and Jennie's five years earlier, the service was held in the Lady Chapel at St. Saviour's, where the memorial window honouring Alice Ayres had never materialized; instead, the chapel boasted a brass lectern with an inscription blessing "that heroic maid-of-all-work." The chaplain's bible rested on it as he led Harry and Mary Anne through their vows, their words echoing off the centuries-old walls. Harry's parents, William and Mary Margaret Deverill, came from Deptford for the ceremony, and though it wasn't a great distance, locals thought the far side of Borough High Street was a world away.

On Charles Booth's poverty map, William and Mary Margaret's Ilderton Road address was coloured pink, like Red Cross Cottages, and people in the immediate area had good ordinary earnings. The streets were clean and broad, with slate-roofed, two-storeyed houses. William was an ambulance coachman at the nearby South Eastern Fever Hospital, and while on shift he lived at the station, taking his meals alongside the other drivers. Besides accommodation for the workers, the station had coach houses, a forge, harness rooms and a laundry, and employed a cook, a housemaid and a laundress. A relatively novel concept, the horse-drawn fleet of varnished wood broughams guided by specialized drivers like William had replaced a haphazard system that relied on police or firemen pushing stretchers to the hospital on foot. Although it separated William from his family for days at a time, it was a good, steady job that kept him in the pay of the Metropolitan Asylums Board, the body responsible for managing London's state hospitals and mental institutions.

Circumstances hadn't always been comfortable for Harry's father. In a society obsessed with moral righteousness, he'd begun life with the scales tipped against him. Illegitimate, his baptism entry included the notation "base born," and it is doubtful he ever met his mother. Raised by non-conformist relatives, William learned the grocer's trade from his foster father, and married his wife in a Methodist church. He opened his own shop, and his wife, herself an entrepreneur, had a toy shop. Unlike a greengrocer, who sold fruits and vegetables, a grocer traded in dried provisions like tea, coffee, sugar and spices, all cut, ground, mixed and blended by hand. Success depended on reputation and word of mouth, and sadly for Harry's father, within a few years a notice appeared in the *London Gazette* advising the creditors of "William Henry Deverill… Grocer" that he was bankrupt. It was sheer luck that it had happened just a couple of years after imprisonment for debt was abolished. Bankruptcy had landed Charles Dickens's father in the Marshalsea Prison, and the rest of the family too – all of them except one sister and Charles, who at twelve went to work in a bootblacking factory. Harry's father had fared better than Charles's, but the proud "grocers shopman," as the elder Deverill had described himself on an early census, was no longer. Harry's mother's toy shop disappeared too, and the Deverills joined the thousands of Londoners who knew how hard it was to escape poverty.

Did William wonder at his son's decision to move to a place like the Borough, criss-crossed with the blacks and purples of Booth's poverty map? Did he visit Harry's shop that day and see the weigh scales and tin pots, smell the turpentine and linseed, and admire his son's determination to succeed where he had failed? Perhaps they walked together to the church, sunk behind the Surrey bank of the Thames, their footsteps lost in the din of the streets. In 1895 St. Saviour's was still being renovated, so William and Harry couldn't enter through the arched Norman doorway, or see the stacks of ancient oak bosses, long removed from the ceiling of the nave, the carvings depicting scenes like Judas Iscariot being swallowed by the devil, his feet dangling out of a grinning, sinister face. Instead, Harry and his father skirted scaffolds and stepped through rubble to await the bride and the guests in the Lady Chapel, where the thin light through the lancet windows showed the sparkle of dust in the air.

There are no photographs of the events of that June day, but a trio of ceramic pitchers made by Doulton have been passed down through the family since that time and may have been a wedding gift from Ellen and potter Fred. Just twenty-six, Ellen had been married nine years already, and had given birth to five children, though one daughter had died of tubercular meningitis. In Lambeth, she and Fred lived in an area not unlike the Borough, according to Charles Booth, who pegged the surrounding streets as "poor and very poor." Fred's fellow pottery workers populated the vicinity; most worked for Doulton and Company, whose big factory on Black Prince Road overlooked the Albert Embankment and employed hundreds, from the kilnmen who loaded the kilns to the grinders who helped purify the clay. The unskilled portion of the workforce was "a very rough lot" according to the vicar of a nearby church. A recent strike at the factory had caused friction between the moulders and the throwers, and when the trouble settled, many of the agitators did not get their jobs back. Fred had probably not been among them, for he continued to work as a moulder, breathing the clay dust that dried his skin and coated his lungs. John Thomas Arlidge, a physician who specialized in occupational disease, would later caution that "Potter's dust does not kill suddenly, but settles, year after year, a little more firmly into the lungs, until at length a case of plaster is formed. Breathing becomes more and more difficult and depressed, and finally ceases."

Fred may have felt the symptoms of the aptly named "potter's rot," but Ellen's disease – alcoholism – was all too visible. It seems Ellen had been drained by the hurry and scurry General Booth warned of, and coped by drinking; Fred, in turn, had been drained by Ellen – financially, emotionally or both. Balancing three-month-old Emily on her hip, Ellen might have stood apart from her husband at the wedding, while their other children gaped at the bride and groom. Perhaps the guests nearest her smelled alcohol on her breath, noticed the crookedness of her gait, and whispered behind their hands that Ellen had always been a bit feeble in the head and took after her mother's elder brother, John, a habitual drinker. John was a haberdasher making a precarious income selling buttons and ribbons. He lived with his family on Red Cross Street, so was likely also at the wedding, the subject of similar knowing glances.

The gossip from that day is gone now, but some years later the *Poor Law Officers' Journal*, a publication that kept officials abreast of cases that effected the laws, printed a surprisingly detailed rendering of the disintegration of Fred and Ellen's relationship. It recounts that one Saturday in October, four months after Harry and Mary Anne's wedding, Fred came home from work to find the bailiffs carting off his goods for nonpayment of rent. Ellen had squandered the money Fred had given her on drink, and not for the first time. Her habit had gotten out of control, to the point that she neglected the children, pawned family belongings and could not be trusted. He moved out of their bed that night and slept with one of his children – no doubt the only boy, Freddie, who was now eight years old. Fred asked Ellen to leave, at least for a while, and said he'd pay her an allowance as long as she remained sober and did her utmost to change. If she reformed, he promised he would take her back.

Such disputes were all too frequent, and often violent. With alcohol thrown into the mix, a domestic argument could quickly devolve into serious assault and even murder. When Charles Booth's investigator interviewed the Southwark police superintendent Henry Wyborn about violent men "with drunken wives," he was told that the courts were too hard on the husbands. "A woman of this kind will provoke her husband until he strikes her, and then have him up before the magistrate." One of the cases heard at the Old Bailey told of a Borough man who, after a drinking binge, longed for a nap but found that his wife (drunk too) had pawned the blankets; he longed for a hot meal but found that his wife had pawned the frying pan. On his enraged insistence, she went out to buy another so she could cook for him, but she stopped at a pub or two along the way; when she finally returned, he stabbed her to death. When the police came to the scene, they found him lying on the floor. "I am a man," he declared, as if that justified his actions. He didn't deny his crime and handed the knife to the officer. "This is what I done it with." According to witnesses he was a "quiet, peaceful man," and "wonderfully kind to the children." Convinced he'd been provoked, the jury recommended mercy, but the judge sentenced him to death.

Fred, too, seems to have been the peaceful sort, and a devoted husband and father, but despite the tawdry details that surface in the journal, there's no way to know what Ellen was escaping when she turned to drink. The accounts tell us that Fred took the children, moved in with his parents and continued to work at Doulton, while Ellen disappeared back into the familiar Borough, staying with Aunt Maggie, surrounded by old friends and relatives. Each week Fred visited Harry's shop to leave a weekly allowance for Ellen, and Ellen entered later to collect it. In this typical way the larger family was caught up in the couple's troubles, hearing one side and then the other in a lengthy, ugly battle that came to a head when Fred encountered Ellen accidentally at Maggie's house. The journal's slim details suggest high drama: Ellen begged Fred to take her back and was very distressed to have lost him. But she had already been drinking that day, and though he was "sincerely attached to his wife," he rebuffed her since she had clearly not mended her ways.

Comparing herself to her sisters, as sisters will do, Ellen came out somewhat inferior. Her marriage had failed, she was often drunk and she no longer watched over her own children. By all accounts she was somewhat simple-minded, and in pictures she lacks the sharpness of Jennie's gaze and the calm of Mary Anne's. Her sisters appear to have lived happier lives: Mary Anne was busy with her new husband and their shop, and Jennie had two girls by now, and a baby boy named Richard, after his shoemaker father. Jennie's children were close in age to the kids Ellen had left behind in Lambeth. When Jennie's Richard took his first steps that autumn, Ellen knew that her own baby Emily would soon do the same, though Ellen wouldn't be there to see it. And when baby Richard died of whooping cough that December, she must have recognized her sister's sorrow, for she knew how it felt to lose a child. But drink soothes all kinds of aches, and makes rights out of wrongs, at least for a while, and Ellen could not get enough of it. When Harry slid her allowance across the shop counter, Mary Anne beside him may have sighed, for there was little doubt where the money would be spent: two doors down, at the Prince of Wales pub, where Ellen was quickly developing a bad reputation. The *Poor-Law Officers' Journal* says that rumours of her promiscuity travelled back to Fred in Lambeth, and when he heard that Ellen was "constantly associating with men in public houses, and with one in particular," he arranged to meet her at Harry and Mary Anne's place. Fred arrived, but Ellen didn't show, so he told Harry that he was discontinuing her allowance, then headed to the pub for a drink. Ellen must have heard the news from Harry shortly afterward, for she found Fred and confronted him in the crowd, demanding to know why he was withdrawing support. He accused her of cheating on him, and she didn't deny it. How could she? The journal tells us "she was visibly pregnant with a bastard child."

That ended things for Ellen and Fred. With no hope for reconciliation, no money and a child on the way, she soon moved in with the man she'd been seeing, John Humphreys, a butcher turned bricklayer's labourer who lived in the Stanhope Buildings and then, with Ellen, in the neighbouring Mowbray. Both bleak tenements stared across Red Cross Street at Harry and Mary Anne's place, at the rooms above the oil and colour shop, and at Harry below in his clean white shirt and long apron, setting out his products for the day: soap and candles and paraffin that gave the shop a wonderful smell, and stiff straw brooms that hung above the entryway. Such shops had evolved in recent years. An oil and colourman still dealt in paints and oils, but he also sold "pickles, sauces,… firewood, tinned goods, jams, brushes, baskets, hardware, lamps, and china."

Harry opened early each morning, around eight o'clock, after he had dusted and arranged his wares, propping open his door on warm days, and fixing signs in his window for items like Zebra Grate Polish, Sunlight Soap and Holbrook's Sauce. His name and trade would have been stencilled above the door in bold capital letters – H. Deverill, Oil & Colourman – and on most days he stayed open late into the evening, putting in at least seventy-five hours by week's end. Soon he had a grocery store in the street as well, and while there was some prestige in running one's own shop, Charles Booth believed: "Among grocers, as among other shopkeepers, the small man has fallen on evil days. In no trade apparently has 'cutting' been fiercer. The competition of 'the stores' has forced grocers to lower their prices until it is now exceedingly difficult for the man with only one shop to make a living; in a few years' time the trade will probably be confined to large firms, and to a certain number of very small shops in poor districts, where the master is on the same social level as his customers." That's where Harry was already – a young man making just enough to get by.

In February 1897, royalty ventured into the Borough when the Prince of Wales officially reopened the renovated St. Saviour's Church in the presence of the Duke and Duchess of Teck, the Archbishop of Canterbury and a train of other dignitaries. It had already been designated "Pro-Cathedral," meaning that it would soon receive the status of a full cathedral, and some £40,000 had been put toward its transformation. The *London Standard* called the reopening a "magnificent spectacle as well as an important historic event," and mused about the church's checkered past – noted poets buried on its grounds, kings married inside and bishops condemned to death at trials in the Lady Chapel, where Harry and Mary Anne had been married. "The variety of its associations and splendour of its history are surpassed only by Westminster Abbey." But "evil times" had prevailed, and "abominable excrescences and ruinous neglects brought about corresponding degradations" that had finally been addressed.

Great crowds gathered in Southwark Street and the Borough Market, which was dressed with flags and flowers. They cheered the prince and strained to get a glimpse of him as he disappeared through the double doors. Inside, the ceremony commenced, with the clergy in all their finest and a choir of men and boys extending the full length of the nave. Later the crowd outdoors watched the prince go, and waved and cheered at him. The look of them and their neighbourhood must have had some effect on him, for the *Evening Telegraph* reported: "It is an open secret that when the Prince of Wales went to open St. Saviour's Church he noticed the poverty-stricken condition of the streets through which he passed, and remarked that it would have been better to do something for the benefit of the poor rather than to decorate the streets with flags and banners." Perhaps he recalled his trip into the slums disguised in workingman's clothes, and how he'd longed to toss some money to a hungry mother and her malnourished children. His companions had convinced him that that would be foolish; he'd have been quickly attacked for whatever else he had.

It was a common enough opinion among the more privileged classes that the poor wanted handouts, that they were simply loafers, to blame for their own dire straits. The poor even believed it of each other, as the "Lazy Mary" slur attests. A week before the prince's visit to the Borough, four small children between the ages of two and nine were brought to the local police station by a woman who said they'd been deserted by their parents and were starving. She'd found them wandering in Red Cross Street, she said, where they'd slept several nights in stairwells, huddled together to fend off the February cold. The police inspector gave them a warm spot by the fire and fed them, and the next day they were given over to the care of the workhouse. Soon, though, it was discovered that the woman who'd brought them to the police in the first place was in fact their mother, and she was summoned to court to answer for her deception. She appeared with a fifth child – this one newborn – and said she'd been unable to feed the children. Presumably to avoid having to enter the workhouse herself, she'd thought up a lie in hopes of procuring food and lodging for them. The magistrate, seeing the woman's manipulation as a shirking of her parental responsibility and an abuse of society's generosity, returned the children to her and admonished her to look after them. Had the article included an illustration, it would have shown the judge wagging a scolding finger at the woman cowering in shame.

When it came to issues of poverty, the scolding went both ways. The Board of Guardians overseeing the Mint Street workhouse had recently brought charges against its master, William Tompson, and suspended him. They claimed he frequently neglected his responsibilities, wasted stores and provisions, failed to follow dietary regulations for his inmates and was often away from the workhouse for lengthy periods of time. While an inquiry into the matter found the accusations true and the master's conduct reprehensible, it was nonetheless decided that, due to his long period of service, he should be reinstated rather than forced to resign; but he should also consider himself fairly warned that any further infractions would cost him his job. The *British Medical Journal* reported on the decision, calling it nothing less than criminal, and a "grave and gross injustice to the poor." The Board's workhouse committee agreed. Just weeks after the decision, committee members announced they could not work with the master after all that had gone on, and that they would take further steps to secure his retirement. Soon after, Tompson's imprinted name was crossed out on the admission and discharge ledger, and a new master, one George Murray, was hired.

Yet the scandals continued. A couple of months into Murray's tenure, a tragic tale of starvation was reported in the *South London Press*, following a coroner's inquest. A forty-three-year-old woman named Emily Mott had been sleeping on doorsteps along Borough High Street for weeks. People who'd seen her around had noticed that she looked ill and weak. One night, around two a.m., a police officer came upon her and asked her to move along. She promised to do so but said she wasn't well and needed to rest a little longer. Eventually she carried on, stopping frequently as she made her way down the street. When another man paused to speak to her, she told him she had no home, and he convinced her to go to the Mint Street workhouse, where she was admitted at around three a.m. by one of the inmates charged with night duty. Once inside, she told the inmate that she had not taken off her clothes in eight weeks, for she'd had nowhere to sleep, and she was so weak that she had difficulty removing them now and donning the uniform. She was filthy and emaciated and hadn't even the strength to feed herself. The court learned that the doctor had not been called until seven a.m., that there was no nurse on staff and that the only person to care for her was the inmate who'd received her. Emily Mott died later that evening. Perhaps the death was not in vain, since the coroner recommended that a nurse be available to receive all female patients, no matter the hour. But would Emily have lived if she'd been seen right away? The real point, it seemed, was that she'd held off entering the workhouse until she was dangerously emaciated – that people would rather starve than go there.

This raises again the question of Mary Evans nee Jones – Ellen, Jennie and Mary Anne's mother – who entered the Mint Street workhouse despite having so many family members nearby. Apart from her children, she also had siblings: her sister Maggie still on Red Cross Street with her cows and her wayward husband, and her brother David living south of the workhouse, running his own small dairy. David had recently become a vestryman for the parish of St. George the Martyr, which, together with the Board of Guardians, conducted the business of the parish and had input into the operation of the workhouse. Annual reports show that David was an active member of the vestry, attending almost all of the weekly Tuesday evening meetings and participating on the General Purposes and Open Spaces Committee, ostensibly mulling the problem that there was little open space to be had in the Borough. When the workhouse was discussed at those meetings – its scandals or the cost "per head per day" of sheltering paupers – did David think of his sister Mary? Did he think of niece Ellen when the Medical Officer of Health deemed the Mowbray Buildings unfit for human habitation?

The corporate owners of the Mowbray had recently been charged with violations of the Public Health Act. Evidence had been gathered during midnight raids, and lawyers argued back and forth over the conditions in the structure. There was an unusually high rate of mortality connected to the property, one side claimed, owing to bad ventilation and foul air and what amounted to open cesspits by the entry doors. The Medical Officer of Health believed the buildings should be closed down, like so many others in the area. Representatives of the Mowbray denied the charges, purporting that the buildings were in fairly good order given the low rents and the class of tenants inside. By virtue of their poor status, the owners seemed to be arguing, the residents of the Mowbray Buildings deserved lower standards.

One quarter of children born in the Mowbray Buildings died within their first year, the court heard, and that very spring – in April 1897 – Ellen gave birth there, to a baby girl. Drunk or confused, or in love with what she'd decided was a pretty name, she called the girl Florence, the same as her third child with Fred, so now she had two daughters registered as Florence Roff. Did her sisters gently chide her, encouraging her to choose another name, reminding her of the existence of her other family? Or did they leave her to her muddled world, mired among the low? On the baby's birth certificate, the box for "father" was stroked through, but by the time Florence was baptized, she had been given the name Humphreys, and Ellen had taken it too, though records show no divorce from Fred Roff, and no subsequent marriage to the new man, John.

When celebrations occurred for Queen Victoria's Diamond Jubilee in June 1897, Mary Anne was pregnant with a baby due soon after Christmas. As the queen's procession made its way through the Borough, she and Harry likely stood in the throng with hands clasped, excited by both the pageantry of the event and the thrill of the coming child. Ten years after the parties for the golden jubilee, this grander celebration meant Harry's shop was closed for the day. The crowds were thick along the parade route that crossed into Southwark at London Bridge and followed Borough High Street before wending west and back across the Thames at Westminster Bridge. A number of viewing galleries had been placed at the Borough Polytechnic Institute, a technical college on Borough Road that offered courses relevant to the local population: oil and colour (Harry's trade), masonry, plumbing and leather tanning, as well as science, music and elocution. The *Morning Post* reported that the exterior of the college had been wonderfully transformed by the decorations. "Flags and banners hung from every possible point, and along the front of the main gallery was expressed in letters of striking size, worked in yellow on a crimson ground, a sentiment which appealed to each individual of the thousands who saw it: 'May children of our children say she wrought the people lasting good.'" The seats were let for a fee to raise money for the school's expansion, with the college reportedly holding out for more than twice what Harrods department store paid to buy the view from the St. Martin-in-the-Fields churchyard.

It seemed everyone with a place along the route was a speculator. In the weeks leading up to parade day, after it had been announced that Borough High Street would be part of the route, landlords began evicting tenants, knowing that the vacated High Street premises would fetch a small fortune as viewing galleries on the big day and that they could easily move another tenant in when the celebrations were over. One couple, a watchmaker and his wife, barricaded themselves in their shop and refused to leave, setting a sign in the window advertising the fact that they'd been unfairly evicted. The police came to remove them, but a surly crowd had gathered in the street, standing in rain and mud, and people jeered as the officers smashed the glass in the door and read out their warrant. When the defeated couple appeared, the onlookers cheered them. The newspaper described the man as "thin-faced [and] undersized...with a deformed back and looks like one who has had a hard struggle for an honest living." Later the watchmaker told a reporter, "This jubilee business has been just the ruin of me...now I haven't got a shilling, or a business, or anywhere to go."

Newspaper accounts of the day acknowledged the Borough as the poor cousin to the areas north of the Thames on the parade route, but they also claimed that if the streets were not so elaborately decorated as those across the river, the enthusiasm of the people was a match. Harry and Mary Anne would have been two of thousands sporting ribbons of blue, red and white. And when the first of the royal procession appeared at the top of Borough High Street at five minutes to twelve, they'd have cheered, Harry holding his cap high with other men doing the same. Wave after wave of military regiments passed, sun glinting on helmets and medals, followed by the carriages of dignitaries and royal guests, with princes riding alongside on plumed horses. Victoria was empress of some 450 million people around the globe – Britannia at its pinnacle – and all the colonies were represented. Her many children and grandchildren had married into nearly every royal house in Europe, ensuring her a tight weave of influence around the world, and members of these families too were present, dressed in their finery and riding in open landaus. Victoria's grandson, Kaiser Wilhelm, had not been invited this time, and despite strong familial links between the German and British monarchies, relations were souring, just as they were improving with Russia. Nicholas II, the handsome new tsar, had married Victoria's granddaughter Alexandra, and Victoria found him charming and delightful.

The crowd roared when the queen's carriage finally appeared, the imperial lady herself sheltered from the sun by a white silk parasol. At seventy-eight she was much frailer than she'd been ten years earlier, and was still shrouded in black, with a bonnet of ostrich feathers and diamonds. She studied the throng through opera glasses, as curious about them as they were about her. It was the first time in her long reign that the queen had visited the Borough, and later, thinking of the multitudes there and elsewhere, she wrote in her journal, "A never-to-be-forgotten day. No one ever, I believe, has met with such an ovation as was given to me…The cheering was quite deafening and every face seemed to be filled with real joy."

Harry and Mary Anne's son arrived on a Monday in January 1898. They named him Joseph William, but he would be Joe, a name suited to the man he'd become: small, round and unassuming. His cries, echoing into the street as he announced himself to the world, were muffled by a damp winter fog that clung to the walls of Harry's shop and shrouded the gaslights in the street. Harry was doing a brisk trade in kerosene and paraffin these days, as people struggled to keep the chill at bay. But with Joe's arrival, Harry's need to succeed in his business expanded. He had a boy to provide for now, and with luck there would be more children coming. When the grocer at 64 Red Cross Street moved on, Harry took over the premises, a full circle for Mary Anne, who had grown up at this address, home of her grandparents, Benjamin and Margaret Jones. There was more and more crossover between the trades these days, so it was a neat arrangement when Harry's younger brother Jack moved into 68 and assumed the trade of oil and colourman, while Harry tried his hand as a grocer, as his father had done years ago. Deverill Bros., he and Jack had become, and neighbours too. Soon the family ties would grow even stronger when Jack married Mary Anne's cousin Meg, eldest daughter of Aunt Maggie.

It must have seemed in those days that they would never leave the street, though indeed they would in just a handful of years. For now, relatives were all around them as the clusters of family grew and over-lapped, and each became caught up in the others' dramas, whether happy or sad. Richard Vanson's sister Emma, one of the girls who'd been with him at Hanwell School for orphans, married a Deptford man, an ac-quaintance of Harry's, and the couple briefly lived with Harry and Mary Anne in the small rooms above the shop. All the talk at 64 was about the latest Vanson family tragedy: in a sorry case of history repeating itself, the children of Emma and Richard's brother Stephen were sent to Hanwell. This time there were three of them: the eldest, thirteen-year-old Stephen, namesake of his doomed father and grandfather and great-grandfather, along with seven-year-old George and four-year-old Louisa. They had several other siblings who, for unknown reasons, were not admitted with them when they arrived in October 1897.

Many years later, Edward Balne, an orphaned Mint Street work-house boy who entered around the same time, wrote his memories of the place as he approached eighty years of age, detailing what chil-dren saw when they first landed at Hanwell. "By the time [the hill] ... was reached, one had had to encounter a very steep climb indeed, but the effort was worthwhile, because just a few steps farther on, one en-tered one of the many lovely leafy lanes of Greenford, with a vista of the wide open countryside spread out before one like some magic and gaily decorated carpet." Another boy there in that period – the soon-to-be-famous Charlie Chaplin – agreed on the stunning scenery, but later wrote that "Sadness was in the air; it was in those country lanes through which we walked, a hundred of us two abreast. How I disliked those walks, and the villages through which we passed, the locals staring at us! We were known as inmates of the 'booby hatch,' a slang term for the workhouse."

The story of Chaplin's early years has a familiar ring. He lived much of his childhood in the Lambeth area, close to Fred and Ellen Roff's place. His mother was a shoemaker's daughter and his father a butcher's son, though they themselves had gravitated toward the music hall stage: Hannah was a singer and character comedienne who went by the stage name Lily Harley and had performed throughout Britain; Charles Sr. wrote and performed his own material – songs like "Oui, Tray Bong" and "The Girl was Young and Pretty" – but drink eventually hampered his success. What with alcohol and violence, the marriage disintegrated soon after Charlie was born. When Charlie was five, Hannah lost her voice on stage, and he performed in her place. She never regained her singing voice, and after her separation from Charlie's father she became increasingly fragile, suffering from migraines and exhibiting manic behaviour. At times she earned money working for a sweatshop, sewing blouses at home and aiming to make twelve every twelve hours. Her skill was great, honed by years of making her own stage costumes, but her income was meagre, and with little alternative she entered Newington Workhouse right around the time that Ellen's troubles with Fred were escalating. Young Charlie and his older brother followed her in. In the usual way with child inmates, Charlie's hair was shorn, and his clothing replaced with a uniform. He was separated from his mother, and when he saw her later, also clad in workhouse clothes, she looked "forlorn and embarrassed." But the workhouse wasn't an unfamiliar concept. Records show that Hannah's mother had recently been in Newington too. An "old clothes hawker" given to drink and worry, she was labelled a person of unsound mind upon her admission. She believed there were rats and mice in there with her, according to the reception orders, and beetles in her bed – which was likely enough; less likely was her certainty that the doctors of the infirmary were trying to poison her.

As was the norm when parents entered the local workhouse, Hannah's boys were sent to Hanwell. Charlie was still there when the Vanson children arrived, and was close in age to the middle boy, George. An 1897 photograph shows a mischievous-looking Charlie with a class of about seventy boys his age, any one of whom might be George Vanson. Charlie mentions none of his classmates by name, but his descriptions of life on the boys' side of Hanwell illuminate an unhappy time. One fourteen-year-old boy – a "desperado" Stephen Vanson's age – hated the place so thoroughly that he stole through a second-floor window and clambered to the roof, throwing horse chestnuts at the officials who chased after him. Though the escape was brave and impassioned, it didn't succeed, and the boy was placed in solitary confinement, awaiting further punishment: a flogging, which all the other boys would witness, and which always landed the recipient in surgery.

Such punishments were a weekly ritual. The bugle was blown, the boys were lined up, the names announced and the cruelty began. For minor offences, a boy was laid across a table and caned. "The spectacle was terrifying, and invariably a boy would fall out of rank in a faint," Charlie recounted. As he learned from personal experience, "the strokes were paralysing, so that the victim had to be carried to one side and laid on a gymnasium mattress, where he was left to writhe and wriggle for at least ten minutes before the pain subsided, leaving three pink welts as wide as a washerwoman's finger across his bottom." The birch – inflicted for more serious infractions like the desperado's – was worse still. A boy's wrists were strapped to an easel; if he was too little to reach the straps, he stood on a soapbox. The strokes were wicked but fast. Three of them and the job was done.

Edward Balne's account of punishments at Hanwell matches Chaplin's, including the onlookers fainting. He would watch "the first heavy swish" and then close his eyes for the rest, but he could still hear the boy screaming if the victim wasn't one of those rare children able to "take the medicine like men." Though Balne found the beatings barbaric, even as a child, he never blamed the yard master who doled them out. He was simply doing his job, and the rules weren't rules he had made. "During the closing years of the 19th century," Balne wrote, "when the poor were literally the outcasts and pariahs of the then robust and most powerful nation in the world, schools of this kind (the Poor Law type) were not only few in number but pretty grim establishments. Frequent administrations of the cane and the birch were the rule and not (repeat not) the exception." This form of punishment happened at posh schools as well, but there had been suggestions over the years that there was "an unnecessary amount of flogging" at Hanwell. Yet Balne had been told that Hanwell was one of the best schools of its kind. He believed it, and furthermore maintained that the school had given him a decent education he would otherwise not have received. There was musical in-struction, taught by a "brilliant" ex-army band sergeant, and children marched to their meals as the brass band played. Students were drilled on the three Rs, and taught to speak distinctly, sounding their aitches. "Woe betide the boy who made a persistent habit in dropping them." Chaplin, too, recalls Hanwell as his first taste of real schooling, where he learned to write "Chaplin." "The word fascinated me and looked like me, I thought."

But young Charlie ached for his mother. Though Balne, who'd never known his own parents, called one of the more fatherly teachers "Daddy Wadsworth," for many of the students there was no replacing family, whether or not the powers that be deemed them unfit or poor influen-ces. Charlie was elated when his mother arrived. "Her presence was like a bouquet of flowers." He went home with her in January, and though it was not long before she was ill again and he was sent to a similar school, for now he was happy to be reunited with her.

With Stephen-the-father still at Newington Workhouse, and his wife Emmie and the other children who knows where, Stephen, George and Louisa Vanson were kept at Hanwell throughout the autumn and on into February, when George died in the infirmary. The death certificate, signed by the school's medical officer, Dr. Salterne Litteljohn, names the cause as "meningitis about 10 days; convulsions 3 hours," but beyond that there are no details. George may have had an infection that sim-ply couldn't be controlled, but there is a possibility that meningitis was brought on by a skull fracture. There were frequent newspaper reports of such cases, and coroner's inquests held to determine if foul play were involved. One piece told of serious allegations against a schoolmistress for hitting a boy who'd done poorly in his lessons. Later the same day he felt increasingly unwell, was admitted to the infirmary and died a few days later. A post-mortem examination determined suppurative meningitis had been caused by a blow to the head. A similar case involved Hanwell and pointed the blame at Dr. Litteljohn, not for inflicting injury but for "laxity of attention" once the patient was brought to him. The girl had received an "accidental blow" in the morning, and then an "accidental knock" in the evening. On waking the following day, the pain in her head was so extreme that she was taken to the doctor and fell unconscious shortly after that. Dr. Litteljohn prescribed ice, left her in the care of a worker who was not a trained nurse, and did not see her again. "He thought there was no need to, seeing that the child was dying."

In fairness, the article cannot give us the full story, and Dr. Litteljohn had many children under his care. An 1897 *British Medical Journal* report on Hanwell called it a "pauper palace" and said its massive size – housing around one thousand children – contributed to the spread of illness. Statistics showed that disease rates were higher at Hanwell, a barrack-style institution, than they were at smaller schools run as so-called village communities. The author of the report detected "a note of sadness, a sense of failure" as he interviewed Dr. Litteljohn, who'd been at the school since the 1870s, even before the previous generation of Vansons were admitted. "For twenty-four years he has given labour and thought, time and strength, to the impossible task of cultivating health in unhealthy subjects under unhealthy conditions." The doctor's own reports to the Board of Guardians show a frustration with the system. If the children were to thrive, both physically and mentally, they needed proper rest and "outings in the pure air," and though their schedule ostensibly allowed for such restorative periods, Dr. Litteljohn claimed that in actuality the children were put to work during many of those holiday hours, and they were worse off because of it. His concern for the children extended beyond their physical health:

If you take the case of a child who comes there when he is four, and remains there over ten years perhaps; he goes to school every day except Sunday, and at the end of ten years all he has been practically taught is reading, writing and arithmetic. My own opinion is that there should be a much more liberal system of teaching; that the children should have something brought under their notice which would interest them more than the "three Rs."... I do not believe that the children in our schools, if you were to ask them, would be able to tell you the names of the trees that grow around them. I know children who have walked down the fields repeatedly to the farm, and who do not know what a turnip is.

Little George Vanson's chances for learning were over. A flurry of activity shows in the records, giving shape to his story. On February 6 he entered the infirmary. Four days later his siblings were discharged from Hanwell to their father, Stephen. Had he come to retrieve them because he'd heard about George? In another six days George was dead, and less than a week after that, his siblings returned to Hanwell, marked as "deserted by father," which meant that Stephen had entered the workhouse again, for reasons unknown. On March 10 the children's mother came for them and made the trip back to the city, a child on each side of her and one forever missing.

By spring, Ellen Evans Roff Humphreys and her man John had their second daughter, Nellie, and Jennie Vanson was pregnant again. Her older girls skipped rope or chased iron hoops along the street with sticks. When they played "Queenie," the child deemed queen stood with her back to her band of ragged subjects and tossed a ball over her shoulder. She had to guess who caught it, and when she failed, subject and queen traded places.

In reality, it was not so easy to change one's lot in life, as became all too clear when Ellen's daughter Flo – the one fathered by John Humphreys – fell seriously ill. With so many other Borough babies dying soon after getting sick, Ellen must have been frightened for the child's life, and her soul: Flo was baptized the very day she was admitted to the Evelina Hospital for Sick Children, next to the Mint Street workhouse where her grandmother Mary still resided. John was probably at Ellen's side, since the baptismal register lists the parents as though they were a married couple. Flo spent more than a week in care, alongside other

Red Cross Street children admitted that month with similar illnesses: whooping cough and bronchial pneumonia. Frank Bottone, the four-year-old son of an Italian ice cream vendor who lived across the street from Ellen, next to Harry and Mary Anne, was there at the same time, with the same sickness. But Frank seemed the kind of boy who could survive anything: he'd been admitted earlier in the year for various ailments, and the following year he'd be run over. The register doesn't say how the accident happened, or who hit him, but he was brought to the Evelina with a concussion, only to be sent home with chicken pox.

The children were well cared for at the hospital, which served regular healthy meals and had bright, airy wards and a playroom for the kids who were feeling up to enjoying it. A photograph shows a ward with floor-to-ceiling windows, the transoms pulled open so that sunlight streams in. The room curves in a gentle arc, and patterned tiles decorate the walls. Several nurses stand at attention wearing white caps and long white aprons over darker dresses with crisp, high collars. Two of the nurses hold babies in their arms, and another rests her hands on a young boy's shoulders. A doctor kneels beside a boy astride a rocking horse, and next to them a little girl with a bow in her hair sits on a child-sized chair. The room appears friendly and clean: rows of tidy cots with pretty iron frames; a palm growing out of the back of a decorative swan; a fireplace for cool weather.

George Carpenter, one of the esteemed doctors at the Evelina, had, that very year, been charged with updating the classic *Advice to a Mother on the Management of Her Children* by Henry Pye Chavasse. The book promised clear, simple information, free from technical jargon, and covered everything from smelly feet to measles. For Flo's illness there were several pages of advice. "If you put your finger into the mouth of a child labouring under inflammation of the lungs, it is like putting your finger into a hot apple pie, the heat is so great." Mothers were urged to lose no time seeking medical aid should the child be so afflicted. Once cured, it was advised that the child should from then on wash in salt water each morning, and wear flannel shirts and lambswool stockings pulled above the knees, and dry shoes of good quality; in appropriate weather she should spend lots of time outside every day, and have plenty of milk and meat in her diet. In the autumn she should travel to the seaside and spend a couple of months breathing the fresh, salty air. Did Dr. Carpenter wonder at the chances of this routine being followed when his impoverished patients were sent home? A local newspaper reported it was sad to see the children return to their "dark, unfurnished, overcrowded rooms…One of the nurses told us the pity she felt [when] she met a child who had not long left her care clinging to a drunken mother's skirts, and following her zigzag plunges from one side of the street to the other."

For most of the children admitted that month, the outcome was "relieved," just as Ellen must have been when Flo was returned to her after an eight-day stay. But even before she came home, her baby sister Nellie had begun vomiting. There was diarrhea also – two dreaded afflictions that were difficult to curtail, especially during summers like this one. It was early September, and temperatures were soaring in London. Papers reported cases of sunstroke, exhaustion and even suicide because of the intense heat. Nellie was not admitted to the Evelina for care, but the church register shows a baptism took place at St. Saviour's Church. Newly blessed, Nellie, just four months old, died nine days later, a daughter dwindling to little more than a statistic: one of the many Mowbray babies who never made it past the first year.

The burial register shows that Nellie was laid to rest north of the Thames, at Manor Park Cemetery, one of a number of garden cemeteries built decades earlier in response to overcrowded churchyards and burial grounds. She was placed in a common grave, since a private plot was beyond her parents' means. Of the burial itself there are no clues, except for the broader fact that even the poor spent lavishly on funerals – as lavishly as they could, at least. They bought burial insurance to avoid the indignity of a pauper funeral paid for by the parish; many contributed weekly to "funeral clubs" in order to save enough for decent trappings: black garments for the family, the use of a hearse and coachman, and the coffin itself – black for an adult, white for a child. Displays in undertakers' windows advertised myriad choices available to the bereaved: elaborate funeral cards to announce the deaths, plumes of black ostrich feathers for the horses pulling the hearse, stone markers carved with doves or broken lilies. But there was no marker for Nellie. That same day, three other babies went into square seven, grave 50, on top of four bodies buried earlier in the month. Jennie and Mary Anne must have prayed for their grieving sister, but also for their own babies-to-be, since both were pregnant when Nellie died.

Even outside of the Mowbray, infant mortality was high in London. While life expectancy in the general population increased, in the late 1890s babies were dying at the rate they had thirty years earlier – 160 small souls for every thousand born. They died of diarrhea and dysentery and gastroenteritis, of whooping cough and diphtheria and tuberculosis. In the Borough, where the death rate was significantly higher, one of the chief causes was chronic wasting disease, produced by malnutrition, and a result of improper feeding. But the Medical Officer of Health cited several other factors that interfered with a Borough baby's failure to thrive, among them overcrowding, and a dearth of parks and open spaces; debility and disease of parents; maternal ignorance and neglect. All these, he said, "play a considerable part in either destroying or crippling the lives of these slum-bred children." He stressed that the death rates of infants under one year spoke volumes about the sanitary well-being of the community at large.

In December, Jennie and Richard's fifth baby, Edith, arrived, but she was dead nine months later, a year and one day after Nellie. And like Nellie she was buried in one of Manor Park's common graves, with seventeen strangers. All that remains of these lives is the curl of ink on a register where the names have been recorded: a curt, inadequate statement of their existence.

It seemed merely luck that Mary Anne's baby – Ethel, a sister for Joe – survived. Mary Anne couldn't know it at the time, but later she would come to depend on this girl for everything. Ethel was baptized at St. Saviour's Church, though there's no sign that Joe was, and baptism wasn't part of Harry's tradition as a Salvationist. It was morally wrong, General Booth believed, to say a person couldn't get to heaven without having been baptized with water. At the same time, he urged those who wanted the ceremony to seek it. "The churches and chapels all round about will welcome you for this, but in our own ranks let us be united, and go on our way, and mind our own business." And so Ethel, and the siblings who followed her, received the symbolic cleansing.

No photographs have been found of Ethel as a baby or even a small child, though some must have been made. A picture of Harry with Joe as a toddler is a tender portrait, though the subjects barely touch and neither smiles. Taken around the time of Ethel's birth, the photograph shows Joe dressed in a wide-brimmed bonnet, a jacket with huge lapels, and a tiny pleated skirt. His shiny boots with all their buttons peer out from the hem as he sits perched on a table next to his father. He looks puzzled by the moment and stares just above the lens, as if wondering why the man taking the picture has disappeared under a dark cloth. Will there be a game of peek-a-boo? Beside him, Harry sits in a chair, one leg crossed over the other. He's neatly dressed, with trimmed hair and a broad moustache. He's a small man, but his hands look strong, with thick fingers. What made him trot out with his son on this day and have an image of just the two of them captured for posterity? This was the first such portrait of Harry and Joe alone, but not the last.

As Joe and Ethel grew, the dizzying sequence of births and young deaths in the wider family continued. When one set of parents was welcoming a child, another was saying goodbye. Shortly after Jack and Meg had their daughter May in October 1900 – an enduring best friend for Ethel, and a cousin on both sides – a female sanitary inspector was appointed for the area, in light of the infant mortality rate. In a way she was the personification of Chavasse's *Advice to a Mother on the Management of Her Children*. She went house-to-house making "health visits," telling mothers how to feed and clothe their children, and how to keep a home scrupulously clean. The idea was "the maximum of health and the minimum of sickness." It was a tricky position, one woman telling another how to do her job, but one that was becoming more common in poor areas throughout the country. Candidates for such posts were usually widowed or unmarried, and not more than thirty-five years of age. "I would not like to be the female inspector," one man quipped in the *Evening Post*. "She will soon find the bottom of the stair."

If such a woman visited Mary Anne, offering sanitary pearls of wisdom with or without tact, it did not save her two boys, born in quick succession in the coming years. According to the death certificates, both babies – Harry, two months old, and then Alfred, just ten months – perished at home, of epidemic diarrhea and exhaustion, which meant quite simply that they were worn out by the relentless illness.

Though Mary Anne seemed more able to cope than her sister Ellen, it wouldn't have been hard to blame herself for these deaths. There was no real substitute for mother's milk, Chavasse's *Advice* stressed, but a breastfeeding mother should know that she could cause her baby's illness by being ill herself, by eating unsuitable food, by taking "drastic purgatives," by worrying, being anxious or angry, or even by being pregnant with another child. A child who had no interest in the breast was usually a victim of "bad management," the book stated, as was the "overloaded" baby who was fed every time he cried. And speaking of crying – the emotional mother should understand that her mind had "a great influence for good and evil" on the body of her baby. "The child's health may be marred and seriously damaged by colic, flatulency, diarrhoea, and sickness, and even its life endangered by convulsions and exhaustion owing to a mother's want of control over her emotions. Women of a highly nervous temperament do not make good nurses. Fits of rage and temper, seasons of fasting, with their attendant emotional disturbance, the worries, anxieties and vicissitudes of daily life, if allowed controlled sway, will induce such changes in the milk as to make it unfit for nourishing the babe." Should she choose not to breastfeed, the mother who could afford the next best option of cow's milk had better boil it well. It was often "swarming with germs…particles of hair, dirt, straws, hay, and so forth" by the time it reached the consumer. Of this, Mary Anne, Ellen, Jennie and Meg – young mothers who were granddaughters of a dairyman – had first-hand knowledge. Aunt Maggie still had her cows, and Uncle David, though no longer on the prestigious vestry, was still turning up in the yearly reports – twice he was suspected of watering his milk, as Benjamin had been, but both times the charges were dropped.

Mary Anne's boys were buried south of the Borough at Nunhead Cemetery, another of the sprawling garden cemeteries that made room for the city's dead. While the details of those services have disappeared, like the graves themselves, there is one tempting clue of the family coming together: right after baby Harry's death, Mary Anne's mother, Mary, was discharged from the Mint Street workhouse at her own request, trading in her uniform for her old clothes, bothersome boots and all. If she trudged up Red Cross Street to assuage her daughter's grief, it was a quick visit. The following day, Mary was readmitted and settled in for a lengthy stay.

The first of several shots taken of Harry and Joe together, likely around 1900. Joe wears the skirt and wide-brimmed hat typical of toddler dress in the Victorian era.

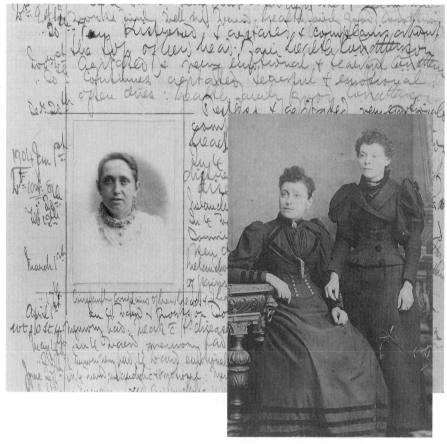

This photograph of Ellen Evans Roff in 1904 was found in a Stone Asylum
casebook, held at the London Metropolitan Archives. The books are full of images
like this one, surrounded by scribbled details of the patients' various troubles.
Courtesy London Metropolitan Archives (City of London).
In stark contrast is the formal portrait of Ellen's sisters, Mary Anne, left,
and Jennie, likely taken around the same time.

Tell Me When Your Mother Drops

In the last years of Victoria's long reign, Britain, too, was showing signs of weariness. The country was locked in a second war with South Africa, which proved to be messier and lengthier than the first. Twenty years earlier, attempting to expand its colonization of the area, Britain had lost its contest with the Boers, but discovery of gold in the region had renewed Britain's appetite for the conflict. Whether her men were cut out for the fight was another matter. Recent studies had shown a serious decline in the health of potential soldiers, not just in London but in other parts of the country as well. The 1899 findings of social investigator Seebohm Rowntree, doing work similar to that of Charles Booth, showed that in a four-year period, almost half of would-be recruits in York, Leeds and Sheffield were rejected on medical grounds. A little later, in 1902, Boer War General J.F. Maurice insisted that out of every five Englishmen who enlisted, only two became effective soldiers. The idea that the might of the British Empire had withered was alarming news.

In his book *Efficiency and Empire*, journalist Arnold White warned that "the first element of efficiency is health … A quarrel between two nations, one of which lives mainly in the open air, and the other mostly in streets and tenement houses, suggests the reconsidering of our own attitude towards the unfit." He listed a full page of ideas the English believed about themselves – Britannia rules the waves, one Englishman can beat two foreigners, the Empire is safe from decay – and then bluntly stated that such propositions were either disputable or entirely false. And while South Africa was its current rival – a lesson to be heeded – there were others in the wings, and none of them were deteriorating in physical stamina. "If we continue for another twenty years as we are going on at the present time, there is little doubt that the delicacy and infirmity of the race will then prove unequal to the maintenance of a great and growing Empire. What was won by a hardy people, fed on their own beef and bread, will scarcely be held by invalids."

The death of Queen Victoria in January 1901 seemed to underscore the country's vulnerability. Accounts of her demise describe the smallest detail, reporting that she lay on her flower-strewn bed at Osborne House surrounded by palms and ferns, and with "a white veil of the purest thin silk" covering her face. A silver crucifix hung on the wall, and a bust of her long-dead husband rested on a nearby table. "The last moments," wrote the Bishop of Winchester, "were like a great three-decker ship sinking." Her eldest grandson, the Kaiser of Germany, later claimed she died in his arms. "She was so little – and so light," he recalled.

Lists were published of the various royal houses that would be attending the memorial – a similar cast of characters as at the jubilees. Tsar Nicholas was ill and couldn't be there, but Germany committed a bevy of princes and counts to the occasion, which was not surprising, given Victoria's German roots and branches. Just days before the funeral, the Prince of Wales, now king, made his nephew, Kaiser Wilhelm, a field marshal in the British army in honour of his birthday. But the relationship with Wilhelm had always been contentious. In recent years, as the royal family's bond with Russia grew, Victoria had written to Tsar Nicholas and confided, "I am afraid [Wilhelm] may go and tell things against us to you, just as he does about you to us. If so, pray tell me openly and confidentially. It is so important that we should understand each other, and that such mischievous and unstraightforward proceedings be put a stop to."

Harry's shop was closed on the Saturday of the funeral, likely only the second time he'd ever shut his doors on a workday. The first would have been for the queen's diamond jubilee, an event equally grand but much less sombre. If Harry and Mary Anne crossed the Thames to watch Victoria's funeral procession make its way toward Paddington Station for the journey on to Windsor, they'd have been struck by the still and utterly silent crowds standing thirty and forty deep, but also by the military pageantry of the affair. Eight cream-coloured horses, their manes plaited with purple ribbon, pulled the coffin on a gun-carriage, while representatives of the army and navy and colonial regiments marched in dress uniform. The weather was fine but cold, and when the new king, Edward VII, rode past, accompanied by Kaiser Wilhelm, the horses' breath plumed white in the chill of the morning. Harry and Mary Anne likely held Joe and Ethel against them to share their warmth, noses red as they peered at the solemn scene. Every eye, the newspapers promised, was turned to the new sovereign and, next to him, to the Kaiser, "a powerful and potential Imperial friend." The fact that Wilhelm had rushed to his dying grandmother's side, and had seemingly been welcomed by her heir, spoke volumes. "All those in Germany and abroad – and there are a great many – who speculated on an estrangement between the German and British Royal Houses, and consequently the two countries, must now see that their calculation was wrong. It does great credit to the political sense of King Edward that he has once and for all nipped in the bud hopes cherished by the adversaries of an Anglo-German friendship."

Two months after the queen's death, newspapers carried the reminder that April 1 was census day, and enumerators would be making their rounds to do "the big count." The papers mused about the reliability of the census, with its blind watchmen and dumb preachers; its ladies who grew mysteriously younger as the decades passed. The question as to who was the head of the family could well cause domestic disputes, they teased, since more often than not "the grey mare is the better horse." Harry and Mary Anne appear at 64 Red Cross Street as head and wife, age thirty and twenty-eight respectively. Harry was "grocer, own account," working at home, with Joe and Ethel underfoot, now three and two years old. Behind them, buffered by the gardens, a couple of policemen lived with their wives and young kids in the well-kept Red Cross Cottages. Just south of Harry was a family of book folders, and one more door down, Jack with Meg and daughter May. Next to Jack lived a German baker and his wife, their English-born children, and their three employees, all born in Germany. And to Harry's north, the family of Italians selling sweets and ice cream; together with their wives, children and other family members, they totalled seventeen people in close quarters, their house joined to Harry's own. Among the many children there was Frank Bottone, the boy who'd been in the Evelina Hospital with Ellen's daughter, and two Lorenzos just Joe's age. Did the children mix? Or did they gobble the goods their neighbours had to offer and play among their own?

Italian ice cream was popular in London at the time, but it was unpopular too. The "penny lick" was served in a sundae-style glass that you licked clean and then returned to the vendor, who typically gave it a quick wipe and used it for the next customer. This serving practice was banned because of health concerns, brought to light by rants that also revealed ethnic hostilities: "Hardly a week goes by," the *Telegraph* reported,

> without an inquest being held upon the body of some luckless child whose death is due directly to this pestilential concoction, which is retailed in dirty glasses by dirty hands from dirty cans... The victims in the vast majority of cases are little children who spend their farthings and halfpence on this most pernicious sweetmeat. The business is almost entirely in the hands of Italians, who herd together in the lowest slums...Their influence in the London streets is wholly mischievous, and England is the only country where their presence would be tolerated...What they produce is poison of the most virulent kind, and no sentimental considerations ought to stand in the way of protecting the children. If they cannot make a living by other means, let them be sent back to their own country, and, for the future, debar their indigent comrades from landing. London has been too long the dumping ground for the refuse of the Continent.

And yet sweets "are to food what tucks and ruffles are to clothing." Not essential but delightful, especially in grim surroundings. The vendor with his painted barrow travelled the streets crying *"Gelati, ecco un poco!"* – "here's a little" – and the children came running with their coins and hungry bellies. They called the treat "hokey pokey" because they could not quite make out what the vendors were saying, but the flavour they understood with ease.

In recent years, Italians had arrived in London in large numbers, fleeing circumstances similar to those Benjamin and Margaret Jones had fled when they'd left Wales with their cows in the 1840s. Though they appeared here and there in the neighbourhood, the census shows that residents of the Mowbray Buildings at this time were largely South-wark-born. The single Italian family there was related to Harry's neighbours – presumably spillover from the packed house – and there were the odd Irish and Welsh groups too. The tenants had jobs like fur puller, bottle washer and rag sorter, card cutter, seed packer and collar stitcher. The very titles point to the minuteness of the tasks. How many rags would you have to sort to collect a decent day's earnings? How many seeds went into a packet?

Ellen and her man, John Humphreys, were two of these folk, living in a single room with Flo, now four, and baby John, just three months old. But young John was doomed, just like Meg and Mary Anne's boys, two of Jennie's children, and his sister Nellie before him. His death certificate shows that he died early in 1902 at the Evelina, though hospital records from that time have been lost. In the Evelina's early days, children under two were not admissible, because caring for them – washing, dressing, feeding them – took up too much of the nurses' time and made it difficult to tend to the rest of the children. Of course the littlest ones were also the most vulnerable, and so the rule was increasingly overlooked and eventually rescinded. Even still, there was not enough money to keep the hospital's beds full, and most children were treated as outpatients instead, often sent home to an unhealthy environment, possibly disastrous for an unwell child. John, a victim of bronchopneumonia, which had killed countless other Borough babes, was buried in a common grave at Manor Park, never to enjoy the changes that were taking place to enrich the lives of the neighbourhood's children.

That January, London County Council officially opened Little Dorrit's Playground in the Falcon Court area, where Benjamin had once kept his cows. The first weeks of the new year had been relatively mild, though by month's end, when the ceremony took place, the days grew bright and cold, with wintry showers. The new playground was close to St. George the Martyr Church, whose vestry had convinced the council a playground was needed. Eight years earlier, the *Standard* had described the Borough's people as "decimated by disease and producing a race of children even more sickly and degenerate than their parents. Child life is, in fact, blighted, and a plentiful crop of pauperism is provided for the future." The parish vestry had appealed to the council for land, pointing out that there were twelve blocks of working-class dwellings in close proximity to the site suggested – buildings full of children who needed their own place to play. In time, a long swathe of slum buildings behind the Mowbray and the Stanhope was razed, and a small patch of the land was tar-paved and named after Dickens's Dorrit.

The changes came none too soon, according to the *Standard*, which had had harsh words for the slums branching off Red Cross Street and the excessive rents charged by landlords who left their buildings in "a shocking state of dirt and dilapidation…The whole locality reeks with noisome exhalations, and the difficulty is to understand, not why the inhabitants look stunted, miserable, and sickly, but how they are able to exist at all, in the utter absence of anything approaching decent sanitary arrangements." The *Standard* found it "satisfactory" that a large number of buildings had been torn down, though it meant that the residents had been displaced. The people turned out were indignant, but they seemed to have "no conception of, or desire for, anything better than the slums in which they have passed their lives." Home, some called it. The writer of the piece admitted it was difficult to understand these folks. They resented all inquiries, he said, and hurled "a torrent of abuse" to questions posed by outsiders. "As for allowing the interior of their dwellings to be inspected, they invariably refuse in the most determined way. Only by chance, or bribery, can one here and there get a glimpse of the inside of one of the houses." Yet somehow he knew "they are all alike – in an indescribable state of filth and squalor." The children were "more woe-be-gone, ricketty, unwashed and unhealthy-looking" than any in the city, and sat on doorsteps staring blankly, looking "as stunted in mind as they are in body."

When Charles Booth's man George Duckworth passed by a couple of months after the playground had been opened, doing his rounds of the Borough, he was not impressed. Nothing had been built on the cleared area, and the local police told him that most of the displaced inhabitants had moved as close as possible to their old home, so the demolition had only caused greater crowding. More lived in one room now, instead of two, and rents had risen. The new playground was cement, surrounded by high walls. It had one gas lamp in the centre and a drinking fountain. "It is essentially a playground for rough children, no seats because of the encouragement to loafers, nor any caretaker. I have only been there during school hours," he admitted, "when few children were about."

Children began attending school in those days as young as three, and while entering at such an age was not mandatory, shooing children off to a teacher's care allowed a mother the freedom to deal with younger siblings or to get more done around the house or to take a job herself. No matter the time of year, if school was in session and a child had passed his third birthday, his mother registered him and he began attending infant classes, learning the alphabet and "drawing apples in white chalk on brown paper." For the Deverill children, Joe and Ethel, that meant a start at the Lant Street Board School, walking with cousins and other students from Red Cross Street across Marshalsea Road and past the workhouse where their grandmother Mary lodged. The Deverills were certainly not the only ones with a relative inmate. Did groups of children pause by the grating in hopes of seeing a family member? Or did they avoid the place altogether, shame guiding them to the other side of the street?

Once they reached the plain three-storey building that housed the school, boys and girls separated, entering by different doors. More than a thousand Borough children attended, making the place seem a "human rabbit warren" of narrow corridors and stairwells and classrooms. The boys occupied the upper floors, supplementing arithmetic and reading with carpentry, while the girls were busy below, learning dressmaking and millinery in addition to letters and numbers. A separate wing housed the youngest, including Ethel and May, two

cousins becoming fast friends. Jennie's girls and Ellen's Flo attended
Lant Street too, under the supervision of Head Mistress Carrie Newbould, who paid attention to the fine details that made a school a welcoming place. "I have allotted off a window in the hall for each class,"
she wrote in her logbook that spring, "so that they can bring flowers in
pots and attend to them daily. Much interest is felt by the children as
the flowers grow and expand, and each class knows a part of the hall
is their very own."

On parent night, if Jennie, Ellen, Meg and Mary Anne visited
with their husbands, they'd have been shown the students' handiwork – drawings, vegetables made of clay, and paper trees – and felt
thankful for the opportunity their children received. Twenty years earlier, only those who could afford the fees attended classes, despite the
Elementary Education Act of 1880 that mandated compulsory education for five- to ten-year-olds. Impractical for the poor, the dictate only
worked when subsequent acts revised the rules again. Now elementary
education was not only free but also compulsory up to age twelve – albeit with lots of wiggle room – and though the details would continue
to shift with the times, children were expected to attend school until
at least that age, or until they'd reached a certain educational standard.
Liberal Member of Parliament Charles Morley, a politician in favour
of government-funded education, wrote that such instruction "softens
the manners, breaks evil habits, [and] reveals a thousand new interests."
After a visit to Lant Street Board School, he was impressed with the
progress, writing of the current crop of Borough girls that "the three R's,
the needlework, the drawing, the drill, the cooking class, the laundry,
the discipline have already raised them high above the Southwark girl of
twenty years ago." Another politician boasted in a speech that he wore
stockings knitted by the girls at Lant Street School, and flashed them to
his friends to make them jealous.

With hindsight, there is something unsettling woven into the
praise – a certainty that, even with schooling, these children would
never transcend their station. "The girls of Lant Street School make
cardboard boxes beautifully," wrote Morley:

TELL ME WHEN YOUR MOTHER DROPS

Each is supplied with a piece of board, upon which they rule exact octagons, hexagons, squares, or whatever figure the shape of the box may require. The results are admirably accurate. With practice, the eye is trained, the hand is trained, and accuracy in measurements soon becomes second nature. Many of them take up the binding business when they have to make a living for themselves, which is very early in life. Not long ago, a grown-up woman came into the school, and, picking up one of the boxes, said to the Mistress: "I'll tell you what it is – your girls is so quick at folding they're cutting us out altogether."

Still, what a thrill it must have been when the wider world breezed in through the classroom doors. Morley wrote of a visit by a young sailor that had the Lant boys riveted. This "sun-burnt, wind-tanned Blue-jacket" was Charlie Ponton, a strapping Borough man who'd gone to Lant Street School as a child, and now had returned there to tell other boys about his work. The boys nudged each other as they gawked at him, with his smooth, friendly face and his carefully clipped hair. He wore his uniform – navy breeches with bell-bottoms, the matching top with its casual open collar and bright white cording. He grinned back at the children and brought out an album of photographs that showed the many places he'd been: Gibraltar, Malta, Alexandria. He sketched a map with chalk on the board to show them where those places were, and the sixty boys listening rested their chins on their hands and travelled with him in their minds. To them, Morley wrote, Ponton was the embodiment of that which the Borough boy loved so well: adventure. And yet he had few "perils by sea and land" to recount. Rather, he spoke about what a typical day was like on board ship: what time he rose, what time he ate and when he went to bed at night. He talked about the time he'd seen donkey races in Egypt, and how Spaniards used their dogs to smuggle tobacco. When Ponton was done, Morley decided he'd never witnessed a better geography lesson.

Seeing how enthralled the boys were, the head master, Feargus Slingo, sensed an opportunity. "I have great trouble," he said, "to keep this school tidy. You boys will scatter paper and rubbish about the rooms, and the steps, and the playground." He turned to Charlie Ponton. "On board ship are you allowed to do that?"

"No," laughed the sailor.

"May you spit upon the deck whenever you feel inclined?"

More chuckles, and the assurance that there were indeed dire consequences for such actions.

When Charlie Ponton had gone, the boys were asked if they'd like to be sailors in the Royal Navy. "Every boy," Morley reported, "except a few very sleepy ones who had probably been hard at work in the early hours of the morning, held up his hand." And while Morley believed "the Borough boys' fancy is fickle," it was encounters like this that sparked the imagination, prodding Joe Deverill and others to don "full togs" at the earliest opportunity. Joe could also look to the Vanson family for seafaring inspiration. Uncle Richard's brother Robert, the youngest of the Vansons put in the Hanwell school for orphans back when their mother had died, was an able seaman now, with tattooed hands and a long string of ships listed on his record. And Richard's nephew Charles was a "fisher boy," learning the ways of the sea at the Home for Smack Boys in coastal Lowestoft.

Some parents may not have minded the school facilitating the recruitment of their children by the Navy, and believed education was an unnecessary luxury that meant one less wage in the jar. Their own employment was not always steady, and it was tempting to add older children to the earners' circle. Teachers tried to accommodate pupils' employment when they could, letting a boy out early so he could get to an after-school job on time, or forgiving absences when they heard a parent was ill or injured. The point was to keep children in school as long as possible, with the ultimate goal of improving their prospects. Alexander Bain, head master of the Webber Row Board School in Westminster Bridge Road, a school similar to Lant Street in the socio-economic standing of its pupils, saw the same marked improvement Charles Morley had mentioned, and not only in academics. Interviewed by one of Booth's volunteers, he contended that the hostility and violence of parents toward teachers that had been common twenty years earlier now was diminished, and fewer children showed up with bruises inflicted

by their parents. Truancy, in his experience, was rare, and when it occurred it could be explained by "something in the blood." Cleanliness
was generally better, although the incidence of head lice among girls
was almost universal, and fleas lived on some of the boys. It was necessary, according to Bain, "to distinguish between surface dirt, got at play
etc., and ancient filth that gives the tramp smell." Notes he made for
the interviewer also cited loose morals, mentioning in particular single
mothers and "the usual evidence of the number of children with uncertain surnames." Ellen's second Florence, first a Roff and then a Humphreys, was a case in point. "Dullness. Disgust. Drink," Bain continued,
jotting on his paper. "Most parents who come up to the school in the
afternoon for one purpose or another, generally women, smell of beer."
Ellen, spiralling downward, fit the profile.

By now she'd taken work at one of the area's several jam and pickle
factories, which sent out the cloying fragrance of overripe fruit, scald-
ed sugar, and vinegar. E & T Pink's was famous for its marmalade; one
advertisement depicted a flock of winged oranges flying from Seville to
London, and another encouraged marmalade lovers to write for an invitation to see the jam being made at "our model factory," not mentioning
the hundreds of Ellens who lacked good working conditions and were
poorly paid. They'd tried complaining. A few years earlier some sixty
women at Pink's had gone on strike when their wages were reduced,
but though the owner was "very sorry to part with his old hands, and he
bore no vindictive feeling towards them," according to *Reynolds's Weekly*,
the workers were immediately replaced by other women eager for their
jobs. Did Ellen's paltry salary go into the Humphreys purse, or was it
spent on drink? Did she squander the rent money and pawn the family's
belongings the way she had when she was with Fred years before? If so,
what did John think? Or was he a drinker too? With the deaths of their
daughter and son, there were even more sorrows to drown.

When Booth's investigators asked pillars of the community throughout London for opinions on the use of alcohol, they often heard un-
forgiving answers. Again and again they were told that women, especially, were drinking to excess. One minister said that a man's drinking
only harmed himself, whereas a drunken woman set the whole street

drinking. "Somehow women are born with the persuasive qualities necessary to make others follow in their steps." He believed that men these days were drinking less, while women were drinking more, and he suggested that "worry is what they suffer from. A woman here never knows whether she will have her money at the end of the week. Anxiety is constant…Drunkenness dulls the sense of present evil and gives a rosiness to what is to come."

A police inspector agreed that the heavy use of alcohol among women was on the rise and even went as far as to separate them into categories. The factory girl drinks once in a while; the prostitute drinks to do business but very rarely gets drunk; the laundry woman drinks because her work makes her thirsty, and there is a tradition of drinking linked to her trade; and finally the married woman drinks simply because her husband does. You need only look around to notice the increase in women drinking, the inspector said. Ten years earlier a crowd would gather if a policeman hauled off a drunken woman, but nowadays, he claimed, "they don't do more than turn their heads."

Henry Wyborn, the burly police superintendent at Southwark Division, concurred. He was the same man who'd said magistrates were too hard on men who beat their drunken wives. The only superintendent with Booth's map framed on his office wall, he seemed pleased to give his opinion of things. He wished women with babies at their breast would be forbidden from drinking in public houses, and he said the sight was common in Southwark. He added that the local jam trade – Ellen's calling – had brought a measure of freedom and independence for women in the area, and now they drank more readily because they had their own money to spend. "The jam girls are a rough lot," he said, and with more factories coming into the area, and more jobs available to women, the problem would only worsen.

What was life like for the jam girl's daughter, Flo, an only child now, whose cousins lived seemingly more comfortable lives than she did, albeit poor ones? Joe and Ethel returned home after school to see Harry behind the counter of his shop, his apron a little grubby from the day's custom, and his sleeves rolled up to his elbows. The Vanson girls' dad, Richard, also worked at home, and so did May's father, Jack, amid the rich scent of linseed and varnish. Fried fish and other food smells set the children's tummies rumbling, but beneath the layered aromas was what social reformer Alexander Paterson termed the "vapour of the slum… the constant reminder of poverty and grinding life, of shut windows and small, inadequate washing-basins, of last week's rain, of crowded homes and long working hours." When Flo, returning from Lant Street Board School, climbed the stairs of the Mowbray, she likely smelled urine and garbage, and wondered if she'd find anyone at home. Pushing the door to the family's single room open, she might have seen the bed in the corner unmade, and crumbs littering the table, left over from breakfast. If it wasn't a workday, Ellen could be found propping up the bar at the Prince of Wales pub, and Flo, going to fetch her mother home, might have ducked past girls skipping rope in the street and chanting, "Cold meat, mutton chops, tell me when your mother drops. I'll be there to pick her up, cold meat and mutton chops." The rhyme surely stung, for Ellen spent more time in the pub than at home. If Flo was able to coax her back to their flat, Ellen probably crawled beneath a blanket and began to snore, leaving Flo to cook dinner for herself and her father.

Alcoholism seemed to run in the family. A few doors along on Red Cross Street, Ellen's uncle John flopped into his bed on a warm July afternoon in 1901 and never got up again. Some years earlier he'd left the haberdashery trade and found work as a hop porter, a job that included a beer allowance as well as a wage – not a good thing for someone who already had a penchant for drink. The inquest into his death says that the doctor visited twice over a seventeen-hour period, and that John finally died of cardiac failure due to "excessive use of alcohol." His death certificate notes "chronic alcoholism."

The pubs were full on any given evening, but early Sunday mornings they were often closed, and in the Borough the streets were quiet and relatively deserted save for the milkman or the odd coster plying a barrow. Empty cigarette packs and a bit of newspaper lay in the gutter, and outside the pubs were the clues to Saturday night's revelries: a lost shoe, a torn bonnet, a greasy bit of chip ground into the cobbles, the vomit of someone who'd had too much to drink. Most of the partiers managed to stumble home to their beds to recover from the booze, but Ellen was among those whose drunkenness had become a perpetual state. One morning in July 1903 she was found unconscious on Queen Victoria Street near the Salvation Army headquarters, on the other side of the Thames and far from her Borough neighbourhood. She must have made her way across Southwark Bridge in the night, and was discovered lying on a sidewalk, her body bruised and filthy. The police brought her to the Cloak Lane Police Station and then to the Bow Road Infirmary in Mile End, east of Whitechapel, where the nurse, Mary Pear, filled in a "Report re Wandering Lunatic." In a dainty script she described "Feet very much discoloured from old boots," despite a shoemaker brother-in-law, and "Head and body in a filthy condition. Rash all over body apparently from vermin bites." It was obvious that for some time Ellen had not been taking care of herself. Two days later she was meant to appear in court on the charge of "wandering insane," but the record shows she was too ill to attend.

By the end of the month, another nurse and the policeman who'd found her in the street accompanied Ellen back across the Thames to Stone Asylum in Dartford, where a subsequent record was begun, adding more pieces to the puzzle: "She is at the present time restless and sleepless. She has loss of memory and cannot collect her thoughts or put ideas into words. She is melancholy and is frequently found crying and when questioned cannot give an explanation for so doing. She is unfit to be at large."

And yet she was not a rarity. Insanity had long been considered a particularly female affliction, and asylums held large numbers of women suffering from mania, melancholia or dementia, diagnosed by the men who examined them. As one clinical text noted, "That there is an excess of female lunatics might be expected from the greater nervous instability of women ... [and from] the greater tendency of mothers to transmit insanity to their female children."

There is much to be gleaned from Ellen's Stone Asylum records, yet every detail that helps tell her story raises still more questions. The greatest prize among the pages of crabbed writing is a photograph of Ellen, framed with red ink, which shows a woman with dark hair pulled back from her face, her eyes bruised with fatigue or despair, and her mouth slack. Wearing a striped blouse with a ruffled collar, she looks directly at the camera. The notes confirm details: colour of eyes, brown; expression, sad. Her physical health was "fairly good," but she had a heart murmur and heart disease. At the top of the page, in black ink, is written "Ellen Evans," and yet she was a married woman, known alternately as Ellen Roff, mother of four, or Ellen Humphreys, mother of one. On her initial admission record she identified her husband as Frederick, but provided no last name. Was the omission intentional? Asked for the names of relatives, she gave just one: "(mother) Mrs. Evans, St. George's Workhouse SE," and via that route, presumably, Mary Anne and Jennie and eventually Flo discovered what had happened to Ellen.

Notes in the casebook penned by various doctors describe her as "suffering from melancholia with marked depression," and state that the cause of her attack was probably epilepsy, though the condition is never mentioned again in her papers. Later notes say she was "listless, apathetic, and emotional," and then "tearful and full of her troubles," but with "no evident delusions." Almost right away she was given tasks in the dormitories, presumably housekeeping, and though the doctors commented that she was a good worker, she soon began complaining of headaches. "Today very depressed," one doctor wrote. "Tells me her mind is going…Very agitated and constantly clutches at her head and says the pain is terrible." The observations of her simple-mindedness and defective memory cycled forward, with the assessment of melancholia repeating week after week. Doctors at the time believed that some people were predisposed to melancholia and had "an unnatural, inborn, inherited tendency to look upon the dark side of life; to make the worst of everything; to conjure up horrors that may never exist; to cross bridges before they are reached; to imagine that an enemy lurks behind every tree and stone, and that even tried and true friends are not always to be trusted." Who were Ellen's perceived enemies? Her siblings? Her husbands? The case notes tell us that she was childish at times, and jealous of other patients, but of her life before the asylum there is no word. The notes never mention sisters, nor either husband, nor children, nor any acquaintances beyond the institution. There is nothing written in Ellen's own hand, though other patients' letters exist. Tucked among the brittle pages of the casebook are samples: "Dear Sir, will you kindly inform me whether my mother Mrs. Dollard is still living as I have not been able to come and see her." And this one, written but apparently never sent: "Dearest Victor...I am so awfully miserable here...They say that I am ill here, and that it's serious...If I hear nothing of any of you within the next few days I shall expect you are none of you going to take any notice."

Behind the scenes, certainly some were noticing Ellen's case. By late November, in the offices of clerks and solicitors, a battle was brewing between the Poor Law unions over who would pay for her care – City of London was where she'd been found, Southwark was where she'd lived at the time, but Lambeth was where her legal husband, Fred Roff, continued to reside. The London Union made a "diligent enquiry" and sent a letter to Fred at Doulton's pottery works, a copy of which remains in her file.

Dear Sir,

I have to inform you that your wife has been admitted to the City of London Asylum at Stone near Dartford, Kent, chargeable to this union. I shall be glad to hear from you as to what would be the best time and place for my clerk to see you, as I wish to get information as to what Parish she properly belongs to.

Yours faithfully,
Clerk

Fred responded right away, attempting equal formality:

Dear Sir,

I shell be glad to meet you anny evening after 6 pm or Satuary after 1 o'clock by Appointment.

Yours faithfully,
H.F. Roff

The following Monday at seven o'clock, London's examinant, Edmund Watson, showed up at Fred's home at 24 St. Oswald's Place. The details of the interview aren't documented precisely, but scrawled notes at the edge of a page in the old tome that contains these Poor Law records suggest Fred told Watson that Ellen had "misbehaved" herself with her drunken habits and friends, that he cared for their four children, and that she had since had "4 or 5 children by ano man," which was an exaggeration but not far off the mark. Following the interview, London decided that Fred had deserted Ellen, and she was therefore Southwark's charge, since she had lived there for several years. Southwark, however, insisted that she had not been deserted, and that therefore London should be pointing its finger at her husband's union, Lambeth. London countered that Southwark's settlement officer had "frightened [Fred] as to the consequences if he admitted desertion – and he tried all he could to support the Southwark contention that they agreed to separate." But there were other witnesses – Mary Anne, Jennie and their husbands – who said that from the moment Fred and Ellen parted, she was distressed and longed to go back to him, and never agreed to the separation Southwark described. If anyone asked for Ellen's view of the situation, her answers were not recorded. While the letters went back and forth between the clerks and the lawyers, and decisions were made and appealed over a period of years, "Ellen Evans, properly Roff," continued sweeping floors and stripping beds in Ward 4 at Stone Asylum. The *Poor Law Journal* says that Fred Roff made the trip to see Ellen at Stone when he first found out she was there, which meant a train ride from Lambeth that chilly, dull December. Arriving at the grand but imposing asylum, he'd have passed through the well-tended grounds and pulled open the heavy doors, offering his name and the reason for his visit. How he felt when he saw his long-lost wife's haggard face, what words were exchanged between them after so many years apart, can never be known.

Around the time that Ellen's sorry life was being documented in the pages of the Poor Law registers, Mary Anne and Jennie had a portrait taken together at the Parisian School of Photography in Old Kent Road.

Looking at the cabinet card with its gold border and elegant subjects, you wouldn't guess how poor the women were, or what had become of their mother and sister. Jennie is standing, in a skirt and jacket with voluminous "leg o' mutton" sleeves, her hand resting on Mary Anne's arm. In her early thirties, she's trim and attractive. Her hair is tightly curled, and while she isn't smiling, her eyes sparkle as if she's pleased or even amused about something. Mary Anne, seated beside her, wears similar clothing, though with more detail: bands of dark trim on the cuffs of her sleeves and the hem of her skirt; a brooch at the collar of her pleated blouse. The sisters' noses are alike, and ever so slightly up-turned, but Mary Anne's jaw is broader and her eyes are larger than Jennie's, and glossy-dark. Her expression exudes confidence rather than mirth. There's a resemblance between Mary Anne and Ellen too – in the eyes and the shape of the face – but it's obscured by the weak, lost look pasted into the Stone Asylum casebook. How different the suggestions of these photographs: the younger sisters posing in their best clothes among the studio's props – ornate furniture and statuary that transform the women for posterity – and the older sister staring lethargically into the lens, a headshot on a plain background that reveals none of her surroundings.

The truth is, though, that Ellen's surroundings had drastically improved, at least in the physical sense. Approaches to treating mental illness had undergone vast reform over the span of the Victorian era. In all parts of the country, large asylums had been built to house the insane poor, and were funded and supervised by the government. Legislation was drawn up to protect patients from abuse, and commissioners in lunacy made regular inspections. Mechanical restraints – manacles, muzzles, chains and "coercion chairs" that strapped patients into place – were increasingly seen as cruel and barbaric, and the emphasis instead was on the healing potential that existed in humane treatment of the insane. Physical surroundings mattered, so sites were chosen with care for both their pastoral beauty and fertile grounds. Gentle hills were ideal, with views of "a landscape reposing in the softened light of an English sun." The buildings themselves were designed to feel like homes rather than the madhouses of old with barred windows and iron gates and dungeons somewhere in the bowels of a bleak building. An 1870s study by the Lancet Commission on Lunatic Asylums found that the creation of this type of homey environment was key to the patients' comfort and happiness. "It is by domestic control, by surroundings of the daily life, by such details as the colouring of walls, the patterns on floorcloth, the furniture and decorations of rooms, by the influence of pictures, birds, and draperies, the judicious use of different kinds of clothing, suitable occupation and diversions, and, generally, by moulding and controlling the life of a lunatic, the psychologist hopes to reach, capture, and re-educate the truant mind, and perhaps reseat the dethroned intelligent will of his patient."

Constructed of yellow brick and with a long gravel drive leading to the main entrance, Stone Asylum had a clock turret and a belfry and a water tower that could be seen above the treeline. There were four airing grounds divided for male and female use. The main administrative block contained offices, kitchens, a grand dining room with high ceilings and long windows, and a recreation hall complete with a curtained stage and pianos. Curved, covered walkways connected the centre core to two pavilions, one housing the laundry and the mortuary, the other the bakery and workshops. Like so many asylums built in the Victorian years, it attempted self-sufficiency in its quasi-rural setting; there was a working farm as well as a chapel and a cemetery. The patients lived in dormitories within wards – the males in the east wing, the females in the west – and these were subdivided according to the patients' behaviour, since "suspicious and violent" didn't mix well with "weak and apathetic."

Ellen, for her part, was fairly consistently dull and despondent, and even facile. Eventually there'd been so little change in her behaviour that she was recertified with chronic melancholia, which is described in psychiatric literature of the day as a "Giant Despair" and "the terminus of all other forms of spirit depression. It is the inevitable goal of continued mental shock, and worry, and brooding, and physical decay."

Stone's odd mix of inmates became a family of sorts to the patients who stayed a long time, and true to the old adage "familiarity breeds contempt," Ellen soon began to exhibit "foolish jealousies regarding the other patients." No further details are noted in the casebooks, and the specific targets of Ellen's jealousy are not mentioned, but flipping through the pages some candidates emerge. Was it Sybil, whose parents had been on the stage and who had "consequently been much neglected and allowed to run wild"? Or Caroline, who had masqueraded successfully as Paul for years? Plucked from the streets for chasing omnibuses on Blackfriars Bridge, supposedly searching for his wife, the infirmary discovered Paul was a woman. She ended up at Stone, photographed for the casebooks, however unhappily, in female garb.

The patient photographs, often framed with red ink, are surrounded by scrawled notes about the person's condition and history, sometimes expanded on by the patient herself. One photo shows a bone-thin woman with great bags under her eyes and a wary countenance. Her file includes a five-page letter she wrote to the chief medical officer, suggesting the reason she had not been allowed to go home was that her doctor had been switched with a look-alike. "Early last August, Dr. Nelis went for a three-week holiday. He was a fat man with a very red face, bright blue eyes with remarkable clear whites and dark hair and moustache with a short clipped beard. At the end of August, his facsimile came back … [with] a pale face, hair greyer, beard much greyer, eyes of cloudy grey with a touch of blue; the whites were dull with brownish splotches; his shoulders seemed broader, and he walked with a quicker step than Nelis… Anyone can see what a muddle such a state of affairs might cause."

The casebooks are full of these delusions and the faces that go with them, some with challenging stares, some with mischievous grins, and one with a nurse in the shot, holding the patient's head and forcing her to look at the camera. Further on in the book a woman in a knitted shawl wearing a timid expression holds a basket in her lap. She has a talent, apparently, for needlework, but she also wrongly believes her children have been murdered. Another woman hides her face from the camera with one hand and stretches an arm across her middle, as though hugging herself for comfort. The notes tell us she insists that all the women around her are actually men, and that she knows "she is here to have her light taken out."

Many of the patients, Ellen included, look as though the light is already gone. Among the pages that contain their checkered histories, a scrap of paper flutters loose, bearing a whimsically handwritten score for a hymn. The notes dance across the staff like balloons that have escaped their strings, and the lyrics, too, suggest a wish for release: "Weary of earth, and laden with my sin, I look to heaven and long to enter in. But there no evil thing may find a home: And yet I hear a voice that bids me, 'Come.'"

Harry, pictured here in 1905 in his Salvation Army bandsman uniform with sons Ernie and Joe, played the tuba and the euphonium in the Borough Band. If he played by Army standards, it was joyful and infectious and came straight from his heart. As General William Booth remarked, "fishy hearts can only make fishy music."

CHAPTER 5

Cracked Eggs

The Salvation Army believed that every light could be rekindled, and throughout London it had any number of projects on the go with the aim of improving the lot of the poor. In the East End it opened a match factory to challenge industry practices of underpaying the workforce and using yellow phosphorous, a chemical that caused a disfiguring rotting of the facial bones, or "phossy jaw." The Army's matches were made with non-toxic red phosphorous, and were packaged in boxes that read "Lights in Darkest England." When the industry finally changed its ways, the Army bowed out of the business. On the south side of the Thames, next to the Lipton jam factory in Bermondsey, the Army ran a combined shelter and paper-recycling depot referred to as the Spa Road Elevator, with the ultimate goal of "elevating" men who were unskilled or unemployed and needed a helping hand. In the short term, the Army expected men could pay for their own lodging, and in the long term they could develop skills that would help them find permanent jobs. The men were paid in tokens that could only be redeemed at participating shops and businesses, so they would not be tempted to fall back into old habits. Charles Booth's social investigator, upon visiting, described the Elevator's deputy as "a choice-looking ruffian, with a pasty face, an unshaven chin, a Salvation blazer, and six feet of flesh." It turned out he was from a well-known Nottingham family but had fallen on hard times and did not want his relatives to know where he was until he'd fixed his life. The Elevator itself, the investigator noted, "was a sad scene, typical of existence not of life, the piles of paper, the muddy yard, the half-finished buildings and, above all, this cargo of what looked like human wreckage."

There were happier Army sites. The Borough Corps of the Salvation Army was headquartered just south of Red Cross Street, and when interviewed for Booth's survey the ensign (yet another of the General's military terms) boasted that it was one of the oldest in South London. The corps had its own brass band, a Young People's Legion, and classes on Friday nights in painting, sewing and knitting. On Sunday afternoons, nearly one hundred people congregated for a service, and more came in the evening. The ensign was a relative newcomer to the Borough from Gravesend where, he said, you almost always knew the faces at the meetings. Here in the Borough there were new people every week, most of them "much more ignorant, especially on religious points," and he said it was often difficult to know how to deal with them. Open-air meetings were held four nights a week and three times on Sundays, and it was here that Salvationists offered their testimonies, sang with faces shining, and blew their horns to catch the attention of lost souls. The louder they could be, the better. When the ensign noticed that the "ordinary march" didn't draw people as it once had, the corps, never stuck for drama, sent the Borough Band out in top hats and pulled in "an enormous crowd, and the Hall full."

Harry must have been among those bandsmen, crisply attired in a navy blue serge jacket with broad white stripes across the front. Band members were required to purchase their own uniforms, costing the equivalent of about three weeks' wages, so the men wore them with pride, and to most important occasions. Harry played the euphonium, the tuba, and other wind instruments, and the fact that his brother and sister also played instruments suggests that he joined as a seasoned musician who could share his knowledge with others, showing bandmates how to press the valves, and tracing his finger along the snaking tubes that carried the music through. For the price of a penny he would have subscribed to *The Bandsman and Songster*, a sixteen-page weekly "devoted in the main to the part which Music and Song play in the Salvation War." It included band-related news items from around the country: "Watford – Band have been specialling at Tring, where a large crowd awaited them on their arrival." There was local news too, of the Borough Band's home performances and its occasional travels farther afield, which briefly took Harry away from the shop, Mary Anne and the children: "Borough – The Saturday night musical meeting at Sheerness was held out-doors. A large crowd assembled. A soldier in His Majesty's army was moved to tears while the Band played 'Songs of Heaven.'" The magazine also listed practices and coming events for the various bands, and reminded members of the rules of engagement: a bandsman must be a "Salvation Army Soldier in good standing… speak, sing and pray for the Salvation of souls… abstain from wearing jewellery and worldly adornment… not be in debt." As well, critiques were included of band performances, pieces Harry might have read aloud to Joe and Ethel. "The other night I visited the Borough Band at practice," and here he maybe paused to waggle his eyebrows, ensuring their rapt attention, "… and was surprised at the good material which the Bandmaster has in the Band. Yet one thing thou lackest – a set of decent instruments." Peering over the paper, he'd have frowned with exaggerated sadness, eliciting giggles, before continuing. "They are however going to do their best to overcome even this difficulty, and would be pleased to receive any help from others who have in the days long past been in a similar unenviable position… God Bless the Borough Band!"

And blessed these bands were, at least by the Salvation Army itself. Time and again the *War Cry* praised the ability of bandsmen like Harry to win souls for God. One issue Harry must have pored over featured a series of such stories – Salvationists who'd written in to tell about their first-hand experiences of the transformative powers of music. One man wrote:

On a Saturday night some few years ago, our band met at the Hall going to the open-air service. It was in good spiritual fighting trim, and held a red-hot prayer meeting. Our special efforts that night were for the reclamation of drunkards. We had several ex-drunkards in the band, and these were especially interested in, and full of zeal for, this effort. We played as we marched to the open-air stand, which had been selected outside a prominent hotel. The crowds gathered round us, and the testimonies, singing, and playing kept the service in good swing from beginning to end. We were in excellent spirits and full of expectancy for something to happen, joy and gladness being dominant throughout. Reluctantly we closed the meeting and marched to the Hall. Unnoticed by us we were followed by one of the hotel frequenters. As we commenced our inside meeting, we noticed a man enter who was the worse for liquor. A soldier conducted him to a seat near the front, where he quietly remained until the testimonies began. Readily, one after the other, the ex-drunkards in the band rose to testify. Suddenly the man to whom it seemed the bandsmen particularly addressed themselves stood to his feet and exclaimed: "Can God save me?" The ex-drunkard who was testifying replied: "Glory to God, brother, He can. He has done it for me; He'll do it for you." In a few moments the inquirer was at the mercy-seat, and after praying for him, and singing helpful choruses, and exercising faith on his behalf, we were joyously rewarded in seeing our capture sobered. He told us his sad story which terminated with his testimony of assurance of God's forgiveness. He had been a military bandsman, but after leaving His Majesty's service, and getting away from the discipline, he became loose in his habits, that of drunkenness gradually fastening itself upon him. This particular Saturday, on quitting work with his wages, he made for the hotel, and there he had remained drinking and paying for the drinks of others. Several times during the afternoon he had resolved to go home to his wife and children, but he could not break away from his companions. He had heard our open-air service in progress, but the three beats of the drum given before the commencement of the playing for the return march to the Hall awakened memories of his better days when he had been a drummer in the King's Service. The glass of liquor ordered he left untouched and followed our march to the Hall, where, as his afterlife proved, God soundly converted him. He afterwards became drummer in our band, beating the very drum which had helped so much in bringing him into the Light of God.

Come Christmas of 1903, Joe and Ethel had a new brother, Ernie, born on Red Cross Street like so many of his relatives before him. But Harry and Mary Anne must already have been packing the family's belongings, for by the time he was baptized at the end of January 1904, they had left the two shops and their familiar rooms and moved to 49 Oval Chambers on Vauxhall Street in Lambeth, just around the corner from St. Oswald's Place, where Fred Roff still lived with his and Ellen's four children. What precipitated the move for Harry and Mary Anne is impossible to know, but it couldn't have been easy to give up the shops Harry had started or the place Mary Anne's family had inhabited for sixty years. Red Cross Street was home, filled with friends and family and neighbours who knew one another's business, who felt comfortable scolding each other's children, and who'd help out in hard times. The familiarity was a safety net, so moving even as far as Lambeth was a big decision, perhaps made easier by the fact that more family – Fred and his children – were nearby.

Did Harry's shops fail, as his father's had, or did he give them up voluntarily? Small shops were being swallowed by larger ones, and trades were changing with technology. It was less common now for the retailer to blend his own tea or grind his coffee and sugar. Many goods these days arrived attractively packaged, with a predetermined price attached, and the shopkeeper's job had more to do with how to market his wares and create artful displays that made it difficult for his customers to walk past. Advertising was changing everything. Writing in that first decade of the century, novelist H.G. Wells pointed out that it had already revolutionized trade and industry, and it was bound to revolutionize the world. "The old merchant used to tote about his commodities; the new one creates values. Doesn't need to tote. He takes something that isn't worth anything… and he makes it worth something. He takes mustard that is just like anybody else's mustard, and he goes about saying, shouting, singing, chalking on walls, writing inside people's books, putting it everywhere, 'Smith's Mustard is the Best.' And behold it is the best!" But maybe Harry wasn't much of a salesman. While he still called himself an oil and colourman when Ernie was born, from then on he and his brother Jack did not appear in commercial directories as proprietors of any shop at all, and Harry's occupation in Lambeth is unknown.

Charles Booth's notes tell us that the family's new neighbourhood was not much of a step up from the Borough. A gas plant was close by the street Harry and Mary Anne settled into, and according to Booth, poverty and gasworks always went together. Of Lambeth generally, Booth determined, "The fairly comfortable have left or are leaving, but the poor or less well off remain, and their numbers are increased and the character of the neighbourhood is still further lowered by incomers." As in the Borough, there were slum tenements rife with bugs, laundry strung between the buildings, and several families sharing a single tap and toilet. Also like the Borough, there were efforts at improvement. South of Harry and Mary Anne's new place, social reformer Octavia Hill's influence could be found in Vauxhall Park, where winding paths and gardens were intended to provide the poor with what she called "the outside peace they so often need." The playground had swings and a seesaw, as well as parallel bars and hand rings for the gymnastically inclined. There was a pavilion and a fancy, pagoda-style drinking fountain made by Doulton, where the Roff and Deverill children could quench their thirst after school.

Doulton had more than just a presence in the area. Apart from its ornate, Gothic-style headquarters on Black Prince Road, whose turrets could be seen from a ways off, some of the streets in Harry and Mary Anne's new neighbourhood were named after men associated with the pottery, and the dwellings housed Doulton workers like Fred and his brothers. Art and functionality were married in these days, and Doulton's "ware" could be found in abundance: as terracotta building panels, decorative friezes and tiles, claddings, drainpipes and fireplaces. The same artistic touch was used on smaller pieces: delicate figurines with swirling dresses, mugs with laughing faces, and stoneware pitchers like the ones Harry and Mary Anne owned, inscribed with inspirational mottos: "Straight is the line of duty, curved is the line of beauty; follow the straight line, thou shalt see, the curved line ever follow thee."

Although Harry had left the Borough, he did not leave the Borough Band, even though the Kennington Lane Band in his new neighbourhood could have used some help, judging by the critique in *The Bandsman and Songster*: "The cornet soloist played with a faulty method, and his tonguing lacked point. The euphonium soloist was fair, but the upper E, F sharp and G were out of tune. The horn player made a plucky attempt at his solo, but unfortunately failed when nearing the end." Perhaps Harry didn't join their effort because the bond was strong enough among his own band members that he didn't want to desert them for another group – and an apparently inferior one at that. Small mentions in the Army's *Local Officer* magazine suggest the Borough bandsmen were a dedicated lot, especially lately, and that the players were "improving wonderfully" under a new bandmaster. "Where a short time back there was a cry for men there is now a cry for instruments. Better still, the spirituality of the Band is going up." *The Local Officer* also reminded bandsmen that their work as musicians for the Army was a steadfast commitment. "Let the bandsman understand that he cannot run in and out like a dog at a fair."

Two photographs show Harry in his bandsman attire – one from the depths of the Salvation Army archive, in which he appears in the middle of the second row with the Borough Band, his thin face unmistakable. There are twenty-seven members in all, including several boys, accompanied by trumpets, cornets, trombones, tenor horns, euphoniums and a huge bass drum with which to make their joyful noise. The other picture comes from the family collection, and again it's easy to recognize Harry with his trademark moustache and his proud carriage. The peaked cap sits smartly on his head; it's masked in sepia, like the rest of the old photo, but in reality it was "the best colour" and "too well known to need describing," according to an ad in *The Bandsman and Songster*. Harry's euphonium is strapped over his torso, and he's holding hands with a very tiny Ernie, his youngest son, who wears a toddler's dress and a puzzled expression. Ernie's other hand clasps Joe's, but most of Joe's body is hidden by Harry's tuba, which stands on the pavement before him. There's a wide grin on Joe's face, as if someone has joked that he should pick up this grand instrument and blow out a tune.

Nothing would have pleased the Army's General Booth more. A handful of years earlier he had released *Salvation Army Music* in book form, with the wish that the songs be played "skillfully and with a loud noise…Never, I entreat you, take this book into your hand without prayer that God may keep your heart up to heavenly concert pitch." The songs were indexed alphabetically and also according to metre, and made regular reference to the ongoing fight the Army waged:

The war is all our souls delight
While battling for the Lord;
We love the thickest of the fight
While battling for the Lord.
We want no cowards in our band
While battling for the Lord;
But call for valiant-hearted men
While battling for the Lord.

Was it the music or its message that appealed to Harry, or could he separate the two? *The Local Officer* reminded him to take his role seriously – that he was a soldier first and foremost, and a bandsman only as part of that career. "Every convert should be tried and proven before he is elevated to the position of a Bandsman of the Salvation Army. Let him first satisfy himself, and satisfy others, that he is a Salvationist by conviction, that he is saved, that God has for Christ's sake forgiven his sins, and that no ulterior motive has brought him into the ranks. After that, give him an instrument."

There's little reason to doubt that Harry was a devout man, and yet it's obvious he disregarded at least one of the Army's rules. The Articles of War he'd signed upon joining required abstaining from tobacco, as well as alcohol and other things that could "enslave the body or spirit." Whether he enjoyed the occasional pint with his brother Jack or brother-in-law Richard Vanson isn't known, but a photograph of Harry with cigarette in hand pegs him as a smoker, and in this, at least, he'd have done well to heed the Army's rule. Around this time Harry began to have trouble with his health – breathlessness or chest pain – symptoms associated with heart disease. He was only thirty-four years old, and trim according to the photos, but this and other chronic illnesses were all too common for residents of the poorer pockets of London, where pollution blackened buildings and contributed to the city's famous fogs. Londoners overall were using more gas and less coal, so foggy days were on the decline, but fog remained a distinct feature of the city and gave it the nickname "the Big Smoke." One writer claimed the fog "stifles the mind as well as choking the body. It comes on slowly and stealthily, picking its way, choosing its direction, leaving contemptuous gaps in its course; then it settles down like a blanket of solid smoke, which you can feel but not put from you." Even with less of the toxic brew filling the air, it made for an unhealthy environment.

Nutrition was also lacking. Britain had a colony for every food group, and improvements in shipping and transportation meant things could be imported cheaply. While that allowed for a greater variety in London's shops and markets, it didn't necessarily mean a better quality. Tinned meats, often cheaper than fresh, were fatty and "corned" or salted, while canned fruits and vegetables had been leached of their vitamins and much of their texture. Cheap sugar and the development of methods to process food resulted in such damage to people's teeth that many could no longer chew tough meat, or crunch vegetables and nuts, perpetuating the need for the softer, nutritionally inferior canned types. In Harry's lifetime, London's working-class men had become shorter and weaker, to the point where the minimum height requirement for joining the infantry had to be dropped, from five feet six inches to an even five feet, so more men could qualify, though later it was again raised. Officers, drawn from the middle and upper classes and better fed, were by 1901 a full head taller than Harry's lower-class brethren. The Committee on Physical Deterioration, commissioned by the British government to study the problem that had become startlingly apparent during the second Boer War, traced the blame back to mothers who were less and less able to breastfeed their babies due to their own ill health, and who raised their families in chronic poverty.

But the situation wasn't utterly hopeless. When interviewed by the committee, school medical inspector Alfred Eichholz spoke of the "plasticity of human material during childhood," and insisted that low physique wasn't hereditary. "Nature gives every generation a fresh start." School life these days could have a positive influence on home life among poor families, and that was happening at Lant Street Board School, where the same master had been in place for many years, and the children were benefiting from his approach. Eichholz showed two photographs of Lant Street children taken in the 1870s and compared them with a more recent one. Back then, during Mary Anne's childhood, they had been "wild, unkempt, loosely built, ragged, barefoot children, who look like savages and not like human beings." Looking at the images, that seems exaggerated, but there is an overall slovenliness, with plenty of bare feet, rumpled clothes and tousled heads of hair. The children pose in ragged lines rather than the neat rows of the later photograph. "There is a more civilized intelligent look about the children. They are better filled out and straighter...There are fewer rough faces." When difficulties with regard to food, overcrowding, cleanliness, drunkenness and general home management could be rectified, the children quickly grew stronger and healthier. "In fact," Eichholz asserted, "all evidence points to active, rapid improvement, bodily and mental, in the worst districts, so soon as they are exposed to better circumstances, even the weaker children recovering at a later age from the evil effects of infant life."

School held that sort of power, he believed. At Lant Street, the boys had better endurance and more enthusiasm for sports. "Though they still come off second best with good schools when they come to a contest...they are readier to fight an uphill game in a greater degree than formerly." This was particularly impressive because, in general, the diets of children at Lant Street were still very bad. With adequate nutrition, the students would improve yet more in every way. Eichholz estimated that 122,000 of London's young students were underfed, and he used Lambeth's Johanna Street Board School as a shocking example. Straight across the river from the Houses of Parliament, 90 percent of the boys there were anemic, and significantly shorter than average. "A good many children suffer from blight in the eyes and sore eyelids. The hair is badly nourished and wispy, the skin is rough, dry, pale and shrivelled, giving a very old look very early in life." Weak academically, the boys were not physically strong enough to get through a full game of football, or a hard day's work. Poverty was rife. The fathers took casual jobs, and often both parents drank. The children arrived at class hungry, and even once school meals were put in place, it was hard for schools to make up for all that was wrong at home.

In Lambeth, as in the Borough and other London slums, the cramped spaces available to families surviving on meagre incomes contributed to poor health and difficult living. Basement rooms were cheap but also dark and damp, so tenants had to burn more coal and gas. Police regulations insisted lower windows be shut to deter burglars (though few had much worth stealing), and this made the tiny units stuffy, too. Those who paid a little more to live upstairs also had problems. More often than not they shared the laundry copper with the landlady, better situated on the ground floor, and had to do the washing according to her schedule. If there was no water on the second floor, housewives had to carry fresh water upstairs and the dirty water down. In some units there was no stove – just a hob and an open grate for cooking. Mice bred in the walls of these houses, which were frequently infested with bugs too; no amount of cleaning could get rid of the insects. Repapering the walls and fumigating – if the landlord was willing to do it – slowed the problem for a while, but the bugs always returned, scurrying to dark corners during the day, and dropping from the ceiling onto sleeping bodies at night. The rats visited too. One man told Reverend Samuel Barnett's wife, Henrietta: "The rats they're getting that cheeky. There's no scaring of 'em... Last night they comed on our bed. My missus, she'd been sadly-like all day, and had just dropped off, when up comes one and runs about quite frisky... What could I do? If I'd moved I should of woke 'er up – but I watched a bit."

The best places to live were in blocks of well-managed workmen's dwellings. But here, too, there were problems: lack of privacy, the spread of illness, and inflexibility on the part of the rent collector. Around the same time that Harry and Mary Anne made the move, Jennie and Richard Vanson did too, settling in close proximity to Richard's older brother Stephen and his wife, Emmie. Stephen's family was more or less intact now, except for George, who'd died at Hanwell, and Charles, who was still a fisher boy in Lowestoft.

Richard and Jennie and their three girls lived just north of Harry and Mary Anne, in a block of artisans' dwellings on Burdett Street off Westminster Bridge Road. You could follow the road west and travel across the Thames to a different world: the Houses of Parliament and the Clock Tower were there, with Westminster Abbey and Buckingham Palace just beyond. Like Jack and Harry, Richard disappeared from commercial directories around this time, so it seems he'd lost or given up his business as a boot repairer.

Whatever his means of income now, Richard didn't earn much. "Round about a pound a week" was a typical amount, and also the title of a book published by the Fabian Society, advocating social justice. Written by Maud Pember Reeves, the book was based on a study undertaken by the Fabian Society's Women's Group, and had originally been titled *Family Life on a Pound a Week*. Spurred on by the high infant mortality rate in London slums, Reeves and her fellow workers spent four years in the Lambeth area, gathering detailed household information from women like Jennie and Mary Anne. The participants were selected from among the patients of the General Lying-In Hospital near Burdett Chambers, where Jennie's daughter Ada was born, the first in the family to be delivered in a hospital. As well as training student midwives, the hospital received poor, pregnant, married women, but they also accepted single women for a first confinement "if of previous good character."

Though they shared circumstances, the subjects of Reeves's study were distinct in personality. Mrs. K. was happy-go-lucky, but her skirts had been chewed by rats; Mrs. P. was pretty and practical – she bought cracked eggs because you could smell them when they'd gone off; methodical Mrs. B. wore a man's cap and loved the new task of keeping rigorous accounts; Mrs. L. was gaunt and deeply depressed but always clean; Mrs. S. was slow and resigned and could only love her family in a "patient, suffering, loyal sort of way." According to Reeves, most of them "seemed to have lost any spark of humour or desire for different surroundings. The same surroundings with a little more money, a little more security, and a little less to do, was about the best their imaginations could grasp."

The women were quizzed weekly on how their income was divied up to cover rent, burial insurance, coal and light, cleaning materials, clothing and food. In the beginning there was sometimes a clash of cultures between the Fabian women interviewing and the Lambeth women being interviewed; many of the housewives (mathematical Mrs. B. excluded) were intimidated by the prospect of keeping accounts, and they sometimes used slang and creative spelling that baffled their visitors. Some of the women were "curiously efficient in a kind of mental arithmetic, though utterly at sea directly pencil touched paper." They were cautious and suspicious at first, and seemed to expect "a teaching of something" from the lady who'd entered their homes. Yet week after week nothing more was asked of them than an honest account of their days. Soon enough they relaxed and offered anecdotes about everything from their husbands – "My young man's that good ter me I feel as if somethink nice 'ad 'appened every time 'e comes in" – to their shopping expeditions along Lambeth Walk with its bevy of market stalls and coster carts – "'E said [the cabbage] was as fresh as a daisy, but it turned out to be all fainty like w'en I come to cook it." One woman told how she'd lain in bed one morning and accidentally "unraveled a mystery which had puzzled her for weeks." A band of mice was crossing the room on her clothesline, thereby accessing the food she kept on the high shelf of a dresser precisely so they couldn't get at it.

Over time, a picture began to emerge of just how difficult it was to escape the vortex of poverty. Once the math was done, it was easy to see the disparity: a poor family typically paid one-third of the father's income in rent, while a rich family paid one-eighth. The wives of men who were paid daily, and in varying amounts, therefore had to shop daily, though it was far less economical, because they could never be certain quite what they'd have to spend. The same went for coal. The poor bought in smaller, more expensive amounts, while the well-to-do had enough cash on hand to buy by the ton or half ton, and they had the cellar space to store it. The penny a week per child that went toward burial insurance was a penny less spent on the children who survived. To add to the indignation, the policies were not interchangeable. If baby Ernie died, as his brothers had, insurance paid for Joe or for Ethel wouldn't cover him. The family who fell behind on these payments and then lost a child had to borrow money to see the child properly buried. "For months afterwards the mother and remaining children will eat less in order to pay back the money borrowed," Reeves wrote. "The father of the family cannot eat less. He is already eating as little as will enable him to earn the family wage. To starve him would be bad economy. He must fare as usual. The rest of the family can eat less without bothering anybody – and do."

Reeves believed that paying burial insurance was a "calamitous blunder" on the part of these poor women, but understood, too, that the alternative was to settle for a "pauper's funeral" paid for by Poor Law funds. The women Reeves spoke to were adamant that "the pauper funeral carries with it the pauperization of the father of the child – a humiliation which adds disgrace to the natural grief of the parents." One woman even said she'd prefer to have the dustcart call to collect her child's body.

Sometime after Ellen's admission to Stone Asylum, six-year-old Flo Humphreys and her father, John, left the Mowbray Buildings and moved into a lodging house nearby. How Ellen's disappearance from her life affected Flo is impossible to know, but it's certain that Flo struggled at school, for records show that in spite of being promoted at the usual age from the infants program to be with the bigger girls, within a few months she was moved back with the younger children. Such a demotion meant that she was schoolmates with her younger cousin May Deverill, whose sweet face beams out from a couple of old school photos. By now, this branch of the family – Harry's piccolo-playing brother Jack and Mary Anne's cousin Meg – had also moved out of Red Cross Street. The Deverill Bros. shop signs had been painted over, and Jack, Meg and May had taken a flat in the well-kept Goodwin Buildings in Marshalsea Road, near the Mint Street workhouse.

Meg's mother Maggie was there too, having finally let go of her cows. The dairy – the family trade since the 1840s – had failed, at least in part because Maggie's husband, William Donnelly, the cabinetmaker cum milkman from Yorkshire, was a ne'er-do-well. Did Maggie grieve the loss of old Benjamin's dairy? Or was it a relief to leave the occupation and the ever-curious sanitary inspectors behind? Without a business to run, it was still Maggie who kept her family going, taking a cleaning job at the Borough Polytechnic Institute over on Borough High Street. It was steady work, which suggests that William's work was the opposite – one investigation into women's employment, *Married Women's Work* by Clementina Black, found that "married women in London, at any rate, do not go out charing unless driven thereto by necessity." The most common reason a woman took a cleaning position was because her husband's earnings were irregular: "You cannot make both ends meet when you do not know what you'll have from week to week." But Maggie wouldn't keep her unreliable husband much longer. Several times she turned William out with the fare back to Leeds in his pocket, but each time he returned instead of boarding the train, having wasted her hard-earned money. In the end she took him to the station herself and was rid of him, or so the story goes. He last shows up on the electoral register for Red Cross Street in 1902, and by 1904 Maggie appears as Margaret Jones of 22 Goodwin Buildings. She'd not only freed herself of a good-for-nothing husband, but dropped his name as well, and reverted to her maiden one: Margaret Jones, the sole breadwinner for herself and her daughter Clara.

For a decade the Borough Polytechnic Institute had been busy in its mission to "raise the dignity of manual labour." Careful planning had gone into the curriculum development, and the school offered training in areas relevant to Southwark-based industries. The baking school had been particularly successful and made up the largest group of students, but there were also courses in typography, boot and shoe manufacture, chemistry, and building construction. There was instruction relating to oils, colours and varnishes, though Harry and Jack no longer needed it, and no longer qualified, given their age. Instruction was open to men and women between the ages of sixteen and twenty-five, and required payment of various fees, the amounts of which the governing body decreed must be "of the most moderate character." Women could learn about laundry, dressmaking, upholstery and needlework. In recent years the school had begun to offer courses for young adolescents as well, giving boys and girls the skills they'd need to continue in the upper-level programs when they were old enough. Photographs show baking students taking hot loaves of bread from an oven; women fitting skirts onto dressmakers' dummies; girls pressing fabric and stitching waistcoats by hand. The rooms look comfortable and well-equipped, with large windows to let in maximum light. What's more, the students in the rooms look happy to be there, engaged in the task at hand.

Maggie was of the class the school was intended for, of course, but age and circumstance meant that she cleaned the rooms rather than learned in them. Six days a week, she began at seven a.m. and finished at four. She worked with a group of about ten women, finishing the week on Saturdays, when the main staircase was scrubbed and all the corridors were thoroughly cleaned and polished. In contrast to her sister Mary, who supposedly chose the workhouse over fending for herself, Maggie was a woman of determination, a trait reinforced by photographs that show a small person with a direct gaze, a slightly tilted chin and a somewhat sardonic expression. Hats soften the look of her, and one picture gives a glimpse of a less severe side. It's taken at the seaside, Maggie in conservative beachwear: long-sleeved, striped blouse; a belted skirt; and a narrow-brimmed hat that looks more like a habit than an effort to shield the sun. She's astride a donkey, and in the background a woman in a beach chair twists to look toward her, drawn by the sound time silences: Maggie bent forward with laughter.

The details of Maggie's sister Mary's time at the Mint Street workhouse are long gone, and no casebook with red-rimmed photographs exists to provide insight. Newspaper accounts reveal a little of what went on in the workhouse during Mary's stay, such as the delicious King's Dinner to the Poor that was served to inmates to celebrate Edward's coronation: roast beef, plum pudding, nuts and oranges, delivered "by the kindness of the guardians." But such chipper mentions about Mint Street are rare. Much more typical is the story of the workhouse porter, who left the house one Friday and returned drunk on Saturday, waving an unloaded revolver and threatening to kill himself; or that of a female inmate who similarly returned drunk and caused an even bigger ruckus. She kicked and spat at workhouse staff, who she said were more cannibal than Christian, and when she was sentenced to twenty-one days' imprisonment for the assault, she declared, "I don't care if it's a lifetime – anywhere but that hole."

Hole or no, Mary Jones Evans stayed at the Mint Street workhouse for years. Like other inmates she occasionally discharged herself, but never for long, and where she went and for what reason we can only speculate. She was still there in 1904, when a serious outbreak of measles lasted several months and kept some of the wards under continuous quarantine. Her final leave-taking occurred in autumn of that year, but it was only to travel to Homerton Workhouse across the Thames, probably because Southwark had more people than it could deal with, and unions made arrangements to ease each other's burdens in such situations as long as the costs were covered. The reality was that a workhouse of one kind or another had become Mary's home, her uniform marked with both her dormitory and bed number. She'd landed at the bottom of the social scale, and as Charles Booth put it, "Easy the descent, but to step back is difficult."

In some regards, however, Homerton was a positive move. It made the news less often than Mint Street, suggesting a more peaceful venue, and the *Reports on Surprise Visits by Guardians* were generally favourable. "I have just been shown over the house and have been very pleased with the comfortable appearance of the rooms and inmates," one such visitor wrote in 1906. "The bright colours on the walls and green trees and creepers much relieve the monotony usually associated with workhouses. I saw several of our Southwark people who expressed themselves very satisfied with their treatment." On another occasion the surprise visitor was present during dinner, and was impressed that "everything was good including the people. NO complaint because no beer was being served."

But even the better places were bleak. Workhouse pictures show large dining halls where the uniformed inmates sat in long rows, elbow to elbow, spooning in the daily pudding – batter, bread, pease, rice or "roly-poly" – from the newly introduced *Workhouse Cookery* recipe book. The food was bland and stodgy, even more so for Mary, who had been prescribed the infirmary diet. But the meals were also warm, constant and more or less nourishing. Often the walls were painted with less-than-subtle reminders to the diners: "God is just," which some must have taken to mean people got what they deserved – the trough-like feeding, the lined-up beds in the dorm, with strangers coughing and farting throughout the night, or shouting out in their sleep.

During the day there was always work to be done in-house, and some inmates had jobs outside in the regular world. They came and went the way others did from family homes. Though not disallowed, "ins and outs" for other reasons were discouraged because they made more work for the staff, who had to dig out the individuals' private clothes – rumpled from being in storage – and run through the lengthy procedure of readmitting the inmates when they returned, steaming and storing their clothes once more and reissuing the uniform. Sometimes staff were reluctant to readmit such people, and cold to their emotional torment; one woman left in the morning and came knocking again at night, "the only reason given…being that she wished to visit her child at Hanwell Schools." But who could not have been moved by the dedication of the "octogenarian pedestrian" whose story appeared in the *Evening Telegraph* in July 1904? A long-time inmate of Homerton, he walked eighteen miles to Colney Hatch Lunatic Asylum to see his wife each Sunday, never missing a visit, and never returning late.

And what of the Evans family? With Mary Evans now farther from the Borough, who made the effort to see her these days? Or to visit Ellen at Stone Asylum in Dartford, even more distant? These were the sorts of absences that altered a family's closeness, like holes in a knitted blanket that can't help but unravel further.

This Lant Street School image shows May Deverill second from right in the second row. Taken in the early 1900s, it may also hold other girls from the family – the Vanson sisters or Ellen's daughter Flo – but the faces have long since become separated from their names.

This candid shot is the only known photograph of Harry and Mary Anne together. Taken around 1907 in Whitechapel, the abundance of flowers and the playful nature of the composition hint at the kind of people they were. Does Harry, posing in his tiny garden, even know Mary Anne peers through the window behind him?

CHAPTER 6

We Are Shadows

Beyond the Borough and Lambeth, the wider world kept changing. The causes and effects were numerous, complicated and interconnected, but could be seen at every turn. In 1905, General William Booth, who'd begun his career preaching in a burial ground, was given the Freedom of the City of London, an ancient and prestigious award bestowed, in the General's case, for his "earnest and conscientious exertions for the moral and social improvement of the condition of the necessitous classes, not only of his fellow subjects of the British Empire, but of other races and peoples throughout the world." Even *The Times* – which the *War Cry* claimed had rarely been kind to the Salvation Army – sounded impressed and noted that the General, wearing his braided frock coat and crimson jersey, had walked to Guildhall from the Army's headquarters, leading a parade of Salvationists. In his address, the City Chamberlain praised the General's now forty-year war against sin and poverty, and said that "no man of feeling" could disapprove of the General being thus honoured. The Army had suffered adverse criticism, ridicule and even outright physical attack, he said, but it had persevered and was now being lauded for its enormous accomplishments. The *War Cry* claimed that Booth was "staggered" by the applause that followed, and as he rose to address the crowd, he could not fail to see the contrast between the Army's humble beginnings and its current place in society.

To a certain extent the Salvation Army had King Edward to thank for its climb up the ladder. The king and queen had apparently taken a quiet interest in the Army's work for a number of years, and in the summer of 1904, Edward had invited General Booth to Buckingham

Palace, marking the first time the Army had been formally recognized by the royal family, or for that matter by any official leader. The visit was just one example of the fact that King Edward couldn't have been more different from Queen Victoria, who had for so long represented stability and constancy, an old mum in lace and brooches. Edward – known informally as Bertie – was an extrovert who'd had decades as heir apparent to refine his diplomatic skills. He'd hunted tigers in India, ridden a timber slide in Canada, tented near Damascus and travelled regularly throughout Europe, all the while deftly solidifying his allies. He favoured the company of new money: beer barons and bankers and entrepreneurs with fortunes. He was a rotund playboy with a string of mistresses, but his charisma was also his most effective political tool, for he made important international friendships wherever he went. In 1903 he was the first British monarch to visit France in four hundred years, and while at first the French public rebuffed him, by the end of his time there – speaking fluent French, charming the ladies and moving among the crowds "like a pacific Caesar," as the *Daily Express* put it – he'd won the people over, and paved the way for the two countries' governments to sign the Entente Cordiale, officially ending the aggression that had knotted their shared histories for centuries. Although his role as a constitutional monarch ostensibly gave him little power, Edward was at the centre of improved relations with Russia too, since his wife, Alexandra, and the tsar's mother were sisters. Within a few years, Britain, France and Russia had locked in as allies through the Triple Entente, a cautious alliance between countries that had been traditional enemies. Such bonds would soon be crucial, for all the while, Britain's age-old ally, Germany, grew more distant.

Edward's nephew, Kaiser Wilhelm, was so familiar to the British public that newspapers called him Kaiser Bill with the kind of affection one reserves for an eccentric old uncle. But relations within this branch of the family had chilled significantly, and Edward's machinations with France and Russia had caused Wilhelm to label him "Edward the Encircler," since the agreement between the three countries had Germany hemmed in on all sides. Unlike Edward, Wilhelm was both insecure and arrogant, and urgently wished to be seen as a powerful warlord. Instead he tended to vacillate and often made contradictory pronouncements that embarrassed his government. Historians claim he had always been hand-wringingly jealous of the British, and that his tormented love-hate relationship with his English mother – Edward's sister – was at the root of all his problems, with enormous long-term consequences for the world. At family events he frequently tried to upstage his uncle, whose ease in social situations was the opposite of Wilhelm's gracelessness. Eager to demonstrate his own importance, he'd created a duplicate of Cowes Week, the pre-eminent social and yachting event of the year, at Kiel in Germany and spent a small fortune on his own racing yachts, always pursuing something faster and better in order to beat his opponents. His competitive nature and his desire for respect from his English cousins had continued until his wish to excel in the world of yacht racing became a need to challenge Britain's domination of the high seas, and this, finally, had caught the attention of the English and set off a naval arms race.

But Germany's bid to become a world power was just one concern among many. In China, peasants rose up against the Ch'ing Dynasty, and in Italy, labour unrest led to the assassination of the king. In Russia, the ill-fated Tsar Nicholas went to war against Japan and lost, adding fuel to the discontent within his country. Socialism, already a force by the twentieth century, made even greater strides, spurred by the shift in political power from the lords in gold epaulets to the ordinary man. In England, a ruling class giddy with the good times of playboy Bertie's reign was learning to accept the members of the *nouveaux riches* who propped up their hereditary rights with their fortunes. But beneath the layers of glitter and the sound of good cheer at dinner parties around the country, the rumble of dissatisfaction from the working classes was becoming audible, and it was paired with anti-German sentiment.

In 1906 the *Daily Mail* serialized *The Invasion of 1910*, a novel by William Le Queux that painted Germans as ruthless enemies and warned that England needed to prepare for war. In the story's opening pages, "the dear old City" is asleep when Germany attacks, unprovoked, and England suddenly finds itself "helpless beneath the iron heel of the enemy." German writers were equally alarmist, publishing works like

Hamburg und Bremen in Gefahr, or *Hamburg and Bremen in Danger,* written under a pseudonym by a retired naval captain who imagined Germany's response to an alliance between France and Britain. With the discord escalating on both sides, some concerned lords had already formed the Anglo-German Friendship Committee, certain that the majority of the population desired a respectful and cordial relationship with the German people. In 1907, when Kaiser Wilhelm visited England for the first time since Queen Victoria's death, members of the committee called on him, and the *Advocate of Peace* magazine reported that they were warmly received and also suitably impressed by the "strong and dignified figure; not a small-made man, as he is often represented," but one with dark hair and broad shoulders, and a keen, alert expression "by no means without the milk of human kindness."

He was fairly gushed over in the press on that visit, and both he and the king made a great show of admiring each other. Reporting on the Windsor Castle banquet, the *Exter and Plymouth Gazette* said that King Edward had fondly recalled the Kaiser's boyhood visits, and the sadness of his last trip in 1901. He called this new visit "a sincere pleasure to the Queen and myself, as well as to the whole of my people, and I not only fervently hope for the prosperity and happiness of the great country over which you are Sovereign, but also for the maintenance of peace." The Kaiser in response lovingly spoke of his "revered grandmother" and his childhood ramblings at Windsor Castle, and stressed it was his earnest wish that relations between the two families be reflected in the relations between the two countries, "and thus confirm the peace of our world."

In hindsight, the delicate flattery underscored the precarious bond, and the unease that existed between England and Germany despite – and partly because of – the German ancestry of the royal family. Plenty of ordinary English families had German roots as well. Two years earlier, Harry's youngest sister Nell, the piano teacher, had married a man named Percy Kraushaar. Percy was born and bred in Rotherhithe, east of the Borough and Bermondsey, and his great-great-grandparents had come to England more than a century earlier, but unlike many other immigrants, Percy's branch hadn't anglicized its name. Percy was employed as a compositor in the printing industry, typesetting the many newspaper articles about warships and lurking Germans, but what he thought of such articles, or of his family connection to Germany, is a mystery now. Actual war was still years off, though, and the parry and thrust of Anglo-German politics had little effect on the personal life of the average working-class man, even one of German descent like Percy Kraushaar. For now, he could easily whistle on his way home from work, ink-stained fingers in his pockets.

If Percy was musical, like his pianist wife, Nell, and her brothers Harry and Jack, he would have taken special notice of storey-high posters plastered on building walls, advertising a variety of entertainments: *The Merry Widow* at Daly's Theatre, or *The Girls of Gottenberg* at the Gaiety. There were posters for the spectacles at the Hippodrome, too, showing elephants sliding into huge water tanks, and seals balancing balls on their noses. The papers carried similar notices interspersed with more serious news items, so on any given day those looking for diversion could find listings for operas or ballets playing at the Savoy or the Alhambra. "Today's London Amusements" also targeted the working man like Percy, more inclined toward a music hall comedy performed by the likes of Charlie Chaplin, who by 1907 was a member of the well-known Fred Karno Pantomime Troupe, bringing slapstick comedy, song and dance to the masses. Almost as popular were amateur productions of comic theatre, with Gilbert and Sullivan's operettas among the favourites. According to one paper, participating in musicals was "an excellent way of acquiring a good knowledge of music if the time necessary can be given." In one writer's opinion, the working-class halls had more to offer than the highbrow ones, even though the singing was often off-key. "The [people] rock with laughter, the whole pit swaying like a field of wheat in a breeze. Those who assert that the London poor are a joyless class, incapable of merriment, should see this crowd when genuinely amused, and consider whether there is not some exaggeration in descriptions of their hopeless gloom."

And yet how gloomy things must have seemed for the Deverill family in March 1907, when Nell and Harry's mother, Mary Margaret, died of pneumonia. Their father, William, was well surrounded after his loss – Nell and Percy lived in the house, and so did another of Harry's sisters, Maud, and her husband, Arthur Jordan. Ada, the eldest of the Deverill siblings, lived a ways south, in Lewisham, the first of several moves that took her increasingly farther from her family. In those days even small distances could render a sister "completely lost to view" according to Maud Pember Reeves.

By this time, Harry, too, had moved again, heading in the opposite direction from Ada and settling with Mary Anne and the children in Whitechapel. Exactly when and why the move from Lambeth happened is a puzzle, for there was no family in this infamous pocket of London's East End. But Harry had found a job as caretaker of a model dwelling there, sporting a cap and uniform somewhat plainer than the one he still wore as Bandsman Deverill.

Like the Borough over London Bridge, Whitechapel lay outside the gates of the old city. Consequently, as with Southwark, slaughterhouses, tanneries, foundries and the refuse and smells that accompanied them came to reside in Whitechapel. For centuries the area had been a perpetual slum, home to the poor and destitute and part of the notorious East End, and therefore a curiosity for the writer George Sims, the same man who'd written of the Borough's "wretchedness." But unlike the Borough, in recent years Whitechapel had become so rich with Jewish immigrants fleeing persecution in Russia and eastern Europe that Sims thought it a "foreign land which is in London but not of it." In 1880 the Jewish population of London was estimated at 46,000, but by 1900 it had swelled to nearly three times that size, with most of the Jews settling in the East End. The men wore beards and fur caps and long boots, and the women draped colourful shawls over their hair. When Harry and Mary Anne arrived in Wentworth Street sometime in 1907, it must have felt as if they'd travelled farther than across the Thames. They moved into College Buildings, with mostly English-born Gentiles, but in the wider community they were in the minority now. Jews made up 95 percent of the area's population, crowding into an already crowded neighbourhood, and bringing their traditions with them. Harry and Mary Anne need only step outside to be immersed in this unfamiliar world.

A little east of College Buildings, across busy Commercial Street, Wentworth Street continued toward Petticoat Lane market, or "the heart of the old Ghetto," according to Sims in a piece he called "In Alien-Land." On Sundays, the one day English shops were typically closed, the Lane thrived with commerce. Many of the Jewish hawkers did business from the early morning until midnight, when the gas-lit streets glowed yellow. They were "old, solemn-looking men," Sims wrote, "calling aloud the price of their poor goods in the lachrymose sing-song of the Eastern pedlar." Those not haggling with customers sat reading Hebrew newspapers, or clustered in small groups playing cards as the commotion went on around them.

Amid the crush of people in Petticoat Lane there were women carrying fluttering birds and baskets of fish heads, accompanied by the whir of sewing machines stitching silk petticoats, suit jackets and trousers, waistcoats and cloaks and gloves. Gold and diamonds were traded in tiny leather bags and cases with precious velvet lining. Houses had been haphazardly converted into stores, so that living rooms bulged with goods for sale. "Every available corner is used," wrote Sims. "One sees the proprietor sitting in a little front room so packed in with rolls of gay-coloured cloths, fancy boxes, and packages that one imagines his only way of getting out must be by a harlequin leap through the window."

Footage of the market filmed around this time shows the press of people between the stalls' canvas awnings, mostly men in flat caps or bowler hats, and here and there a woman with a basket over her arm. The men grip their lapels and stare at the camera recording them, occasionally glancing over their shoulders at a vendor gesturing from a platform above the crowd, trying to draw attention to his wares. "D. Isaacs" is painted above a door, while farther down a banner proclaims "This is Levy's." Frequently those being filmed are laughing and elbowing one another, and one man makes a concerted effort to remain in the camera's eye, shifting as it pans the crowd. Another with white mutton-chop whiskers, and a pot-belly filling his vest, lifts his hat and appears to call out a greeting to the person filming, then balances with his hat in the air, as if posing for a photograph.

These images are the grey scale of the time and don't convey the fact that in spite of the poverty of the neighbourhood, the young Jewish women wore fashionable clothes in bright colours, and the children were well cared for, with white pinafores and good boots. A number of years earlier, when Charles Booth's investigator had wandered the same streets, he'd noticed a positive change underway. Though the gutters were a mess with fish heads and bread and orange peels, it struck him that the children were well-fed and happy, playing with their skipping ropes and hoops. "Great improvement in this district since the incoming of the Jews," he noted. But where Jews and Gentiles mixed, "neither are pleased and quarrels result."

Sims's view of what remained of English Whitechapel was harsh:

One sharp turn out of the gay, crowded street and the scene is changed. Here everything is gloom…We pass quickly by the group of loafing tramps who have come out of the lodging-house kitchens to gossip, and make our way up a narrow, tortuous passage to another street of evil fame, where lodging-houses of the lowest class still remain. Battered wrecks of lost humanity, male and female, flit to and fro in the darkness. A woman pauses under the solitary lamp and we see that her face is bruised and her eyes are blackened. The door of one lodging-house stands ajar and the English tongue salutes our ears once more. It is not a welcome relief, for the sentiment of the words is foul and blasphemous.

The descriptions were just like those written of Whitechapel when the infamous Jack the Ripper murders had taken place twenty years before.

With the massive shift in demographics came massive resentment. The sense that the Jews were taking over – stealing not just jobs but places to live – resonated enough that the government formed the Royal Commission on Alien Immigration, and an array of people from all walks of life were called and examined. One woman who owned a lamp and oil shop said that her earnings had dropped dramatically because her usual customers were leaving the area, and the Jewish customers frequented the Jewish shops. They could pay higher rents, too, "because they have so many living in the same house. We could not live crowded like that. Where four people lived to a room there are now eight, and they can afford to pay the rent more than we could."

Another person said the overcrowding was "disgusting...Twenty years ago there was not a single Jew in the whole street, from end to end, but now there is not a house without one." One man – a carpenter born and raised in the East End – had been a census taker many times over the years. Early on, he'd encountered a purely English population when he knocked on doors, and then later it was half and half. By 1901 it was almost entirely foreign. "Our people are not philosophers," he told the commission, "and we see these people taking our place and one by one we are driven out. It causes a feeling, and the racial feeling, I'm sorry to say, is very bad."

The Reverend Samuel Barnett, the same man who'd advocated for brighter streets at the time of the Whitechapel murders, and long an eloquent voice for the troubled area, spoke well of the Jews, who according to him were on the whole clean, sober, hard-working and dressed "with rather more colour." Their children came regularly to school and did extremely well. As to overcrowding, he claimed conditions had been much worse thirty years earlier, and that now the standards were higher, so people noticed the crowding more. It was only natural for Jews to wish to live among Jews, he said, and if it was a solution to move some out to the country, where there was more space, then the solution worked for Christians as well.

A local schoolteacher agreed that Christians were slowly being replaced by Jews, but "in some streets the advent of the foreigner tenant has brought about a distinct change for the better, where respectable and hard-working foreigners have replaced a rough or vicious population." Some claimed the English-born were being pushed out, while others claimed they left of their own volition. Lord Nathan Rothschild, a wealthy Jewish philanthropist who built model dwellings in the East End, presented a letter written by a Christian tenant to his landlord. "Dear Sir – No doubt you will be surprised to hear that I am thinking of giving up the house, but the neighbourhood is so bad now that it is crowded with the foreigners that I shall try and get further away...We made up our minds to go in a hurry, or the wife would have told you on Monday, but our own people are leaving the street, and I cannot stand the foreigners. Hoping this will meet with your approval."

CHAPTER 6

As their kind left the area, Harry and Mary Anne moved into it and took a ground-floor flat in College Buildings, a red-brick, five-storey structure with Tudor roses on its lintels. Owned by the newspaper proprietor Harry Levy-Lawson, College Buildings was a vast improvement when it was first erected in 1887. It backed on to the Toynbee Hall university settlement, which had been founded in 1884 by Reverend Samuel and Henrietta Barnett as a place where university men could live, meet and study and offer culture and educational courses to the local population. The idea was that some semblance of university life, complete with quadrangle, diamond-paned windows, and scintillating lectures, could be transplanted to Whitechapel, and that the privileged should live among those they purported to help – "to learn as much as to teach; to receive as much as to give."

Both College Buildings and Toynbee Hall were the work of architect Elijah Hoole, the man who'd designed Octavia Hill's cottages in Red Cross Street back in the Borough. With its Gothic features and charming terracotta details, College Buildings had been designed "with some regard to beauty," and could therefore attract a better sort of tenant than those who'd lived in the rickety houses that previously stood on the same spot. As part of the Toynbee plan, many of Whitechapel's derelict structures were condemned and demolished, and property had been bought up by wealthy philanthropists and building companies – friends of Samuel Barnett, who agreed with his vision.

Henrietta Barnett had worked for Octavia Hill – they called each other Yetta and Ockey – and had originally met Samuel at Octavia's birthday party. Shortly after they married he became rector of St. Jude's, the small church next to what would become Toynbee Hall. At the time, the Bishop of London called it "the worst parish in my diocese," but Barnett was up for the mission. And there were plenty of like minds. In this challenging but hopeful atmosphere, the philanthropic circles continued to overlap, for Toynbee became a base for Charles Booth, and Samuel Barnett proved an enormous help opening East End doors for Booth's studies. Some of the people residing at Toynbee became deeply involved in Booth's extensive inquiry.

When Harry and Mary Anne moved into the neighbourhood,

Barnett was Canon of Westminster Abbey. He had retired from St. Jude's, and Toynbee Hall was well established, its courtyard behind College Buildings a quiet oasis where students read in the shade of ivy-covered walls. The pulpit next door at St. Jude's was manned by Reverend Ernest Carter, a modest clergyman of middle years who made a point of calling on every newcomer to the parish. Though he was neither an intellectual nor a particularly gifted speaker, nor a visionary like Barnett, Reverend Carter was noted for his enthusiasm, good humour and generosity of spirit, and was admired by his fellow churchmen for his approach to what they saw as a difficult task: leading a Christian ministry in a largely Jewish parish. He too had been interviewed for the Royal Commission on Alien Immigration, as had a number of other clergymen, and he'd testified that Christian people really were feeling displaced by the shift in the neighbourhood. "When a Christian moves out, a Jew does move in," he told the Commission. In his view, "the Sunday question is the great question." If Jews and Gentiles rested on the same day, "very great trouble and difficulty would disappear."

A little before that he had written an article on "the Jewish question" for Oxford's *Economic Review*. The act of writing such a piece was "a distasteful task, for it is most unwillingly that I seem to write hard words about those whose lot in life is none too happy, and who find in England a liberty and justice unobtainable elsewhere." He was proud to live in Whitechapel, he wrote, but "deplore[d] the present serious and dangerous state of affairs." Overcrowding for both Jews and Christians was scandalous, and "the owners of many of these fever-traps have practically achieved the feat of putting the contents of a quart into a pint." Lately, he saw an erosion of English ways, which was partly the result of English complacency and partly a logical extension of the fact that most of the people in Whitechapel were now Jewish. Thus, on the Lord's Day, there was no sign of religious observance or rest from work, and the school holidays were arranged to coincide with Jewish fasts and festivals. "'Why don't they keep our laws when they come to our country?' is not an unreasonable observation which can be heard daily, and can be only fully understood when the bitter feelings behind it are adequately realized."

Carter's solution to the problem was prescriptive. He believed that the Jewish population of any area should not be allowed to exceed 50 percent. "The Christian would then feel more kindly about them, for he would, at any rate, be on equal terms with them...he will feel more secure in his home, become less suspicious in his sentiments, and more apt to recognize undoubted Jewish virtues."

What his wife Lilian thought of his plan isn't recorded, but once in Whitechapel this reportedly brilliant woman studied Hebrew and Yiddish, and started a class so policemen of the area could learn Yiddish themselves. Unlike Ernest, she was a dedicated orator and lecturer, especially on women's issues, and when she spoke, her face came alive with passion. Lilian was known among the academics at Toynbee Hall as the youngest daughter of Thomas Hughes, once a member of parliament and county court judge, as well as the author of the hugely popular novel *Tom Brown's Schooldays*. The Hughes family moved in the same circles as the Barnetts and Octavia Hill, who had tutored Lilian's older siblings for a time to help them overcome what their learned father called their hatred of lessons. Thomas Hughes owned a country mansion in Cheshire and a house in London's elegant Mayfair – an area Booth coloured comfortable pink, well-to-do red and wealthy yellow on his poverty map – so by the optics of the day, Lilian had married beneath her when she wed the former schoolteacher Ernest Carter. And yet her father saw it differently: "I hold a parson's work done as it should be done to be just about the noblest given to the sons of men, so rejoice in the match which most folks would call a very poor one."

Hughes, like many of his class, was a social reformer, and his idealism helped shape his children. His exceptionally bright, somewhat eccentric daughter Mary had kept house for an uncle in Berkshire for many years and become a member of the Board of Guardians there. Accounts say she was stunned that the Guardians could enjoy an ample dinner, and afterward, on full bellies, discuss cutting workhouse bread rations. When her uncle died, she moved in with Ernest and Lilian in Whitechapel and began to champion the cause of the poor yet more vigorously, joining the Stepney Board of Guardians and walking the streets to befriend "the dirty, the thriftless, the profligate, liars and loafers, and the habitually intemperate." Mary often signed as a witness to the marriages her brother-in-law Ernest presided over at St. Jude's, stepping in when there was no one closer to the bride and groom to fill that necessary role. Though she'd inherited more than enough money to keep her comfortable, she disdained the family wealth and claimed, "We Hughes[es]...feel rather like the receivers of stolen goods." She firmly believed that "in service lies greatness," and as her work went on she seemed fuelled by the notion of selflessness, living as if poor herself, a "shabby and sometimes verminous woman...radiant with love."

Her sister Lilian sought to reach people in a different way. She and Ernest opened their home to parishioners, Ernest setting aside Thursdays for any who cared to call, and Lilian hosting her little band of truth-seekers in the great room of the vicarage. The room was nothing fancy. The vicarage had been decorated with many paintings and fine objects when the Barnetts resided there, in keeping with their belief in the uplifting power of beauty and the importance of bringing it to the people. The Carters followed a different philosophy. Lilian's sister Mary once wrote that when the girls were young, their father, Thomas, "was always telling us that we were in God's *lowest* class because we had so much and so many people waited on us and served us." Hence, the sparse rooms at St. Jude's. Once, when a wealthy friend of the Hughes family visited the vicarage, he was struck by how bare the place was, and afterward sent along Turkish carpets and beautiful drapes to dress it up. Another time he sent £2,000 each for Lilian and Mary, and a diamond pendant that Lilian quickly sold. "Suppose I keep this," she apparently mused. "I should only put it in the cupboard. It would be no good to anyone, and a temptation into the bargain. Instead, we could electrify this room and put a stove in the pantry!"

Mary Anne Deverill was one of the regular visitors to the vicarage, drinking tea from china cups with Lilian and the other women of the parish, and perhaps sharing stories about her children – funny little Ernie, already showing his eccentricities, or Joe and Ethel, who'd been enrolled in the Church of England school on nearby Brick Lane. The school backed on to the massive Christ Church, with its towering spire, and the churchyard everyone called "Itchy Park" because it was a home for vagrants who liked to scratch themselves on the railings. By day the homeless slept leaning against each other on benches, and at night the iron gates were closed to keep them out. If Mary Anne – worried for her children – asked Lilian about Itchy Park, she'd have heard that parents forbade their children to go there (though some loved to sneak in anyhow, and spy on the strange inhabitants). Only a few years earlier, the American writer Jack London, dressed incognito in rags to research *The People of the Abyss*, had wandered into Itchy Park one Saturday afternoon and seen "a welter of rags and filth … sleeping bolt upright or leaning against one another in their sleep … It was this sleeping that puzzled me. Why were nine out of ten of them asleep or trying to sleep? But it was not till afterwards that I learned. *It is a law of the powers that be that the homeless shall not sleep by night.*"

In order to avoid Itchy Park and other squalid corners of the neighbourhood when they walked to school, Ethel and Joe would have stuck to the main streets, going east along Wentworth, then north on Brick Lane to just past Fashion Street, where the small school sat a little back from the road, a single storey of classrooms suspended above a covered playground. The playground had once formed the eastern edge of Christ Church's graveyard, and according to surveys the ground was densely packed with bodies; thus the school itself had been built on arches to avoid disturbing the graves. It was a pretty, red-brick construction with a steep slate roof and a neat row of dormer windows overlooking Brick Lane. The playground below was separated by a brick wall into boys' and girls' sides, and when the bell rang, Joe climbed one set of stairs and Ethel another to get to their respective classrooms. Though this was a Church of England school, many of its students were Jewish, and a discreet Star of David can still be seen on the building, gracing the top of a drainpipe. One of the teachers interviewed for the Royal Commission on Alien Immigration said that local schools increasingly had to cater to the Jewish population when it came to curriculum and holidays, otherwise they would be largely empty. Lately the classrooms were bursting with well over three hundred students, sixty more than the facilities were meant to handle, and the head master and his staff were in regular battle with the Board of Education as to what should be done about it.

The staff insisted they managed well and had enough room for every-one, despite the official numbers of what the school could and couldn't hold. But rules were rules. Eventually the board ordered a stay on ad-missions until the numbers fell within acceptable limits.

Meanwhile, the children crowded in for their classes, the girls with the infants of both sexes, and the older boys on their own. When the school day ended, some of the Jewish kids walked steps north, past the Seven Stars pub, to the next block for lessons in Hebrew and Judaism at the Spitalfields Great Synagogue. Ten years earlier, when the synagogue was new, the policeman doing the rounds with Charles Booth's inves-tigator had said this centre stretch near the school and the synagogue was the best part of Brick Lane, and that it got much rougher at the north and south ends, where there were plenty of brothels and com-mon lodging houses of ill repute. In all, Brick Lane was "a mixture of good, bad, and indifferent," with a heavy Jewish presence – not just the stately synagogue, but the bagel sellers and Schewzik's Russian vapour baths, the kosher restaurants and the shops selling salted herring and pickled cucumbers. Friday afternoons brought a sense of flurry to the street, and to much of the East End, as families prepared for the Sab-bath: the mothers cooking and the children rushing to and fro to fetch necessities; the fathers coming home from work as early as they could get away. And then, with sundown, a hush descended and candles ap-peared in windows. Even the non-Jewish residents were swept up in the weekly rituals. Women like Mary Anne, or kids Joe and Ethel's age, were hired on Fridays and Saturdays by the more religious families to turn the gas off and on or to put coal on the fire, allowing the Jewish family to observe the rule of no work on the Sabbath. These were "Jews' pokers" to the Gentiles, and "Shabbat goys" to the Jews. So plentiful were the Jews that their customs became East End customs.

And yet before the influx of Jews, the Brick Lane synagogue had long been a Methodist church, and before that, a Huguenot place of worship. Fleeing religious persecution in France in the late 1600s, the Huguenots had once formed the bulk of the neighbourhood's immi-grant population, bringing with them their culture and their formidable skill in the silk-weaving trade. Soon the area became known as Weaver

Town, where French was widely spoken in the streets. Along with chapels, the Huguenots built a number of elegant houses distinguished by their large windows, designed to let in enough light for the weavers to work, and they grew mulberry trees in the yards for the silkworms they imported. But times changed. By the early 1800s the silk industry had fallen into decline, unable to compete with machines and cheaper imports. The Huguenots slowly assimilated, migrating to other areas of the city. The cultural shift showed in the history of the Seven Stars pub that pressed up against Joe and Ethel's school: once run by a Parisian Huguenot, now it was in the hands of a Russian Jew, who served up drinks to a largely Gentile clientele. The distinct weavers' homes still existed, but they held well-to-do Jewish residents now, in the midst of "a thoroughly vicious quarter." As the sundial on the church-turned-synagogue attested, *umbra sumus*: we are shadows. The same sentiment appeared often in the Bible, which Mary Anne liked to read to her children while sitting near the fire. There was James 4:14 – *ye know not what shall be on the morrow* – and Job 8:9 – *our days upon earth are but a shadow*. This she and Harry had seen first-hand as family members old and young passed on.

Death and circumstance meant that the core in the Borough was nothing near what it had been. Troubled Ellen had now spent five years at Stone, her days recorded in repetitive detail in a casebook. Though no particular behavioural changes were noted in her files, and a 1909 entry stated "memory uncertain…she says the year is 1906," soon she'd be sent for a trial stay at Newington Workhouse, not far from the Borough. Mother Mary was there already. She'd left Homerton for Newington – her third workhouse – so she was closer to the old family home, yet the very concept of such a place had continued to disintegrate. Family was far-flung now, and Mary Jones Evans had been a workhouse inmate for so long that she fit the typical profile: old, poor and widowed.

According to Emmeline Pankhurst, one of the founders of the Women's Social and Political Union, women like Mary and Ellen spurred on the aggressive suffragette movement. Pankhurst believed the vote was a right for women in general, but "a desperate necessity" for the poor. The struggles of workhouse women were "potent factors," she wrote, in her decision to take a militant approach to women's rights. For years the non-violent suffragists had been politely trying to change the way people thought about a woman's place in society, but lately they'd been losing the publicity race to Pankhurst's ilk, the suffragettes, who grabbed headlines by throwing rocks and chaining themselves to the gates of the prime minister's residence. They carried signs and shouted "votes for women!" and staged a huge rally at Hyde Park, complete with all-women brass bands. Music was a powerful motivator, as General Booth had long ago discovered, and the suffragettes were taking a page out of the Salvation Army's playbook.

Forty bands performed at the event that summer of 1908, and tens of thousands attended, wearing sashes or hats of suffragette colours: purple for dignity, white for purity, green for hope. Posters in shop windows en route to Hyde Park demanded the vote for women, and delegations arriving by train unfurled banners that they carried through the streets to the rally. Emmeline Pankhurst had been instrumental in organizing the event, but even she was shocked by the crowds that poured in from every corner of the park. One of the many speeches that day explained "It is for sweated work and reforms respecting women's work that we want the vote." Some listeners began to come around to the suffragettes' stance with that statement, and the *Hull Daily Mail* quoted one man saying to another, "Did you hear that, it's the working women they are working for, not the propertied women." Others were not so polite and shouted disparaging remarks: "What's the old man doing? Home washing the dinner plates?"

By the time Ellen Roff/Humphreys nee Evans left Stone Asylum in January 1910, the suffragette movement was in full force, and though they aimed to be a voice for all women, "whether they be with us or against us in this fight," it's unlikely Ellen had much awareness of them. Apart from taking exercise in the yard at Stone, or going on supervised walks with other patients, Ellen hadn't been away from the asylum since her admission seven years earlier. There she'd been among people she'd come to know, both staff and fellow inmates, her days revolving in a familiar pattern. How did the journey from Stone to Newington Workhouse feel to Ellen, pegged by her doctors as simple-minded and confused? The asylum was remote from the bustle of London, so as she travelled toward Newington the sights and smells and sounds of the city she'd grown up in were not only new again, but magnified. The streets had changed dramatically in her time away, with horse- and motor-powered vehicles vying for space on the road.

Did Ellen realize her mother Mary was at Newington? And did Mary know to expect Ellen that winter day? By chance or design, after more than twenty years apart, the two women had arrived at the same destination by different routes, both clad in shapeless workhouse garb and taking a bed in the female ward, with the laundry nearby. The long, T-shaped main building housed men at the opposite end, and a dining hall and cookhouse formed the centre. A cluster of buildings near the men's section included the mortuary and the casual wards – for so-called tramps and vagrants who only stayed a night or two – as well as sick wards and "lock wards" for people with venereal disease. The workhouse had been built in 1850, with much less care and attention to detail than at Stone and other public asylums, but there had been improvements of late: there were married couples' quarters now, and a nursery, and Master William Swinnock, whose family lived and worked with him in the workhouse, permitted elderly couples to make their own meals at breakfast and tea time, and to stay in their rooms when not doing work for the house. They were also allowed to light a small fire there between seven a.m. and seven p.m., giving them a feeling of independence and privacy. The *British Nursing Journal* applauded these "cosy corners for married couples" and said it was a shame that so few poor couples lived to be old enough to enjoy such thoughtful provisions. These luxuries didn't extend to widowed Mary, and even after the renovations there were complaints of overcrowding and understaffing – one nurse, for example, in charge of four wards with more than three hundred inmates. The nurses' duties were sometimes more than they could manage. A little before Mary arrived, a nurse had placed a stillborn baby in the bathroom of the lying-in ward and then seemed to forget about it. When the child – a twin whose sibling had survived – was discovered two days later, the nurse was asked to resign, and the matron and the head nurse responsible for inspecting the bathroom were reprimanded.

The staff-inmate ratio was lopsided for sure, but the needy extended be-yond workhouse walls as well. Outside, long lines of poor people waited to collect out-relief in the form of sugar, tea and flour, hoping not to slip off that last rung that would land them inside the institution's doors.

That Mary was still in the workhouse when she had relatives seem-ingly able to take her in suggests that either her family callously aban-doned her or she was too difficult to care for. There are no records remaining to confirm she was a drinker or foul-tempered or mentally unstable. The only clue to her personality is the anecdote that she was too lazy to put on her own boots, and that this story survives a century on compels the image of a cantankerous old lady unwilling to help her-self. The truth must be multi-layered and many-hued, but one fact is clear: wayward mother and wayward daughter now shared an address after long separations from family.

In Whitechapel, Harry was farther still from the Borough than he'd been in Lambeth, and yet he remained a member of the Borough Band. He was now living in the Salvation Army's very birthplace, the area General Booth had come upon by chance almost fifty years earlier, when he was asked to fill in for another evangelist preacher who'd fallen ill. "I've found my destiny!" Booth told his wife on his return home, and from then on he became a fixture on East End streets, delivering powerful sermons in the open air. One biographer wrote that in those early days "he was the finest-looking gentleman you ever saw – white-faced, dark-eyed, and a great black beard over his chest…There was something strange about him that laid hold on a man." As his fame grew, other preachers became curious about William Booth. Henrietta Barnett wrote that occasion-ally she and Samuel would wander out from St. Jude's on Sundays to listen to the street sermons "in the hope of finding what both attracted and fed sick souls."

All these years later, General Booth had retained his charismatic intensity, though his beard blazed white now, and his work took him farther afield. Music was still vital to Army culture, and whether sung or played on an instrument, he insisted it come from the heart. "The secret of cold, icy fishy singing is heartless formality. Fishy hearts can only make fishy music," he said, shunning choirs and singing classes that brought forth a "mincing, proper set of sounds." Though he played no instrument himself, he recognized the power of a band in drawing onlookers, and in profoundly moving them too. There was a bond that existed between the players as well, for music was like a language. Musicians performed for the audience, yes, but in the act of playing, they also connected with each other.

Day or night, travelling back across London Bridge to the Borough to take part in practices and concerts was a busy commute for Harry, toting his unwieldy tuba or the slightly more compact euphonium. By 1896, London Bridge had been carrying more than eight thousand pedestrians and nine hundred vehicles of varying description every hour, and the city's main streets were hectic. Horses pulled omnibuses and trams and hansom cabs and rickety carts, and also the ambulances that Harry's father had steered through the snarl, with a sick patient and an attendant bumping along in the back. It took a single horse to pull the lowliest of carts, but eleven to pull an omnibus. The clip-clop of hooves spread out in all directions, and the droppings left along the way made constant work for the street cleaners of every borough – poorly paid men who walked everywhere because they couldn't afford the transit they tidied up after. By the early 1900s the network had evolved into a relatively efficient system that included working-men's trains, the deep-level tube – a marvel of the 1890s – and electric trams that could carry large numbers of people quickly through London streets. For a time, traffic congestion comprised both animals and engines, as well as the daring "New Women" weaving through it all on bicycles, wearing knickerbockers or split skirts. "We dares not drive over them, wotever they do," an omnibus driver once commented to author Thomas Hardy. "They do jist wot they likes. 'Tis their sex, yer see; and it's wot I call takin' a mean adventage. No man dares to go where they go." And of course there were motorcars too, spoke-wheeled Vauxhalls and Crossleys with running boards and flat windscreens and polished brass horns. Even General Booth used a motorcar and travelled widely both in England and abroad, stopping to preach from the comfort of his open-top vehicle.

Indeed, the streets were changing. In 1910 the *Grantham Journal* reported that the London General Omnibus Company planned to auction four hundred of its remaining horses. Since the motor buses had come into general use, the company had been disposing of surplus animals at the rate of one hundred a week. Such efficiencies were yet another arm of social reform. Less dung on the streets meant fewer flies, and fewer deaths from the diseases they spread; and the working classes could now afford the cost of travelling by means other than foot, since trams were fast and cheap, and helped bring down the costs of competing forms of transportation. This meant people with a reliable income could move from poor, crowded areas like the Borough and Whitechapel to the suburbs, where it was thought they'd enjoy a healthier lifestyle in quaint cottages with multiple rooms. Many did move, Harry's sisters included. Others, like Harry, Mary Anne and Jack, stayed put, navigating the chaotic streets with extra care, and paying the fare of a motorized bus to get to work or across the bridge to band practice. Karl Baedeker's 1908 guide *London and Its Environs* described the newly widened London Bridge as a must-see for travellers, because of "the steady stream of noisy traffic" day in and day out, with the edges reserved for slow-moving vehicles, and the centre for quick ones.

Despite the congestion, it would have been easy to find Harry in the crowd, a thin man in a threadbare coat, his dark hair neatly combed and his moustache tidy as he climbed onto the tram with his euphonium tucked beneath his arm. If it was concert day, or the wedding of a bandmate and his songster, he'd have exchanged the coat for his uniform and cap, the peak "lined green leather, improved in shape, and placed at an angle of about sixty degrees to protect eyes from the sun, and lessen the tendency of the Cap to blow off." As he rode, standing to allow ladies the seats, he'd consider the words he'd read in the latest *Bandsman and Songster*, praising the Borough Band's work in aid of the Self-Denial Fund. They'd played at the Surrey Square Mission Hall, pieces like "The Good Choice," "Songs of Comfort" and "The Old, Old Story," the performance an appeal to supporters to give up an item of food or clothing they would normally purchase and instead donate that money to the fund to aid the "suffering and lost." "The music was much appreciated by a large audience," the writer in the *Bandsman* noted, which was good, because listeners translated to donors.

But not all Harry's trips across the river were for band practice or recitals, or the outdoor meetings held to lure drinkers from pubs. One day in April 1910, word came from his sisters in Deptford that his father had suffered a stroke. Harry likely boarded the tram that day with an air of agitation, his shoulders stiff, impatient with the press of people. Anxiously counting the stops until he came to the one he needed, he might have recalled the times they'd spent together as father and son, and his earliest memories in his father's grocery store before the business went under. Harry had been too small, then, to see over the counter, but was well acquainted with the great tin canisters and their contents, the weigh scales and the thick roll of brown paper used to wrap the items people purchased. It was a link between them, son following in father's footsteps, but both those paths had ended abruptly. William Henry lingered three days before he died, and Harry, eldest son, was now the patriarch of the Deverill family.

William was put to rest at Nunhead Cemetery, buried a foot above his wife in a plot that had been purchased when she'd died three years earlier. Built by the London and Highgate Cemetery Company, Nunhead was the second largest of the seven established in a ring around the outskirts of London. It boasted fifty-two lush acres planted with towering lime, ash and sycamore, and was situated on a rise with a magnificent view of the city and St. Paul's white dome. The gates at the main entrance off Linden Grove bore examples of the symbolism favoured by the Victorians of the time: upended torches signified lives extinguished, while the snake swallowing its tail suggested eternity. A broad gravelled lane sloped up from the gate, drawing one's gaze to the chapel, a pinnacled stone structure of Gothic design with a crypt below. Lining the way up the hill and all around the chapel stood the most ornate monuments of gleaming granite and pink marble topped with draped urns, Celtic crosses and angels in flowing robes with faces downturned. The inscriptions gave the graves' occupants an anchor in the living world: "In Memory of Our Darling Sydney," "In Fondest Remembrance of Our Dear Brother," "Beloved Mamma." The Deverills couldn't pay for such luxury, so the memorial for William Henry and his wife, marking an unassuming plot at the far eastern boundary of Nunhead, was much humbler, and has long since been swallowed by glossy ivy, brambles and soft moss. For Mary Anne and Harry, the graveside service must have stirred old sorrows: their baby boys were buried at Nunhead too.

William's funeral was a great contrast to the farewell for the king a month later. When his death was announced on May 6, 1910, Head Mistress Newbould at Lant Street School wrote in bold letters in the centre of the page of her logbook "Death of His Majesty King Edward VII," and drew a box around the solemn entry. The children, she noted, had been "quietly dismissed."

As usual, details abound about royal deaths while ordinary deaths disappear into the past. No one knows what Harry's father had been up to in his final days, but King Edward had been travelling in Europe, as was his habit, and had fallen ill with bronchitis. He was recuperating at Buckingham Palace when he suffered several heart attacks in a row. When the public heard he had died, crowds gathered outside the palace to pay their respects to the king. In the distance a hymn could be heard, and soon a Salvation Army procession appeared, white mourning ribbons fluttering from their flag. The crowd was astonished to see the gates open for the band, and its members march straight into the palace grounds. There they formed a circle around the flag, bared their heads in prayer and then played "with a softness and delicacy of tone that was greatly appreciated by the listening crowds outside." It turned out that the concert had been General Booth's idea, because the king had admired the Army's work for the poor. Queen Alexandra was moved by the request and readily agreed to their visit. With her daughter Princess Victoria, she stood behind the closed drapes, listening to the instruments played so beautifully by mechanics, cab drivers and Covent Garden porters – men like Harry Deverill, who'd given their shoes an extra buff in reverence for the dead king.

A trail of royalty later followed King Edward's coffin through the streets and included contingents from nearly every corner of the globe. In addition to the European houses, the Russians were there, represented by the tsar's mother (who was also Queen Alexandra's sister) and several grand dukes. There were factions from Japan, Egypt, China and Persia. The newspapers were full of kind words for Kaiser Wilhelm and even speculated that he was the next great peacemaker, now that his gregarious uncle was gone; he'd been seen grasping hands over Edward's coffin with the new king, George, and this subtle gesture was taken as a good omen. Edward's lavish funeral showed off the fact that there were currently more European monarchs than ever before. Later this solemn parade of kings would be remembered as the largest royal gathering ever, and also the last of its kind.

A week after the funeral, Harry Deverill turned forty. He and Mary Anne, thirty-seven, had been in Whitechapel for several years now, and she was pregnant again – a surprise baby most likely, given the gap between this child and Ernie, born more than six years earlier. Did Mary Anne worry as the due date approached? Great strides had been made in battling infant mortality, so the baby's chances of surviving were much better than her siblings' and cousins' had been. But it was difficult to let go of the memory of your babies dying in your arms. No one knows if Mary Anne exchanged such fears with Harry, or confided them to Lilian Carter over tea at the vicarage, but passed down through the years is the story that Lilian was more than the vicar's wife; she was Mary Anne's friend, a woman of influence but also of genuine kindness. Though Lilian had no children of her own, she was an active member of the Mother's Union and often lectured under that organization's banner. The fervently Christian union sought to unite mothers of all classes; it saw motherhood as a profession that required training and that gave women enormous power over the home and their child's character and, by extension, over the country and the country's character. Did Mary Anne, a mother several times over, need advice from Lilian, mother of none? Probably not. But a thread connects these two women who were from such different worlds. When the baby arrived in July 1910, Harry and Mary Anne named her Doris and chose Lilian for her middle name.

Later, Doris would hold fast to the story of her naming as one of the few things she could be certain of regarding her earliest years. Like the tale of her great-grandparents, Benjamin and Margaret Jones, walking to London from Wales with their cows, it helped to define her history, but something more too: it marked her own personal beginning.

Harry's brother Jack and Jack's daughter, May, around 1912,
likely taken at College Buildings in Whitechapel. Jack lived next door
to Harry and Mary Anne, but May was only ever a visitor there.

CHAPTER 7

The Blaze of Day

In a photograph taken in Whitechapel in the summer of 1910, Mary Anne looks into the lens, her hand on her hip in the classic pose of maternal authority. The scalloped leaves of geranium dot the open window behind her, and in the foreground Ethel, fine hair twisted into soft ringlets, cradles her new baby sister, Doris, who is asleep in Ethel's arms, swathed in white. Seven-year-old Ernie wears a sailor suit and hat and stands alongside, a tentative thumb on the arm of the chair. With soft smiles, brother and sister stare down at the baby as if not quite sure she's real.

Was this picture taken to mark the occasion of her baptism? The family wears Sunday best: Ernie looks dapper and Ethel wears a bow in her hair; Mary Anne has a brooch pinned to the high neck of her blouse. Maybe it's Harry behind the camera, a borrowed Brownie or even his own. Such cameras were cheap and easy to use; "You push the button, we do the rest," the early ads claimed, and soon these simple yet magical contraptions were everywhere, well within the reach of even the working classes. In the image, Mary Anne's honest gaze hides nothing, and her slight smile is careworn but intimate too, the kind of glance shared with a husband. It's easy to imagine the scene as they left for St. Jude's that Sunday morning in August, amid the throngs heading toward the market on Petticoat Lane. Doris tucked into Harry's arms while Ethel walked proudly alongside, sneaking glances at her tiny sister. Ernie holding Mary Anne's hand, pressing his sailor's cap to his head with the other, and Joe, the eldest and too big for a similar costume, bringing up the rear in his young man's suit.

By the time Doris was born, the family had been in Whitechapel several years, long enough to be regulars in Ernest and Lilian Carter's little congregation at St. Jude's, and to befriend a spinster neighbour named Martha Bedford. Born in 1865 to a shoemaker and his wife who already had a large family, Martha was a twin and had grown up a little farther east on Baker Street. When she was twelve, her mother died, and Martha stowed the memorial card among her things, an elaborate black and cream announcement with a relief of drooping wisteria and a woman kneeling before a tombstone. The household shrank and expanded as her siblings married and left, and her father found a second wife and had yet more children. Martha's twin sister married in 1887 and moved to Essex, and it was around this time that Martha also left the family home to live on her own in Whitechapel. She found a job as a cork sorter and took a flat in the brand new College Buildings on Wentworth Street, at the top of George Yard, a narrow alley connecting Wentworth with Whitechapel High Street. But her independence was marred by trepidation when Martha Tabram's body was found gutted on a landing in George Yard Buildings, directly behind College Buildings. Within a few months, five other women had been similarly slain, including Catherine Eddowes, whose daughter Annie was friends with the Vansons. Catherine's was the first of the victims' funerals for which huge crowds turned out, so perhaps Martha Bedford, drawn by morbid curiosity or swept up in a public grief, stood at the roadside as the carriage carrying Annie and her aunts followed the hearse to the cemetery. Did Martha shiver with fear as the coffin passed? Though the murdered women were reportedly prostitutes at least part-time, that fact was cold comfort to residents like Martha. The whole city was in a frenzy, but Martha lived at the core of it. Venturing into the street on her way to and from work, she would not have been alone in casting cautious glances over hunched shoulders and taking extra care to throw the bolt at night.

Women took to walking in pairs or threesomes, but the murders had not frightened people off the streets entirely. George Sims, writing under the pen name Dagonet for the *Sunday Referee,* recorded his visit to Whitechapel Road one October night in 1888, shortly after Catherine Eddowes had died, and found the district "remarkably lively." He decided people "relieved their overstrained nerves by laughing." When a cry was heard from an alley, everyone rushed toward the noise, and a young boy, grinning, shouted, "'Ere ye har, guv'nor! This way to the murder! Triple murder up this court!'" The sound was attributed to a quarrel between two ladies, and the gathered crowd laughed, but Sims detected a thin line between the humorous and the horrible. The name "Jack the Ripper" was on every tongue. "The costermonger hawking his goods dragged him in; the quack doctor assured the crowd that his modern medicine would cure even Jack of his evil propensities; and at the penny shows, outside which were the most ghastly pictures of 'the seven victims,' all gashes and crimson drops were exhibited."

The newspapers reported every detail they could find of the investigation, and also some that were fabrications. After one of the murders, witnesses came forward with myriad descriptions of the man supposedly last seen with the victim, and so Sims and his ilk could say Jack was "a tall, sandy-whiskered man of rough appearance; a short man of German appearance; a gentleman with a black bag and moustache; a foreign-looking man with a brown paper parcel under his arm; a swell, with spats on his boots, a gold watch chain, and an astrachan collar to his overcoat; a blotchy-faced fellow who looked like a labourer; and an elderly, respectable-looking man with the appearance of a clergyman." Sims himself was put forward as a suspect after a coffee vendor saw his picture in a bookshop window and recalled a conversation he'd had in the middle of the night with a man "of strange and wild appearance" who resembled this one. The fellow had bought a cup of coffee, and as he stood drinking it, the two had engaged in a bit of small talk about the recent murders.

"I dare say we shall soon hear of another," the coffee-stall man said.

"Very likely," his customer had replied. "Perhaps you may hear of two tomorrow morning."

When he reached to pay for his drink, the sleeve of his coat rode up, and the vendor saw blood stains on the cuff of his shirt. In the morning, news of a double murder committed in the dark hours convinced the coffee seller he'd conversed with Jack the Ripper himself. When he then saw Sims's photo, he took it to Scotland Yard and to the press, claiming the man with the blood-stained shirt had looked just like him. There was no evidence to support Sims being Jack, and the coffee seller later clarified he'd only meant they *looked* alike, but Sims himself had a fascination for the story, and for murder in general, and repeated it often over the years. As one fellow journalist put it, "his curiosity was greater than his horror."

Then again, when it came to Jack the Ripper there was curiosity from all corners, not to mention speculation and paranoia. A plainclothes policeman was walking on Commercial Road when someone accused him of being the murderer. An angry, burgeoning mob attacked him, and he was narrowly rescued. A laundress sent a pair of bloodstained cuffs to police, attaching a note: "These cuffs come in the washin from Mr – . There is a stain on them which looks like blood. He is a queer-looking man, my dorter says, as she as seen him when calling for the bill, an is wife is a inverlid. If he is not the Whitechapel murderer, please return, as I do not want to be mix up in the affair."

Others strove to cash in on the notoriety. At a pub called Dirty Dick's a drunk was arrested for boasting he was Jack the Ripper, and in Hanbury Street, where Annie Chapman was murdered and her intestines straggled across the yard, people with windows over the site did a fine trade charging the public for a look even long after the mess had been cleaned up. Maybe those in George Yard did the same. It no doubt chilled Martha Bedford to read in the papers that at least two suspects frequented the Princess Alice pub at the corner of Wentworth and Commercial Streets, just north of St. Jude's and Toynbee Hall. Nor could it have been comforting to see that the police inquiry thought the murder weapon might have been a cork cutter. Martha's job as a cork sorter gave her firsthand knowledge of the tool mentioned. A cork cutter was a sharp knife with a broad blade and sturdy handle, but the men who wielded the instruments were "on the steady side," according to Charles Booth's inquiry, and because there were few health issues related to the trade, many of the workers were comparatively old – certainly not the profile of the usual Jacks described in the dailies. And yet it must have seemed that the murders permeated nearly every part of Martha's world.

When Harry and Mary Anne arrived in Wentworth Street nearly twenty years later, Whitechapel was still synonymous with Jack the Ripper, and the killings remained unsolved and present in the public consciousness. Martha Bedford's situation, too, was unchanged: she was not married and had the same flat and the same job. She accompanied the Deverills that August Sunday when they headed to St. Jude's for Doris's baptism, and her name appears as a sponsor on the baptismal certificate, an ornate document with gold-leafed edges, decorated with biblical illustrations and the message that "By one Spirit are we all Baptized into one Body."

Doris's baptism must have been a welcome event for Reverend Carter as well; the church books show he performed just a couple of baptisms in the span of each month, and weddings more rarely. At St. Jude's, the members of the choir often outnumbered the parishioners, and even under Samuel Barnett, so charismatic compared to plodding Ernest, the "empty brown benches" had been a constant, disheartening reality. "Why do the people not come!" Barnett exclaimed in his diary after he'd worked so hard to improve the church, both physically and spiritually. Originally it was "a cheap structure, built by cheap thought and in cheap material." But Barnett had the galleries that blocked the windows removed, and outside, on the wall of the church tower facing busy Commercial Street, a huge mosaic intended to offer what Barnett called "the influence of beauty." There was a tiled Doulton fountain beneath the mosaic, inscribed with the reminder that "With God is the Fountain of Life," but according to Barnett's wife, Henrietta, some locals used it for more practical purposes. The thirsty drank from it, mischievous children splashed each other, and "sometimes the tramps would wash their clothes and utensils as well as their bodies." Early one morning, Samuel Barnett watched from his window as a woman undressed her baby and tenderly bathed the child in the fountain.

Though low numbers of parishioners were discouraging for ministers, from the Deverills' perspective St. Jude's likely seemed an intimate place, where Harry and Mary Anne could chat with neighbours and fellow parishioners after Sunday service. George Biss, whose large family had several rooms in College Buildings, had recently taken on the role of verger at St. Jude's, assisting with services and maintaining the building. Others from College Buildings show up in the church's marriage and baptism ledgers. Some of the residents hailed from Poland or Germany or Russia according to census records, but most were English-born and of familiar circumstances. They were cork sorters, like Martha, and charwomen; they were tea chest nailers, as well as tea packers, cigarette makers, machine minders, barbers, tie makers, waistcoat makers, bakers, button-hole hands, shape makers or hawkers. One small unit contained a widowed cap maker who'd drawn her children into the profession: her daughter was a cap machinist, her son a cap cutter and her youngest boy a cap traveller, selling the finished product. These College Buildings residents were quite a contrast to the tenants of the surrounding buildings, who were people affiliated with Toynbee Hall: curators, architects, medical practitioners, science students, analytical chemists and engineering draughtsmen.

Due north, the Rothschild Buildings, two well-kept, massive blocks of flats that dominated Flower and Dean Street and Thrawl Street, were almost entirely Jewish. The Rothschild and College Buildings, and other model dwellings with fastidious caretakers and tenant rulebooks, had altered the flavour of the area, but the poorest of the poor still lived in seedy homes and decrepit lodging houses, and some made no attempt to hide a less than respectable way of life. Occasionally children of the neighbourhood were drawn in, and given a pittance to stand guard while a prostitute and client made their exchange. Even kids who heeded their parents and avoided disreputable people knew about the haggard women everyone called "four-penny bits," and the drunks sleeping off a night's binge in the alleys. And it wasn't always easy to judge. Sometimes the prostitute from the lodging house was the same woman who did washing for the woman in the model dwelling next door – both jobs had put money in Catherine Eddowes's skirt pockets.

Whitechapel was a neighbourhood in flux. Though there were still plenty of rough edges, there were also Toynbee Hall's Sunday concerts and Shakespeare plays to which so many people came that some had to be turned away. Toynbee also offered classes in Spanish, Greek and Italian literature, as well as clay modelling, musical analysis and "life saving." For some, the experience was just that. A book binder named Joseph Dent claimed "my whole being was transformed" when he began to take courses at Toynbee Hall. When Harry and Mary Anne came to Whitechapel, Dent had moved from book binding into publishing. Appropriately, he called the house Everyman's Library, and produced small pocketbooks of great works that could be had for a shilling.

There was something for all interests at Toynbee. One could learn about astronomy, hygiene and needlework, dressmaking, bandaging and brass bands. Musicians like Harry arrived with their tubas to demonstrate playing the instrument – raise the mouthpiece to your lips rather than bowing your head toward it; fill up your diaphragm, not just your chest, and keep it so taut you could withstand a punch to the stomach; and whatever you do, don't puff out your cheeks like a blowfish.

Pleasant as it is to place Harry in such a role, it's unlikely he had much to do with Toynbee's ambitious education programs. By the early 1900s, holes were starting to show in what architect and disillusioned Toynbee resident Charles Ashbee termed "top-hatty philanthropy." With hindsight, it's easy to see the flaws in Barnett's vision of "developing the high in the low" and "bringing out the manlike qualities in those who live as animals." The classes and workshops were popular, but not with the people for whom they were intended. A 1905 report shows that only 4 percent of members in Toynbee's wide-ranging clubs actually lived in Whitechapel. Most who benefitted from the rich array at Toynbee were of the middle class and came from farther afield. The wall that wrapped around Toynbee Hall was meant to give the settlement an oasis-like feeling upon stepping in – but people living in the area saw it as a barrier and stayed on the outside, failing to identify with such refined splendour. Yet sometimes the children of Commercial Street School performed their plays at Toynbee Hall – *Sleeping Beauty* or *Puss in Boots* – and parents herded in to see the show. Harry and Mary Anne would have been proud guests, with Martha Bedford there too, the neighbour who had become like family. Perhaps Mary Anne and Martha took turns holding Doris, and Doris, giggling, squirmed to be free to wriggle around the floor of Toynbee Hall, crawling between the legs of the grown-ups who watched the play so steadfastly. She was little yet, so the carefully rehearsed lines delivered by the students would have made no sense to her, but in this she was not alone – many of the parents were new immigrants, who relied on their children when communication in English was necessary.

Charles Booth's study includes an essay called "A Life in Buildings" that is thought to describe, in its early days, the very place Harry and Mary Anne lived. The piece was anonymously authored by "A Lady Resident," who lived in a pretty, five-storey, red-brick building, in two tiny rooms, each nine feet square. The front room opened on to a common balcony, and the back room to a smaller private balcony. One of the tenants kept pigeons in his, fluttering and cooing as pigeons do, but most decorated the space with flower boxes that gave the building a cheerful, well-cared-for look. The rooms were clean and painted in bright colours. Unlike other buildings the Lady Resident had lived in, this one had been designed to let in as much air and sunlight as possible, "and I think the great difference I noticed in the cheerfulness and temper of the children must have been largely due to this cause." The walls were thin, so there was no mistaking the wee hour when dressmaker Mrs. A stopped work at her sewing machine, or the consequently late hour she rose in the morning, calling to her husband to feed the baby before he left for work. At some point through the day the Lady Resident could also hear Mrs. B telling Mrs. C how late Mrs. A had risen – omitting the reason – and Mrs. C in turn embellishing the jab. One woman complained about the curate visiting when no one had invited him, and another about the "shocking temper" of Mrs. C's child. But the Lady Resident also writes of neighbours presenting gifts of food to each other, and taking turns to sit with poor Mrs. D, who was "wandering in her head"; of the schedule tenants followed, sharing the tasks of cleaning and whitening the stairs, and using the wash house and the roof to dry their clothes on fixed days. There were sometimes squabbles, but more often than not the rows were outside, among "a distinctly lower walk of life," and their ferocity drew the tenants to their balconies, "where we can look down exactly as from boxes in a theatre on to a stage." They could look down from the back of the building too, into the asphalt courtyard where their children played, chalking wickets against the walls for a makeshift game of cricket. The building grew quieter when the children left for school, and filled again with the sounds of their play when they arrived home for tea. The smells of Mrs. A's cooking drifted through Mrs. B's rooms, and vice versa. Life "in buildings" meant you could never quite escape each other, so in that sense there was something to be lost if you'd given up even the shabbiest home. But the advantages far outweighed the drawbacks, our Lady Resident decided: "Cheapness, a higher standard of cleanliness, healthy sanitary arrangements, neighbourly intercourse... and, perhaps above all, the impossibility of being overlooked altogether."

Despite the many improvements model dwellings like College Buildings offered, the amenities were not thoroughly modern. Octavia Hill condemned the idea of running plumbing to every flat, declaring, "If you have water on every floor that is quite sufficient for working people," and so College Buildings offered just a tap per floor, and shared lavatories. Still, this was a step up for Harry and Mary Anne, who'd come from antiquated living conditions in Red Cross Street. And Harry was caretaker here, which offered some perks. As the reverend at Christ Church had said at the Royal Commission on Alien Immigration, "In the great buildings... there is always a most competent man as caretaker, and he is constantly on the watch to see that the people are cleanly in their habits, and any defect is at once put right." The Lady Resident agreed. It was down to the caretaker to set the tone for the building in general – whether it was rowdy or genteel, spotless or filthy, or anywhere between, was in his power to determine. At College Buildings, Harry was responsible for ensuring that applicants for tenancy fit the criteria, and he'd have handed over a list of rules when they moved in. It was his job to ensure the rules were followed, and time and again he'd be called on to sort out arguments over whose turn it was on the roof, or who had failed to whiten the steps, or who (other than he with his music) was making too much noise in the late hours. And he was probably liked and loathed on a rotating basis, depending on where he sided.

At night, when the day's work was finished, the lamplighter rode along Wentworth on his bicycle, stopping at each lamppost to set the street aglow. And before Doris had been tucked into her cradle at

Harry and Mary Anne's bedside, Harry lifted each of his instruments in turn and played them. The sound of his music reverberated around the rooms of College Buildings, then out through the window, blending with the noise of the street.

Baby Doris had no idea, of course, but a few months after her baptism, in the autumn of 1910, the suffragettes fighting on her behalf fell into battle with the government. A conciliation bill, proposing the right to vote for some prosperous, property-owning women, had been put before the House of Commons and made it to a second reading. The suffragettes had set aside their militant activities in hopes of a good outcome, but in November, Prime Minister H.H. Asquith shelved the bill and announced there would be no more time devoted to discussing the issue in the current session. Right away the suffragettes protested against this policy of "shuffling and delay." On November 18, three hundred of them stormed the House of Commons on what came to be known as Black Friday – but there were six thousand policemen to meet them. The women put up fierce resistance. According to *The Times*, several of the officers had their helmets knocked off and received kicks to the ankles. "As a rule [the police] kept their tempers very well, but their method of shoving back the raiders lacked nothing in vigour. They were at any rate kept warm by the exercise, and so were the ladies who flung themselves against the defending lines."

Public response was less condescending. When news of the event filtered out to the masses, people were shocked that women had been assaulted by the police. The increasingly militant activities of the more extreme suffragettes were still unpopular, but by and large people believed the government and its bullying protectors had sunk to a new low. Newspapers showed women struggling with police, or lying curled on the ground, gloved hands clutching their faces. For the government, it was political disaster. The suffragettes stepped up their campaign of violence, throwing rocks and smashing windows and setting fire to postboxes, but there were troubles within the group too. The daughters of Emmeline Pankhurst embodied two factions. Christabel focused on getting the vote for more privileged women, while her sister Sylvia advocated for the working class and aimed to include them in tackling a wider array of social issues that affected them. A rift grew between the sisters. The more militant Christabel, dubbed Queen of the Mob by fellow activist James Joseph Mallon, believed that any effort to include the less fortunate would only dilute the suffragist cause. According to Sylvia, Christabel felt that a working-women's movement would be pointless, for they made up "the weakest portion of the sex: how could it be otherwise? Their lives were too hard, their education too meagre to equip them for the struggle."

It's true that daily life wasn't easy for Mary Anne and her kind. Shortly before Black Friday, her sister Jennie Vanson, who was still in Lambeth, balancing the needs of her four girls, learned that her husband, Richard, had tuberculosis, the same disease that had killed his mother and father and put him in Hanwell School. Sometimes called the white plague, because of the pallor of the sufferer, or, more commonly, consumption, owing to the person wasting away, tuberculosis often struck working-class men like Richard, who toiled for long hours in unventilated workshops and had little opportunity for fresh air and exercise. Despite being romanticized by poets and novelists as a glamorous illness, the afflicted making a refined exit from life, with time to order their affairs, the reality was much harsher. Consumption was indeed slow to kill, but its symptoms were far from gentle. Richard had seen his parents suffer through fevers and night sweats, coughing up blood and taking delicate breaths that ripped painfully through the chest, and now it was his turn to suffer those same symptoms. Newspapers advertised a variety of bogus cures, among them "Specialist" Derk P. Yonkerman's Tuberculozyne. This latest "product of science" promised to cure where other treatments failed, but even if Richard could have afforded the liquid, it wouldn't have done him much good. The British Medical Association analyzed Yonkerman's concoction and pronounced it "little more than coloured, flavoured water." In October 1910, Richard entered Lambeth Infirmary, next to the workhouse, and remained there until he died the following February. He was forty-five years old.

Jennie's handwriting on the census a couple of months after his death appears cramped and childish. She listed herself as head of the household and scrawled the names of her daughters beneath. Only two of them were left at home – eighteen-year-old Florence, who worked as a tailoress, and four-year-old Ada, the girl born at the Lying-In Hospital when Richard and Jennie had moved to Lambeth. Jennie's occupation, undertaken when Richard got sick, was office cleaner, so she either worked nights, with Florence taking care of her sister, or days, with Florence doing piecework at home. Nineteen-eleven marked the first year women were required to specify the number of children they'd had from their present marriage, also noting how many were alive and how many had died. Jennie dutifully filled in the numbers – six, four and two – but an official drew a line through the details because Jennie's was not considered a "present marriage" anymore, and such information was not requested from widows.

Over at Newington Workhouse, the information her sister Ellen provided on the census didn't give a complete picture either: she used the name Roff again, offered the marriage to Fred as her current one and said four out of four children from that "present marriage" were still living, rather than four out of five. There was no slot to record her Humphreys children, living or dead, and so they went unacknowledged, seemingly forgotten.

The doctors at Stone Asylum had deemed Ellen "improved," and her trial period at Newington had ended successfully, meaning Ellen was now a permanent workhouse resident. Yet she was one of the few inmates who had no occupation; others were charwomen and laundresses and picklers and artificial flower makers. Her mother Mary was also unemployed, but she was elderly now, and occasionally moved to the infirmary; on later documents she was listed as a factory hand, so she still worked at least some of the time. But there is no sign that either woman had contact with the family. Ellen's John continued to live in Causeway Place, head of a household that contained his shoe-black brother and his "bastard daughter" Flo, as the census reported. Fred, meanwhile, remained in Lambeth, still a moulder at Doulton's. Except for the eldest, his children were all with him. Son Freddie was twenty-two now, working as a railway porter. The middle girl – the first of Ellen's Flos – was twenty, and a "housekeeper at home," which would have been Ellen's role had things not gone awry all those years ago. Emily, a baby when her mother left, was sixteen. A thorough search of the census has not turned up Fred and Ellen's eldest daughter, Ellen Elizabeth, twenty-five years old in 1911, and single, since she married a few years later. Might she have joined the massive boycott of the census that year?

Just days before the count was taken, the feminist newspaper *Votes for Women* wrote that suffragettes had long been looking forward to this stellar opportunity to send a message to the government. Plans were complete for widespread protest, and the paper's tone was gleeful. "An army of women very much larger than was originally supposed, running into many thousands, will resist or evade the census." The boycott encouraged women to stay away from home that night and the following morning – or, if they stayed at home, to avoid giving the information requested. One woman claimed to be "the daughter of a sister of an earl," but would say nothing else about herself, forcing the registrar to guess at her age and add a note to her page that said "information refused for political reasons." Her neighbours – two sisters who claimed their surname was MacIrone – likewise kept mum. Occasionally men took part in the subterfuge. One man offered his own details for the census but wrote a blunt message on the form as well: "Decline to give information about the women of my household in protest of the fact that Englishwomen are not granted the full rights of citizenship." Women who avoided the count altogether slept in broom closets and bicycle sheds. One particularly determined activist, Emily Davison, went so far as to hide herself in the crypt at Westminster Hall so she could claim to be the sole occupier of the House of Commons. The stunt worked, but not without cost: written on the top of the census schedule is the notation "apply Common Row police station for more details." Most made their point in a somewhat less dramatic fashion, meeting at prearranged venues and listening to concerts and speeches to pass the hours away from home.

In London, hundreds gathered in Trafalgar Square, where police stood watch alongside the statues. It had rained all evening, but the showers stopped by eleven or so, and the pavement gleamed in the pale moonlight that pushed through the clouds. Shortly after midnight, police began to urge the crowd along, but the women didn't mind. The square had only been intended as a meeting place for a protest that would go on through the wee hours. In a herd, they made their way along The Strand to the Aldwych Skating Rink, where, said Emmeline Pankhurst, "we amused ourselves until morning." They were entertained by some of the suffragette movement's brightest stars, not just inspiring speakers but also dancers, singers and actresses reminding them to "open your eyes to the blaze of day."

And the day was dawning. While the women roller-skated and laughed their way through potato races, the sky brightened through the windows, and Covent Garden began to fill up with carts and flowers. The city was waking up after what *Votes for Women* called "a delightful and never-to-be-forgotten experience." The night had been memorable elsewhere too. "If one could have taken the roofs off houses on census night, the scenes would have been extraordinary ones!" the paper reported. "Houses which looked most innocent to the passersby were filled with recumbent forms in every available corner, wrapped in rugs, sleeping in arm chairs, on landings and stairs; while others, more hardy, were spending the night in delightful fashion – talking with friends, playing cards, listening to music, taking meals at most weird hours, doing things they would never otherwise have dreamt of doing in the night, sleeping on lonely moors, travelling through the quiet country in a caravan, when all the rest of the world were asleep! There is no doubt of it – census night was a huge success."

A sense of optimism imbued the movement that spring. After the disaster of Black Friday, and looking ahead to the coronation of King George in June, the government had introduced a second conciliation bill with an eye to placating the restless suffragettes. So far, the plan was working.

The census that year shows Mary Anne's dogged aunt, Maggie Jones Donnelly, at the Goodwin Buildings, with her daughter Clara and granddaughter May. By this time Maggie was fifty-four, and had been working at the Borough Polytechnic Institute for almost ten years. Benjamin's dairy was long gone, but Clara supplemented the household income by working as a book folder. The monotonous job, folding and ordering sheet after sheet at home on the dining table, brought in very little money, but anything helped. Both Clara and Maggie called themselves "Jones" on the census, as if the name of hapless father and husband William Donnelly was no longer worthy of them. Maggie had been without him for years now, presumably happier that way, and resolutely single. A photograph taken on the rooftop of the Borough Polytechnic shows her to be rather tired-looking, front and centre in a line of her co-workers clad in identical patternless smocks. Their hands are folded, and though the picture doesn't show the detail, their skin must be rough and chapped and reddened, the calling card of a char. Behind the women, in a less tidy string, stand their male counterparts – the caretakers and refectory workers, neat in their jackets and ties but slope-shouldered and thin-chested. Beyond the rooftop, another building is faintly visible through what looks like the smog of London, but may just be the grey wash of time. Between 1908 and 1911 the Institute reduced their work staff from eight full-time cleaners to three, but Maggie was among the lucky ones who held on to her position, a relief with May being an additional responsibility, and no husband sharing the load.

Ten-year-old May tied the families together: she was related to both Harry and Mary Anne, and hints of both families could be seen in her unusual, heart-shaped face. So distinct is May that she can easily be spotted in school photographs – a girl with large, heavy-lidded eyes, and a full, downturned mouth that somehow doesn't diminish her joyful expression. Yet these were some of May's hardest years. By her own account, she and Ethel were more like sisters than cousins, so she'd been lonely when Harry and Mary Anne left the Borough, taking Ethel, Joe and Ernie with them. And then her mother, Meg, just thirty, had died of heart failure, and her father, Jack, had moved north alone, crossing the river to Whitechapel, his application for tenancy at College Buildings readily accepted by his brother Harry. He'd left May in the Borough with Maggie and Clara, and while the decision was made for May's own good, it was the beginning of a kind of emotional distance between father and daughter. Family legend says they saw little of each other for many years, and a rare photograph of the two of them taken during this time suggests an estrangement. Bubbly May barely smiles and leans ever so slightly away from Jack, a small, wiry man so like his brother Harry, standing with a pipe in his mouth, arms hanging at his sides. But May was in capable hands with her grandmother. Maggie was caring and kind, and embraced all of the family's children as her own, earning her the nickname of Gran, whether she was grandmother, great-aunt or something else altogether. "Let's have a treat today, shall we?" she'd tell Clara and May. "We'll butter the bread on both sides."

Harry likely knew how Ethel and May missed one another now that the Thames drew a line between them, and saw how much worse it must be for May, an only child now living with neither parent. Perhaps his own failing health spurred the idea of a holiday with his family, and when the opportunity came, it was decided that May must come along. May's letters, written a lifetime later, tell of the extended Deverill family going to Canvey Island, crossing from the mainland at low tide on flat stepping stones.

Canvey in the first decade of the century was as different from Whitechapel and the Borough as the moon. Some five miles long and two miles wide, it became an island at high tide and a peninsula when the water ebbed. Situated in the middle of the Thames Estuary, it lay across from the village of Benfleet, which was easily reached via the London, Tilbury and Southend Railway for the sum of less than two shillings. Yet most Londoners were unaware of the island's existence. The *Royal Magazine* in 1899 called it "the most curious place in England," while the *Portsmouth Evening News* in 1901 reported that in spite of recent developments of a hotel and bungalows on the island's south side, it remained "the most primitive corner that can be discovered within fifty miles of London." How Harry and Mary Anne came to bring their little group there is guesswork, but it's telling that in 1906 the *Penny Illustrated Paper and Illustrated Times* ran a series of photos of Canvey, depicting it as the simple life, and showing scenes from the Salvation Army Girls Holiday Camp. The 1901 census counts just 301 permanent residents occupying sixty households, as well as a number of uninhabited bungalows that were most likely rented out as holiday homes. And though the numbers climbed over the next decade, by the time of the 1911 census there were still fewer people living on the whole of Canvey Island than occupied the Mowbray Buildings, back in Red Cross Street.

Harry's beloved Salvation Army arranged sojourns to the seaside or the country for London's less fortunate, and Sunday and Ragged Schools, established to provide a rudimentary but free education to poor children, had also been sponsoring day trips to the countryside for their students since the middle of the century. But Samuel and Henrietta Barnett were among the first to begin sending "pale-faced boys and girls" from St. Jude's off for two weeks at a time, an effort that grew into the Children's Country Holidays Fund. The "weak, ailing children, too poor to get a holiday otherwise," were boarded at country homes and seaside cottages for two-week stays, paid for by the fund. Parents, while not invited to accompany their children, were encouraged to contribute to the cost, and according to *The Sunday at Home, A Family Magazine for Sabbath Reading,* most did, especially when it was pointed out that they'd be saving money with their children away. The Children's Fresh Air Mission had a similar mandate and captured the recipients in a photograph, clustered round a signboard that read "Off to the Country." The Islington Board of Guardians also took pictures of their efforts when they sent hundreds of London schoolchildren to Canvey Island for three weeks each summer, the boys sleeping in small bell tents, and the girls in larger marquees. One photo shows a group of girls in white pinafores and boys in dark shorts on their knees cleaning dishes, a tent in the background. In another, boys stripped to the waist bend over buckets and sluice themselves with water. The Salvation Army Girls Holiday Camp on Canvey Island is represented in a montage that includes an image of a shed used as sleeping quarters, and another of the girls at dinner, sitting in long rows on benches and smiling over their shoulders at the camera.

May and Ethel are not among any of these groups, despite a similar social status and Harry's ties to the Salvation Army. May's letters suggest a different kind of vacation: one with less structure and a more familial setting. The thrill of the trip comes across in her penned words. "We had the train to a place called Benfleet, then we had to cross over to the island. If the tide was out, we used to walk across on stepping stones, but if the tide was in, then we had to cross by rowing boat, and there would be a horse-drawn carriage waiting for us. Oh yes, we did enjoy that. There was no electricity on the island, so of course no lights, there were very few houses, one or two farms, a Church and very little else … When we went to the beach we had it mostly to ourselves." Such a memory provokes a different picture of the Deverill children: Joe, Ethel, Ernie and May, shoes and socks discarded, the sun and wind tanning their skin. Joe with his eyes to the sea, scanning for ships on the blue horizon; Ethel and May intent on building a sandcastle, their chatter and laughter constant; Ernie dunking pebbles in water to see how the colour changed, then carefully loading them into a pail, a collection to be cherished. Canvey Island was Ernie's first taste of travel – of being somewhere other than home – and the beginning of his lifelong wanderlust.

The children would stay on the beach all day, until a flag flying from the distant house signalled the time to return – "Uncle Harry used to hoist it there" – and the group made their way back, with the sun starting to slant in the sky. Their route took them past a farm where geese chased them, honking, wings spread wide. It was almost a game, deciding whether to creep past or run, but no matter the choice the geese came after them, and they fled with hearts pounding.

Harry and Mary Anne must have treasured this time away from the tangle of Whitechapel, given Harry's increasingly frequent breathlessness and fatigue. He'd have been rejuvenated by the warmth of midday, seated outside in a garden chair in the shade of their rented house with his eyes closed, the sea breeze lifting his hair. Perhaps Mary Anne sat beside him, her fingers loosely laced with his, one ear turned to the open window of the room where Doris napped.

The time at Canvey sped by for everyone, as holidays do, and before long the Deverills were back in London, the shrill cries of seabirds and the tang of saltwater replaced by the call of street vendors and the odour of fish shops and smoke. May returned to the Borough and Aunt Maggie, but her letters tell us she stayed with Harry and Mary Anne often, and that, since the death of her mother, they were like her own family. With Ethel and Joe and Ernie she was sometimes among the groups

of children who walked to Victoria Park together for a bit of an outing – four miles out and back – toting packed lunches and bottles of
water. There were very few closer choices: certainly Itchy Park was a
poor alternative and a world away from Canvey.

It took forty minutes to walk to Victoria Park, trudging north along
Brick Lane past the school and Flower and Dean Street with its lodging
houses and hawkers' barrows. Almost anything could be had along the
way, if one were buying: one man wheeled a barrow laden with plaice
and haddock, another sold hot bagels, another toffee-apples. Each seller had his own cry: "Bananas!" "Coconut!" and sometimes he'd slip
the children something to munch on as they passed. There were small
shops, too – one was run by an old Jewish woman who sold bacon, despite kosher dietary laws, and many of the Jewish children passing by on
their way to Victoria Park held their breath so as not to breathe in the
smell of the pork.

After the bustle of the neighbourhood, Victoria Park seemed like
some kind of small heaven when the children arrived. Joe, with his
fondness for plants and flowers and the way ivy turned a wall lush green,
would have admired the gardens and wished that the window boxes at
College Buildings could hold such abundance. He and Ethel and May
kept a close eye on Ernie, for there was plenty here to lure a curious
explorer. Baedeker's guide described the park as "Prettily laid out with
walks, beds of flowers, and two sheets of water, on which swans may be
seen disporting themselves." The sprawling grounds also held "bathing
lakes," pleasure boats and cricket pitches, as well as swathes of cool grass
in which to bury hot feet. At summer weekends and bank holidays the
park attracted thousands, who came not just to enjoy an expanse of nature, but to listen to bands playing, or reformists spouting opinions at
the Speakers' Corner. One writer noted: "On this lawn the listener, as
his fancy prompts him, may assist on Malthusianism, atheism, agnosti-
cism, secularism, Calvinism, socialism, anarchism, Salvationism, Dar-
winism, and even, in exceptional cases, Swedenborgianism and Mor-
monism." By 1911 suffragism was a common topic, too.

But for the children, play was paramount, and the rest drifted into
the picturesque background. Victoria Park was about the size of all of

Whitechapel, and school logbooks tell us teachers often took their students there by the busload during the summer session so they could play cricket and football outside their cramped playground. Ethel and Joe must have gone on those chaotic trips, and young Ernie too, three in a passel of noisy adventurers bound for greener pastures.

By this time the Deverill children were attending Commercial Street Board School, since the much smaller school on Brick Lane had been closed to new students when Ernie was old enough to go there with his siblings. Commercial was closer, too, just a block south of College Buildings, and farther from Itchy Park. In keeping with the neighbourhood's general population, most of Commercial's nine hundred students were Jewish, and so, to Reverend Ernest Carter's chagrin, both Christian and Jewish holidays were observed, causing what he called constant breaks in the schedule; every Friday, school ended early for Sabbath.

Commercial Street School had recently been rebuilt along narrow, cobbled George Yard, where Martha Tabram had been murdered, and the modern building was a welcome addition to an otherwise dreary small street. The new school had large airy classrooms with big windows and a modern heating and cooling system that did away with the dirt and smoke of fireplaces. As one student recounted, "There were no fireplaces, and they explained to us that…in the winter, 'You see these fluttering streamers? You get warm air blown in and it's very healthy for you,' the teacher went on about it: 'And in the summer you'll have cool air blown in.'" Negating the effect were the soot, fumes and a shower of ash from the mechanical "dust destructor" that had been erected nearby in the 1880s and remained a persistent problem for decades, dictated only by the whims of the wind. College Buildings was affected by the loathsome thing as well, as were Toynbee Hall and the vicarage at St. Jude's. Henrietta Barnett had renamed it "the dust distributor" in her day, and had claimed it did more harm than good. "The additional cost of clearing gutters, cleaning windows, and washing curtains was considerable in our large establishment, a minor evil compared with the permeating dust in the homes of the thousands who lived under the smoke-shadow of that giant chimney." But the chimney chugged on through the years. The smoke in the school was sometimes so bad,

according to the head master's jottings in the logbook, that students and
teachers alike fell ill.

Still, the large, bright rooms of the new school must have awed the
children, some of whom were so poor they came to school barefoot.
Students four to fourteen were separated into Boys', Girls' and Infants'
classes, with four- to seven-year-olds attending the latter, and marched
into separate assembly halls each morning, to piano accompaniment.
Sometimes toddlers came too, if their mothers had to work and there
was no one to care for them at home. There was an aquarium in the
girls' hall, and birds and flowers in the boys' hall, all of which pleased
the school inspector. Plants brightened the rooms, he noted in his annual report, and the children themselves took good care of them. The
infants' walls were covered with drawings the little ones had made, and
also some rather accomplished pictures by their teachers. In all, the inspector was impressed by the goings-on at Commercial Street School,
especially considering "the number of foreign children...is large, so
that special difficulties have to be overcome."

The inspector found "considerable originality" in the school's approach to teaching the older boys English and arithmetic. "That they
are being soundly taught is evidenced by the intelligence shown by the
boys in the first class, which could only be built on a good foundation
laid in the lower classes." Even the "backward children" were being well
cared for, in the inspector's opinion, and getting the special attention
they needed. Records show that attendance was usually good, especially among the boys, and sometimes prizes were doled out to encourage kids to come every day. For the "necessitous children" – those who
didn't get adequate food at home – meals or a cup of warm milk was the
best incentive.

More and more (and not without controversy), schools were taking
on responsibilities that had traditionally belonged to families. London
County Council school nurses visited regularly and checked the state
of the children's hair and clothing, and their general health and cleanliness. The nurses drew up a list of "verminous" children and gave it to the
head master, who then passed on a warning to the parents, along with
details of how to cleanse their child. But problems like lice and fleas

were notoriously difficult to get rid of, and scabies frequently recurred. Sometimes parents tried to avoid the checks by sending their children to another school, but sooner or later a nurse would pop up there, too, and it became obvious that escape was near impossible. One mother complained that previously it had been enough to send her daughter to school in a clean pinafore, and "now she must be sent clean right down to the skin, because she might be examined by the nurse at any time."

If, after fair warning, children returned to the school in an unclean condition, they would be taken away by the nurse to a nearby cleansing station, where they underwent a thorough professional scrubbing. According to the 1910 report of the Medical Officer of Health for the London County Council, "There the child's clothing will be removed and exposed for ten minutes to boiling temperature moist steam, then thoroughly dried and brushed. Meanwhile the child will be washed with soft soap and hot water and given a hot bath. The hair will also be treated with paraffin and if necessary portions cut...The cleansing of the child at a centre is ineffective whilst the home is untouched and so a mechanism is arranged whereby the unclean child in the school will be followed up in its home by the sanitary authorities and cleansing of the home achieved." It was through this process that many a squalid home was discovered, but the prescription – scouring, fines or even imprisonment – was often no solution. The report mentioned one widow who lived with her children in particularly harsh circumstances. "The little girl might be cleansed over and over again and never be clean; yet prosecution in such a case means imprisonment and the loss of what little means the parent has of earning a livelihood." On the positive side, the Jews of Whitechapel were once again singled out as exemplary. "There are not many troublesome parents in the neighbourhood, as foreign parents take or send their children for voluntary baths."

Were the Deverill children filthy, with lousy hair and bug-bitten skin? Were their shoes too small and their bellies empty? From what can be inferred more than a century on, the answer is no. Whether it was Mary Anne's good childrearing or the fear of being trotted out of school by the health nurse, Ernie was fastidious in his grooming. May wrote that he was "very particular" and "would never sit on any grass unless he put his handkerchief down to sit on." Ernie himself recounted his memories of lining up for inspection at school and having to show clean hands and polished shoes. He was nervous in those moments, heart thumping, for he was an introverted boy, eager to stay in the shadows, and something as obvious as dirty nails could pull him out.

How one went about achieving high standards of cleanliness while living in a two-room flat without dedicated plumbing can be partially explained by the existence of public baths like the one a block or two over on Goulston Street. Part of an effort to improve the living conditions of east London's poor, the Goulston Street baths had opened in the 1840s as one of the city's first public bathhouses. There were sixty-eight baths for men and twenty-one for women, which were further divided into first and second class; swimming baths were added later. By the turn of the century, baths were common throughout the city, and well used. It was not unusual, at peak times, for bathers to expect a wait of an hour or more for a private hot bath, the premium choice and the most expensive. The management of facilities varied, and sometimes the costliest bathing option gave no guarantee of cleanliness. Usually a half hour was allowed per bath, but on weekends, supply frequently could not keep up with demand, and bathers were limited to a quarter hour, with the hygiene of facilities suspect. Some bathhouses excluded children on weekends on the grounds that their time was more flexible; other places gave vouchers to bathers who were turned away due to overcrowding, or lowered their rates on weekdays, providing an incentive to those for whom every penny counted. If one wasn't choosy or had less to spend, one could opt for tepid or cold water, or simply take a plunge in the public swimming baths alongside shrieking and laughing children.

Ernie was not the type to be rowdy in a public bath. More likely he'd float off to his own corner and lose himself in a daydream. May described him as "a very quiet boy, and very nice," and photographs taken in these early days show a small, thin child with a shy smile, eyebrows often raised in private surprise. Unlike May, who was gregarious and friendly, Ernie was quirky but reserved. He sometimes muttered to himself, and had the funny habit of rubbing the ball of his nose with the palm of his hand. He was the type of child who gets teased but has the temerity to withstand it, or to escape it by letting his ears slip below the waterline so that the tormenters became a muted blur. Even a partial dunking was a thrill. He couldn't swim well – the best he could do was a bit of a dog paddle – but with his ears in the water, he'd hum a tune to himself for comfort: notes Harry was practising at home, or a ditty he'd learned at school. Ernie and Ethel were always singing, said May, and they had beautiful voices, which May attributed to their Welsh roots. Singing was part of the curriculum at Commercial Street School. The inspector who had commented on the tending of plants and the challenge of so many "foreign children" also noted in his report that "singing is excellent due [to] attention being given to breathing exercises and voice production." Ernie and Ethel must have been among those students who excelled.

If Joe went to the baths, he would have avoided the children's pool if possible. He was as poor a swimmer as Ernie, and, being older, perhaps he attended with Harry, to wash rather than frolic, taking his turn in a second-class private bath to scrub himself clean. In 1911 Joe was thirteen, old enough to quit school, as the leaving age was twelve. Mary Anne and Harry must have encouraged him to stay, since the census that year counts him a "scholar." Yet it was around this time that he posed with Harry in a photo that marks his departure from the rank of child. Joe is in a suit similar to Harry's, complete with waistcoat and pocket watch. Harry props his arm casually on Joe's shoulder, a stance that suggests camaraderie rather than paternalism, but while Harry appears happy and self-assured, Joe looks awkwardly proud, a little rigid in his stance, but pleased with himself just the same. He's almost a head shorter than his small father, and he won't grow much taller in the coming years. Both look directly at the camera and reveal the headiness of the moment as the shutter opened and closed, capturing the image of father and first-born son in perpetuity.

But *was* Joe the oldest son? The creased page of Harry and Mary Anne's census return presents a fact that did not live on among the stories passed down through the generations: a seventh child had been born and died, making three that Harry and Mary Anne buried over the course of their fifteen-year marriage. Whether boy or girl, whether first-born or something in between, no record of the child's existence has surfaced, save that small acknowledgement penned by Harry on the schedule. Once again, a new discovery fits a piece into the puzzle, but pushes open more empty spaces.

This photograph of Harry Deverill shows him in his caretaker's uniform, smoking a cigarette the Salvation Army would have frowned upon. The boy beside him is unknown, but the girl depicted with her doll is Doris at age two, around the time of her first great sadness.

Ready for the Call

In 1911, England sweltered in record heat that reached from one end of the country to the other and beyond. Outside the cities, birds stopped singing, pastures turned brown and wells dried up. Fires erupted spontaneously along railroad tracks, and the asphalt melted on the roads. In the cities and towns, people sought the shady side of the street, but there was little relief, as the brick and stone soaked up and held the heat. Each day the sun rose into a cloudless sky and burned with a relentlessness that began to kill. One newspaper reported that in London, in a single week, 629 infants died of the heat. The usual weekly mortality rate for infants was eighteen. Newspapers ran regular columns listing "Deaths by Heat," such as the demise of a Lambeth woman whose throat had been cut. The inquest resulted in a verdict of "suicide whilst of unsound mind, through the intense heat." In the East End, people waited for the relative cool of the evenings and sat outside on the steps of their tenement buildings, avoiding the oppressive heat of narrow, airless rooms. Sleep was elusive; the streets were almost as noisy by night as by day.

Even without the extreme weather, 1911 was a time of unrest. Social change was pushing up as determinedly as weeds between paving stones. In addition to the agitation caused by the suffragettes, there were 872 different strikes that year, including coal miners in Wales; seamen, dockers and carters in the ports; and eventually railway workers countrywide. Other workers were soon drawn in, among them cleaners employed by London County Council and fifteen thousand women in sweated workshops. Butchers, bakers and grocers closed their doors, not necessarily in solidarity, but because the delivery of goods had all but ceased. Signs were hung on shut factories blaming the strikers for the closures, while across narrow Leroy Street near Pink's jam factory a paper banner warned landlords "No Work, No Rent!" Throughout Bermondsey, jam, biscuit and confectionary factories emptied of the women employed there, and outside Pink's, striking women held a banner that read "We are not white slaves, but Pink's slaves!" The jam workers, Ellen's lot before her admission to Stone, were fed up with years of poor treatment.

The women's strikes began spontaneously, and one group flooding into the streets encouraged another. There was a gaiety about the processions, with much singing and laughter and shouting. Defying the heat, some dressed in feathers and fur tippets, and their jauntiness drew criticism from the press, who decided the women were merely irresponsible and had been "drawn in [by] the excitement and the chance of a holiday." Suffragette Emily Davison – the same woman who'd hidden in Westminster Hall at census time – objected, and in a letter to the *Morning Post* replied that "the wit and banter displayed by the girl strikers was no sign of…holiday gaiety." Instead, she insisted, it was "the staunch and brave attempt to put a good face on a very serious matter." Within a few weeks the factory girls returned to work, with the majority of employers conceding substantial wage increases.

Yet calm did not prevail. In early September, less than a month after the women's strikes, a group of boys in Wales walked out of their school to protest the caning of a classmate. The action spread, first by word of mouth and then by the newspapers and within larger cities by groups of "pickets" moving from school to school. Before long, pupils of all ages and throughout Britain abandoned their classrooms, emulating the striking railwaymen, dockers, car men and factory girls they'd been watching throughout the long hot summer, and airing their grievances by marching in the streets and picketing their schools. Like the adults they carried banners and shouted their demands: "no cane," "free boots" and "no home lessons." Though their wants were legitimate, particularly for children who worked after school to contribute to the family's earnings and so had no time for homework and little money for pencils, they were not taken very seriously. The strikes were merely "an eloquent sign

of the times," declared the *Evening Telegraph and Post,* adding, "The rod
is spared and the child is spoiled." Boys in particular, the paper decided,
were "devoted patrons of moving picture shows," and being "an imita-
tive animal," they were simply reproducing scenes they had witnessed
there. The same report singled out the cry "Down books!" as the demand of London schoolboys, and with a scolding tone, accused them of
"adopting the methods, in quaint miniature, of the Transport Workers'
Federation, even to picketing."

Likely the children did not need moving pictures to incite them to
pick up sticks and stones, which they did in more than a few locations.
They struck in sixty-two cities and towns, often smashing the glass out
of lampposts, breaking windows and marching from one school to the
next, where they recruited more bodies to their cause. In Whitechapel
and the wider East End, children added iron bars and belts to their arsenal of sticks and stones, and one small fellow carted three half-bricks
beneath his arm, proof that he meant business despite his size. The children were menacing enough that police were called in, but in the end it
was mostly mothers who put an end to the strikes, plucking truants out
of the crowds and taking them home by the collar.

Earlier that summer some of those same mothers – including Mary
Anne, perhaps, and her sister Jennie – had dressed their children in
their best clothes, scrubbed their faces, shined their shoes and trotted
them out to join the throngs witnessing the coronation procession of
King George and his consort, Queen Mary. The newspapers described
everything in detail: the lightly falling rain, the state coach drawn by
cream-coloured horses with royal blue rosettes woven into their manes,
the queen in a magnificent robe of ivory satin, embroidered with gold
thread. "Never such a crowd, never such enthusiasm," gushed the *Daily
News,* though of course the papers had written much the same thing ten
years earlier for the crowning of Edward VII, and a few years before that
for Queen Victoria's diamond jubilee.

There were suffragettes among those watching, but they made no attempt to disrupt the grand procession and were still adhering to a truce
with the government as they awaited the outcome of the second conciliation bill. A week earlier the women had staged their own coronation

procession, marching five abreast in a seven-mile-long parade from the Victoria Embankment to the Albert Hall. Tens of thousands of women took part, and bands played along the route, and aside from sheer numbers they made their point by dressing up as women of historical importance: Queen Elizabeth marched, and Joan of Arc, as did Abbess Hilda, Florence Nightingale, Jenny Lind and Charlotte Bronte. It was a pageant of colour and inclusion, with contingents from near and far. Each London borough was represented, while the Irish wore green and carried harps and shamrocks, and the Indians dressed in saris and lofted carved elephants on rods. Banners fluttered overhead, sewn with emblems and rich fabrics. One bore a grim reminder of the suffragettes' methods – "From Prison to Citizenship" – while others touted the diversity of the participants: "Home-maker," read one; "Actress," another. The organizers promoted the parade as a patriotic demonstration and hoped it would sway the minds of the politicians, soon to cast ballots that could give the vote to at least some privileged women.

The suffragettes were still derided, but they had their admirers, who noted that the women's coronation procession included representation from all sectors, including art, science, trade and commerce. Politician Keir Hardie, championing socialism and the plight of the poor, was a long-time supporter of the suffrage movement. He claimed that the king's procession, "with its pomp and show of tinsel and pasteboard ceremony, was planned to conceal the fact that behind the barricade, behind the soldiers guarding the route, there was a sweltering mass of poverty that would disgrace a savage nation."

Nineteen-eleven slid into 1912 with little changed but the weather. The conciliation bill had once more failed to pass, and another doomed one would soon be put forward. Discontent among workers still simmered: a miners' strike in Wales, thought settled in November, reared again in January when owners refused to negotiate a minimum wage, and weavers in the north continued to agitate. A Cheltenham newspaper reported that there was trouble brewing again in the shipyards. Yet another publication ran the headline "England – Restive" and said that the mood throughout Britain was one of "uneasiness and almost despair."

Did Harry Deverill concern himself with the news of the day? Did he read about the worries of the railway workers or the weavers and picture himself in their shoes, fighting for things that could make a life decent? Did he see the suffragettes throwing stones and breaking glass and going to prison for their beliefs and think of his daughters, Ethel and Doris, wondering what might lie ahead for them if the women did not succeed? Or did he dream of what might be possible if they did? Did he look at his sons, Joe and Ernie, and expect bigger things for them than he himself had accomplished? Or was he a plain man whose world was not many-faceted, who was content of an evening to sit by the warmth of the grate after dinner, picking up and playing each of his instruments in turn, striving for the perfect tone and the sweetest music?

He'd done just that one Friday evening in February 1912, and no one listening to the music he made knew that it would be the last time they heard him. On Saturday, he and Ernie were at the table, talking. Harry had put his instruments away and was polishing his boots, one foot up on a chair. There was no indication that anything was wrong, no pained cry or clutching of his chest. He simply fell to the floor and died. And although it was an inconspicuous death, for eight-year-old Ernie those moments became a vivid memory that surfaced every time he bent to rub scuffs from his shoes.

Nothing else survives of that day, but one can imagine the scene: Mary Anne's anguished cry when Ernie summoned her; the sound of Jack's boots as he ran from his flat next door; Martha Bedford, dear friend and neighbour, rushing in as soon as she heard the news, watching Mary Anne and Ethel embrace, pulling a puzzled Doris into her lap. Lilian Carter would have come too, her husband, Ernest, making special mention of Harry to the sparse congregation at St. Jude's the very next day, a Sunday.

For the following week Harry's body rested at home, in the room where he'd died, laid out in his bandsman uniform until the Salvation Army's Borough band led his coffin to a graveside service at Nunhead Cemetery, where so many of Harry and Mary Anne's family members had been buried before him. Mary Anne and the children followed, as well as Jack, Aunt Maggie and her daughter Clara, and May, whose heart surely ached for the uncle she loved, and for Ethel, too. Perhaps Martha carried Doris and Lilian Carter held Ernie's hand, small and dry in sadness. Mary Anne's sister Jennie, who'd lost her husband, Richard, just a year before, must have come with her daughters from Lambeth, and potter Fred Roff may have been there too, but the register for Newington Workhouse shows no sign of Ellen or mother Mary discharging themselves for the occasion. Harry's siblings looked on as their brother was lowered into a grave shared by his mother and father. The group of mourners stood beneath leafless trees in the February breeze – a breeze too warm for the season, and so unsettling. Under a grey sky that refused to release rain, Harry's friends and family listened as the Borough band offered a musical goodbye. Traditionally, Salvation Army funerals were infused with joy through music, since the deceased, after all, was being "promoted to glory." White, not black, was the colour of the day, worn as arm bands over the men's uniforms, strung as ribbons fluttering from the Army flag, and covering the large drum that made such a thundering sound. Before Harry's coffin was covered with soil, his bandsman cap, his bible and his songbook were set upon it to accompany him.

Later the Salvation Army's *War Cry* magazine published a short eulogy under the heading "Bandsman Deverill – Borough": "There came the news that Brother Harry Deverill had suddenly passed away while cleaning his boots. But – glory to God! – he was ready for the call. His life and daily conduct proved him to be a son of God. As his comrade-Bandsmen sang over his grave, 'Safe in the arms of Jesus,' we thanked God for having known him and heard his testimony and seen his many little acts of service."

The words were meant as a comfort, but the truth was Mary Anne was left alone in a world harsh and unsympathetic to the plight of widows. If Harry's employer provided a death benefit to Mary Anne, or allowed her a small pension, then she was among a minority. How she supported herself and the children in the time immediately following Harry's death is not clear, but she stayed in Whitechapel, with Joe and Ethel being old enough to help her, and Jack and Martha Bedford close by. By now Martha was "Bebbie" to Doris. Joe, Ethel and Ernie had always called her Miss Bedford, as was proper, but Doris couldn't manage that mouthful, and the nickname stuck, symbolizing a bond between them. Bebbie still worked at the cork factory, and Mary Anne took an evening job as a cleaner, or washed clothes for some of the women in buildings nearby.

The mothers in the largely Jewish Rothschild Buildings often had large families, and while they were far from wealthy, their husbands had steady employment, so they looked to women from respectable model dwellings like College Buildings for domestic help. Monday mornings the heaps of clothes were taken away, and by week's end they were returned, washed and ironed. If Mary Anne took on such tasks at College Buildings, she'd have climbed to the roof for her washing and drying on her single designated day and finished the rest in her two-room flat, in an already busy and tiny household. The cramped scullery was too small for such chores, and the main room served as living room, dining room and also bedroom for the older children. Mary Anne would have heated the water over the grate, boiling the whites, then scrubbed the clothes by hand, rinsing them, wringing them out and hanging them from every possible spot in the flat. The iron would be heated on the coals until it was hot enough to sizzle out each wrinkle. She was fastidious, and each of her children grew up to be people who took care of even the most ordinary things that passed through their hands. A scratch on furniture was quickly polished, a torn sleeve carefully, invisibly mended. It was a point of pride to have things look just so, no matter what they had cost.

Joe left school and got work as a porter after Harry died, but what he carried, and between which destinations, no one knows. He'd just turned fourteen, and he was the man of the family, small for a boy his age, and capable. Less lost in his own world than Ernie, and quiet rather than shy, Joe emanated kindness and couldn't bring himself to fib. He giggled over silly comics, but he wasn't particularly funny himself; he didn't like being the centre of attention. He was practical and good with his hands, and he didn't mind following rules. But he was squeamish, too, so there were certain tasks that were never given to him – treating a sibling's oozing sore, or scooping up dead mice snapped in a newfangled mousetrap.

Those duties likely fell to his sister Ethel, who had always been a help to Mary Anne, but who now, with Harry's death, was indispensable. There were thousands of girls like her, so many that they were commonly called "little mothers" in the press, or even "the drudge of the family. She nurses the baby, she helps with the washing and charing, she runs the errands; her work, poor mite, is never done." Not quite thirteen, Ethel was capable of caring for Doris and Ernie when Mary Anne couldn't, and she soon looked older than her years, with a long, thin face, and large eyes that were a family trait, but sadder on Ethel than on sparkling May. In the few photographs of Ethel that exist, her smile is uncertain, as if she expects happiness to be short-lived. The weight of her mother's worries had shifted to her, and for the rest of her life she'd appear careworn.

Doris, though too young to understand the uncertainty of her family's circumstance, must have sensed it. A photo taken around 1912 shows her in a knitted hat, suggesting cooler weather despite the flowers behind her. She holds a doll in one arm, face out, as if sharing the portrait. The doll has full hair and a painted face, and fills the role of a special friend, played with on happy days, clutched on hard ones. But Doris herself stares at the lens with a child's candour, unsmiling, sad, even frightened, as if she knows how precarious her life will be.

Martha Bedford – Bebbie – had turned forty-seven the day before Harry died, a plain woman with a hard face that hid a generous soul. For widowed Mary Anne, she proved a fine example of the strength of a woman alone. There are several formal portraits of a young Bebbie, all dressed up, with curled hair that looks awkwardly done and never quite meets the style of the day. Though whispers survive of a beau in her past who died in the Boer War, there is nothing to substantiate the rumours. For decades she'd supported herself with a respectable job, living on her own in an area of London that many women with a choice avoided.

She'd been a friend to Mary Anne for some time, but she enters the saga most prominently from this juncture, bringing with her a bevy of extended family. Her older sister Frances was particularly close, and it is Frances's daughters' postcards that offer some insight into how important the nieces were to her. Though the cards read just a line or two, offering birthday greetings or Christmas wishes, Bebbie stored them away as keepsakes, and they remain, a hundred years on, sepia-toned images of long-lashed girls, floral sprays and idyllic country scenery.

Perhaps it was the growing transience of people that prompted Martha to hold on to the postcards. Two years earlier, one of Frances's daughters had shipped out for Canada. It was half a world away, and yet these days it seemed people travelled the oceans in greater numbers and from all walks of life. Many, like Martha's niece, took a one-way ticket and emigrated to Canada or South Africa or Australia. Some journeyed for commerce, especially between New York and London, while others crossed the sea for a holiday. There were regular columns in the newspapers advertising the various routes and the ships that plied them: Ellerman's Hall Line was a choice if one wished to travel to Karachi or Bombay, while the Allan Line, "unsurpassed in cuisine and service," would whisk you to Canada, which was a popular destination.

Some of the poorest travellers found their way with the help of the Salvation Army, the Church of England's Waifs and Strays group or the East End Emigration Society, to which Ernest and Lilian Carter belonged. Such groups were sometimes accused of what had long been called "shoveling out paupers" to deal with social ills, and on the receiving end, in some Canadian cities that were filling up with less-than-desirable newcomers who gave the rest a bad reputation, signs appeared in factories stating "Englishmen need not apply."

In England, though, the relocation schemes seemed a positive endeavour. One paper reported that the East End group's annual report made for "cheerful reading" because it showed that "steady progress is being made in planting our surplus population in the Colonies." England itself would have more elbow room, but the travellers benefited too. "A few of them do not succeed, but that is not remarkable. The vast majority, however, do infinitely better in the new country. This is largely due to the care with which the Emigration Society chooses its cases. A man must be physically suitable, and possess a good character. For such there is a healthier and happy life beyond the seas, and one has only to read the letters of the emigrants to wish that there were many more such societies to relieve the hideous congestion of our great cities."

Potential emigrants were thoroughly vetted by Ernest and other society members in order to assess their character and willingness to work. The Canadian agent who received them was pleased overall and stated that East End and other groups like it sent over a superior class of emigrants. Notes went back and forth between agents in England and in the destination country, promising worthy folk and decent treatment.

WILLIAM LICKFOLD, 21 and LEONARD, 18. These two young men are very respectable and superior and they would like to be placed together if possible. William has done Carpentering work and he has also worked in a garden, and so has his brother Leonard. They are highly spoken of by all their references as very superior young men and I hope that you will be able to place them where they will have a good home and be thoroughly taught their business. You may give them £1 each for landing money...
JOSEPH STEVENS, 28. This man is a Carman and he thoroughly understands horses. He is quite ready and willing [to] work on the land and expects to get placed on a farm. He is a good strong fellow and ought to do well. You may give him £1 for landing money.

There's record of Ernest and Lilian making the trip as well, travelling first class on a Montreal-bound ship carrying Salvationists, children from the fostering organization Dr. Barnardo's Homes, and a passel of other emigrants. Clergymen were often invited on these excursions and taken to visit new immigrants once they arrived, in the hopes that the clergymen would return enthusiastic and eager to spread the word about the bonuses of emigration. It seems Ernest did. Sometimes he and Lilian's tireless, altruistic sister, Mary, went to the railway station to see their parishioners off to Canada. Once, on a hot night in June, a friend accompanied them and witnessed Mary's fury that there was no water for the travellers. "The little families of East Enders were all packed into the carriages," she later recalled, "and [Mary] came to me burning with indignation that these people – emigrating because of their very low standard of life and unemployment – could only get lemonade at sixpence a bottle to give to their thirsty children on the train."

A passenger liner was the only way to cross the ocean, and it was a lucrative business that had the shipping companies in fierce competition for the biggest, fastest and most luxurious ship. Third-class tickets were the cheapest, but sold in such vast quantities that they were the most profitable, too. Cunard's *Mauretania* and *Lusitania* were among the first of a new breed of luxury liners, which were quickly adding cachet to travel no matter the class. After them came the White Star Line's fleet of three enormous vessels, *Olympic, Britannic* and *Titanic*.

Titanic's maiden voyage was scheduled for Wednesday, April 10, 1912, but a nationwide coal strike put most vessels out of service in the days prior. *Titanic* was berthed in Southampton, and it seemed unlikely she would sail as planned, causing uncertainty for passengers like Ernest and Lilian Carter, who'd bought tickets in anticipation of a holiday to visit Lilian's brother in America. But over the Easter weekend, between Good Friday and Easter Sunday, the strike was settled, and the White Star Line began recruiting the crew to man the mammoth vessel. Ernest likely preached that Sunday's sermon at St. Jude's mindful of the suitcases standing open at the vicarage, ready for his shirts and dinner jacket. Lilian, teaching Sunday school, probably reassured the Deverill kids and her other young charges she'd be back from vacation before they knew it, and left them in her sister Mary's care, with bible passages to learn. She might have hosted Mary Anne and Bebbie and other parish ladies for tea later that day, even drawing the new widow aside and squeezing her hand, knowing her heart still hurt. Did Mary Anne envy Lilian this trip with her husband, still alive and well, and wonder what such an adventure might be like?

On Wednesday, Ernest and Lilian took the seven-thiry a.m. train from Waterloo Station, arriving dockside in Southampton by nine-thirty. Boarding for those in first class came later, and included a personal greeting from *Titanic*'s captain. Ernest and Lilian held a second-class ticket, so they boarded early with hundreds of others, shuffling down the red-carpeted stairway with its curling oak banister, or riding the maple-lined elevator to find their cabin. Third-class passengers had a separate entrance and were closely scrutinized by a medical officer for ailments, lest they be refused entry to the United States and then have to return to England on the White Star Line's dime. Shortly before noon, *Titanic* slipped her moorings and slid away from the dock.

There were many wonders to be explored on board this ship, no matter the category of your ticket. A first-class passenger who travelled from Southampton to Queenstown, Ireland, published an account in the *Cork Constitution*: "It is useless for me to attempt a description of the wonders of the saloon – the smoking room with its inlaid mother of pearl – the lounge with its green velvet and dull polished oak – the reading room with its marble fireplace and deep soft chairs and rich carpet of old rose hue." In the morning one could plunge into a swimming pool or exercise in the gymnasium while working up an appetite for breakfast, and at dinner an orchestra played beautiful strains. "But if the saloon of the *Titanic* is wonderful," the passenger wrote, "no less so is the second class and in its degree the third class…Lifts and lounges and libraries are not generally associated in the public mind with second class, yet in the *Titanic* all are found. It needed the assurance of our steward guide that we had left the saloon and were really in the second class."

Ernest and Lilian were quick to make acquaintances. In the smoking room on the first night, Ernest, an Oxford graduate, struck up a conversation with Lawrence Beesley, a Cambridge man who taught science at a private school in London. They discussed the merits of their alma maters and agreed that both institutions were much more than mere academic houses, providing excellent opportunities for the development of character. Eventually the conversation turned to Ernest's parish work. Despite the shrinking size of his congregation – he'd performed just a dozen marriages over the past year – Ernest remained optimistic, though he admitted to Beesley that he would not have accomplished much at St. Jude's without the efforts of his wife. Later, upon meeting the charismatic Lilian, Beesley "realized something of what [Ernest] meant in attributing a large part of what success he had as a vicar to her."

In addition to Lawrence Beesley, the Carters befriended others on board: Stuart Collett, a theology student joining family in Port Byron,

New York; Marion Wright, a young lady from Somerset who was en route to her fruit farmer fiancé; Kate Buss, a Kentish girl who'd worked in a grocer's shop and was also going to America to marry her intended; and Robert Douglas Norman, an engineer from Glasgow joining his brother on a farm in Canada. Kate's ongoing letter home to her parents indicates these passengers encountered one another regularly, and that she "chummed up" with "Miss W" early on, when Marion offered to share her steamer rug that first chilly day on deck. Together they gossiped about the passengers they met in the "mixed-up assembly" that was second class. One fellow they called "Mr. Sad Man" because he was sailing morosely away from a wife and children and would not see them again for at least two years; and another was the flirtatious "Doctor Man" who had adeptly removed soot from Kate's eye with his finger. Stuart, the theology student, "tries to teach us all religion," Kate wrote, but she had nothing but kind words for Ernest and Lilian Carter. And Lilian, in return, had advice for the emigrant bride. "She tells me that I must admire everything that is American for a start, or I shall not be well received."

The new friends may have shared a table in the dining hall, or recommended books to one another in the mahogany-panelled library with its white fluted columns. They chatted as they relaxed in deck chairs, wearing their steamer rugs to ward off the cold. Marion later wrote that Lilian was "exhausted" and had confided her worry about how her Sunday school class would fare during her absence. Nor was Ernest feeling his best. He'd picked up a head cold before boarding, and the bothersome symptoms were crossing the ocean with him. Kate was tired too. She hadn't been seasick, but the vibration of the ship kept her awake at night, and late on Saturday she wrote in her letter, "I must go to bed now, eye neuralgia coming bad. That means a bad day tomorrow, I'm afraid."

That Sunday, April 14, two days from New York harbour, the purser held a morning service in the second-class saloon. Later it would seem as though the service had been preparation for "that awful experience," but for now there was no sense of doom. The sun shone brightly and the sea was calm. The temperature had dropped, and Kate, Marion, Ernest and Lilian were among the few who ventured out on deck when they strolled together after lunch. Lilian noticed how drained Kate seemed, with her problem eye and her windburned cheeks, and insisted after their walk that she have a good rest in Ernest's chair. Ernest, meanwhile, wandered to the library.

As children played in the covered promenade that ran alongside the library, Ernest paused to read the charts that showed the ship's progress and detailed the day's run. Because of the chill outside, the library was full and bustling, and the steward, "thin, stooping, sad-faced, and generally with nothing to do but serve books," was busy passing out baggage declaration forms in anticipation of the ship's docking. There was a lot of congratulatory talk about how smooth the trip had been so far, the weather nearly perfect, if cold. It was expected to be equally tranquil overnight and indeed for the remainder of the voyage, and when Lawrence Beesley joined Ernest by the charts, Ernest mentioned that a hymn sing might be a pleasant pastime and wondered if Beesley would help arrange it. That evening, with the purser's blessing, nearly one hundred guests gathered in the saloon. Ernest, used to the tiny congregations at St. Jude's, was no doubt exhilarated by such a turnout, though his cold still plagued him. He'd swallowed some tablets offered by Marion, who by chance had a lovely singing voice and had agreed to perform. It was a collaborative effort: the theology student, Stuart, assisted with prayers, and Robert Norman, the Scottish engineer, played the piano. Ernest led the singing, prefacing each chosen hymn with words about the author and, if he knew it, the circumstances surrounding its composition. The room was impressed with his knowledge and his eagerness to share it. When Marion sang her solos, the singing was so beautiful that Kate saw tears in the eyes of some of the passengers, and noticed that Lilian briefly covered her face with her hands. Lawrence Beesley detected "the hushed tone with which all sang the hymn 'For Those in Peril on the Sea.'"

Shortly after ten p.m. the stewards brought biscuits and coffee, and Ernest drew the meeting to a close. Thanking the purser for the use of the saloon, he added a few words about the "confidence all felt on board this great liner with her steadiness and her size, and the happy outlook

of landing in a few hours in New York at the close of a delightful voyage."
The gathering ended, the crowd dispersed, and Lawrence Beesley and
the Carters had coffee together and said goodnight. It was ten-forty-five
p.m. *Titanic* pressed westward through black water, beneath a black sky
lit with stars.

The story of *Titanic*'s demise has been told and retold, the tale no
less heart-rending with the passage of time. A century on, it's less the
details of the iceberg's sudden appearance, the desperate effort to avoid
a collision and the tearing of the ship's hull than the accounts of the
passengers that continue to fascinate. And of course it's the words of the
survivors that remain, so we know that Kate Buss had just climbed into
her berth when the collision occurred at 11:40 that night. The noise was
like a skate on ice, and she paused and heard the engines reversing. She
got out of bed, put on her slippers and dressing gown, and went into
the hallway to find Marion Wright, who was in turn coming to find her.

For Marion, the sound had been like crashing glass, but the shud-
der of the engines stopping alarmed her more. She and Kate went up
on deck together and met up with Robert Norman, who told them the
ship had hit an iceberg, and that he had seen the thing himself and regretted not having his camera. They agreed to return to their cabins for
warmer clothing so they could stay on deck to see how things unfolded,
and when she slipped on her coat, Kate put the letter to her parents
in her pocket. Back up on deck, passengers were donning life vests,
people were crying, shots were fired, and through the crowd – "quite by
chance" – Kate and Marion heard an officer call out "Any more ladies?
Ladies first." She and Kate were herded into Lifeboat #9, but Robert
Norman was not allowed to board, though Kate protested since she
saw that several other men were already in the boat. Stuart Collett, the
young man who'd assisted Ernest Carter at the hymn sing, afterward
told the *Toronto Star* that he'd guided Kate Buss and Marion Wright to
a lifeboat, and climbed in himself after explaining to the crew that he
was responsible for the ladies. But neither Kate's nor Marion's account
mentions Stuart, and another passenger in the same lifeboat later said
Collett "appeared out from under a seat. He must have gotten in even
before the lifeboat left the deck. He sat with his chin on his walking stick

moaning on about all the years of sermons he lost. One woman all but turned and flew at him – 'if you can give me back my husband and my son I'll pay you for your sermons.'"

Before the collision, Lawrence Beesley reclined in the upper berth in his cabin, reading. Outside in the corridor he could hear the muffled sounds of stewards moving about and talking, the normal noises of the crew settling for the night. At about 11:45 he felt the ship's engines give an extra heave, and his mattress moved with "a more than usually obvious dancing motion...[but] nothing more than that...no sound of a crash or of anything else: no sense of shock, no jar that felt like one heavy body meeting another." He continued reading, but in a few minutes felt the engines slow and stop. He got out of bed, put on a dressing gown and shoes and went out into the hallway, where a lounging steward told him he didn't know why the ship had stopped, but that it couldn't be "anything much." Beesley decided to go above to see for himself, to which the steward replied, with an indulgent smile, "All right, sir, but it is mighty cold up there."

On deck Beesley hung over the rail, but there was little to see apart from calm water and a moonless sky. In the smoking room a card game was ongoing. The young men reported seeing an iceberg slide alongside the ship and tower above it, and told Beesley they'd paused in their game to watch it pass, then resumed their play. One estimated the berg at sixty feet tall, another at a hundred. Most agreed the ship had had a near miss and maybe lost a bit of paint, and that the captain had stalled the engines as a precaution. One fellow, gesturing to his glass of whiskey, suggested jokingly that they check the deck for ice shards, as he could use some for his drink. In fact, the forward deck was covered with ice, and circumstances were far more dire than anyone in the room realized.

Beesley returned to his cabin but soon heard a shout summoning passengers onto the deck with lifebelts on, and he went above to find a motley crowd, some dressed in furs and wraps, others in little more than nightclothes and dressing gowns, shoes without socks. According to Beesley, there was no sign of alarm or cries of fear, no panic or hysteria. The crew organized the boarding of lifeboats, and people waited calmly on deck for their orders to alight. Beesley's own words offer the best

READY FOR THE CALL

light in which to view the scene: "If the reader will come and stand with the crowd on deck, he must first rid himself entirely of the knowledge that the *Titanic* has sunk – an important necessity, for he cannot see conditions as they existed there through the mental haze arising from knowledge of the greatest marine tragedy the world has known…he must get rid of any foreknowledge of disaster to appreciate why people acted as they did." There was no iceberg visible, no obvious gaping hole with water pouring in, no indication of the scope of the disaster, and no reason to question that there wouldn't be sufficient lifeboats with enough capacity to save everyone, and adequate time to do it. Then a rocket lit the sky, and

a sea of faces upturned to watch it, and then an explosion that seemed to split the silent night in two, and a shower of stars sank slowly down and went out one by one. And with a gasping sigh one word escaped the lips of the crowd: "Rockets!" Anybody knows what rockets at sea mean. And presently another, and then a third. It is no use denying the dramatic intensity of the scene: separate it if you can from all the terrible events that followed, and picture the calmness of the night, the sudden lights on the decks crowded with people in different stages of dress and undress, the background of huge funnels and tapering masts revealed by the soaring rocket, whose flash illuminated at the same time the faces and minds of the obedient crowd, the one with mere physical light, the other with a sudden revelation of what its message was. Everyone knew without being told that we were calling for help from anyone who was near enough to see.

Lawrence Beesley left *Titanic* in Lifeboat #13, and from the relative safety of the crowded boat watched the liner's broadside as she sat in the still water, her bright lights illuminating the lifeboats bobbing around her. At about two o'clock in the morning she tilted slowly up, and her lights extinguished. For some minutes she hovered that way, stern in the air, and then slid slowly down. The sea closed over her and heaved gently as if *Titanic* had never been.

205

Most survivors agreed that apart from the sight of the ship sinking, the thing that stayed in their minds was the cry of those in the water. The sound carried, loud and plentiful at first, but within forty minutes there was silence. On board the rescue ship *Carpathia*, Kate wrote to her parents that "heaps died of exposure." She couldn't bear to think of the lifeboat pulling away from Robert Norman and her other *Titanic* friends, and how they'd rowed hard for fear of suction from the sinking ship. Once far enough away, they'd drifted until morning. Afterward it seemed as if she had known her fellow shipmates for years. "If you ever see those names mentioned as living, be sure and let me know; also, of the Rev. and Mrs. Carter, who, I believe, went down on the vessel."

In the ensuing days a Nova Scotia undertaker led the gruesome task of pulling the dead from the water and meticulously recording everything that might be used to identify them. Each body was assigned a number, and a list was drawn up: *Male, estimated age 10-12, hair light, probably third class; Female, estimated age 25-30, hair fair, wearing a red striped skirt and a green petticoat and blue flannel drawers and with a chemise marked V.H.* Robert Douglas Norman was recovered as body #287: *Male, fair-haired, high forehead, wearing dark trousers and vest, no coat, and a green striped flannel shirt.* If Ernest and Lilian were found, they were never identified. But survivors remembered them. Lawrence Beesley, writing his account of the sinking just weeks after the event, felt compelled to mention the couple by name for the sake of those who would miss them. "While [these details] have perhaps not much interest for the average reader, they will no doubt be some comfort to the parish over which he presided and where I am sure he was loved…They were good people and this world is much poorer by their loss."

There is no witness who can say why Lilian did not climb aboard a lifeboat with other women. But almost every tribute written to the couple after the sinking agreed that one would not go without the other, and that the two chose to stay on board together so others could have a place in the boats. *The Times* wrote that "between the first shock and the last plunge, there is no question as to what these two would wish to do. They were childless, and in Commercial Street they lived their lives for others. Ernest Carter would pass round with his words of artless and ardent comfort, and his wife would say, 'Let the mothers get to the boats first; you and I must see this out together.'"

Months later, in December in Whitechapel, St. Jude's Church filled with mourners for the dedication of three memorials to the "keen-eyed, beaming lady" and her modest husband, who was "just the one to let others go first." Neighbours and friends found seats in the normally sparse pews, alongside distinguished guests from farther afield. Togeth-er they listened to the Lord Bishop of Stepney delivering his address from what had been Ernest's place behind the pulpit. The ceremony was described in detail in the *East London Observer*, so it's not hard to picture Mary Anne and the children among the mourners, with Bebbie and Jack there too, and Harry noticeably absent at the end of this long, hard year. Despite the difference in their backgrounds, the Carters had been friends of a sort, especially Lilian to Mary Anne, two women close in age if not in circumstance. A memorial tablet, worked in gun metal, showed Ernest and Lilian in relief, with an inscription that commem-orated the fact that "in death they were not divided." There was a brass tablet added to the font, given by members of Lilian's bible class, with the inscription: "This font was carved by Lilian Carter. The members of her Bible class have placed this tablet in grateful remembrance of her wise counsel and loving friendship." Third came a stained-glass window of "extraordinary beauties," and here the younger Sunday school chil-dren in the church came forward and gathered around the bishop to sing a song Lilian had been teaching them before her departure. Doris was still too little to join in, but Ernie would have been there, singing his best.

Afterward, walking back along Commercial Street toward Went-worth, fresh from the solemnities at St. Jude's, the group of Mary Anne, Bebbie, Jack and the children might not have noticed the relative quiet of the neighbourhood. The noise of their footsteps on the pavement was a hollow echo, but it was an appropriate sound and fit the sadness of the occasion. Only when they reached the corner of Wentworth and the usually raucous Petticoat Lane market would someone remember that today was Saturday, the Jewish Sabbath, so the stalls were closed, their awnings folded, the cobbles bare. A chill breeze sent debris scuttling along the gutter, and Mary Anne and her little band walked the remaining distance to College Buildings, where a cup of hot tea was in order.

On a sunny afternoon the following June, St. Jude's was again hosting a funeral for one of its masters. Canon Barnett left instructions in a letter that he wished to be cremated, and to have a service in his memory performed not at Westminster Abbey, where he was sub-dean, but at the humble church in Whitechapel where he'd spent thirty-three years. He'd suffered a "long and painful illness," which his wife Henrietta referred to when apologizing for her neglect of the flood of letters she'd received with messages of sympathy: "To reply to so many letters was not possible, for I was crushed by sixty days of terrible nursing." As with Ernest and Lilian Carter's recent memorial service, there was no polished coffin hung with draperies at the front of the church. Instead, Samuel Barnett's ashes were enclosed in a copper casket "made by a man whose soul he had rescued long years ago," and carried into St. Jude's by men associated with Toynbee Hall. The news accounts of the day listed the distinguished guests who were present, but more important, according to Henrietta, "was the crowd of humble folk that thronged the church. Not an idle curious crowd, but each one personally admitted as a known friend, a recognized fellow-worker." Later, she was visited by a St. Jude parishioner to whom she'd once given a jet brooch. The woman had kept the piece, wrapped reverently in wool. "I want you to take it," she told Henrietta, "in memory of our Canon; it's the best thing I've got"; and, she added, "you can wear it now."

To those who'd spent their lives in social work, trying to fix the world of the poor, these were sad times. Henrietta's old friend and colleague Ockey – Octavia Hill – had died of cancer the preceding August, leaving behind the legacy of community gardens and the concept of social work as a profession. And on the same day newspapers were reporting on her memorial service held at Southwark Cathedral, where the "lady's good works were particularly well known," other headlines grabbed the spotlight to announce that William Booth, founder of the Salvation Army, had died. In the main entrance of the Army's headquarters on

Queen Victoria Street – close to where a bedraggled, unconscious Ellen Evans-Roff had been found by the police – a simple typewritten message was posted: "The General has laid down his sword. God is with us."

Booth's memorial was much grander than Octavia Hill's, and much wider in scope. By the time of his death on August 18, 1912, the Army he'd begun in Whitechapel more than forty-five years earlier had expanded into a worldwide church and charity, and gained respectability and admiration. So it was only his due when tens of thousands filed past his casket at Clapton Congress Hill over the three days prior to the funeral, and tributes poured in from leaders all over the world. King George sent a personal telegram to Booth's family, as did his mother, Alexandra, who wrote that "the irreparable loss you and the nation have sustained in the death of your great, good, and never-to-be-forgotten Father, [is] a loss which will be felt throughout the whole civilised world." The procession to the cemetery assembled on the morning of August 29 in a drenching downpour, and for hours the bands that would accompany the cortege stood silently, taking what shelter they could from the rain. Shortly before eleven the precipitation let up, and the procession began, winding through the four quarters of London so that "City men saw it from their offices," "clerks and typists bareheaded crowded the roofs of the Royal Exchange," and at Shoreditch, factory workers swelled the numbers paying their respects to the General. Handel's "Dead March" was played by the bandsmen, and at Abney Park Cemetery the sun broke through, shining on a platform decorated with wreaths. King George and Kaiser Wilhelm each sent one, laid amongst less noble accolades: "A small tribute from the Fleet Street Tavern, Derby," and "With love to the General, from Joey, Jimmy and Joe."

PART TWO

The Noise of War
1913–1919

When he joined the Royal Navy in 1915, Joe Deverill was four foot eleven and a half inches, and tiny around too. His wasn't the ideal sailor's physique, but allowances were made for the fact that, at seventeen, boys were still growing. In Joe's case, no growth spurt was forthcoming.

CHAPTER 9

Bang, Crash, Tinkle

Early in June 1913, the Derby Stakes horse race was held at Epsom Downs, and everyone who was anyone attended. Film footage shows people arriving by motor car, horse-drawn carriage and over-loaded omnibus, and settling into the stands for one of the country's greatest annual spectacles. But something more was captured by the camera that day, and analyzed for years to come. The film's jaunty piano accompaniment picks up tempo as jockeys and racehorses soar past. Suddenly the music takes on an ominous tone; a woman steps from the sidelines into the path of King George's horse and is thrown to the ground. The horse somersaults, and his rider is tossed off his back and lies unconscious with the woman as people stream forward into the racecourse from both sides.

Newspapers soon revealed that the woman was Emily Wilding Davison, the suffragette who'd thrown stones, hidden in the House of Commons at census time and starved herself repeatedly in prison. She had two flags in suffragette colours on her person that day at Epsom, and died of her injuries four days later. Speculation over her intentions varied. Some believed she'd tried to grab the horse's bridle, hoping to attach one of the flags there. Others thought she'd found a dramatic and public way to commit a martyr's suicide – Emmeline Pankhurst had no doubt that "she threw herself at the King's horse, in full view of the King and Queen and a great multitude of their Majesties' subjects, offering up her life as a petition to the King, praying for the release of suffering women throughout England and the world." And yet the return train ticket in her pocket and holiday plans with her sister suggested otherwise.

213

Whatever her intentions, her rash actions were severely criticized. Anonymous hate mail sent to Davison as she lay dying labelled her "a person unworthy of existence in this world ... I hope you suffer torture and tears until you die." The words would not have fazed her had she been able to hear them. In a posthumously published essay she wrote zealously about the "price of liberty" and her belief that "the perfect Amazon is she who will sacrifice all even unto this last to win the Pearl of Freedom for her sex."

Of course, many women of the day had little time or energy to contemplate such pearls. If Mary Anne Deverill appreciated the efforts of the Emily Davisons of the world on her behalf, the difficult truth was she was a widow with a family, surviving on a paltry income. Who could consider votes for women or imagine change when what time she had apart from paid work she spent with her children – teaching Ethel to cook and Ernie to sew on a button, and ensuring Joe was a dab hand at housework. One of Doris's earliest memories was of sitting by the fireplace, listening to her mother tell stories about Jesus, a task of the utmost importance to Mary Anne by October 1913, since even three-year-old Doris was attending Commercial Street Board School by then, with her siblings and a wealth of Jewish neighbours. Doris's school record tells us that Mary Anne worked as a cleaner, but either the work wasn't steady enough, or the pull homeward to the Borough was too strong to resist now that Harry was no longer with her. Early in 1914, Mary Anne and the children returned, leaving Bebbie and Jack behind at College Buildings. That separation could not have been easy, but being closer to Aunt Maggie was a consolation. The family took a flat in the Goodwin Buildings on Marshalsea Road, where Aunt Maggie lived with May and Clara, just at the base of Red Cross Street. Ethel and May were reunited, and Ernie was happy enough anywhere now that he'd discovered roller skates and his own agile abilities. He'd strap them on and sail through the streets of the Borough, the wind lifting his hair and whistling in his ears. Joe was fifteen and already had his eye turned to the wider world. That his family was settled and secure was what mattered, so the move, in Joe's eyes, was probably a good thing, with Aunt Maggie nearby to steady the ship.

Back in Whitechapel, Jack worked as an accumulator maker, probably for Hart Accumulator Company, building batteries for train lights. Hart was located in Marshgate Lane off Pudding Mill, a tram ride or a brisk hour's walk from College Buildings. Jack had always been good with his hands, and was a bit of an inventor, so perhaps he used the morning commute to plan his creations, like the thin piece of metal that fit around a brass keyhole to prevent polish spoiling wood, or the bagatelle board that had amused Joe, Ethel, Ernie and Doris on rainy days. If he'd ever considered bringing May across the Thames to live with him in his two-room flat, the departure of Mary Anne and her brood would have settled the question. Their presence in the Borough was one more reason to leave her at the Goodwin with her gran.

Bebbie too was dealing with an exodus of family, although her relatives were continuing to cross the Atlantic instead of the Thames. Nieces and nephews had gone, and now her sister Frances left, she and her husband declaring on the ship's manifest that their intended occupations were farmhand and domestic servant, the two types of workers Canada most desired as immigrants. Tom had no experience with farm work, though, having been employed as a bar steward at a workingmen's club in Stepney. They settled in London, Ontario, the descriptions of which must have sounded funny to Bebbie. It was such a new and tiny city when compared with her own ancient, swarming London, and yet it had a river called Thames, a Victoria Park and a Covent Garden Market.

If Bebbie was tempted to follow her sister, she made no move, but she did travel frequently to the Borough to stay in touch with Mary Anne and the children. In this way she became a part of Mary Anne's wider family, getting to know Aunt Maggie and Clara, and also May, who'd often come to Whitechapel. So though Bebbie lived at a distance now, the bond grew stronger, especially between her and Doris. Mary Anne had given Bebbie a photo of Doris standing before a studio prop and clutching white flowers. Her hair has been set in bouncy curls and is topped with a bow. She wears a slightly rumpled dark skirt and top, and she stands knock-kneed and smiling. On the back of the card Bebbie has penned in black ink "my little pal," and drawn a line beneath the words as if in happy emphasis. Despite Bebbie having her own rather large family and collection of nieces and nephews, Mary Anne's cluster adopted her, so she was as much a dear aunt to the children as Maggie was – someone they rushed to share their news with when she visited: a stitch Ethel had learned at school, the porter job Joe had procured, Ernie's latest roller-skate moves and Doris's close call with a tram.

She'd been about four then, out walking with Ernie, when she dashed away from him and into the busy street, chasing a leaf or a pigeon or an imaginary friend. Too late she saw the tram approaching, and in the aftermath it seemed a near-death experience: the tram's bell clanging, the massive car heading toward her, and the driver's mouth opening in slow motion as she fell. Thank goodness for the "cowcatcher" – a safety grill placed on the front of trams in order to prevent such gruesome but all too common accidents. The contraptions were basic things that looked like out-of-place bed slats, and they didn't always save lives. The victim had to fall in just the right place, and the driver had to quickly reach for the lever to lower the fender in time to avert a tragedy. Too often that did not happen, as in the case of a girl Doris's age who was killed right around the time Doris was struck. "With commendable presence of mind, Driver Shepherd applied the brakes and dropped the cowcatcher but for some so far inexplicable reason the child was drawn under the car wheels. Jacks were speedily procured, and after the car had been raised sufficiently high, boards were taken from the floor inside and the little victim extricated."

Luckily Doris's fall had less tragic consequences. The cowcatcher scooped her up, the streetcar came to a halt and any onlookers exhaled with relief as she was lifted out, unhurt, and returned to her brother's care. She must have been shaken by the event – Ernie too, for he'd been charged with caring for the baby of the family and had been just a whisker away from going home without her. The incident wasn't his fault, but he took the blame, or it was placed on him, as when "someone" had dipped her finger into the can of condensed milk and left telltale dribbles down the side.

"Who touched the milk?" Mary Anne asked Doris.

And she blinked her big eyes and answered, "Ernie did!"

With Ethel and May, Ernie was attending the old Lant Street Board School, which had recently been renamed for Charles Dickens. The suggestion had first been made back in 1894, when the annual school report noted that "in a low locality like this" a distinctive name connected to the history of the area might be beneficial. Dickens had lived on Lant Street as a boy and was already commemorated in many place names in the Borough. "Would not therefore Charles Dickens School, Lant Street, Southwark, be an appropriate name for this school?" Though the change took years, it was in place by the time the Deverill children returned to the Borough. Like Commercial Street and Brick Lane schools, Charles Dickens got good reports on its visits from the inspector, who praised the head master and the staff, most of whom had been at the school for many years. They were committed and kind, and their efforts often extended beyond school hours. But the curriculum and the methods of teaching it were not always suitable "for this type of boy," the inspector wrote, no doubt meaning a poor child was less capable than a privileged one. Formal lessons in grammar and history were often too difficult for the students to grasp, the inspector found, though they were quick at arithmetic and their handwriting was neat and careful. While there was "much to commend and little to criticise" on the girls' side, arithmetic and history might be simplified to better suit "this type of school." In all, "the refining influence which the work of the teachers has on the habits and manners of these poor children, is in itself one of the best tributes." Another report found the children clean and tidy, and well-mannered. "The head mistress appears to be wholeheartedly supported by her staff, who succeed extremely well in gaining the goodwill of the children."

A head mistress wasn't always supported by the system, however. A few years back, as an experiment that had the blessing of Octavia Hill, then-Head Mistress Newbould had begun taking students on field trips to Red Cross Gardens, next to the Deverills' old abode. The children – May, Flo Humphreys and their classmates – would spend an hour at the garden, not just observing but "digging and raking" under the supervision of two teachers. The fresh air and the connection with nature appeared to do the children good, and they always behaved well, according to Miss Newbould's writings; but when she put forward a formal request to include the outings as a regular part of the curriculum, it was denied. In her logbook she copied the letter of rejection: "'I regret very much to say that though I have the fullest sympathy with the object for which you make the application on Form 237, it is not possible to accept the suggestion under the conditions.'" After that she jotted, "Re – gardening in Red X Gardens one hour a week as per Scheme. We shall, therefore, discontinue the visits."

On the boys' side of Charles Dickens School, Ernie fit the profile the inspector outlined. Not brilliant academically, he was nevertheless always tidy and relentlessly committed to detail both at school and at home. Given a can of paint he'd ensure every spindle of a chair was equally and carefully covered, twice over if there was a sufficient amount in the tin. It was a pastime he loved: the smooth pull of the brush over a surface, the glistening wetness of the fresh paint and the way it renewed things, covering the dirt and grime. The solitary nature of the work suited Ernie too. As he stroked and blotted and dabbed, his imagination was free to roam at will, setting him on a bicycle and darting round the city's streets, or crossing the ocean even, where Bebbie's relatives had gone. When he was finished the job, he'd step back and admire his handiwork, then set about cleaning up, meticulously scrubbing away any paint that got on his skin. At school, lining up in the morning for inspection – tidy collars, polished shoes, clean hands – Ernie could hold out his palms with confidence, certain no paint remained, even if the odour still lingered in his nose.

Girls Ethel's age, mostly reaching the end of their studies, devoted half their time to domestic endeavours undertaken outside the school so as to further their skills in typical women's work. Over the years their schooling had more or less prepared them for becoming wives and mothers, but first these girls would work for pay, too, as domestic servants, or in a home-based workshop, making anything from boots to clothes to cardboard boxes, or folding books, as Clara did at Aunt Maggie's flat in the Goodwin. Upon leaving Charles Dickens School at fourteen, Ethel worked as a box maker for a large firm called Cropper's in the Borough. It was the kind of work Charles Booth and his ilk termed "sweated labour," because it was poorly paid and the hours were long whether you worked on the premises or took the cardboard home. Usually the materials were prepared by men who worked machines that cut the paper; boys who scored it for folding; and girls and women who made the pieces into boxes. Often young, unmarried girls worked onsite in the factories, with the men and boys, but most of the employees were married women or widows like Mary Anne, who took the pieces home to assemble and then returned the made-up boxes in exchange for pay. "A few minutes spent outside one of these establishments any afternoon towards the end of the week will give an observer an idea of the extent of this trade," Booth wrote. "Numbers of women and children may be seen returning the finished work to the warehouse, carried in carefully covered parcels or wheeled thither in perambulators."

Hours of work in the factories varied. Eight to eight was common, with ten minutes for lunch, and half an hour for tea; but, Booth noted, "it is very difficult to get the women and girls to start punctually, especially those who have household duties to perform before going to work." Conditions hadn't improved much over the years, in his opinion, and the need for workers had substantially increased because more and more industries – confectioners, chemists, soap makers and bootmakers – were packaging goods in boxes. Such changes meant there was no real slack season. Year round, girls like Ethel were busy making boxes of every shape and size, and mothers with children in tow rushed to and fro to meet quotas at home, where they could also manage the household duties. In 1906 a Sweated Industries Exhibition had been held at Queen's Hall "to acquaint the public with the evils of sweating." An exhibition handbook described the various jobs associated with sweated labour, including buttonhole makers, shawl fringers, glove stitchers, bible folders, sack sewers, chain makers and rope washers. The chapter about box makers explained that: "Boxes enter very largely into our commercial life. They meet us everywhere. Boxes for shoes, for handkerchiefs and gloves; boxes for matches, for hair pins, for correspondence cards; for sweets, chocolates, and the thousand-and-one things sold at a thousand-and-one shops." Of all the home industries, this was the largest, despite the paltry pay. The article described the typical day of a widowed box maker, who worked some twelve to fourteen hours with quick fingers, bending the cardboard, pasting the paper on and throwing the pieces over her shoulder to dry on the bed behind her. When she walked to the warehouse to deliver and retrieve more cardboard, she picked up dinner from the fish shop for her family and rushed home again, but there was barely time to eat it if the quota of boxes was to be made. A picture shows her at work with her daughters, all of them gathered around the table in a cramped room, with a teetering stack of boxes behind them. "Very remarkable is the skill required by these box makers, and wonderful the precision with which they work; though the widow's fingers be dirty and coated with glue, she will not soil a single box."

Bringing work home like this was sometimes the only way of getting by. But Clementina Black, in her 1907 book *Sweated Industry and the Minimum Wage*, had claimed that the practice too often involved children. "The temptation to press children into the service is very great. The tedious process of fetching and carrying work from and to the factory or workshop generally falls to their lot; indeed, workers who have no children of their own not infrequently hire a child, for a few pence, to perform that duty. The time of a child is generally considered to be of little value… Not a few children are habitually late for school, in consequence of being thus employed." Among her pages of examples were Esther S., aged ten, and her six-year-old sister, who helped their mother lining and covering boxes at home, and often missed school because their assistance was "absolutely necessary." Black believed that sweated labour was "a running sore that affected the entire fabric of society." Such workers made everything from tassels to safety pins, which meant "their work, in some shape or form, comes into every house in this country… The taint is everywhere."

A few years later, Black wrote again about box makers in her book *Married Women's Work*, and discovered after visiting with forty-two of them that their lot was poorer than before. Because the work wasn't heavy and didn't require much in the way of materials, it was more and more often done at home, "and it is commonplace that trades in which home work prevails tend to become ill-paid." Some of the women had been at it for years, and Black was amazed by their skill and speed. One reported making 430 boxes in a day, along with running her household. But many of the women had cramped, rheumatic hands "bent almost into claws, and incapable of ever opening out again into flatness." No matter: all of the women interviewed said their work was essential "if the family was to be kept above the barest level of subsistence." Mary Anne hovered right around that level too, her own earnings combining with Joe's and Ethel's to pay for rent, food and other necessities.

Despite having little money to spare, she was presented with an increasing number of ways to spend it. As politician Philip Snowden noted in his 1913 book *The Living Wage*, "new expenses have come into the category of necessities," including halfpenny newspapers, trams that led in all directions and cheap books and magazines. "People cannot see tramways without wanting to ride sometimes; they cannot see newspapers without at least buying one occasionally; they cannot see others taking a holiday into the country without desiring to do the same." But the additional costs came out of wages that remained stagnant, so the struggle to make ends meet only grew.

The choice of entertainments was hard to resist and arguably well worth the money for the pleasure incurred. Even the local pub, seeing that it had to offer more than just a well-pulled pint to attract and hold customers, began to organize games and family outings. There is a photo of Aunt Maggie, her daughter Clara, and granddaughter May, smiling beneath their hats, seated in a crowded charabanc that reads on its side: Hart Motor Co., For Hire. An early version of a bus, a charabanc was a long, open-topped vehicle fitted with low-backed seats and a folding canvas top stowed in the back in case of rain. Clara and Maggie are seated safely in the middle, but May is perched on the top of a seat at the very back of the charabanc, leaning toward the camera as if barely able to contain her thrill.

Entertainments still included music halls these days, offering the usual fare of jugglers, ventriloquists, dancers and comedians. But establishments were finding they could forego live performances and draw yet a larger crowd by showing films, the earliest of which were often slapstick comedy. One of South London's own had risen to the top of the genre, and in 1914 Charlie Chaplin's soon to be signature character, The Tramp, made his first cinematic appearance, becoming a huge hit. Chaplin was twenty-five now, and the get-up was his own inspired creation: a bowler hat, a too-small jacket, baggy pants and huge shoes. One of the earliest films shows him at a cart race, more interested in the camera ostensibly filming the race than in the event itself. Time and again the tramp walks into the frame, staring into the lens and wiggling his eyebrows or adjusting his hat, begging to be noticed. The scenes are obvious comedy, but there's truth here too – an echo of the men posing and preening in the Petticoat Lane footage, itching to be captured on film. Theirs was a world Chaplin understood, because it was his world too.

The Chaplin family's trials had continued after his stay at Hanwell. His mother, Hannah, had gone in and out of Lambeth Workhouse, and Charlie had been sent to yet another Poor Law school and then to his father, a man he barely knew, though he lived not far from the family in Lambeth. In time, Hannah's mental struggles had grown so severe that she was admitted to Cane Hill Lunatic Asylum in Coulsdon, Surrey, a sprawling Victorian-built institution like Stone Asylum, where Ellen was sent at around the same time. And like Ellen's, her behaviour was assessed in lunatic examination reports. "She was sent here on a mission by the Lord," one Cane Hill record states. "She says she wants to get out of this world." The reception orders for lunatics at Lambeth list her as a stage artist and say, "She is very strange in manner and quite incoherent. She dances, sings and cries by turn. She is indecent in conduct and conversation at times, and again at times praying and saying she has been born again." Charlie later wrote that when he first saw her at Cane Hill, when he was about fourteen, the wait in the visiting room was "almost unbearable." The nurse was condescending when she brought Hannah in. "It's a pity you came at such a time," she told him, glancing at Hannah. "We're not quite ourselves today, are we, dear?" Glibness aside, Charlie could see it was true. Hannah's lips were blue and her face was pale, and she did not seem cheered by the visit. Although she recognized him, "it was without enthusiasm; her old ebullience had gone."

No one knows whether Ellen Roff's children saw her at Stone Asylum, or whether anyone visited her and her mother, Mary, at Newington Workhouse, but pictures taken in such places show just the sort of woman Charlie described – depleted, and undoubtedly carrying some sense of shame. Though conditions in both types of institutions had continued to improve, the stigma remained for those entering, and for their relatives too. In the Newington Workhouse records, Fred Roff appears consistently as Ellen's husband and next of kin – with not a mention of John Humphreys – but it's hard to believe Fred had much to do with her after their worst years and the legal turmoil that followed when Ellen was brought to Stone. Aside from his one visit to her there, mentioned in the asylum's records, there was apparently no contact. Fred was fifty now, and Ellen just a little younger. They had spent more years apart than they'd spent together, and he had raised the children alone. Baby Emily was nearly twenty, and if she and her mother passed on the street, they might not have recognized each other. But such a moment was close to impossible, for Ellen rarely left the workhouse. In April 1914, when Fred succumbed to bronchitis and asthma cardiac failure – so-called potter's rot, caused by long-term exposure to silica dust after years of working at Doulton's – Ellen did not stand with their children at his burial. The singular change for Ellen was that Mary Anne's name replaced Fred's as next of kin in Newington's records.

All three of the Evans sisters – Ellen, Jennie and Mary Anne – were now widows. But this was the eve of the Great War, and there were plenty more widows to be made.

By 1914, tension in Europe was palpable. Disputes over trade and land, resentments from old grievances and suspicions of motives had broken the continent into camps, with Germany and Austria-Hungary forming the so-called Central Powers, later including the Ottoman Empire and Bulgaria. Britain was still firmly allied with France and Russia, but within her own dominion there was trouble everywhere. The Irish were bucking British rule, the Scots grumbled about independence, women bemoaned the lack of respect for their cause, and class wars rumbled ominously, stirred by events like the Lena Massacre in Russia, where the tsar's troops slaughtered striking gold miners. Despite the growing unrest from so many quarters, few thought the possibility of war with Germany a serious threat, and people took little heed of the news pasted on signboards outside smoke shops. The danger of war had become such a commonplace idea that it no longer had the power to disturb. H.G. Wells, later observing that an entire generation had grown up listening to talk of war, noted that "a threat that goes on for too long ceases to have the effect of a threat." Politicians also grew complacent, certain that the network of alliances they'd negotiated would maintain the status quo.

But at the end of July, the chain reaction began: following the assassination of Austrian archduke Franz Ferdinand, Austria declared war on Serbia, and a couple of days later Germany declared war on Russia, and then on France. The Salvation Army's new general, William Booth's son Bramwell, appealed to Salvationists all over the world to pray for peace. But on August 4, Germany invaded neutral Belgium to get to France, and Britain warned it would declare war if Germany didn't cease its attack by eleven p.m. Staff at the Central Telegraph Office, where Harry's brothers-in-law worked, put in long, anxious hours, and that evening people gathered in Trafalgar Square, at the War Office and outside Buckingham Palace, waiting out the ultimatum. The crowd at the palace was large but more or less orderly, especially when police put out an appeal for silence because the king was in a meeting inside. The minutes and hours ticked by, and at eight o'clock the king and queen and the Prince of Wales appeared briefly on the balcony and waved with their handkerchiefs, then slipped back inside. Late in the evening, as the music halls and theatres let out, still more people joined the throng, cheering and singing "Rule Britannia." Once the deadline had passed, a last direct cable message was sent to Berlin from the Central Telegraph Office, reading simply "GN" for "goodnight." The news made its way through the gathering: Britain was officially at war with Germany.

Beneath the somewhat exaggerated headline "World Wide War," one newspaper began its account of England's declaration of war on Germany with the sober statement "the die is cast," and counselled, "Be steadfast; unafraid." The tone of the writing was one of regret, the author claiming that "there is really no hatred of our enemy as a whole," and reminding people that "for the first time in the life of the present generation, Great Britain is at war with a first-class Power, and our skill and resources and endurance will be matched against the other branch of the Teutonic Race." Another paper announced the arrival of war more matter-of-factly, the headline reading simply "War." Largely confident in the might of the Royal Navy, journalists of the day advocated striking at Germany "swiftly and effectively" after rumours of firing off the coast of Scotland were confirmed, adding that "the appearance of the German fleet in the English Channel is the signal for action to the English fleet, the greatest and most effective naval fighting force that the skill and foresight of man has ever called into being."

And the first clashes were indeed at sea. Even before many Britons knew their country was at war, the German steamer *Königin Luise*, dressed up in the black, buff and yellow of the ferries that regularly plied the channel between Harwich and Holland, was spotted in the night by fishing boats, apparently dropping something overboard. When the fishermen later encountered the scout cruiser HMS *Amphion* on patrol with two destroyers, they reported the suspicious nighttime sighting. Unbeknownst to the fishermen, *Königin Luise* had been pressed into service as a minelayer, with orders from the German navy to spike the mouth of the Thames Estuary, and she managed to lay some two hundred charges below the surface of the water off the Suffolk coast before *Amphion* closed in and sank her, taking eighteen survivors on board. For the remainder of the day, *Amphion* continued her patrols without incident, but in the wee hours of the morning, headed for home, she hit one of the mines laid by *Königin Luise,* losing one officer, 150 sailors, and the eighteen rescued Germans before sinking herself. The war was just thirty-two hours old, and Germany and England were at a draw.

There are many descriptions of the summer day that war began for England in 1914, most of them from the perspective of the middle and upper classes. It was sultry and warm, the kind of weather that spawns cricket matches and lawn parties and leisurely outings to the countryside or the beach. A photo taken in the south of England shows three white-clad ladies seated in beach chairs, their feet encased in kid leather, their wide-brimmed hats shielding them from the sun. One holds an umbrella. Their heads are turned to one another as if in conversation, and none appear to notice the newspaper seller behind them, wearing a newsboy cap and carrying a signboard that reads "War Declaration Official." And though people generally were not oblivious or surprised, they were unaware of what England would be like once her khaki-clad soldiers began to disappear across the Channel to the trenches of France, and her sailors took to the sea, where the Royal Navy would find a formidable foe in Germany's submarines.

Soon recruitment posters began to appear in the streets, and in red, white and blue, with bold block-capital lettering, they urged men to OFFER YOUR SERVICES NOW. One quoted the king: "We are fighting for a worthy purpose, and we shall not lay down our arms until that purpose has been fully achieved." Men enlisted – or "rushed to the colours" – in droves in late August and early September, spurred on by a sense of duty or a sense of adventure, or both. Newspapers carried advertisements for a history simply titled *The Great War*, published serially as the conflict progressed. "Are *you* reading it?" the ads asked. "You can secure the book at trifling expense in sixpenny weekly parts which in due course will grow into handsome volumes and be one of your most treasured possessions in the years to come." There was no telling how many volumes there would be, because no one knew how long "the stupendous drama" would last. "The great war of 1914 may be short and sharp, or long drawn out. It may be rapidly concluded by a series of sweeping victories, or victory may incline now to one side, now to the other. But however it ends – and Britain is confident that it can have but one end – Europe will never be the same again."

Within those first weeks British soldiers left Southampton by the thousands, unaware of the statistics – underestimated – that suggested one in ten men would not return. Finished with practice drills and parading, they boarded the huge ships that transported them across the Channel to France, vessels also laden with field guns and horses and the stuff of war. When the soldiers arrived in Boulogne, they marched through the narrow streets in their khaki uniforms, chanting slogans and singing the latest music hall songs. "I can see them again with their brown jolly faces full of laughter," reported a special correspondent for the *Daily Mail*, "and hear them still shouting and singing 'It's a Long Way to Tipperary... it's a long way to go.'" Just a couple of days later the lyrics were printed in the *Daily Mail* under the heading "Song of the Moment." In a matter of days the song's publishers received a rush of orders for sheet music, and soon it was billed as "the Marching Anthem on the Battlefields of Europe...sung by the soldiers of the king."

The Salvation Army was likewise gathering its troops. Days after Britain had joined the fray, Bramwell Booth called on all Salvationists throughout the country to volunteer for Red Cross and ambulance work at home and abroad, and within a couple of weeks, papers reported that five hundred had come forward to form a foreign service contingent. People from all walks of life were finding ways to contribute to the cause. Long lists in the papers told of a doctor giving free first-aid lessons; a rich man offering an unused villa as an emergency hospital; a reverend giving over two motor cars; and a dog breeder offering his superbly trained bloodhounds to trace wounded men missed by the Red Cross. "They will wear a khaki-coloured coat, marked with a red cross."

The willingness to pitch in was balanced by a collective determination to live by the motto "business as usual," a catchphrase that began to appear at the tops of advertisements for all kinds of items. "With the exception of some of our staff who have gone to the front," read one ad, "we are working full hours and with full strength. Keep smiling, and make your homes bright and healthy by using Lightning Soap." Another said: "Those who intended to buy a PIANO and are putting it off because of the WAR – which we hope will soon be over – take our advice: buy NOW. You will save money, and help to keep men in work."

Even the suffragettes, for the most part, supported the troops and stopped stirring the pot. Emmeline Pankhurst and her daughter Christabel became avid supporters of the fight against Germany, though it meant a rift with two other daughters who were committed pacifists. Paradoxically, the shift in focus from women's rights to war work could only help the suffragettes' cause. Long before the mainstream accepted it, the first wartime issue of *Votes for Women* recognized that "everywhere women will have to take the public places left vacant by men... Necessity will compel men to accept the offer. There will be work of all kinds that will want doing, and women will have to do it." The writer warned, though, that women must not revert to their old subordinate roles but hold fast to the new ones once war was over. "The new spirit of women inculcated during the last decade must shine through all their labours and illuminate all their actions." And so it happened that as vast numbers of men left for training or actual battle, women stepped up as mail carriers, shopkeepers, clerks and even police officers. "Business as usual," yes, but the people conducting it had changed. A Britain's War Workers postcard bore images of the uniformed women and a little rhyme to describe them:

> *Behold the smart post lady*
> *Who brings letters to our houses;*
> *Also the tram conductor*
> *And these sweet things in trousers.*

Everyone was adapting to meet the needs of a country at war. Industries began converting their runs from the domestic to the military, so tailors sewed uniforms instead of dress shirts, and box makers swapped hat boxes for ammunition containers. The Borough Polytechnic where Maggie worked joined in to support the war effort too, putting students to work manufacturing gas masks and medical supplies, and running courses for the army in wheelwrighting and farrier skills. Throughout the country there were boundless opportunities for women, but some, like Maggie, preferred the status quo. She carried on at the school, and records tell us that Mary Anne was also part of "the army of charwomen" at this time. In the grainy rooftop photo of Aunt Maggie with her co-workers at the Borough Polytechnic there's a woman at the end of the row of cleaners who resembles Mary Anne, though any who could confirm it with confidence are long dead. Still, the likeness is striking. She looks harder now than in earlier photographs when Harry was alive but wears a similar almost-smile and a knowing, albeit mysterious, expression. Charing was work every able-bodied woman could perform with little training, according to *Married Women's Work*, "therefore in her hour of direst need every able-bodied woman turns to it." It was certainly preferable to the workhouse.

Ellen and her mother, Mary, were still at Newington, but that autumn Mary was staying in the sick ward, suffering from enteritis, an inflammation of the small intestine with symptoms of diarrhea and vomiting. One Tuesday, while crossing the ward, she was "seized with giddiness" and collapsed onto the floor. She was taken to the East Dulwich Infirmary, but she died two days later, at age sixty-seven, and the coroner deemed the cause was "syncope, due to enteritis, accelerated by the fall." The death certificate lists her as "widow of David Evans, brewer's stoker." Nearly thirty years had passed since David's death on Red Cross Street, and poor "Lazy Mary" had spent much of that time in workhouses, growing old in institutional care and becoming just the kind of person Samuel Barnett had lamented: "The world loses more than it knows when such lives are left in our workhouses to wear away in sorrowful uselessness." Charles Booth agreed it was no way to finish out a life. During his inquiry, touring even the better workhouses brought on "a feeling of utter depression; so monotonous is the existence; so essentially comfortless; so often unrelieved by pleasant human relationships." One hopes this was not the case for Mary, since her daughter was in the workhouse with her, but there's no telling whether Mary and Ellen encountered one another very often in a place that held hundreds of people, or whether they were even close. Mary's connection to the rest of the family at the end of her life is also unknown. But she was buried in a common grave at Nunhead Cemetery rather than at Brookwood, the designated resting place for many of London's unclaimed workhouse inmates. Does this mean that the family held at least a rudimentary funeral when Mary died? Or had she been more or less forgotten, her quiet death a harbinger for Ellen's own in the years to come?

Outside the workhouse walls, Ellen's remaining family went on living their lives without her. The second Flo, her daughter with John Humphreys, was seventeen, the age Ellen had been when she'd married Fred Roff and moved from the Borough to Lambeth. Her two eldest daughters with Fred had each married that year, Florence number one in the summer and Ellen Elizabeth, possible census dodger, at Christmas. Son Freddie had joined the Royal Sussex Regiment just a few months into the war as part of the "rush to the colours," but more surprising was the fact that Fred Roff senior's brother Charles had also enlisted that October, giving his age as thirty-four when actually he was almost fifty. He was a short, somewhat wide man according to his service record, with grey hair, a fresh complexion and an anchor tattooed on his left forearm. To make his application convincing, he left off mentioning the first six of his children and included only the youngest four, but he gave his correct wedding date, which would have made him a seven-year-old groom. The authorities either missed or ignored this oddity, and Charles was taken on as a driver, but his army career lasted only 160 days, into March 1915, when he was discharged as "not being likely to become an efficient soldier." There is a clue that he made an impression on someone, though, because the very next record under R belongs to his taller, slimmer, twenty-four-year-old son, also Charles, joining one month after his father's unceremonious exit.

Failure to enlist often earned men the gift of a white feather, a symbol of cowardice encouraged by the Order of the White Feather. Founded in 1914 by Royal Navy Admiral Charles Fitzgerald, the movement was also championed by women with opposing views on suffrage, such as Mary Ward, the first president of the Anti-Suffrage League, and Emmeline and Christabel Pankhurst. Though they disagreed on the issue of votes for women, they all agreed that a man out of uniform must be a coward, and should be publicly labelled as such. One London newspaper ran a sarcastic want ad calling for "petticoats for all able-bodied youths in this country who have not yet joined the Navy or Army," while another looked for recruits to hand out feathers: "Oyez! Oyez!… Ladies wanted to present to young men…who have no one dependent on them the Order of the White Feather for shirking their duty in not offering their services to uphold the Union Jack of Old England."

Such tactics were so successful that men whose skills were needed at home were no longer around, and the void had to be filled by women. But it would only be temporary; the war would be done by Christmas, people said, and then by spring. It kept on and on, though, and the casualties mounted. In 1914 alone, between August and December, nearly 90,000 men of the British Expeditionary Force were killed or wounded, or had gone missing. The two Bottone boys – sons of the Italian ice cream vendor who'd been Harry and Mary Anne's neighbour in Red Cross Street – enlisted, but only one of them would return: Frank, who had gone in and out of the Evelina Hospital with pertussis and bron-cho-pneumonia and chicken pox and a concussion from being run over. He and his less fortunate brother Lorenzo were close to Joe's age, as were so many others who looked older and wiser in uniform, and sud-denly carried themselves differently. In Canada, Bebbie's sister's young grandson enlisted but was later discharged as being physically unfit. The record doesn't give the reason – perhaps something happened to George in service that made him no longer viable. That was the case for Bebbie's nephew, Tom, who started out as a fair candidate for a sol-dier. He stood nearly five foot ten and had an impressive girth when fully expanded. His vision was good, and his hearing was satisfactory; he was assigned to the Royal Garrison Artillery as a gunner. But he was discharged when he suffered hearing loss in his right ear. His medical re-port says his deafness was not attributable to his war service, but points instead to a depressed scar on his forehead incurred twenty years earlier when he was hit with a stone. Several times the report mentions the stone and the deafness together, so the implication is that the old injury caused Tom's hearing loss, which was aggravated by his service in the artillery to the point that the drum was perforated and oozed mucous for a time.

The noise of war truly was deafening, and for gunners especial-ly. The sound of thousands of shells bursting, of grenades exploding, of the constant firing of small arms – all of it melded into a sickening "storm of noise" that shuddered through the body. The sound was so loud that some men described it as a physical thing: a wall or an oppres-sive ceiling. "It did not move; it hung over us … It did not begin, inten-sify, decline, and end. It was poised in the air, a stationary panorama of sound, a condition of the atmosphere, not the creation of man." How-ever it was described – "a diabolical uproar," "a sustained crescendo," "a symphony" – the noise of war was loud enough to actually split the eardrum. And then there were the noises soldiers wished they couldn't hear: the screams of the freshly wounded, the groans of men who took forever to die, the squealing rats and the buzzing flies drawn by the stench of decay, and in quiet moments the birds, whose singing made the violence more awful.

As Bebbie worried about her nephews, and about neighbours' sons in College Buildings, and about co-workers at the cork factory, she added Joe Deverill to the list and commiserated with Mary Anne. Joe had turned seventeen in January 1915, and by the end of March he'd joined the Royal Navy. The only hint that Mary Anne didn't want him to go is a granddaughter's impression that he "ran away to sea." And yet Joe entered with the rank of Boy 2nd class, and the Royal Navy's publication, the *Navy List*, stipulated that "every boy must obtain the consent of his parent or guardian, or nearest relative to his entering the Navy and engaging to serve until he shall have completed 12 years' continuous service from the age of 18." If she didn't forbid him from going, perhaps she just wished he wouldn't, like many mothers. A number of recruitment posters appealed to "the Women of Britain," implying they were being selfish by keeping their men at home. Consider what the Germans had done in Belgium, the posters urged, and what they would do in England, given the chance. "Do you realise that the safety of your home and children depends on our getting more men NOW? ... When the war is over and someone asks your husband or your son what he did in the great War, is he to hang his head because you would not let him go?"

Joe's certificate of service says that, "on entry as a Boy," he had brown hair, grey eyes and a fair complexion. He stood four foot eleven and a half inches, and measured thirty-three and a half inches around the chest, well shy of the ideal sailor's physique. The *Navy List* stated only that his height and chest measurement be "sufficient," and allowances were made for the fact that a boy this age was still growing. (Joe, however, was pretty much done and only managed to stretch three-quarters of an inch more by the time he reached manhood.) Aside from being "of robust frame, intelligent, of perfectly sound and healthy constitution, free from any physical defects or malformation, and not subject to fits," it was essential that Joe be of good character, able to read, write and recite a short passage, and aware of the first four rules of arithmetic. He was already tidy and particular, and the Navy would only hone those skills. All of his clothes and bedding had to be marked in a specific way – blue clothes with white paint, white clothes with black paint, hats and caps in the crown, towels and handkerchiefs diagonally across the corner; the list went on in excruciating detail. The rules were equally strict about what he could wear and when. He had a ceremonial uniform, "on leave" clothes and ordinary working-day clothes. For general cleaning of the ship, or "when better clothing would be spoiled," he was to wear his white working jumper and duck trousers. For the dirtiest jobs, such as coaling and refitting, he had overalls. There was a special, rather complicated way to tie his neckerchief so that the tails were just so. His hat or cap had to sit squarely on his head, not dashingly off to the side however tempting that might be, and the ribbon around it must be tied in a bow over his left ear, perfectly placed so that the centre of the lettering lined up with his nose. Glove, mitts and comforters could only be worn in especially raw conditions and during night watches; if he was unwell, though, he could apply for special permission from the medical officer to wear a comforter in the daytime provided he placed it "one turn round the throat, and a half hitch, the ends being tucked inside the jumper and trousers." If in mourning, he could wear "a band of black crepe two inches wide, and of double thickness, round the left arm, midway between the point of the shoulder and the point of the elbow." Last but not least in his kit came life-saving gear: a swimming collar and an inflated belt best worn just under the breast and above the waist – though of course the shorter the man, the less room he had there. On Joe's certificate of service, beside the query "can swim," the answer is "yes" but should have been qualified. He could only swim poorly, family lore tells us, so the inflatable belt was a doubly valued possession. Given his aversion to water, once he was out at sea did the vastness frighten him? If he thought he was invincible, the 1915 issue of the *Navy List* gave strong evidence to the contrary. In with the regulations, the descriptions of medals and the alphabetical account of active officers, the *List* published the names of all the Navy's men killed in action between September and December 1914 – seventy-two pages' worth in those first few months of the war.

For training, Joe was stationed to HMS *Vivid*, a sprawling barracks at Devonport on the south coast of England. Joe had never been so far from home, but he was used to cramped London slums, so the barracks, filled with a thousand or more men and boys learning to be sailors and sleeping in hammocks 125 to a room, might not have been too daunting. Each room was three storeys high and laid out to mock a ship's mess deck, with tables that could be hauled up on ropes, and stowaway hammocks hung in rows in the middle. There was a clock tower with a bell that struck the hours, and a gymnasium, and galleys for cooking. There was a canteen, a large parade ground and a drill shed so the boys could exercise in wet weather. Reminiscent of the Goulston Street baths in Whitechapel were the heated swimming baths used year-round, purpose-built for recruits years earlier when the Navy realized many of its sailors-in-training could not swim.

By May, Joe had learned how to mend, patch and wash his own clothes, keep his locker tidy and obey orders, although it seems he'd been rather good at those things before joining the Navy. He'd risen from Boy 2nd class to Boy 1st class and moved from HMS *Vivid* in Devonport to HMS *Ganges* in Shotley on the Sussex coast, close to where the *Amphion* had met her end and also nearer to home, though he wouldn't be visiting. He was busy learning knotting and splicing, and how to "heave the lead," read a compass and pull in a boat. For a two-month stint he had the rank of Signal Boy, meaning he'd passed an examination and been given a chance to learn the code of flag signals used by ships to communicate with one another. But Joe was not cut out for the job. A notation in the margin of his service record states "rating altered," and on the next line Joe's status is returned to Boy 1st class, where he remained until his eighteenth birthday and automatic promotion to Ordinary Seaman. This would have suited Joe just fine. By all family accounts he was without ambition, content to get by rather than get ahead. A photograph taken of Joe around the time he became a "Boy" shows a young man in a sailor suit, his hair parted on the side and neatly combed. It's a head and shoulders shot, so it's not obvious how small he is, but his eyes are large and his expression is earnest.

Around the same time that Joe "ran away to sea," Doris was enrolled at Charles Dickens School. She was nearly five years old and walked to and fro with Ernie, who held fast to her hand ever since the incident with the cowcatcher. Once at school, though, Ernie and Doris separated, she entering through the Infants' door on the ground level, he watching her go with the other small children and then climbing the stairs to the Boys' entrance. Before letting go of her hand, he might have knelt in the asphalt playground and pointed out the door, directing her gaze to the grey stone letters over the lintel.

"Infants is you, Dor. Boys is me."

Even if she was nervous, Doris would have teased him. "Infants is *I*, you mean," pointing to the big letter that would help her remember where to go. She was only just learning to read, but she relished the idea that letters made words, and that the word above her door was longer than the word above Ernie's. Right from the beginning she loved school, both the hard work and the play. Recently the London County Council had begun providing schools with dolls and model houses and makeshift nurseries in order to teach the girls to be efficient mothers one day – though they had new role models too, in the skirted bus drivers and letter carriers.

On account of the war, Ernie and his fellow classmates were learning to knit, a task Ernie didn't mind and, in fact, was rather good at. It was solitary work, and the repetitive motion of looping the wool round the needle and creating a neat row of stitches was satisfying in the same way painting was. The things the students made – scarves if they were just learning, socks when they'd mastered the trick of turning a heel – were sent to the soldiers fighting across the Channel, and so they knitted in brown and grey and khaki. The class was quiet while the needles clicked, as boys imagined who would wear the items they made. Ernie would have thought of Joe and wondered if sailors needed scarves even more than the soldiers did.

Knitters could buy manuals like the one put out by yarn manufacturer John Paton, Son & Co: "Directions for Knitting Soldiers' and Sailors' Comforts." Inside were detailed instructions for making balaclava helmets with and without ear slits, chest and neck protectors, cholera belts, hospital stockings and hospital slippers. The children of Charles Dickens School were only one small part of a large population of diligent knitters. Across the country, men, women and children of varying skill fashioned items that were sometimes "of unusual shape," according to Constance Peel, a novelist who also wrote about domestic matters for newspapers and magazines like *The Lady*. "We knitted at theatres, in trains and trams, in parks and parlours, in the intervals of eating in restaurants, of serving in canteens. Men knitted, children knitted, a little girl promoted to four needles anxiously asked her mother, 'Mummie, do you think I shall live to finish this sock?'"

Knitting was serious business. One manual stated firmly that the money from its sale supported the soldiers, and "anyone lending the book to a friend who can afford to buy one defrauds the Allies." On an emotional level, the handmade items connected those who made them with those who received them and gave a sense of comfort to both groups. Often the gifts arrived with messages tucked inside, but even without good wishes, warm, dry socks were appreciated by men in the trenches. For people at home, it was gratifying to make something useful; the more accomplished knitters found the act itself therapeutic, as the journalist and poet Jessie Pope noted in "Socks," one of her many motivational wartime pieces:

> *Shining pins that dart and click*
> *In the fireside's sheltered peace*
> *Check the thoughts that cluster thick –*
> *20 plain and then decrease.*

> *He was brave – well so was I –*
> *Keen and merry, but his lip*
> *Quivered when he said goodbye –*
> *Purl the seam-stitch, purl and slip.*

> *Never used to living rough,*
> *Lots of things he'd got to learn;*
> *Wonder if he's warm enough –*
> *Knit 2, catch 2, knit 1, turn.*

Hark! The paper-boys again,
Wish that shout could be suppressed;
Keeps one always on the strain –
Knit off 9 and slip the rest.

Wonder if he's fighting now,
What he's done an' where he's been;
He'll come out on top somehow –
Slip 1, knit 2, purl 14.

In the spring of 1915 the peril for fighting soldiers increased. High explosive shells were being fired off faster than they could be produced,
and more factories and workers were crucial. A Ministry of Munitions
was created to deal with the catastrophe and to oversee weapons production throughout the war. At its head was former Chancellor of the
Exchequer David Lloyd George, who'd had plenty of run-ins with suffragettes over the years, but now joined forces with them in his quest for
a solution to the shell shortage. Two years earlier, Emmeline Pankhurst
had happily announced "we have blown up [his] house" – an exaggeration, but just one example of the suffragette militancy so rampant at
that time. Her daughter Christabel had declared Lloyd George a fair target for suffragettes because "he is always betraying us." But now Lloyd
George enlisted his old foe to help him urge women into munitions
work. As one newspaper put it, "Once They Were Enemies, War Has
Made Them Friends."

Though it had been *he* who'd asked for *her* assistance, Emmeline
Pankhurst turned that notion around when she approached her followers. "So grave is our national danger, and so terrible is the loss of
precious lives at the front due to shortage of munitions, that Mr. Lloyd
George, as Minister of Munitions, has been asked to receive a deputa-
tion and hear women's demand for the right to make munitions and
render other War Service...Will you help?" Together thousands of
women marched to the Ministry of Munitions, and though it poured
rain, one paper called it "one of the most successful outdoor demon-
strations that London has ever seen." As the crowds assembled, Lloyd

CHAPTER 9

George's impish young daughter peered down on the women from the balcony and blew kisses. Women carried Union Jacks rather than suf-fragette flags, and their banners boasted slogans like "Shells made by a wife may save her husband's life." Lloyd George was surely delighted. "The women of this country can help," he assured them. "On behalf of the nation I am entitled to thank you for the services you have offered." Though he refused to implement all of Pankhurst's demands regarding equal pay, he agreed that a fixed minimum wage was only fair, so that munitions work wouldn't be one more version of sweated labour.

Despite the novelty of women doing men's work, the entire nation knitting in khaki and patriotic posters plastered across entire blocks of buildings, Londoners were only now experiencing first-hand the fright-ening thrill of real war. Although columns of men had drilled in the parks, and talk of combat had been on everyone's lips, war had been the stuff of newspaper reports and gossip, somehow set apart from daily life. And even the newspapers did not print or always know the whole story. The Defense of the Realm Act, or DORA, passed shortly after Britain entered the war, outlawed kite flying and required pubs to shut at nine-thirty p.m., but also declared that "no person shall by word of mouth or in writing spread reports likely to cause disaffection or alarm among any of His Majesty's forces or among the civilian population." With DORA's authority, the government held the power of censorship and shared official information stingily. Newspapers made what they could of it, and were even complicit in the public's ignorance: horrific and sometimes fictitious accounts of death and destruction were re-served for the German side, while the heroic "Tommies" soldiered on, their battle success portrayed with some exaggeration. And although casualties were reported, the numbers were optimistically low. As the months wore on, however, the evidence began to return home, and there was no way to hide the trains that pulled in to Victoria Station bearing the wounded, or the stretchers lined up on the platforms, or the predominant red and white of Red Cross ambulance markings, banda-ges and blood. And there was no way to deny the experiences of the soldiers themselves: the awful "no man's land" between the trenches – tracts of churned mud and barbed wire where snipers targeted any sign of movement – or the greenish yellow chlorine gas clouds that killed without a bullet fired.

For Londoners, the greatest fear so far was of an attack by air. Powered, controlled flight was still a relatively new concept, but as H.G. Wells had written in his novel *The War in the Air*, published in 1908, "There isn't a big Power in Europe, or Asia, or America, or Africa, that hasn't got at least one or two flying machines hidden up its sleeve at the present time. Not one. Real, workable flying machines." The writing was a work of fiction but wasn't far off the mark, though some countries were savvier than others in seeing the potential such machines held. Germany's Zeppelins – giant floating airships buoyed by hydrogen-filled gasbags – were developed in the 1890s. And in 1909 the British government contracted Vickers, Sons and Maxim to design and build a similar model as an aerial scout ship for the Royal Navy. The *Mayfly*, as she was known, broke in half while being transported to her testing grounds and never actually took flight. Following that disappointment, British emphasis shifted to the development of "aeroplanes." By 1911 the War Office was still "not yet convinced that either aeroplanes or airships will be of any utility in the war." Flight was still in its infancy, but war would more than help it grow.

In January 1915 two Zeppelins raided the southeast coast of England, attacking Yarmouth and Sheringham and King's Lynn, and killing four people. An attack on Southend-on-Sea in May killed just one woman and a dog and a cat. From a military perspective the raids were trivial, but they were both ominous and dramatic to a public that so far had been protected from the ugliness of war by geography. As attacks continued, terrifying stories spread: one woman was stepping off a tram when a bomb dropped on her head, killing her instantly. Another died when a bomb fell in the street in front of her house. She opened her door and was struck by a shell fragment. A little girl died in bed when an incendiary bomb came through the roof, the petrol from the bomb lighting her bedclothes on fire.

The War Office assumed that London's docks would eventually be a target and used the attacks to aid recruitment. Posters showed the eerie shape of a Zeppelin lit by searchlights in a night sky, St. Paul's

CHAPTER 9

unmistakable dome in black silhouette. Below the picture the caption read "It is far better to face the bullets than to be killed at home by a bomb. Join the army at once and help to stop an air raid. God save the King." In spite of the War Office's own propaganda, it did not count the Zeppelins a viable threat, expecting that the ponderous machines would be vulnerable to the British planes that would jump to the country's defense. Before the war began, Winston Churchill, then First Lord of the Admiralty, overseeing the Royal Naval Air Service, boasted that "any hostile aircraft, airships, or aeroplanes which reached our coast during the coming year would be promptly attacked in superior force by a swarm of very formidable hornets." What Churchill and others in authority did not take into consideration was the great height at which the airships travelled – some ten thousand feet in the air – and the fact that they could navigate at night, when other aircraft had difficulty taking off and landing.

As a precaution against the Zeppelins, London's street lights were dimmed, householders were told to pull curtains across the windows of lighted rooms, and searchlights raked the skies over the city each night for a few hours. But there was no dimming the winding sparkle of the Thames on a starry night, and on May 31, 1915, a Zeppelin did float over the city, dropping close to one hundred bombs on north and east London, killing seven people. One newspaper gloated that "the heart of the city has not yet been reached," but then warned that the attack was most likely experimental; more would follow. The paper claimed that there was "no panic or fuss" in the city during the bombing, but in the next breath scolded the War Office for releasing only the barest details. As a result, "a large number of absurd and exaggerated rumours were quickly in circulation, among them being that hundreds of people had been killed, that Liverpool-street Station had been destroyed, and that the bombs had been dropped in the busiest thoroughfares in London."

Censored British papers weren't allowed to print exactly where the Zeppelins dropped their bombs, but Mary Anne likely knew. One of the districts hit in that first London raid was Whitechapel, so from Bebbie she'd have heard that a shoe factory was destroyed and that a bomb went through the roof of St. Mary's church, not far from Bebbie's flat in College Buildings. When the attack was over, people flooded into the streets to peer at the rubble and the torn buildings and to exchange tales of heroisms and near misses. It was exciting but also frightening, and although the damage would not have surprised men who'd seen the carnage of the trenches, for Londoners like Mary Anne and Bebbie it was a shock to realize that their island city, protected by the might of their legendary Navy, could be breached. Though there was apparently no panic, there was dismay and then anger that their enemy would target civilians, and that no reliable system of defense existed to protect them from further attacks. Soon posters appeared with silhouetted images highlighting the difference between German and British airplanes and airships so people wouldn't be alarmed over every aircraft spotted. The posters also advised what should be done if they saw a German craft: "take shelter immediately in the nearest available house, preferably in the basement, and remain there until the aircraft have left the vicinity: do not stand about in crowds and do not touch unexploded bombs." Naval guns were installed at Tower Bridge and Regent's Park and manned by Royal Marines, and volunteers were armed with machine guns and some acetylene searchlights that reportedly had less candlepower than a car's headlamp. Alfred Rawlinson, appointed Lieutenant-Commander of the Royal Naval Volunteer Service soon after the attacks, later wrote that the defense was completely inadequate, "as not only was it quite impossible for it to inflict any injury upon Zeppelin airships, but it was equally impossible that these guns could be fired over London without causing considerable injury to the unfortunate people whom they were intended to protect." But resources were needed at the Front and elsewhere, and the May attack and earlier Zeppelin raids on the coast had shown that the airships too were ineffective on a large scale, and the actual danger they posed was statistically small.

Yet the psychological impact was significant. For much of the summer of 1915 the Zeppelins approached no closer than England's coast, but the mere sight of an airship plunged towns into darkness, halted trams, delayed newspapers and interrupted plays and music hall performances. In displays of bravado, audiences stood in the dark and sang "God Save the King." And in London, people waited, wondering when the airships would ghost up the Thames, moving almost silently because of their great height, then hover over their targets and release death. As the daylight faded each evening, Mary Anne must have peered past the curtain and out her window in the Goodwin, knowing that the best time for a raid was a clear but moonless night and, like countless other Londoners, hoping for rain or cloud. On those nights, and when there was a full moon, everyone slept more soundly in their beds.

Summer passed quietly. The blackouts continued and people remained vigilant. Zeppelins visited the coastal areas but did not venture up the Thames. Mary Anne, busily scrubbing floors, had plenty to occupy her thoughts. Ellen's son, Freddie Roff, had completed his training with the Royal Sussex Regiment and been sent to France, from whence so many of England's boys never returned. Then there was Joe, afloat on black seas that hid mines and submarines. Enemy destroyers threatened his days, but he'd chosen the life of a sailor and seemed content. And if it was any consolation, propaganda appeared in all forms to assure Mary Anne she'd done the right thing by letting her son go to war. As the song said, "We don't want to lose you, but we think you ought to go." On the practical side, Joe's livelihood meant there was one less mouth to feed at home, and more money coming in.

Ethel was still working for the cardboard box factory, and war had boosted her wages. Cardboard was in great demand: boxes of all sizes were needed for care parcels for the soldiers and sailors, for the boots and shoes and hats that made up their uniforms, for the medals that got pinned to them and for the ammunition they used. Cardboard discs hung in windows, proudly announcing that the man who lived there was off fighting for king and country. Inspired by such fellows, the War Game Co. churned out tiny cardboard soldiers that came in batches of one hundred, complete with authentic uniforms, armoured cars, tents, nurses and horses illustrated at full gallop. Ethel's work hours were likely longer than they had been, and when she came home with the smell of glue on her clothes, she still had plenty of chores to do.

And Ernie – dear, worrisome Ernie – Mary Anne's diligent knitter, particular and careful, satisfied with his own company and his roller skates. Others in the family thought him strange and somewhat slow, and it was true that he did not have Joe's pragmatism or Ethel's steadiness. Even little Doris, just five, could get one up on him, though he was almost twelve now. Doris, Mary Anne's baby, was clever and eager to learn, and unhampered by old sadnesses. It had been three years since Harry died, and Doris didn't remember him at all. She viewed the world around her, with its smart military uniforms, war songs and slogans, Red Cross nurses and air raids, as if this was the way things had always been.

It was not the world Mary Anne would have chosen for her children. In September the Zeppelins targeted London again, raiding two nights in a row, dropping thirty-five bombs in Bermondsey and another fifty in the East End. The earlier warning to people to stay inside seemed to have been forgotten, and the curious gathered in the streets, craning their necks at the spectacle in the sky, oohing and aahing at the "brilliantly white flashes of shrapnel." War correspondent William G. Shepherd wrote the following account for American newspapers:

Traffic is at a standstill. A million quiet cries make a subdued roar. Seven million people of the biggest city in the world stand gazing into the sky from the darkened streets. Here is the climax to the twentieth century! Among the autumn stars floats a long, gaunt Zeppelin. It is dull yellow – the colour of the harvest moon. The long fingers of the searchlights, reaching up from the roofs of the city, are touching all sides of the death messenger with their white tips. Great booming sounds shake the city. They are Zeppelin bombs – falling – killing – burning… At the gateway [to St. Paul's] stands the old verger, half dressed. It has been his duty for the last fifty years to guard the church against thieves and fires as other sextons have guarded it for centuries past. But he's got a bigger job on his hands than any of them ever had before. The verger's white-haired wife stands beside him. They are talking with three girls such as never come into the lives of church sextons except on nights like this. They are pointing out to the aged couple, with cheaply jewelled fingers, the slowly fading yellow form of the Zeppelin.

The very next day the demand for a better defense system grew loud. Disregarding DORA, people signed petitions and staged protests, and by the time the Zeppelins revisited in October, the Anti-Aircraft Defense Force had been formed and training had begun, and Lieutenant-Commander Rawlinson had secured a single high-powered mobile anti-aircraft gun from Paris. A plan was established that included the selection of searchlight stations and fixed gun locations, and the Anti-Aircraft Mobile Brigade was set up, complete with high-speed vehicles that would do fifty miles per hour while blaring their klaxons. When five Zeppelins were sighted motoring into British airspace on October 13, Rawlinson and his crew leapt into action. They raced through London to the pre-selected gunning site in Moorgate Street in a convoy that consisted of Rawlinson's armoured car, a vehicle bearing ammunition for the French gun, and another towing the gun itself. The streets were filled with vehicular and pedestrian traffic, but the Brigade careened through, and people jumped out of their way. Rawlinson later wrote of the night with almost boyish delight:

I feel quite confident that no man who took that drive will ever forget any part of it... I had such an anxious job myself that I had no time to laugh, but I am sure I smiled all the way... The noise of our sirens being as deafening as the glare of our headlights was dazzling, the omnibuses in every direction were seeking safety on the pavement. I also observed, out of the corner of my eye, several instances of people flattening themselves against the shop windows, the public being at that time infinitely more fearful of a gun moving at such a terrific speed than they were of any German bombs, of whose possibilities they had then but little experience.

The enemy had no idea London had finally acquired a high explosive anti-aircraft gun, and when the commander of the Zeppelin spotted the illuminated gun, parked in a pool of light from the armoured car, he steered his craft toward it, assuming it was one of the harmless, short-range guns used against them previously. The Brigade fired several shells at the airship, seeing with satisfaction that although they did not hit their target, they burst above and quite close to it. The ship then passed into some fog and disappeared, but Rawlinson wrote that the German commander had been made nervous enough by the shells bursting around him that he'd dropped all his bombs at once, and also his water ballast, giving him the lightness and speed he needed to escape. Lieutenant-Commander Rawlinson was pleased with the night's work, and noted as an aside that the bombs dropped so hurriedly by the Zeppelin "fell close together in the neighbourhood of Petticoat Lane."

Bebbie's perspective on the night differed from Rawlinson's. So close to Petticoat Lane in her Wentworth Street flat, she must have felt each thump and heard the boom of explosions and the crash of glass. The raid claimed seventy-one lives in various locations as the Zeppelins dispersed, and although not naming areas specifically, a newspaper reported that one damaged neighbourhood consisted entirely of "working class property, with small, low buildings, some of them used as small shops or businesses, but in most cases occupied, and in many cases overcrowded ... One group of small houses in this area was entirely destroyed by a single explosive bomb, and in the ruins, above which floats an evil smell of gas and drains, are to be found, torn and covered with dust, the account books and documents of some small business which, up to half-past nine on Wednesday night, no doubt kept alive the owner and his family." Seeing the piles of rubble, Bebbie might have considered chance, and the randomness of the destruction, and marvelled that a family on one side of the street remained alive while neighbours on the other side died.

Now living in Croydon, south of the city, Harry's sister Ada also had a close-up view of the ruin a Zeppelin could leave behind. A couple of hours after the raid on London, at about eleven p.m., a local man thought he heard a hissing sound that might be gas as it was syphoned from a street lamp. He listened harder and wondered if it was just steam escaping from a factory's chimney. When the noise grew louder and deeper, he decided it must be a vehicle approaching from a distance – but all three times it seemed to him that the sound was coming from the sky. Before he had time to process that thought, a flash brightened the entire neighbourhood as if it were daytime, and an explosion shook the ground. More explosions followed as a Zeppelin crossed over Croydon, dropping bombs that might have been meant for the railway lines or the munitions factory in Cherry Orchard Road, but that fell instead on homes and the families inside them. One family lost all three of its sons that night: "The youngest was dead when they reached him, the second was dead when he reached the hospital, and the eldest died a little later from shock, while the father was injured and in mental collapse from his terrible loss."

Loss had become commonplace, especially for the very young, whose formative years were being shaped by war. At school, air raids and their accompanying destruction became folded into the curriculum like any other childhood experience. Student essays from Princeton Street School in Holborn in London's West End detail the collision of feelings boys like Ernie experienced with the arrival of the "Zeps." "I was shivering like a jelly," one boy confessed, and another recalled how "each one of us were tremberling" at the sound of the explosions and the shattering glass. One boy's description is peppered with the sounds of the attack: "shrieks and screams that would have done credit to a hyena" and "Bang! Crash! Tinkle! Tinkle!" and "Boom! Whiz!" and finally "Sizzle! Sizzle! Siz – zzzzzz! Sizzle!" as the firemen quelled the blazes resulting from the bombs. Once the Zeppelin had drifted out of sight, the fires became the focus. "The National Penny Bank was blazing like a bonfire," the boy recalled, and a fireman ran up the rungs of his ladder "like a monkey running up a tree." Another boy described the flames as both terrible and terrific, and said that as soon as one fire was subdued, another had burst out. The boys wrote about the attacks and their aftermath in the days immediately following their occurrence, while the details were still fresh, and their hearts, no doubt, still pounding.

"All of a sudden I was awakened by a reverberating roar, like lions when they are hungry," one boy recounted:

I leapt out of bed like a slice of greased lightning and slipped into my clothes. I then heard a sound like a tattoo on a kettle drum. I looked out of a window and saw a searchlight flitting about. Someone shouts "Put your lights out!" and I obeyed…I went downstairs and looking up I saw an elongated shape not unlike a cigar and of a silver grey in colour. There were little splashes of flame around it but none appeared to hit it. After a while I thought I'd like to have a look at a gun. I went round the first turning on the left and in front of me was a reservoir. Standing on the pavement I could see the gun with short sharp pieces of red flashing from the muzzle. After a time the airship sheered of[f] into a southwesterly direction. I watched it for a while and then I went home to bed.

But sleep wasn't always quick to come, for once the Zeppelins had attacked, the possibility of another raid was hard to ignore. That was evident in the account of the "Bang! Crash! Tinkle!" boy, who wrote of his cousin watching warily through the window long after the Zeppelin had left.

"'Look Jack,' she said pointing to the Pole Star.

'Isn't that a Zeppelin's light?'

'Silly,' said I, 'that is a star.'"

He was confident that the raid was over for now, but in its aftermath he noted that "all was dark and silent as the tomb."

By the light of day, everyone found ways to carry on, and humour eased the burden. After the September raids, *Punch* ran a cartoon of an old man painting a sign on his ruined shop: *Business as usual during alterations*, though there was nothing left standing but part of one wall. Games and books appeared that poked fun at Germany and the Kaiser. In the Trench Football board game, the idea was to guide a soccer ball through a maze of falling, bumbling German officers and into the gaping mouth of Kaiser Bill. The poem "Swollen-headed William" spoofed the well-known nursery rhyme "Shock-headed Peter," and included a bulbous caricature of the Kaiser, with this scolding text:

Look at William! There he stands,
With the blood upon his hands.
His moustaches daunt the sky,
Pointing to his great Ally.
What of Heaven William thinks
Is no riddle of the Sphinx,
But a matter much more dim
Is what Heaven thinks of him.

Tales of battlefield glory were repeated in the streets and at school, encouraging patriotism with even the youngest souls, and on Empire Day teachers and their charges went out parading, wearing vests of Union Jacks and waving smaller versions of the flag. Miniature rifle ranges were set up in church crypts so boys could learn to shoot, and girls parcelled up knitting and tinned food for the soldiers at the Front, enclosing letters of encouragement. Boys could join the Boys' Brigade or the Boy Scouts and wear a soldier-like uniform, and members of these organizations were chosen to deliver messages for the War Office and guard railway lines and water reservoirs. Before too long they were recruited as part of the Zeppelin defense system, riding bicycles through London's streets and calling out air raid warnings, and afterward riding again, blowing bugles to signal all clear.

Nothing was left to chance where the hearts and minds of the youngest citizens were concerned. The Women's Emergency Corps converted Bedford College in Baker Street into a toy factory, teaching unemployed young women how to make wooden toys in a military theme. Their creations included battleships, wagons, ambulances and figures such as Jack of the Navy and Lord Kitchener, whose face and pointing finger adorned recruitment posters. Each toy bore the trademark of a lion's paw – the historic English symbol synonymous with bravery – so whether you'd built the toy, bought the toy or played with the toy, you were assured of doing your part for "Old Blighty."

Ernie might have owned a wooden battleship or even a Jack of the Navy figure, but the Deverill household had little money to spare, so such a toy in Ernie's possession would have been something handy

Uncle Jack had built. Jack was close by again, having taken a flat in the Goodwin, where May continued to live with Maggie and Clara, and where Mary Anne and her lot stayed at number 4. Why Jack came back to the Borough is unclear, but he was one of the few men in the family left nearby, and his presence was likely appreciated. Many of his own generation – Harry, Fred Roff and Richard Vanson – had died early, never to know of the war, and the younger ones – Joe, Ellen's son Freddie, and Richard's nephews – were at war or going.

Freddie had been lucky when he'd arrived as a fresh recruit on the Western Front in June. The summer had been quiet, but by September the Battle of Loos was raging. On the first day alone, 8,500 British soldiers were killed, and through October, amid showering shells and poisonous gas clouds, the numbers soared. The army was hungry for soldiers, and recruitment was dwindling so much that the government was inching dangerously near conscription, an issue that divided both politicians and civilians even though simple math, subtracting casualties from recruits, made the problem obvious.

Jack was thirty-nine when, in autumn 1915, men eighteen to forty received a letter from Lord Derby, Director-General of Recruiting, announcing a campaign "to induce men who can be spared to come forward for voluntary service in the army." Then came the sense of *or else*: "If this effort does not succeed, the country...will have to decide by what method sufficient recruits can be obtained to maintain our armies in the field at their required strength." Jack's sisters' husbands – Percy Kraushaar and Arthur Jordan – were in their mid-thirties now, so the call included them as well. In November and December, canvassers visited the homes of the potential volunteers. They were often pillars of the community with special powers of persuasion: clergymen, municipal councillors or union leaders. They were urged to underscore the benefits of serving – bonuses over and above the regular pay for men who signed up right away, possibly pensions in the long term, and of course the satisfaction of doing one's duty for the country. The canvassers were expected to be firm, too, if the situation required. "If the man is not at home, the orders are to keep on coming until he is found, to tackle him by asking and discussing the reasons of his resistance...after which, if the result is negative, a fresh start is to be made, this time indirectly, by trying to put pressure upon him through his family, his friends, or his employer." Shame, fear and intimidation were useful tools. One cartoon titled "The Conscript" showed a forlorn dog being carried off by the scruff of his neck. The caption read, "Lor', how I wish I'd come when I was called!"

Arthur Jordan came and promised to serve should he be called up in the future. A medical exam showed he was a little deaf in one ear, but the flaw wasn't enough to reject him from the stock of reserves. For now, he continued in his work at the Central Telegraph Office, and though the mechanics of his job stayed the same, the nature of the dots and dashes he transmitted changed greatly. As messages poured in about the dead and wounded, did he ever come across a name he knew? He had plenty of friends, family and acquaintances off fighting, and the guilt of being without uniform was its own kind of burden. Arthur's brother-in-law Percy Kraushaar suited up. He'd risen to a supervisory position in insurance but would eventually head to the Western Front with the King's Royal Rifle Corps, leaving Nell and their two boys behind. The Roff sisters' husbands heeded Derby, too. Enlistment records give the tiniest details about these men: one stood five foot three, weighed 108 pounds and had a scar on his lower jaw; the other had varicose veins and an old toe injury that still plagued him. "Hops well" the record states, as if with a shrug.

A photograph taken that December at Southwark Town Hall shows a crowd of men squeezed into the corridor, staring into the camera and struggling to see over each other's heads. A man at the front, with gappy teeth and stand-out ears, beams at the photographer, as if nothing could be more exciting, and the three police officers guarding the mass look as though they've had a long, busy day. As the photograph suggests, men responded to Derby's call in droves, with more than 300,000 enlisting during the six months of the campaign. But there were still not enough of them. The enlistment records that remain tell only a fragment of the story: more than half of the Great War's service records were lost when the War Office repository was bombed in 1940, and history began to repeat itself.

Joe Deverill and a lanky, unnamed friend in a photo dated January 12, 1918. Such portraits of fellow soldiers and sailors abound, and convey the camaraderie that grew from a shared experience of war, and a desire to record that bond.

*In 1916, Mary Anne's cousin Clara Donnelly married Bert Morel,
who was employed as a munitions worker throughout the war.
Though the names of many in this portrait have been lost to time,
Doris sits on the floor at bottom left; her cousin May is next to the bride
and Aunt Maggie stands behind her; Ernie appears slightly blurred
behind May's left shoulder; Ethel is seated far right, second row;
Mary Anne stands behind Ethel with Jack beside her. The picture
doesn't reveal it, but Mary Anne is already alarmingly unwell.*

CHAPTER 10

You Made Life Cheery When You Called Me Dearie

By spring of 1916, Joe had been made Ordinary Seaman and left the training establishment in Portsmouth to join HMS *Royal Sovereign*, a newly built battleship assigned to sail with the Grand Fleet in Scapa Flow off the Orkneys. Historically, the Fleet had been stationed in the south of England in anticipation of attack from the European continent, but with Germany the enemy instead of France or Spain, the remote islands north of Scotland were a more logical location for defense against a power that would come at them via the Baltic Sea. The islands in the vast expanse of water were only sparsely inhabited before the Navy arrived, the landscape bleak and nearly bare of trees, the waters empty but for fishing trawlers. These days the place teemed with vessels. Rows of battle cruisers, destroyers and minesweepers sat at anchor, and hundreds of shuttle craft delivered mail and supplies and ferried "liberty men" – sailors on leave – to and from shore. Gun emplacements dotted the coastline, while barrage balloons, meant as a defense against aircraft attack, swayed on metal tethers.

The YMCA was quick to see an opportunity, and with stone quarried from one of the islands' cliffs erected a stout-walled recreation hall that boasted pool tables, an upright piano and lounging chairs. A generator provided electricity, and a separate system gave heat and hot water, and together with its tennis courts and golf course and hot baths, the hall drew the off-duty "tars" in droves. But while the YMCA did a brisk business in chips and egg with tea, most places throughout the islands dotting Scapa Flow were off-limits to the sailors, and there was little else available in the way of recreation. An anonymously penned ditty described the base this way:

Sure a little bit of wastage fell from out the sky one day,
And it fell into the ocean in a spot up Scotland way,
And when the Sea Lords saw it, sure! It looked so bleak and bare
They said, "Suppose we start to build a Naval Base up there."
So they dotted it with colliers, to provide the tars with work,
With provision boats and oilers, that they dared not dodge or shirk.
Then they sprinkled it with raindrops, with sleet and hail and snow,
And when they finished, sure, they called it Scapa Flow.

Tens of thousands of sailors and dozens of warships were already there when Joe arrived, and at the end of May the Navy's commander, Admiral John Jellicoe, ordered the Grand Fleet to sea to engage the Germans in what would prove to be the largest naval contest of the war, the Battle of Jutland. From the afternoon on May 31 until late at night on June 1, the enemies clashed in the North Sea near Jutland, Denmark, and when the battle finally ended, the British fleet remained in control of the High Seas and the Germans retreated, though they claimed victory in their newspapers with a loss of eleven ships to Britain's fourteen. The Germans were closer to home and quicker to share their version of the outcome, which meant the first news many in England heard was that gleaned from German wireless broadcasts. The Admiralty itself shared the barest facts, reporting only ship losses on the two sides.

Thinking better of suppressing information that was out there anyway through rumour and German broadcasts, the Admiralty issued a late report confirming its victory despite the massive loss of life – just over 2,500 German seamen and more than 6,000 British, with more dying later from their injuries. Some news agencies tried to put a good face on the result. One paper counselled almost apologetically, "What we have to do is to face the news of the battle in the light of the latest facts, and looking at the odds against us we have grounds for seeing in the results of the engagement, a substantial victory." Another writer pointed out, "After the most terrible action ever fought, our command of the seas is unimpaired." But no matter the spin, the general public was stunned. The Royal Navy, whose skill and prowess they'd counted on to defend them for centuries, might have claimed a victory over the

German fleet, but it was a qualified victory at best – and debatable long into the future. The *Daily Mail* offered the harsh criticism that "after relating our losses [the Admiralty's report] becomes curiously vague and contains what we never were accustomed to see in British naval reports, namely, excuses."

Mary Anne needn't have worried for Joe, though. He and the rest of the sailors on *Royal Sovereign* had remained in port after Jellicoe deemed the crew too green for the fight. But how did Joe and his shipmates feel about missing the battle? And how did the details affect their imaginings of what lay ahead? Two hundred and fifty ships clashing; six thousand of their own burned in explosions or plunged to their deaths in the sea. Ships that were meant to be unsinkable sinking, and taking their crew with them. HMS *Indefatigable* shattered. HMS *Invincible* snapped in half. Despite such destruction and loss of life, the Navy insistently slotted the battle into the win column on the grounds that the German fleet had retreated and Britain retained control of the seas, and added the victory to the banner of its historic conquests: Trafalgar, the Spanish Armada, the Battle of the Nile and now Jutland.

Before the battle, the Admiralty had hired author Rudyard Kipling to write propagandist articles, and these appeared in newspapers soon after Jutland, spinning the event in a positive, almost quixotic, light. "The records give an impression of illimitable grey waters, nicked on their uncertain horizons with the smudge and blur of ships sparkling with fury against ships hidden under the curve of the world," Kipling wrote. "One comprehends, too, how the far off glare of a great vessel afire might be reported as a local fire on a near-by enemy, or vice-versa; how a silhouette caught, for an instant, in a shaft of pale light let down from the low sky might be fatally difficult to identify until too late… Then blanket the whole inferno with the darkness of night at full speed and see what you can make of it!"

Even without reading Kipling's musings, sailors like Joe, young and eager, were inclined to believe in the romance of the legend. The expectation was that both soldiers and sailors should feel the thrill of adventure more than the fear of death, and above all should understand their duty to king and country. If Joe and his ilk considered their mortality in the face of such staggering casualties as those seen at Jutland, they tempered it with bravado and pragmatism. The Navy expected courage, and the sailors had no choice but to measure up.

Two years in, though, the war had begun to feel endless. Jaunty songs – "Pack up your troubles in your old kit bag, and smile, smile, smile" – and patriotic slogans – "Rally round the flag, boys," and "Do or die" – seemed strained from repetition, and posters plastered on omnibuses and trams, in shop windows and on statues continued to use bullying tactics to shame people into participation. One depicted a post-war scene in which a man looks away from his children as they ask, "Daddy, what did *you* do in the Great War?" The 1914 ditty "Fall In" had included the lyrics

> *How will you fare, sonny, how will you fare*
> *In the far-off winter night,*
> *When you sit by the fire in the old man's chair*
> *And your neighbours talk of the fight?*
> *Will you slink away, as it were from a blow,*
> *Your old head shamed and bent?*
> *Or say, "I was not with the first to go,*
> *But I went, thank God, I went."*

By the summer of 1916, however, there was no longer a need to coax men to enlist voluntarily. Lord Derby's scheme, officially called the Group Scheme, had failed to draw enough men by voluntary enlistment, and now the Military Service Act gave the government the right to conscript into the army all men between the ages of eighteen and forty-one who were not widowed with children to support – like May's dad Jack – or already serving in the Navy, or ministers of religion, or doing work deemed necessary, such as farmers, train and bus drivers, and shipyard and munitions workers. Men could also be excused for poor health, which exempted Clara's beau, Bert Morel.

Bert was a relatively tall man with broad shoulders and a wan, melancholy look that underscores the family lore that he was rejected by the army due to a shoulder injury. As a man out of uniform, he was given work deemed of national importance in the munitions industry and wore a badge issued by the War Office that proclaimed "On War Service" in stamped brass, and bore a crown and an emblem consisting of three canons and balls. He'd have possessed an exemption certificate, too, issued by a tribunal that had heard his case and made a judgment: "Sir, I beg to inform you that this case has been considered by the Local Tribunal and that they have decided that this man be exempted from Military Service." The documentation may not have protected him from shame. Letters to the newspapers complained of "shirkers" and "slackers" who were "hiding behind munitions badges," and some members of the Order of the White Feather were so vehement that they continued their ritual of humiliation even after conscription.

The story of how Bert met Clara is long forgotten, but if Clara, like so many other young women of the time, took a factory job during the war, she and Bert might have met at work. Once conscription came into effect, the need for female labour in previously male-dominated jobs became still more pressing, so women were working on the docks, and as lathe operators, welders, mechanics and carpenters. The most dangerous job belonged to the "munitionettes" first wooed by Emmeline Pankhurst and David Lloyd George as minister of munitions. Under Lloyd George, munitions production had dramatically increased, and many civilian factories had been secured for war work. Eventually female munitions workers would produce 80 percent of the ammunition and weapons used during the entire war – though not without some serious side effects. Those who worked with the sulphur-laden compound trinitrotoluene, known as TNT, were called canaries owing to the yellow tint of their skin from handling the toxic chemical. Some died from the effects of TNT absorption, or from workplace accidents and explosions. A violent explosion at a shell factory in Leeds in December 1916 killed thirty-five girls working the night shift. Dozens more were maimed. A burst steam pipe created a stew of blood and gore, and in many cases the bodies could only be identified by the tags the workers wore round their necks. Another peril existed when the plants became the target of air raids, the enemy hoping to knock out the factories supplying the army with weapons and ammunition.

There were perks to munitions work – organized entertainment, and extra pay for those in the most hazardous jobs. By the fall of 1916 each worker was ensured a hot meal – bangers and mash or "two Zepps an' a cloud" at the canteen – as well as milk or cocoa. Regulations were put in place that gave workers time away from "poisonous dusts" so as to limit their exposure, and every worker was to have "a suitable costume, which must be washed regularly and chemically purified." But the cases of accident and illness continued. The fate of two men who worked at a Bermondsey factory making neutralizer for poisonous gas was written up in the press after the war. Bill and Dan, as the paper pegged them, had apparently sworn to "see it through," even though few could stand the fumes and burns of the process, and the article stated that "the health of the two men became seriously affected, and long after they had ceased to make the mixture, Bill's mind became deranged, and he put an end to his existence." Dan, presumably, lived on to tell the tale.

Hospitals throughout the country scrambled for the space and beds necessary to care for the casualties of war, whether munitions workers or soldiers or victims of bombing raids, and they were quickly overwhelmed. With wounded soldiers arriving in London from overseas by the trainload, civilian hospitals were turned over to military use, and grand houses, public buildings and asylums were converted for the treatment of the injured. After the devastating Second Battle of Ypres, the War Office appealed for use of some Poor Law infirmaries as well. It was a sign of the times that there were fewer destitute people in recent years, which left space to accommodate more wounded. East Dulwich Infirmary, where Mary Anne's mother, Mary, had died, was the first such institution slated for war use, and most of its civilian patients were hurriedly evacuated to the infirmaries at Newington and Lambeth workhouses. The building was renamed Southwark Military Hospital, with a beefed-up staff and an increased number of beds, and even tents on the grounds outside.

These unusual sights became commonplace around the city. At Charing Cross Hospital a banner was hung across the street requesting "Quiet for the Wounded," and heavy traffic was diverted. Smaller hospitals became specialist units, so there were places for limbless men, for facial reconstruction, for typhoid and venereal disease, and others for cardiac patients and mental patients. Despite all of these changes, London was still inundated with wounded, and the sight of ambulances streaming from train stations to hospitals was distressingly common. Only the injured were shipped home from the Front; the dead remained in the mud where they'd fallen; or if their bodies were recovered from the battlefield, they were buried near the place they'd died – in a farmer's field or a village churchyard. Repatriating dead bodies would have been a logistical nightmare, and a statistic was less shocking than the visual horror of trainloads of corpses. Even so, that summer of 1916, during the early days of the Battles of the Somme, hospitals in London were warned that they would soon see casualties in unprecedented numbers, and that they should free every possible bed in preparation. In many cases civilians were accommodated amongst the soldiers, and non-military patients must have fretted that this was the worst possible time to fall ill, when the hospitals were overflowing with bandaged soldiers.

Mary Anne was one of these civilians, a forty-three-year-old charwoman of small means when some alarming symptoms compelled her to visit a doctor – first at Guy's Hospital behind Borough High Street in Southwark, and then, in November 1916, at St. Bartholomew's – or Barts – across the river. The longer trek suggests she was worried and searching for answers that hadn't come from Guy's, or that the doctor there had referred her case. The Barts record says she had "fits" and that she was under the care of Dr. Howard Henry Tooth, a neurologist known for his work in epilepsy and cerebral tumours. These days he was also deeply involved in the study of shell shock, and St. Bartholomew's, like so many other hospitals in London, was crowded with soldiers wounded in all kinds of ways. Tooth kept Mary Anne at Barts for almost three weeks, and if she was at all herself during her stay, she must have gathered some sense of the frantic work that went on at London's oldest hospital in this third year of war. The record doesn't say whether Tooth believed she was cured when she went home, or how he diagnosed the fits. But such spells must have been as frightening for her, a widow with young dependents, as for Ethel and Ernie and Doris witnessing them.

Perhaps they hoped she had nothing more complicated than the "war strain" that Tooth was so familiar with, and that got written about in the papers – women were anxious about their men, and men were anxious from repressing their anxieties. Almost everyone was overworked and wracked with worry. So prevalent was war strain that there were all sorts of theories as to how you could banish it. Supplements "as nice as caramel" recharged the nervous system and were mysteriously billed as "scientific preparations of many of the most nourishing food elements." Pink pills restored the weakness that came from a prolonged, unnatural period of nervous excitement. There was even a cream to keep war strain from spoiling the complexion. "Anxiety for relatives at the Front, grief for those who have 'gone west,' and the stress of war work are all bad for the skin … Ven-Yusa brings back the sweet freshness that the skin has been robbed of by anxiety or trying atmospheric conditions."

Mary Anne's stay at Barts would have seemed an eternity for the children, but she was home in time for Clara's Christmas Eve wedding to Bert Morel. In a group photo taken at the wedding, Mary Anne looks out at the camera with a serious gaze. She wears a straw hat with a ribbon and bow and a fitted dark coat over a high-collared blouse, and her hand rests lightly on the back of the chair where Ethel sits, almost smiling. Jack is beside Mary Anne, looking so much like Harry, his moustaches falling in a frown around his mouth. May, his daughter, sits next to Clara in bridesmaid's white, her hair coiling over her shoulder, her gloved hands in her lap. May's smile stands out among sombre faces, while behind her, small Ernie has moved slightly, and his image is blurred. The bride and groom form the centre of this shot, arms linked. Bert leans toward Clara and eyes the lens, while Clara looks to the left. Days earlier a terse announcement had appeared in the newspaper, headed "All Munition Badges to be Returned – Drastic Government Action – Grave Warning as to Lost Time." The article went on to state that certificates of exemption were to be withdrawn, since men were more urgently needed on the battlefield than for munitions work. Other articles specified that the change only applied to men who were physically fit and performing unskilled or semi-skilled tasks, which meant that Bert stayed on, though neither course was a happy one: marching into the fray not knowing whether you'd ever return, or staying home because you were too weak to be of use to your fellow soldiers.

In this rather joyless wedding portrait there are many faces with no names attached, but in front, on the floor, sitting cross-legged with two other children, is Doris. She's the flower girl, and a circle of tiny ribbon blossoms lies on her dark hair. Her dress has a sash and pin tucks, and a frill over each shoulder, and she wears white gloves, white knee socks and black shoes with a strap over the instep. A fur rug adorns the floor before the children, placed by the photographer for effect. Doris stares back at the cameraman with a resigned expression that calls to mind so many of the photos of her mother. She cannot know how much will change in the coming months, or that to those looking at the scene a hundred years on, Joe's absence holds special weight. Following the wedding, everyone made merry and sang "When You Wore a Tulip and I Wore a Big Red Rose," and afterward, at home in her bed at 4 Goodwin Buildings, the words ran through Doris's head, cementing the memory of the day:

When you wore a tulip, a sweet yellow tulip,
And I wore a big, red rose,
When you caressed me, 'twas then Heaven blessed me,
What a blessing, no one knows,
You made life cheery when you called me dearie,
'Twas down where the blue grass grows,
Your lips were sweeter than julep when you wore that tulip,
And I wore a big red rose.

Four days later, Mary Anne checked herself into the infirmary at Newington Workhouse where her sister Ellen still lived. "Alleged lunatic," the register states. The doctor who saw Mary Anne thought the cause might be epilepsy, so perhaps the fits she described were somewhat like seizures. He wrote, "Strange in her manner, but not very bad. She says her fits have caused her to be strange." The next day he jotted, "Appears much better," but did not release her and added no further comments on her condition during the rest of her stay. She gave Jack as her contact, but it was "to daughter" that she was discharged two weeks later, for the third time having found no cure for her puzzling symptoms. As Ethel and Mary Anne made their way home to the Goodwin from Newington that winter day, they must have known that the trouble was not yet over.

Whether Joe was aware of his mother's strange illness at this point is a mystery. In November 1916, while she was still at Barts under the care of Dr. Tooth, he'd been transferred to HMS *Mary Rose*, an Admiralty M-class destroyer that had seen action at the Battle of Jutland. In naval tradition, warships inherit the honours of earlier warships sharing the same name, so while *Mary Rose* was a brand new vessel, she boasted a plaque on her bridge that listed battles from Henry VIII's time, as well as a passed-down soubriquet: "the flower of all ships that ever sailed."

The two others boarding with Joe were Frederick Toms and John Bell, young men about his age who'd also moved from the training ship *Victory* to *Royal Sovereign* and now to *Mary Rose*. The trio of able seamen had only recently been promoted from "ordinary." Fair-haired Toms was a Hampshire shop boy who'd been working on ships since 1913, and Bell was darker, a coal miner from Nottinghamshire with a scar on each side of his forehead. On *Mary Rose* they joined men from a variety of backgrounds. Many were as young as these three, but others were in their thirties and forties and had a wealth of experience on the sea. There were gardeners and sewermen and labourers, bakers and clerks and chandler's boys. The sailors often had tattoos – Petty Officer Arthur Bolton had a butterfly and a woman's head inked into his arms, and stoker Harry Smalley wore the names Kate and Rose. Able Seaman Harry Griffin seemed born for the job: the second and third toes of each foot were partially webbed. There were Londoners from all pockets of the city, as well as Scots and Liverpudlians and Mancunians, and even an American from Nebraska. Many of the men had come on board in January of the previous year and had taken part in the Battle of Jutland, though no one on *Mary Rose* had died that awful day.

Once settled, Joe's days were spent routinely. Breakfast was at 7:15 and cleaning was the order of the day. At 9:30 there were prayers, and then it was back to cleaning – quarters, decks, guns. Some days *Mary Rose* escorted merchant ships for a distance through the grey water of the North Sea and handed them over to the next patrol, recording speed, position, weather and sea condition in the grid-lined logbook. One of the seamen, an older hand named John Bailey, referred to these escort missions as "mail runs" because they were so boring. The ship was darkened at six p.m., and supper was an hour later. At ten p.m. the men not on watch were piped down – two short notes and a long trill on the boatswain's whistle dismissing the sailors to their berths for lights out.

Christmas came and went uneventfully, and around the time Ethel retrieved Mary Anne from Newington Infirmary, the *Mary Rose* log states: "Passed derelict, bottom up. Strong SE wind and confused seas. Vessel labouring heavily...Cloudy and showery. Darkened ship." Joe, nearly nineteen, would have lain in his narrow hammock with the sea tossing beneath him, missing his family, probably; but then again, he'd been gone from home a long time, and a sailor's life was not solitary. There were more than ninety men on board, and a picture taken of some of them gathered on deck hints at a motley mix of personalities. Propped on their elbows in the front of the shot, two men lie on the deck with their heads stuck through the lifebuoy lettered HMS *Mary Rose*. One winks at the camera. Others hold cigarettes between curling lips, and a couple clamp their teeth onto pipes. In the centre of the picture, a fellow with too-short sleeves and wrist bones protruding grins widely as if the photographer has told a great joke. Beside him stands John Bailey, every inch the seasoned mariner with broad shoulders, a sardonic smirk and his arms crossed over his chest. Bailey wears his flat-topped sailor's cap pushed far back on his head, ignoring regulations. Down in the bottom right corner of the photo sits Joe, hands clasped round his knee. Unlike Bailey or the men with their heads through the lifebuoy, Joe looks serious and gazes past the photographer as if his thoughts are elsewhere.

And well they might have been. News from the home front was spotty for those afloat on the cold waters around Scapa Flow and elsewhere, but once in port they'd have read in the newspapers of a massive explosion in London's East End. While the papers were vague on the exact location of the blast, they devoted columns of print to the lurid details, and those returning from leave confirmed that the disaster had occurred at Silvertown on the north bank of the Thames, a few miles east of Southwark in West Ham. The area was just beyond the geographic limits of London's Metropolitan Buildings Act, which controlled the establishment of noxious industries, so factories that handled dangerous substances such as sulphuric acid, creosote and petroleum set up there. The densely packed row houses of the workers threaded through the industrial establishments and hugged the docks and railway lines. Brunner Mond Chemical Works, which manufactured caustic soda, was among the industries located in Silvertown, and two years into the war, when the army found itself with a serious shortage of shells, the War Office directed Brunner Mond to begin production of TNT, despite the company's alleged reservations to take on such a dangerous assignment given its location in a heavily populated area.

On January 19, 1917, a fire broke out in the factory, and fifty tons of high explosives detonated, destroying part of the factory and the surrounding area, including the local fire station that should have responded to the catastrophe. Far-off houses trembled and soot whooshed down chimneys. One woman wrote in her diary, "I am still shaking from the shock of a terrible concussion and distant roar which occurred ten minutes ago. It seemed to me as if our roof were giving way." The explosion was heard a hundred miles away, but those up close saw the gruesome consequences: masses of wood and metal thrown blazing into the sky and tumbling back down, starting new fires wherever they landed; the dead and the dying; hundreds stumbling away from the site, panicked and confused. Sixty-nine people died on the spot, four more within days. Hundreds were injured, and thousands left homeless. The *Stratford Express*, recounting the story of the explosion, wrote that "the whole heavens were lit in awful splendour. A fiery glow seemed to have come over the dark and miserable January evening, and objects which a few moments before had been blotted out in the intense darkness were silhouetted against the sky. The awful illumination lasted in its eerie glory only a few seconds ... but down by the river roared a huge column of flame, which told thousands that the explosion had been followed by fire and havoc the like of which has never been known in these parts."

People wept as they dug through the rubble for loved ones. A woman who ran a laundry in Silvertown took in the wounded, and they lay there on ironing boards or stretched out on the floor. Firemen, soldiers, nurses and ambulances from all over London rushed to the scene. The YMCA sent vans with hot drinks and food; the Salvation Army offered its many shelters and sent companies of cadets to assist where they could. They commandeered damaged houses in several streets as places of refuge. According to the Salvation Army's *War Cry*, among the most trying tasks was that of the cadets assigned to the mortuaries. "Here, too, hot refreshments were provided for the people, while the Cadets were also able to whisper into the ears of the sorrowing, broken hearted women and children words of comfort and consolation. 'Never shall I forget,' says one Cadet, 'the dear woman whom I went with to try and identify her husband. She was only able to do this by the condition of his feet – he had had frostbite while in the trenches and had lost all his toes!'" At the mortuaries and elsewhere, the *War Cry* reported, the common refrain from those helped was "God bless you, sister," a sure sign, the *War Cry* claimed, that the Salvation Army uniform had become synonymous with aid to the needy.

As details of the disaster made their way across the city, the mood at the Goodwin Buildings would have been sombre indeed. Despite being newly wed, Bert's munitions work had taken him to a factory in Birmingham, nowhere near this blast, but he was still vulnerable and too far away for Clara to hold. Birmingham, 125 miles distant from London, had long been home to a couple of large munitions manufacturers, but since the war had begun, many of its other factories had been converted for war use as well, prompting Lord Mayor Neville Chamberlain to boast that his city had become "a huge workshop for the manufacture of munitions." There were students, too. Thousands passed through the Birmingham technical school to train for their jobs, taking short, intensive courses in tool making, gauge making, precision grinding, and welding. At first the courses were offered for men only, but later women were encouraged to take them, too. Birmingham and its surroundings swelled with these new workers from all parts of Britain, billeted with residents or housed in temporary huts on site.

CHAPTER 10

Bert's brother Henry was there too, and he and his wife, Ethel, called themselves "machinists" when they were married in the summer of 1916. They lived on Cooksey Road, Small Heath, very near the Small Arms Company on Armoury Road, which manufactured the Lewis machine gun as well as "motor bicycles" and a specially designed military bicycle that could be folded up and carried on a soldier's back. Many of Ethel Morel's counterparts were women who had never been far from home and were entering the workforce for the first time. Other employees were men whose particular skills were vital on the home front, or who were unfit for active service, or who had served already and been discharged. These last had a different perspective on the weapons being made: the powerful shells; the small, complicated fuses that made them explode; the cartridges and bullets; and all the pieces of the airplanes that would eventually bomb enemy territory. Men in munitions factories usually worked the heaviest machinery, or had jobs in the foundry, or were foremen who taught skills to the women workers.

Whatever the task, it was dangerous, made more so by the fact that thousands were doing work they'd never done before, and the pressure was on to produce quality items in massive quantities. Because of what was at stake, safety regulations were stepped up, but whether they were always followed was another matter. In later years it was revealed that TNT had been sloppily stored at Silvertown – and of course it never should have been used in such a densely populated area. So though the country gained experience in war, and greater attention was paid to protective clothing and top-notch first aid, accidents large and small continued. That was where pluck came in. In her 1918 book *The Woman's Part: A Record of Munitions Work*, Lucy Keyser Yates recounted an incident when a piece of metal had jammed in a press, and the woman working it had lost her thumb and forefinger. Six weeks later she was back at her machine "and getting an even greater output than before." Another woman was wiring a large battleship when "a drill came through from the deck, piercing her cotton cap and entering her head." She was seen by the factory's medical staff and then sent home. But her co-workers were surprised when she showed up at six a.m. the next day, laughing off the incident and telling them it was better to lose a little hair than one's whole head. "The heroism of the battlefield," Yates mused, "has frequently been equalled by the ordinary citizen in the factory, whether man or woman."

Politically, the new year had begun with optimism. Unable to find common ground with his coalition partners, and increasingly viewed as a weak and vacillating war leader, Prime Minister Asquith had offered his resignation to King George, expecting that no one would fill his shoes and he would be asked to return. Instead, in a somewhat sleight-of-hand move, Lloyd George stepped into the role and headed up the coalition government. His work as minister of munitions and then secretary of state for war had vastly increased his popularity, and he was seen as a strong and capable leader. Papers reported on his "winning way," his roll-up-your-sleeves attitude, his magnetism and sincerity, and his courage, which they said the Kaiser had good reason to fear. One article announced, "It is realized that in Mr. Lloyd George we have at last found a leader…Get on with the war!" *Punch* ran a cartoon depicting him as "The New Conductor," his baton raised for action, a look of fierce determination on his face.

Up in Scapa Flow, HMS *Mary Rose* had likewise found a new conductor. Charles Leonard Fox was a man in his late thirties who'd had a somewhat checkered career. In his early years he'd been lauded as "keen and zealous" and "a very good officer," but other superiors had deemed him "not recommended for fully manned flotillas" and cautioned that he should pay more attention to detail. Later, in March 1916, he had been relieved of his command and found guilty of "gross carelessness" for having lost the signal flags that identified his vessel. By September, though, while on board HMS *Ajax*, he'd received a rave endorsement from the ship's captain: "An extremely good and trustworthy officer. Although I shall be very sorry to lose his services in this ship, I would most strongly recommend that he be reinstated in c[omman]d of a destroyer. Very able, hard-working and tactful and has a very good c[omman]d of men." In February 1917, Fox joined *Mary Rose*, and the "mail runs" continued.

A little while later, in March, *Mary Rose* sustained some minor damage to her lifeboat davits when she pulled up alongside the ship

Obedient, so she put in at Glasgow to make repairs. The ammunition was off-loaded, the confidential books, logs, charts and compasses locked up for safekeeping, and except for a small party left behind for security, all hands received nine days' leave and a chance to visit home. Joe re-tuned to London, his appearance timely, for Mary Anne was ill again, or had worsened since her last stint at Newington Infirmary. He'd only been at home three days – barely long enough to accustom himself to the noise and dirt of the city and the feel of solid footing and a bed that didn't sway – when she was readmitted. If Joe had heard of his mother's strange malady in letters from Ethel, now he saw it for himself and understood something of its nature: the "strangeness," the epileptic-like seizures. As the oldest son, it would have been Joe's turn to bring Mary Anne to the infirmary, and to provide details as to her age, her address, her next of kin and her symptoms. But he would not have been able to see her home again; a scrawled note stating the dates of her admission and discharge – March through June – suggest she was seriously unwell, and Joe's leave was short in the scheme of things.

He took the train back to Glasgow, just one in a press of soldiers and sailors and hurrying civilians at King's Cross station. Some cried or kissed sweethearts; others clasped hands with friends or waved to family. Little children clung to fathers, and parents embraced sons, per-haps for the last time. Many men were there alone, kit bag or duffle sack slung over a shoulder, searching out their platform in the mass of navy blue and khaki green. What was in Joe's heart as he left can only be sur-mised, but likely he thought of Mary Anne – thinner now, her face a little harder, eyes haunted – and felt thankful for the long journey north to Scotland and *Mary Rose*, and the chance to settle his thoughts.

With her crew returned, *Mary Rose* threw off her ropes and steamed back up the Clyde, travelling north to rejoin the fleet at Scapa Flow. The routine of pipe calls and rounds were good distractions, as were the men who made up the ship's company – a "typewriter" from Pimlico, a fruit-erer from Islington, a bricklayer from Sussex, a stagehand from Dublin. *Mary Rose* resumed her patrols, hunting submarines and policing North Sea shipping channels. But by the end of April she embarked on a secret mission to Queenstown, Ireland, as part of a team of destroyers chosen to officially greet the United States Navy, a long sought, welcome addition to the Allied forces.

The Americans had so far held out as a neutral party, though they'd supplied both munitions and money to aid the Allied cause. In 1916 the United States had protested Germany's practice of attacking passenger ships and not allowing merchantmen to abandon ship prior to an assault. Wary of making an enemy of the Americans, the Germans had agreed to cease, but the pledge had been short-lived. In January 1917, some in the German navy convinced Kaiser Wilhelm that a lifting of restrictions on maritime warfare would end the war in a matter of months. Targeting passenger and supply ships in addition to vessels of war, they argued, would quickly intimidate and starve the British into submission. They reasoned that the agreement made with the United States should not be binding, since the Americans had aided the Allies by supplying arms and financial aid. In the end, unrestricted submarine warfare had resumed, and through February and March 1917, several American ships, crews and passengers went to the bottom of the ocean as targets of German submarines. Even these actions alone did not persuade the Americans to enter the war. But the submarine attacks were coupled with the US discovery that the Germans had attempted to convince Mexico to take Germany's side in return for helping the Mexicans regain territory they'd ceded following the Mexican–American War almost seventy years earlier.

For the British – and so for Joe and the others aboard *Mary Rose* – the reason and the politics behind it were immaterial. The assistance of the United States was welcome indeed to a nation worn down by almost three years of warfare. In a matter of days the British contingent would give the Americans "fresh impressions" of destroyer fighting and impart any bits of wisdom that might be helpful to the newcomers. As *Mary Rose* rounded the most westerly coast of Ireland, the men encountered calm seas and relatively clear skies, all of which were noted in the log. What wasn't included was the trepidation some of them felt as they drew close to one of the allies' busiest shipping routes, where U-boats were a constant threat. Statistics were grim and getting steadily worse.

In the past few weeks, 152 British merchantmen had been sunk, so it was no surprise when, one day out from Queenstown, *Mary Rose* encountered lifeboats carrying survivors of HMS *Tulip*.

The *Tulip* was purpose-built to look like a small merchant ship, when in fact she was a heavily armed convoy sloop. She was one of the Navy's many decoy ships or "Q-ships," the moniker a reference to their home berth of Queenstown, and she functioned as a wolf in sheep's clothing, ready to sink an unsuspecting U-boat to the seabed should her crew see one approaching. In his 1922 book *Q-Ships and Their Story*, Lieutenant-Commander E. Keble Chatterton wrote that the ideal captain of a Q-ship had to have "something of the cleverest virtues of an angler, the most patient stalker, the most enterprising big-game hunter, together with the attributes of a cool, unperturbed seaman, the imagination of a sensational novelist, and the plain horse-sense of a hard businessman. In two words, the necessary endowment was brains and bravery." But the best U-boat commanders were a rare breed as well, and when Captain Ernst Hashagen of *U-62* spotted the *Tulip* through his periscope, *Tulip*'s commander, Norman Lewis, and his crew had little time to react. They watched the torpedo flying toward them; it hit amidships, between the engine room and the stokehold, and all the men in those stations were instantly killed. The boilers exploded, and some of the ship's disguise fell away, exposing the guns, which were useless now anyway. *Tulip* was more or less split in two, and it was obvious she would sink in a matter of minutes. As the submarine circled them, the surviving crew climbed into lifeboats, the sailors looking all the more pathetic for their merchantmen's disguise of dirty clothes and stubbly faces. Finally *U-62* surfaced and ordered Lewis on board. In his grubby jersey and slippers he was ushered below to meet with Hashagen. The *Tulip* crew had an agonizing wait for Lewis, and when he finally returned it was only to bid his men farewell. They watched from their lifeboats as Lewis disappeared into the sea with the enemy.

The next day the men on *Mary Rose* spotted the lifeboats, according to the cursory entry in the log at 6:12 a.m. "Stopped. Picked up 3 boats containing 80 survivors from HMS *Tulip*. Sunk all 3 boats." As the men climbed aboard, Joe and the others heard their stories: how suddenly the attack had happened, how Lewis had said goodbye, and how the German captain had confirmed that the men had enough provisions to see them through until they were rescued – though there was no guarantee they would have been seen or saved. The act of picking up survivors was risky, only to be undertaken if the rescuers could be certain no enemy lurked nearby. Chatterton claimed that "it was a favourite ruse for the U-boat, having seen the survivors row off, to remain in the vicinity until the rescuing ship should come along, so that, whilst the latter was stopped and getting the wretched victims on board, Fritz could, from the other side, send her to the bottom with an easily-aimed torpedo."

Four hours later *Mary Rose* halted again. "Picked up 27 men of sunk Italian ss *Fortunata*." *Fortunata* was an ocean liner used mainly to transport immigrants between Italy and Brazil, and she'd been empty but for a crew of twenty-seven when she was torpedoed by Hashagen's *U-62*. *Mary Rose* continued on course with more than one hundred extra men on board, huddled under blankets, their wounds freshly bandaged. Around noon she stopped a third time, now screening HMS *Marne* as she rescued survivors of a burning oil tanker. Soon *Mary Rose* moved on, marking her passage through Irish waters by the lighthouses dotting the rocky coast. "Great Skellig" and "Fastnet" and "Kinsale" were noted in the logbook, sights Joe could carry with him to counter those of the sinking ships and men adrift in lifeboats: Skellig a towering crag of sandstone, slate and green moss rising out of the sea like a cathedral; Fastnet a solitary rock tooth with a lighthouse built from Cornish granite; Kinsale a giant spit of green protruding into the ocean and topped with the Old Head Lighthouse. Joe and his fellow sailors might have known the Old Head as the point from which the passenger liner *Lusitania* had taken her last bearing before being torpedoed and sunk two years earlier. She'd disappeared in under twenty minutes, taking 1,201 souls with her. *Mary Rose* passed through the same waters, arriving at Queenstown near midnight. The harbour, too, was an ominous site; one sailor described it as "a graveyard of wrecked, partly sunken ships."

The American division that approached Queenstown comprised six small destroyers commanded by Joseph Taussig, a veteran officer with plenty of naval warfare experience behind him. As well as being a decorated commander, Taussig was a prolific writer and kept a personal diary where he recorded the details of the trip. The voyage hadn't been easy; the flotilla had spent much of a week battling severe winds, and Taussig wrote about it on May 3 in a diary entry titled "At sea." "The past week has been a most uncomfortable one. For six days we traveled eastward with half a gale, the wind blowing steadily from SSE, giving us a rough sea on our starboard beam...We have been rolling so much that the mess table has not been set up since April 25th. We have been holding our plates in our laps." Two days previously, in hazy weather, the destroyers had come upon the *Adriatic* of the White Star Line. A passenger liner, she'd been in New York when the *Titanic* went down and had returned many of the survivors to Britain. These days she was one of many boats requisitioned to carry troops and supplies for the government's vast merchant fleet. Taussig noted that "she started to run away, but when we hoisted our colors, she resumed her course and dipped her colors in salute as she passed." The Americans pressed on, connecting by radio with HMS *Parthian*, the British ship sent to find them, but because of poor visibility they did not meet. Instead, a day later, Joe and the boys on *Mary Rose* had the honour of greeting their new allies 350 miles out of Queenstown. As Lieutenant Commander Fox brought the ship alongside the flotilla, signalling "Welcome to the American colours," Taussig's ship *Wadsworth* replied "Thank you, I am glad of your company." Taussig then inquired about the course, and whether the ships should zigzag as they approached Queenstown – a general rule to keep submarines from plotting a ship's position – but Fox reportedly replied in the negative. "It is safer to zigzag, but it is a terrible nuisance."

Thus, with another day's travel, *Mary Rose* led the Americans straight to Ireland, arriving in the harbour on a clear blue afternoon upon glittering seas. The scene was captured by moving-picture man Frederick "Val" Engholm, a sailor turned camera operator who already had a list of newsreels to his credit. The government had recently realized it could use film as a propaganda tool. To ensure optimum control of the message, it had purchased a consortium of newsreel companies and directed them under the auspices of the War Office Cinema Committee. Engholm, who'd made a name for himself in the business, was commissioned as a sub-lieutenant and came to be stationed in a tugboat that day as an official news-film cameraman. His camera steady on the deck of the tug, he filmed the ships passing. The British destroyer with its three smokestacks is immediately distinguishable from her American counterparts, which have four stacks and the ability to travel longer distances without refuelling. Crowds of white-capped sailors appear as *Mary Rose* passes the camera. They stand in the middle of the ship, looking out at the tug as it travels by.

In port, all the glory belonged to the Americans. As Taussig recorded in his diary, "the authorities and people are making considerable fuss over our arrival." But there was little time for heroics; soon, both the British and American ships would be sent out in pairs to hunt submarines and escort merchant ships wherever possible. The next several days were busy ones, in which all of the men, no matter their rank, worked "like beavers," Taussig wrote, the British having much to teach and the Americans much to learn about submarine warfare. British signalmen gave instruction on each US ship twice daily, as did British radio gunners, so that communication would be flawless. Throughout the preparations, there was the awareness of the perilous task all hands were working toward. In a long and solemn address to the US commanders, the formidable British Vice Admiral Lewis Bayly offered some frank advice.

In two days you will go out on a war mission. When you pass beyond the defenses of the harbour you face death, and live in danger of death until you return behind such defenses. You must presume from the moment you pass out that you are seen by a submarine and that at no time until you return can you be sure that you are not being watched. You may proceed safely, and may grow careless in your watching; but, let me impress upon you the fact that if you do relax for a moment, if you cease to be vigilant, then you will find yourself destroyed, your vessel sunk, your men drowned.

He detailed their duties: they would search and destroy for six days, then rest for two in port; out again they'd go for six days, rest for two, and so on until they had either logged five hundred hours or a month had passed, at which point they could rest for five days and ready their ships for the next patrol. He underscored that while at sea their main aim was to destroy enemy submarines. Secondly, to protect merchant ships. And lastly, "to save lives if you can." But they were to pick up survivors only if the area had been thoroughly explored and there were no submarines in sight. If one was spotted, "be sure you go after the submarine. The rescue work must wait…To lose an opportunity to sink a submarine means he lives to sink other peaceful vessels and destroy more lives." He cautioned that the men must avoid using searchlights even during rescue missions, and he forbade the lighting of matches at night. "You would marvel to know how small a flicker of light might show, and the distance spanned." When travelling, they must "zigzag always. Never for a moment neglect this. Your course must be irregular so that the submarine cannot plot your position."

If Taussig's thoughts turned to Fox's comment about the nuisance of zigzagging, he did not make note of it in his diary or in later articles he wrote about his experience at Queenstown. What he did say was that Bayly's talk made an "indelible impression" on him. "Surely we had seen and heard enough in our first four days' stay in Queenstown to appreciate the gravity of the work before us, and to realize that patrol duty in submarine waters was a dangerous undertaking."

On May 8 the ships departed Queenstown in the early afternoon, moving out in pairs to their assigned areas. Standing on the rooftop of Admiralty House, on a hill overlooking the harbour, Vice Admiral Bayly watched them go. One British commander later commented that he imagined every captain must have warily glanced aft to assure all was as it should be, for if even the tiniest thing was amiss, Bayly's eagle eye would find it.

Mary Rose had been paired with the destroyer *Sarpedon* for her tour of duty. The area had been divided into squares, each named with a letter and number, and the patrolling ships might be assigned one, two, or even three squares at a time. They escorted merchant vessels to the edge of the patrol area and radioed ahead to have the neighbouring vessel meet them at the dividing line. But that didn't always work, and often enough the merchant vessel had to go on alone. Taussig wrote that in those cases "it seemed that the vessel always had a sad dejected look as it steamed away by itself."

Ever present was the threat of U-boats, and all eyes were trained to look for them. Birds, fish, driftwood, even a boat hook were mistaken for periscopes. Sometimes the things that floated past were all too clear: boats adrift and empty, dead horses, miles of lumber, barrels and boxes, and great swathes of oil spreading out from the place a ship had gone under. And somewhere out there, Ernst Hashagen lurked in the *U-62*. In the week that followed the *Tulip* disaster he had sunk four more ships in the area and damaged a fifth, with the *Tulip*'s Norman Lewis as his captive passenger. What couldn't be known yet was that Lewis was fine. Hashagen treated him kindly and gave him clothing, cigarettes, food and wine; "We learned to understand each other," Lewis later claimed. "Peace would have been concluded immediately if it rested only with us." For nineteen days after his capture, Lewis remained on the *U-62* as it hunted and sank allied vessels. Until he was delivered to Wilhelms-haven as a prisoner of war, "he saw us waking and sleeping," Hashagen later wrote, "searching and fighting, and found to his astonishment that these U-Boat fellows were not indeed so very different from his own fellow-countrymen."

Lewis's reality would have stunned the Queenstown patrol. For men of all ranks, the job of searching out submarines was exhausting. Constant vigilance was necessary, but sometimes for long stretches there was absolutely nothing to see. At other times the sea was so rough that sleeping and eating were difficult chores. The wind howled and the rigging clanged. And yet neither the monotony nor the irritations could erase the fact that a submarine could appear at any time. Most men slept in their clothes so they would always be prepared to respond to a call to duty. When a British commander mentioned that he'd gone on the bridge in his pyjamas after a submarine sighting, Taussig was shocked.

"Do you mean to tell me that you take off your clothes at night?"
"Certainly," the commander replied. "When a call comes I throw on a dressing gown, and up I go."
"How long have you been doing this duty?" Taussig asked him.
"Nearly three years."
"Well, when I have been doing this patrol duty for three years, I am going to put on my pajamas too."

Mary Rose didn't remain nearly that long. Soon Joe and his shipmates returned north to the Orkneys and the base at Scapa Flow; they were famous now, though no one knew their names. The film Engholm had made at Queenstown played to audiences in London a few weeks after the Americans arrived, their support a secret no longer. The *New York Sun* reported that audiences in one theatre went wild with enthusiasm at the announcement of the US involvement, while English newspapers commented that "the film sensation of the week in London has certainly been the release of the pictures of the arrival of the American torpedo boats at Queenstown. There has been so much censoring of war pictures that the very frankness of this film, with the revelations of the internal mechanism of a torpedo boat, have excited unwonted enthusiasm. The film has had a great reception."

Ethel and Ernie might have been in one of the audiences, two of many viewers seated in the dark, packed theatres, eyes turned to the grainy images moving across the screen. If they saw the film, did they know their brother was in the crowd of sailors lining the deck of the vessel marked only "29"? The ship was singled out for an onscreen mention as having gone 350 miles to meet the US destroyers, but it remained unnamed. The camera pans the length of the ship as it slides past, and despite the grey-scale of the footage, some details stand out: the crisp white of the sailors' caps, the dinghy-like "Carley float" life raft strapped to the side of one of the smokestacks, and the sun sparkling on calm water. Those images, and the ones that follow of sailors bustling about on deck, grinning for the camera as they sort ropes, grease guns and hang off the side with paint cans and brushes, belie the fact that these were dangerous times. Even in port things could go wrong. An entry in the *Mary Rose* log after she'd returned to the Orkneys states tersely "11:15 pm HMS *Vanguard* blew up. Raised steam for taking up station for submarine attack on base."

Lying at anchor on sheltered black water in Scapa Flow, *Vanguard* had exploded without warning, killing all but three of more than eight hundred men on board. At first it was believed to be the work of a submarine, the opening salvo of an attack on the Grand Fleet's base where *Mary Rose* was berthed. Joe and his fellow crewmen, roused from sleep, scrambled to their posts. Wreckage and human remains from *Vanguard* landed on nearby ships, and one of her turrets was discovered a mile away. The defensive measures that summoned *Mary Rose* and other ships remained in place throughout the night, but it was soon apparent that the explosion had not been a submarine attack, and further investigation blamed the disaster on deteriorated or heated cordite in one of *Vanguard*'s magazines. Those on neighbouring ships injured in the blast were sent to recuperate at HMS *Pembroke*, the shore barracks at Chatham, Kent, where, coincidentally, a very similar accident in 1914 on board HMS *Bulwark* had killed almost the same number of sailors.

There were countless more tragedies yet to come, in which great numbers of lives would be wiped out in one go. But on the personal scale, back in the Borough, a single grave concern had ballooned in Joe's absence, and now it overshadowed everything.

The war and their mother's illness brought big changes for Doris (top),
Ernie and Ethel, who lived separately for much of the time and sent postcards
with long strings of x's to express how much they missed each other.

CHAPTER 11

A Person of Unsound Mind

Mary Anne had been discharged from her March hospitalization in the middle of June 1917, but it wasn't a happy occasion, for two days later she was admitted to Lambeth Infirmary. It was a Monday, and it followed the hottest day of the year in London so far, with the thermometer reaching 89°F in the shade. The small flat in the Goodwin was stifling, the heat creating a steam bath after a violent thunderstorm the previous night. The downpour was so heavy that water flowed into the tube tunnels and halted the trains, while bursting water mains rendered sections of above ground roadways impassable. Nothing of that, of course, made it into the ledger that records Mary Anne's admission, nor does the record reveal her illness. In fact it says very little about the patient herself. But there is one curious detail: the same June day that Mary Anne was admitted to Lambeth Infirmary, her sister Ellen left Newington Workhouse for the first time since 1910 and was discharged, the record states vaguely, to Lambeth. In all of Ellen's years inside institutions, this is the only evidence ever found of her discharging herself, though many other inmates come and go. After so many years apart, had the sisters been company for each other at Newington, though Mary Anne was so unwell? And then did Ellen follow Mary Anne to Lambeth and sit by her bedside, calling up stories from childhood, or singing the Welsh songs they'd learned together?

Mary Anne had been at Lambeth Infirmary just over a week when her particulars were recorded in the examination book with the help of Ethel. The experience was probably intimidating for eighteen-year-old Ethel, and prompts a vision of her with hands clasped tightly in her lap as she perches on the edge of a chair, dutifully supplying answers to the questions put to her. The scratch of pen on paper in an otherwise quiet room must have caused her to imagine that the person across the desk, scribbling in the ledger, could hear the loud thump of her heart. She named the birthplaces of the Deverill children, the schools she and her siblings had attended over the years, the addresses where they'd lived and the date of Harry's death, and she recited a list of Mary Anne's previous hospitalizations. She gave pertinent employment details: her work as a box-maker, including her earnings; the rent paid at the Goodwin; the fact that her brother was in the Navy.

With Joe far away, the worries for Ethel were enormous, so it's understandable that during this time a shadow grew across her face, a sadness that would linger her entire life and darken her eyes even when there was something to smile about. Her mother had been sick for months. What if she never got better? There was a cluster of relatives in the Goodwin to lend support – Uncle Jack at number 30, and Aunt Maggie, May and a pregnant Clara at number 36 – but due to the war, everyone was working, and for longer hours. Family stories peg Ernie during those difficult years as slow, or troubled – "not quite right in the brain," one relative said, and a follower rather than a leader – so although he was twelve now, he was not deemed capable of being fully responsible for himself and Doris, nearly seven. Both were of an age to be sent to Hanwell School, the fate of Charlie Chaplin and so many poor children with parents unable to care for them. But thankfully family stepped in. Joe sent money regularly, and for a while during Mary Anne's long hospitalizations Ethel muddled through, keeping Doris and Ernie with her. Aunt Maggie, in her role as matriarch of a shrinking brood, helped where she could, as did May and Clara. Martha Bedford continued to be a stalwart friend despite her location on the other side of the Thames, and Doris sometimes stayed with her in Whitechapel – trips she loved, but which never lasted long enough. No one could keep Doris indefinitely, and she felt the strain from others as she moved from place to place, a small being who'd become a large burden. She was shunted between College Buildings and the Goodwin until Harry's sisters Nell and Maud, in Wimbledon, agreed to have her for a longer stretch.

Uncle Jack took Doris there on the train, depositing her at the spacious three-storey house the aunts shared on Worple Road, a street lined with leafy trees and large, fenced yards full of flowers. This place was unlike anything Doris had known, a suburb far removed from the crowded, noisy Borough and the multi-ethnic warrens of Whitechapel. The house was big, but it was full of boy cousins she didn't know very well, so instead of seeming grand it seemed hollow, the opposite of home. Though the neighbourhood was pretty, it was unfamiliar, and Doris had no friends there. The boy cousins teased relentlessly, but Doris's unhappiness had less to do with them than with missing the people and places she knew and loved.

The one solace came when Aunt Nell played the piano. Nell was a product of a society that loved its music. In the seventy-some years since Queen Victoria had ascended the throne, pianos had gone from luxury items in the parlours of the privileged to commonplace fixtures in the homes of the working class. There was a piano for every ten to twenty people by 1910, and women like Nell could bang off music hall tunes and tinkle Chopin with equal skill. Nell gave Doris her first lessons and never knew the effect she had in doing so. Doris listened to Nell play and worked to copy the pieces, pressing her own fingers on the smooth keys and hoping for the same beautiful music. But her attempts couldn't match the sounds Aunt Nell coaxed from the instrument, and the disappointment only added to Doris's melancholy. She was miserable away from Bebbie and her siblings, and cried nightly for her mother, whose stay at Lambeth threatened to be truly interminable.

A 1913 issue of the *British Journal of Nursing* describes Lambeth as one of London's oldest infirmaries, tucked within a maze of city streets, with bridges connecting various wings of the building. It had nearly seven hundred beds and had become for all intents and purposes "a great State Hospital...for in truth that is what our poor law infirmaries are nowadays." From some vantage points you could see the domes of St. Paul's Cathedral and the Bethlem mental asylum, as well as the Clock Tower at Westminster. Though the patients admitted to Lambeth Infirmary received "every care," according to the journal, they were often incurably ill, as Jennie's husband, Richard Vanson, had been when he was admitted with tuberculosis, "and little can be done for them except to ameliorate their condition as much as possible." In this task the staff succeeded well, and the matron made a point of knowing her patients' illnesses and concerns, and offering words of comfort as she passed through the wards.

The Lambeth Board of Guardians minute book reveals a little of what was going on in the institution at the time of Mary Anne's admission, with some nurses leaving for military service and another away indefinitely due to a nervous breakdown. Just before Mary Anne arrived, a long-term infirmary patient "in a dying condition" had suddenly risen from his bed and jumped out the window. The fall had killed him instantly and was afterward ruled a suicide by reason of temporary insanity. Another man had died in the infirmary after being struck by a military vehicle; the truck had been travelling in a convoy when its driver inexplicably veered off course and hit the man, smashing into a shop window. There are other more cheerful mentions that illuminate workhouse life: a charity organization bringing pots of flowers and entertaining the patients with songs and poems; a letter received from a patient, "thanking the Guardians for the very generous treatment and kindness received by him whilst an inmate of the Infirmary." And there are the humdrum details of the workhouse grocery list: 90 lbs margarine, 100 tins sardines, 2 doz. tins peas, 50 doz. tins beef, 146 boxes raisins, 40 cwt. Swede turnips. The minutes also report the occasional problem of blown and leaking tins of milk, and fish that was "coarse in quality and strong in flavour, with the result that the patients wasted the greater part of it." Owing to the war, there was a dearth of both potatoes and male porters. A new supply of one thousand women's bed-gowns contained two hundred that were made from calico of an inferior quality, but whether Mary Anne's was one of these, no one knows. Her name does not appear in the minutes among the occasional mentions of patients suffering from tuberculosis or pneumonia, or certified insane, but within a month of her arrival at Lambeth Infirmary she received a definitive diagnosis.

"I personally examined the said Mary Anne Deverill," wrote Dr. Arthur Baly, "and came to the conclusion that she is a person of unsound mind and a proper person to be taken charge of and detained under care and treatment." Facts indicating her insanity were as follows: "Patient says that she has been to a young man at the place where she works (untrue, patient has not been out of the ward); she says she is going out as she has promised to meet him. She does not know where she is or how long she has been here." The following day, Baly's recommendation was passed, the official "Order for the Reception of a Pauper Lunatic" was filed and Mary Anne was sent to Cane Hill Asylum. At the same time, Ellen Evans Roff returned to Newington Workhouse, presumably because she could do nothing more for her sister and could not follow her to Cane Hill.

In Wimbledon, Doris received a postcard for her seventh birthday from Bebbie, showing a girl on the front cuddling a cat, and a poem that read "A happy day, a happy year, And glad years following ever, May hope light all your path with cheer, and love forsake you never." On the back, Bebbie wrote, "With kind thoughts and good wishes, M.B." It was a small bright spot in an otherwise horrible time.

By now, Charlie Chaplin was a major star, making movies and living in Hollywood. Despite his enormous popularity, he was frequently accused in the press of being a slacker and had received plenty of white feathers in the mail for having failed to enlist. Contractual obligations conveniently kept him in the United States for the duration of the war, but shortly after the Americans joined the conflict he filled out his draft card – occupation, "moving picture comedian"; dependent, "mother." Apparently he failed the physical, but the white feathers continued to come. And yet Chaplin's popularity swelled among both civilians and men in the trenches. They couldn't get enough of him. His films showed in cinemas at home, in makeshift movie houses at the front and even on the ceilings in military hospitals, so that wounded men could lie on their backs and enjoy the medicine of laughter. The self-described "struggling young nondescript from Lambeth" had come a long, long way and later credited his mother, Hannah, as his greatest inspiration. "She imbued me with the feeling that I had some sort of talent." But as her son's celebrity status rose, she continued to decline mentally. Years after her death,

Charlie wrote about a visit he and his half-brother, Sydney, had made to Cane Hill in 1912, intending to see her. "It was a depressing day, for she was not well. She had just got over an obstreperous phase of singing hymns, and had been confined to a padded room. The nurse had warned us of this beforehand. Sydney saw her, but I had not the courage, so I waited. He came back upset, and said that she had been given shock treatment of icy cold showers and that her face was quite blue."

By the time Mary Anne entered Cane Hill, Charlie's success meant he could afford to move his mother to a private institution, and many of Cane Hill's beds were now taken up by soldiers unable to cope with the trauma of war. The military records of these men offer glimpses into their struggles: one young man from Bermondsey had been a motor driver in France and was diagnosed with 100-percent disability. It was clear to the examiners that his mental state had been altered by war. He'd been "peculiar and stupid in France. Is dull, slow in mind, careless, irresponsible and happy. His mind wanders incoherently from one subject to another and his speech is indistinct." Another was a gunner who was sluggish, slurred his words and had "little to say for himself." He was deteriorating rapidly.

At Cane Hill the noise of war was no longer audible. The asylum sat in a peaceful spot, occupying 148 acres on an elevated plateau in the Surrey hills, overlooking lush countryside. Its longtime medical superintendent, Dr. James Moody, had been in charge of the institution since it opened in 1883 until his death in 1915, and he was buried on its grounds. He'd considered Cane Hill his life's work and had been knighted for the great advances he'd made treating the insane. Moody might have been in agreement with the ideas written by a contemporary, Dr. Maurice Craig, in his 1905 reference *Psychological Medicine: A Manual on Mental Diseases for Practitioners and Students.* Craig, like Moody, was considered a pioneer in psychiatry and was of the opinion that mental disorders should be viewed in the same way as disease in general. He discouraged the use of "antiquated terms, such as 'mad' and 'lunatic,'" writing that "once the fundamental principles of insanity have been learnt, the disorders of mind will at least be intelligible, and no longer a mere concatenation of strange symptoms."

In the asylum's early days, Moody had written enthusiastically about the design of the building, with its wards radiating from interconnected corridors. The wards varied in shape and size, which was unusual for such institutions. Depending on the needs of the patients within, the furniture varied too. Two of the wards had been specially designed for epileptic and suicidal cases and had beds that locked to the floor. "The patient is unable to pull this bedstead about, and should a fall take place the padded edge prevents injury; the height from the floor is only eight inches." Another ward reserved for acute cases contained single padded rooms – where Hannah Chaplin had once stayed. There was attention to aesthetic detail as well: a mirror graced the mantel of each ward's day room, and bright linoleum covered the floors in varying patterns. Here and there were "engravings, oleographs, plaster figures, china ware, aquaria, fern cases, and bird cages," and the patients themselves assisted in making curtains and crocheted doilies that gave the rooms a homey feel. Each ward had a supply of games – chess, dominoes, bagatelle – and two of the women's wards had pianos. A photograph shows a group of men and women seated at easels, carefully dabbing at landscape paintings with one hand and holding their palettes with the other. "As little uniformity as possible" was the rule when it came to patients' garb, so the fabric varied somewhat in type and colour, and on special occasions, or when taken walking beyond the grounds, patients "able to appreciate the privilege" could wear Sunday best. "Strong clothing" – used to restrict movement or prevent self-harm and destructive behaviour – was used sparingly, but in certain cases "the moral effect was very good, for when it was put on for a short time the other patients laughed the wearer out of his habits."

By 1917, two years after Moody's death, the asylum had grown. It held 2,367 patients just a couple of days before Mary Anne arrived, when Commissioner in Lunacy Sir Frederick Needham arrived for his yearly inspection. Needham was a tall, distinguished man just past eighty, known for his keen sense of justice and his perpetual return to one key question: "How will this affect the patients?" At Cane Hill he was pleased with what he saw, though no one had yet stepped permanently into Moody's shoes. The temporary medical superintendent,

Dr. Edward Salterne Litteljohn, oversaw the institution "with energy and conspicuous efficiency." The other medical officers working with him were also at temporary posts, but "the state of the books and the knowledge which they have of their patients show how well they are discharging their temporary duties." Over two days, Needham visited every resident patient and found little to criticize at Cane Hill. "Having visited all parts of the Asylum and its dependencies I am able to report that it continues to be maintained throughout in excellent order and to afford ample facilities for the successful treatment of the patients. The day rooms were everywhere bright, cheerful, and comfortable and generally supplied with adequate objects of interest and occupation. I thought, however, that in many rooms a larger provision of books would be acceptable to the patients and contribute to their happiness." He was impressed with the food, too – one night a dinner of boiled beef, potatoes, rice and bread, and the next a hearty soup served with bread and a dessert of rice pudding. He conceded that not everyone was happy; there were those who asked him to discharge them as he visited the wards, but they were "obviously unfit for it," and not once did he notice a patient being neglected or treated roughly by staff. In all, "the patients throughout the Asylum were remarkably quiet and free from excitement, and in none of the wards was there any general restlessness or noisy confusion."

Yet there were always patients who balked at being restricted, no matter how comfortably, and longed to get away. The minute book mentions two escapes during Mary Anne's stay – one man crept into the shrubbery while working on the grounds, and another broke a chain that locked a ground-floor window and slipped away to freedom. For them, the "airing courts" and the walks through the ample grounds would never lessen the sense of confinement that came with living in an institution, despite the fact that Cane Hill's buildings alone sprawled across twelve acres and contained more than three miles of corridors. The chapel held eight hundred and had a vaulted ceiling and polished wood pews; the recreation hall was larger than most London theatres and boasted a stage, a visitors' balcony and an orchestra pit. Concerts were usual. But much of each day was spent routinely, since in essence

Cane Hill was a working estate, and, where possible, patients contributed by working on the farm or in the greenhouses or at any number of
jobs that supported the operation of the asylum. Men could assist the
baker, tailor, shoemaker, carpenter, painter or bricklayer, while women
were required in the needle room, laundry and kitchen, and as ward
workers and knitters. As an incentive, men who worked received tobacco, and women received extra morning and afternoon tea.

Although seen as therapeutic, employing patients as workers was
not without risks. Owing to the nature of the trades, workers were
frequently trusted with sharp blades, tools and dangerous machinery.
One particularly gruesome incident involved a cabinetmaker suffering
from delusional insanity, whose steady improvement earned him a spot
in the asylum's carpentry shop. It was thought he might soon be discharged altogether. Instead he died of self-inflicted injuries after a fellow
worker found him hammering the sharpened edge of a plane into his
neck with a mallet.

Moody had had several close calls during his long tenure at Cane
Hill. Once he'd been attacked by a female patient wielding a knife; another time a male patient struck him so violently that his upper jaw was
fractured. And then there was the story he told about a time he'd come
upon some patients working in the laundry, who decided, on seeing
him, that he should be boiled. "Let's put the doctor in the copper," the
women goaded each other, all of them gathering round. "Oh, that will
be fun," Moody replied. "But, I say," he paused, looking down at his feet.
"I have a pair of new boots on, and it seems a pity to spoil them. Suppose I go and change them first." The women agreed to this, and Moody
escaped, boots and all.

His temporary replacement, Dr. Litteljohn, had grown up in the Poor
Law system, though on the privileged side of it. His father was Salterne
Litteljohn, the medical practitioner at Hanwell School, who had tended
to Richard Vanson and Charlie Chaplin when they passed through his
infirmary doors, and also to Richard's young nephew, George, who had
died in the doctor's care. Edward Litteljohn had lived on the grounds
too, although in the doctor's house, separate from the poor boys; on the
census reports a distinct line is drawn between his family and the pages

that list "workhouse child" one after another, with the census taker's scribble of frustration: "It is absolutely impossible to give this information as the children have not any clear idea where they were born."

Litteljohn's sister Edith was a nurse at Barts, but had left her position to join the Territorial Force Nursing Service. Loss of staff due to military work was one of many new problems Litteljohn and other medical officers faced during the war. At Cane Hill, as male attendants and labourers became soldiers, former employees who'd retired returned to fill some of those places. Age-old rules were relaxed, and nurses obliged to resign because they had married were invited to take up their old posts. Women worked on male wards since there were not enough men left to do so. The shortages affected all areas of the community that was Cane Hill; Moody, foreseeing trouble, had purchased more cows and sheep when the war began, but there were still food shortages, and the asylum's farm bailiff had an increased workload with fewer trained workers – more than thirty pigs died in the summer of 1915 because the man put in charge of them was inexperienced.

And yet even in these challenging circumstances, the effort was made to maintain the asylum's standards. A month or so after Mary Anne arrived, one nurse accused another of slapping a patient. Dr. Litteljohn wrote that "the Assistant Matron, Miss Lakeman, reported having seen Nurse Celia Gertrude Spinner strike one of the patients. The nurse now denies it. As this is a serious offence, I ask the Committee to see Miss Lakeman and the nurse and come to some decision as to how she shall be dealt with." During that meeting, Nurse Spinner continued to deny the slapping, but claimed she had "pushed the patient's hand away from the patient's boot which she was putting on and which the patient was persistently endeavouring to take off." Patients often tried to take off their boots, it seemed, and for that reason wore a special type that locked closed – but getting them on in the first place could still be difficult. The committee decided that the nurse had indeed slapped the patient, albeit without any intention to hurt her, and as punishment she was reduced in rank, which also meant a reduction in wages. Litteljohn was to report on her conduct in three months' time to see if she might be reinstated to her old position, but by then she had resigned altogether.

That summer, London fell victim to the first daylight raid by Gotha bombers. Gothas were airplanes rather than airships, able to fly at heights comparable to Zeppelins but much faster and with a range that outstripped other airplanes of the time. Daylight missions didn't require the heavy and distracting wireless radio sets used in some craft as direction-finding equipment, which also revealed their approach to the enemy. London was caught off guard. The sound of the engines could be heard for ten minutes before the planes appeared, and Londoners came outside to see what was making such an "impressive noise." Even after they spotted the planes overhead in a diamond formation – and British planes rising from all directions to chase them off – people didn't recognize the enemy or understand what was about to happen. One witness said the Gothas looked like enormous silver dragonflies sparkling in the sky. Looking down from his vantage point, German squadron leader Ernst Brandenburg saw "with perfect clearness, the Thames bridges, the railway stations, the city, even the Bank of England ..." England's attempts at defense were useless. "Our aircraft circled round and dropped their bombs with no hurry or trouble," Brandenburg later wrote. "The effect must have been great."

He was right about that; the East End was hit hard. The Commercial Street School logbook stated that parents rushed to the school in a panic, eager to be sure their children were all right. They climbed over the wall around the school and burst into the classrooms to retrieve their little ones and take them home. Physically, the children of Commercial Street School were fine, but others did not fare well. A bomb landed on a school in nearby Poplar, crashing through the roof, through the girls' third floor, then the boys' second floor, and exploding on the ground floor, in the infants' rooms. As the building collapsed in on itself, eighteen students died, most of them under six years old. One of the teachers said that after the blast, all was instantly in darkness, and there was the smell of fumes. "I thought I was being buried alive and suffocated at the same time."

Bombs had fallen in Southwark and Bermondsey, too. At Newington Workhouse, the master recorded that there was no panic among the inmates that day, and he was able to get them indoors and away from shrapnel. Afterward, he found fragments on the workhouse grounds. Farther north, at Charles Dickens School, the boys in Ernie's class hid under their desks when the whistle was blown and stayed put until the firing stopped. As at Commercial Street School, parents had run to the gate but were prevented from entering by a policeman sent to guard the school. On the girls' side, "the children behaved splendidly," the logbook reports. "National songs were sung during the period and the majority of the children had no idea that enemy air craft were in neighbourhood of the school." It was the parents whose behaviour required correcting. After the devastation at the Poplar school, London County Council posted notices that cautioned parents against storming their children's schools during air raids. "During danger from an air raid, all children will remain inside the school buildings; all gates will be shut and no one will be admitted. Crowding round the school premises only increases the danger. No place is absolutely safe, but experience shows that children are safer in school buildings than if sent out into the streets. The London County Council is doing all it can to secure the safety of the children, and it is hoped that parents will help by leaving their children entirely under the control of the teachers until all danger is over."

All across the city, adults were in anguish over what had happened. In total there were 162 deaths and 432 injuries from this single raid, but it was the loss of the children that sent the public into a period of collective mourning. The children were buried together and given a public funeral; flags flew at half mast, shutters and blinds were closed, and the Bishop of London officiated. Six little girls in white dresses with black sashes and hats, and six young boys in Scout uniforms represented their playmates, carrying bunches of flowers to place on the common grave. Five hundred mourning wreaths graced the Town Hall, offerings from teachers, neighbours, the mayor and even "theatres, picture palaces, music-halls, military hospitals … soldiers … the crew of a destroyer, Customs officials, workmen of various unions … Sunday schools and day schools, cripples' homes, and other children's homes." The king sent a message that the Bishop read aloud, assuring the parents that he and the queen were "thinking of them in their saddened homes … The early ending of young, innocent lives, at all times pathetic, is more than ever so in these cruel and tragic circumstances."

The message seemed genuine, but it came on the heels of some tactical manoeuvring by the king at the urging of his private secretary, Arthur Bigge, Lord Stamfordham, who recognized a general discord among the lower classes of the world and saw that the discontent could easily spread to Britain. Royalty everywhere were nervous these days, and bolstering their thrones as best they could. In Russia, revolution had broken out, the tsar had been forced to abdicate, and with his wife and children had been placed under house arrest. Tsar Nicholas was George V's cousin, and the two men not only looked remarkably alike ("Nicky" was "wonderfully like Georgie," Queen Victoria had once swooned) but had been close friends as well; their mothers were sisters, and as children the boys had holidayed together in Denmark. George was related to Nicholas's German wife, Alix, too: in the tangled web that was royalty, Alix's mother, George's father, and Kaiser Wilhelm's mother were all children of Queen Victoria. But George was loosening family ties. When the Romanovs requested asylum in Britain – and were guaranteed safe passage by the Kaiser – Stamfordham urged George to likewise urge the government to reject the request. He advised detachment elsewhere as well: given the raging anti-German sentiments, the fact that the royal family's ancestry was German through almost all of its branches could be a liability. That the current reigning House bore the name Saxe-Coburg-Gotha and, by coincidence, the planes dropping their loads on innocent children were Gotha bombers didn't help matters.

In fact, in the weeks following the raid, newspapers reported riots in the East End that matched the ferocity of outbreaks that had occurred at the beginning of the war. Angry groups of men and women smashed windows of German bakers and butchers, throwing loaves of bread into the street and demolishing furniture. A shop owner with "a continental name" had his window cracked before he could convince the rioters that he was French rather than German. Another felt compelled to chalk in big block letters on the wall outside his store "WE ARE RUSSIANS," but even when police managed to get in front of the crowds, stones were thrown over their heads and glass shattered. Dwellings were attacked too. In one case, the mob carried off a piano and set it on fire. Once the situation had been brought under control, police still found the demeanour of the crowd so menacing that they kept all available men on watch throughout the evening.

Within a month of the raid the king had followed Stamfordham's advice to distance himself from his Germanic roots and take the name Windsor after one of his oldest castles, a royal residence since the Norman Conquest almost a thousand years earlier. On July 17, 1917, the king issued a proclamation "relinquishing the use of all German Titles and Dignities." *Punch* ran a cartoon of a determined King George vigorously wielding a broom, sweeping crowns and dust and the words "Made in Germany" before him. The caption read "A Good Riddance."

Some of the king's subjects felt a similar obligation to shun their German-sounding names, and notices appeared in the papers of Charles Henry Reissmann becoming Charles Henry Rivers, of Eliazer Duizend becoming Eliazer Dyson, of Anthony Philip Hecht becoming Anthony Philip Heath, and so on. Two of Percy Kraushaar's cousins changed their names, though their great-great-grandfather had come from Germany more than a century earlier, long before Benjamin and Margaret Jones arrived in the Borough with their cows. Quoting one of the men, the *Gazette* reported, "I, Albert Henry Crawshaw, a natural-born British subject of 11 Howley-Road West Croydon, Surrey, Confectioner, now serving in His Majesty's Army, heretofore called and known by the name of Albert Augustus Henry Kraushaar, hereby give public notice…I absolutely renounced and abandoned the use of my former Christian name of Augustus and my former surname of Kraushaar, and then assumed and adopted and determined to use and subscribe the name of Albert Henry Crawshaw."

Among the soldiers admitted to Cane Hill, one man, born to German parents in Whitechapel, suffered delusions connected to his ancestry. According to his military record, "He began to imagine some months ago that people in the streets gesticulated at him and made disparaging remarks about him. Subsequently he imagined that the men at his regiment poisoned his food. Since admission he has…voices telling him that he is to be made away with because he is a spy." The doctors believed this was a constitutional tendency that had been aggravated by war service. "The man is of German parentage, hence the nature of the delusions."

Few records exist to describe Mary Anne's experience at Cane Hill, but she does appear in one of only a handful of surviving medical registers, in an entry that notes her general health was poor. The Lunacy Commission code listed in her record – II5 – means that her mental disorder was diagnosed as "confusional insanity occurring later in life." Other codes indicate the doctors believed her insanity was brought on by mental stress and heredity. In many ways she fit the profile of someone with what Dr. Craig called "organic dementia," the result of "some gross disease of the brain," and described by him in *Psychological Medicine* as "disoriented for time and place, together with severe loss of memory, incoherence of ideas, and imperceptions, and a general condition of confusion of mind." One such patient told her doctor that "things did not fit together properly in her head." It isn't known whether Mary Anne spoke of plans to meet her young man again, or if the young man existed outside her delusions, or if he was Harry come to life in her bungled memories, but her fits must have continued since the Cane Hill prescription register says she was treated with eye drops and unguents, as well as aspirin for pain – but she was also administered bromatropin, a drug used to control convulsions, and sulphonal, a powerful sedative for which psychiatric manuals urged cautious use. In his 1917 work, Dr. Craig wrote that it was the most commonly used hypnotic in both institutions and private practice, a tasteless, odourless powder best given with hot milk or arrowroot. It was dangerous, too, though, and often resulted in vomiting, diarrhea and urine the colour of port wine. The drug sometimes failed utterly, another manual explained, and other times "act[ed] like a charm," its effects lasting to some extent for a full twenty-four hours. Still, "except for the purpose of aborting an incipient attack of mania, hypnotics are inadvisable...Much better results are obtained for the patient by open-air exercise and hot baths." But Mary Anne was likely in need of stronger relief than exercise and baths. The codes in her record imply that she experienced constant mental stress and also some sort of sensory deprivation from August on. As her illness progressed, her symptoms surely worsened.

Dr. Craig wrote that of all possible symptoms of organic dementia, memory loss was the most prevalent. "In some cases the amnesia is very great and renders the patient totally unable to look after himself... Many patients with organic dementia mistake the identity of those about them. As the disease runs its course they become more and more confused, and finally become bedridden and hopelessly demented." In keeping with contemporary ideas about hereditary traits – you could inherit feeble-mindedness and criminality – he pointed out that the family's mental history had its role to play here too: "If the statistics of these organic cases are examined, it will be seen that a very large proportion of the patients have a neuropathic inheritance and are therefore predisposed to mental disturbance."

The codes in Mary Anne's file suggest the doctors at Cane Hill agreed. Did they know about Ellen, and did the family also draw some link between the sisters' illnesses? For Mary Anne's children was there shame in the fact that their mother was at a lunatic asylum, that their aunt had been at a similar facility and that their grandmother had spent so many years in the workhouse? Knowledge of mental illness continued to evolve, but there was still much to learn even at the medical level. Dr. Craig stressed that "our nervous system, like any other system of the body, bears in all probability the stamp of our ancestors upon it. If our parents or grandparents have had an unstable nervous system, the *tendency* is that we shall be unstable in the same direction. We would especially emphasise the word *tendency*, for, after all, it is nothing more. Because our ancestors were of unsound mind, it is no reason why we should become insane." And yet the term "hereditary insanity" prevailed. The physician Frederick Walker Mott wrote about it at length in a 1911 article for the *Eugenics Review*. One of his conclusions was that mothers were far more often the genetic transmitters of insanity than fathers, and that daughters were especially susceptible. A year earlier the medical officer at Barming Asylum in Kent reported that "one cannot fail to observe the large number of our patients who are related to each other. We have at the present time in this asylum examples of brothers, sisters, father and daughter, father and sons, mother and daughter, uncle and niece, aunt and nephew, besides many cases of more distant relatives." On analyzing his numbers, he found evidence of "insanity in the family" in 42.7 percent of the asylum's patients. "Our asylum population is constantly recruited from and maintained by persons who have some inherited defect of brain-cell which renders them unfit to meet the ordinary stress of life, and until the State is able to devise some suitable means for the permanent care and control of such persons the ranks of the insane will continue to be filled and to burden the ratepayer."

The perceived link between insanity and heredity was even stronger in the general population; newspapers regularly wrote about murder and suicide cases in which familial insanity was a factor. Knowing of both his mother's and grandmother's madness, Charlie Chaplin once confided to his cameraman the fear that he, too, would eventually go insane.

Did Doris have such fears when she finally visited her mother at Cane Hill? Was the visit "almost unbearable" for her, as it had been for Chaplin the first time he'd seen his mother there?

Doris had been lonely enough in Wimbledon that her aunts hadn't kept her for long, and she returned to the Borough in August, around the time Joe came home on leave. Given the fact there was a war on, compassionate leave was rarely allowed, even for deaths, but the logbook shows that several men were granted a long break in that same period. The respite was once again timely, and Joe grasped the opportunity to visit his mother at the asylum. Perhaps he'd had word of how sick she was – a letter from Bebbie or Aunt Maggie or Ethel that prepared him for seeing a much-changed woman. He collected Doris for the difficult visit, travelling by train to Coulsdon, he in his Navy uniform, she in her Sunday clothes. The train ride out of the city and into the country and the tree-lined platform where they disembarked were like Doris's Wimbledon trips, but nothing else of the visit was similar once Doris found herself with her hand in Joe's, walking up the path to the ivy-covered asylum, their footsteps crunching gravel. Inside, doctors, nurses and attendants were busy at their tasks, and patients milled about. Despite the strangeness of the day, and its lasting significance, the memories all but left her. Or did they? Later, all she claimed to recall was that she'd sat in a chair beside her mother's bed, and her mother had looked at her and said, "I must ask the nurse to bring you a cup of tea."

More vividly shared memories were those of standing with Bebbie on the balcony at College Buildings and watching flames fall through the night sky. In late September, Gotha bombers launched attacks on London on three consecutive nights, with newspapers mentioning the use of star shells, artillery that burst in the air and illuminated the sky with a magnesium flare. Since the summer raids when so many children had died, the authorities had decided that warning people of impending danger would at least give them a chance to take cover, so police stations were equipped with maroons – sound rockets that were fired in quick succession when enemy planes were spotted. One writer described the sudden boom shattering the relative silence of the night, and the subsequent trail of red sparks that expired just as the second rocket confirmed the warning. "Then everyone quickened his step homeward, or, if too far from home, took cover in one of the places which had been set aside as air-raid shelters. People who owned basements betook themselves to them. Others vacated top floors, turned round arm-chairs with their backs to the windows – and waited."

Lieutenant-Commander Rawlinson, in charge of London's defenses, had a different perspective and gave a more detailed explanation for the flames Doris saw from the balcony on Wentworth Street, writing that on the third night of the attacks, some of the city's defensive gun stations had run out of ammunition to use against the planes. They did have incendiary shells, usually used against Zeppelins, and as Rawlinson later described it, "in a few moments magnificent clouds of burning gas were to be seen hurtling through the sky, with the result that the London newspapers next morning announced, with a bloodthirsty 'glee' which they made no attempt to conceal, that towards the end of the attack enemy aeroplanes were observed 'falling in flames' in several directions!" Despite the chaos – the boom of sound rockets and Scouts running through the streets banging on doors to warn people to take shelter – Doris and Bebbie stayed put and watched the drifting flames, which to Doris seemed both frightening and beautiful.

It must have been hard to decide whether to stay at home or run for cover – to the underground tube stations or the railway viaducts. Larger premises, deemed safer because of their size, were also pressed into service, so breweries, schools and even hospitals opened their doors to those seeking cover. The jury was out on the wisest course of action. One leaflet cautioned that "no shelter is bomb proof" and promised that most people would be "quite as safe in their own homes or in the homes of friends or neighbours if they would keep behind walls and away from doors, skylights and windows." Despite such advice, hundreds of thousands descended underground each night, the crush creating its own problems. At Liverpool Street Station a woman was trampled to death in a stampede. Fights and arguments broke out. Anyone trying to use the trains found the platforms frequently impassable, every space having been taken up by people bedded down for the night. Across London, some 300,000 people were sheltering below ground, bringing with them their inevitable noises and smells. Not until the end of the year did privacy screens go up around the sand buckets placed as makeshift toilets, but the screens only addressed the visuals and did not dispel the stink or cleanse the filth. For most Londoners, crowding, filth and bad smells were nothing unusual.

The *Daily Mail* reported on what it termed "tube camps," claiming that those who took refuge in the tunnels were "the happiest people in London." There was some "crowding and crushing," the writer admitted, but "the men calmed the fears of the women, and after a time stolid British silence was the prevailing note among the people." Whole families gathered, the paper claimed, bringing rugs to sit on, and before long they were passing the time singing songs until "the stations were echoing to rollicking choruses," oblivious to what might be going on above ground.

Perhaps Bebbie never read the *Daily Mail*'s account of the tube camps, or heard first-hand the other version that included stinking makeshift toilets and pickpockets and fights. Her decision to remain at home during air raids created some of Doris's only memories of the war, and a feeling of safety. Bebbie would squeeze Doris's hand reassuringly and nod toward the kaleidoscope of flame and light. "There's a sight, my girl, and one we'll not soon be forgetting."

Doris was still with Bebbie on October 12, when harsh news came with the cold wind and rains of autumn. History remembers that day as the First Battle of Passchendaele in Belgium, with thousands of men falling to their deaths in relentless mud. For Doris's family it was a day of personal tragedy: Mary Anne had died at Cane Hill Asylum. The news must have come to the Goodwin by telegram, delivered by a cycling youth no older than Ernie and, because of the war, well used to bearing sad tidings. A message was sent to Bebbie, and also north to Joe, but days passed and there was no response from him. What did come was news of the post-mortem examination, certified by Dr. Litteljohn, stating that Mary Anne had died from a cancerous brain tumour. The autopsy also revealed breast cancer, so no doubt the disease had been lurking for some time and had metastasized, affecting the brain and causing the "fits" that had sent her in and out of care until she was finally admitted to Cane Hill. A lesion of the brain can cause any number of uncomfortable symptoms: clumsiness, lethargy, headaches, double vision, distorted speech, seizures, vomiting, fever. Hardest for loved ones, perhaps, were memory loss, mood swings and personality changes. However her illness affected her, she was surely very changed by the end of it, and not the mother her children had known.

So many at Cane Hill were buried quietly on the grounds, abandoned by next of kin who wished to avoid the stigma of the asylum, or else with no family left to claim them. But Mary Anne's death was registered by Jack three days after she died, and arrangements were made for her burial at Nunhead. There was room for her with Harry in the family plot, but it must have been too costly to dig a single spot, so Mary Anne was laid to rest in a common grave in a section of the cemetery where the interments were of people with very little money. Before the funeral, Bebbie took Doris shopping for clothes appropriate to the occasion. She bought her a black poplin dress and a white felt hat with a black ribbon, items that Doris would always remember with clarity, though her own mother's features would soon be hard to picture, as would many in the uncertain group she walked with: Bebbie and the bits and pieces of family – Jack and Aunt Maggie, Clara and May, her siblings minus Joe – all strolling Nunhead's stately avenues, past the towering lime trees and stone angels, a place of such sorrowful beauty and solitude, and yet with the roar of London audible beyond its gates. Someone – Ethel, perhaps, as the eldest child present – chose the verse for the inside of the memoriam card issued by the undertaker, and a black-bordered copy made its way into Doris's keepsakes.

A loving mother, how we miss her,
None but aching hearts can tell,
We have lost her, Heaven has found her,
Jesus doeth all things well.

Within a week such faith was put to the test when a telegram arrived from the Admiralty, addressed to Mrs. M.A. Deverill.

This shot of some of the crew of the Mary Rose in 1916 features a few of the key players in Joe's time on board, and in the tragedy to come: Ernest Grummitt stands fifth from left with a pipe in his mouth; dimpled John Bailey stands third from right, arms folded, hat pushed back; and William MacLeod kneels in the centre of the image, with a crewmate's hands on his shoulders. Joe is here too, in the lower right portion of the photo, behind the man with the cigarette in his mouth.

CHAPTER 12

Down-Hearted and Shivery

As the news of Mary Anne's death travelled toward him that October in 1917, Joe unwittingly moved farther away from it. On the morning of the 15th, *Mary Rose* and her sister destroyer *Strongbow* left Lerwick, accompanying a convoy of merchant ships to Norway with the help of two British fishing trawlers fitted out for escort purposes. The trips were sometimes boring, as Joe's crewmate John Bailey had noted, but also potentially dangerous. The convoy system hadn't been perfected yet, and many of the merchant ships, or "packets" as they were known, had little experience travelling in such a regimented way. Sometimes the fast ships pushed too far ahead, and the slower ships lagged behind, making the destroyers' job to guard the whole group not just challenging but maddening because of all that could go wrong while the gaps in the convoy widened. Sometimes, too, the destroyers were purposely sent in different directions. By the morning of the 16th, after an uneventful sail, *Mary Rose* and *Strongbow* were approaching Norway with their group. As per their instructions on leaving Scotland the day before, they parted ways when they encountered a second westbound convoy. *Mary Rose* took up this new convoy of twelve ships, and with the trawler *P. Fannon* started back toward Lerwick. *Strongbow*, with the trawler *Elise*, carried on with her original charges. Once she'd seen them to shore at Bergen, Norway, she would turn back and rejoin the westbound group.

Evening had come by the time *Strongbow* and *Elise* drew close to the others again. Several times through the night, *Strongbow*'s Lieutenant-Commander Edward Brooke attempted to reach Charles Fox on *Mary Rose* but was unable to make contact. Fox, for his part, did not know that *Strongbow* had returned, but he zigzagged ahead anyway, staying close to a couple of the faster ships in the convoy and drawing farther away from the bulk of the packets lagging behind. With Lerwick in reach, the convoy grew uneven. By dawn the two destroyers were close to ten miles apart, with most of the merchant ships between them. The sky was lightening but cloudy, and the sea was rough. Just before six, *Strongbow*'s officer of the watch sighted two ships coming closer. He assumed, from their dark grey colour, that they were British light cruisers. But when *Strongbow* flashed its recognition signals, the ships answered by opening fire.

A couple of hours earlier, on board *Mary Rose*, John Bailey had taken his place as lookout on the after searchlight platform, between two long pairs of torpedo tubes he was trained to man during battles. *Strongbow* and most of the packets were still out of sight. At 5:50, flashes of light rippled and fluttered in the distance, in the direction of the convoy. Bailey stared. He listened hard but all he could hear was the churning of the *Mary Rose* engines. The lights kept flashing. He was certain the distinct rippling meant something even more daunting than a U-boat attacking with its single gun; this was "salvo answering salvo," the work of German light cruisers raiding the convoy. Speaking through his voice-pipe, he reported what he'd seen to the officer of the watch, and Lieutenant-Commander Fox was summoned. From his place on the bridge, Fox put up his binoculars and peered into the distance but apparently missed the distinctions Bailey had so quickly spotted. "I think it's a submarine," he said to the men around him. He ordered the ship put about and the crew to action stations.

As the ship turned, the green water pushed with all its might against her, as if to stop her from her mission. She couldn't be forced to full speed, for if the decks were flooded the guns and torpedo tubes would be useless.

It soon became clear that they would need all possible forms of defense: the swan bows and three straight funnels that were typical of German light cruisers could now be seen about four miles off, a foreboding image for the men, who knew that *Mary Rose* was no match for such fast, well-armed foes. As the crew readied itself, some hurried to the forecastle gun just in front of the bridge, or the midship gun between the second and third funnel, or the after gun behind the torpedoes. Joe went down inside the ship, under the forecastle, one of a team who'd send ammunition up to the two foremost guns. It would be tense, frantic work, done without the ability to see how the battle was progressing, but at the same time hearing its noise: men shouting, the boom of the guns, the throb of the ship's engine and the reverberation of shells as they exploded under water.

Bailey, for his part, left the after searchlight platform and headed for the torpedo tubes. Engineer Lieutenant-Commander William Howie Cleghorn passed him and asked what cruisers he'd seen, but before Bailey could answer, Cleghorn disappeared below to the engine room. With the voice-pipe gear fitted to his ears, Bailey positioned himself between the foremost torpedo tubes. His shipmate Albert French was with him, and from here they could see that some of the shots sent out by the gunners came close to the cruisers, but none were a definite hit. So far the German ships hadn't fired back. He waited for instructions to come from the bridge via voice-pipe. He knew his own moment was coming, for Fox's plan had to entail getting near enough to fire a torpedo. It was their only hope, and a slim one at that.

Just then the cruisers fired – first a shot that landed far off, then a closer one, and then a third so near to *Mary Rose* that the noise was massive when it hit the sea, and a wall of water erupted to momentarily block out the approaching enemy. As Bailey and his pal French launched the torpedo, *Mary Rose* took a direct hit in the engine room that stopped the ship and nearly lifted her straight out of the water.

Many of the crew were blown overboard by the force of the explosion, or killed by shrapnel. Others lay wounded and writhing. Bailey felt a piece of shrapnel enter his thigh, but strangely the sensation was nothing more than a simple prick. His voice-pipe was swept away, and he could hear only the sizzling, spurting sound of steam in his ears. French fared worse and lay collapsed beneath the tubes. There was no blood visible on French's limp body, and Bailey had never seen a man die before, but he knew immediately that French was gone. The hit must have killed Cleghorn and all the men in the engine room instantly, and a boiler exploded soon after. On deck, too, the dead outnumbered the living; others floated lifeless in the water or soon died from ingesting oil. Plumes of black cloud billowed as *Mary Rose* was enveloped in smoke and steam. She was listing to port and sinking rapidly, and the enemy continued to fire. The torpedo tubes were out of action now, as were the midship and forecastle guns, and there was no crew to man them anyway. Only the after gun continued firing, but not for long.

Suddenly Fox appeared, seeming calm and even cheerful, obviously trying to boost spirits. Bailey watched as he spoke to some of the after gun crew and clapped them on the backs. When he got to Bailey's station, he seemed not to notice that Bailey was the only one left there. "Stick it, lads," he sang out. "We're not done yet." But the cruisers were less than a mile away and still firing, and it was only moments until Fox gave a different order, quickly passed from man to man: "Abandon ship! Every man for himself!"

Mary Rose heeled slowly to port as if reluctant to give up. She was ablaze now, and the men still alive were rushing to save themselves. Oil gushed from the holes in her side and blackened the water. And then she lurched and turned over and sank beneath the sea.

The first newspaper headlines were calculated to shock: "German Fast Raiders' Criminal Inhumanity" and "Crews Left to Drown." The stories gave scant, sometimes erroneous details, but praised *Mary Rose* and *Strongbow* as "gallant," while condemning the fact that "no effort was made to rescue the crews of the sunken British destroyers, and the Germans left the doomed merchant ships, whilst still sinking." If anyone reading held out hope for the crews of the destroyers, the last paragraph quelled it. "It is regretted that all the 88 officers and men of HMS *Mary Rose* and 47 officers and men of HMS *Strongbow* were lost. All the next of kin have been informed."

But they hadn't been. By October 20, when those articles were printed, no telegram had arrived at the Deverill address. Ethel, Ernie and the rest of the family must have been in acute anxiety, knowing Joe was on *Mary Rose*, yet not having received any terrible news in spite of the newspapers' claims. Their only hope was that Joe had been transferred to another ship, or that the news reports were wrong. But two days later, as the papers published a story of some bedraggled *Mary Rose* survivors reaching Norway, a telegram finally came, its contents dashing their thin hopes. The message was from the Admiralty and addressed to Mary Anne, a painful aberration that surely made Ethel's throat close as she read the words and saw Joe's name. "Deeply regret to inform you…" Though it hardly seemed possible, the world had grown bleaker still.

Shortly after dawn on the morning of October 17, Joe had been cleaning out the wardroom, a mess cabin reserved for officers above the rank of midshipman. He'd have been wiping tables and mopping the floor and whistling while he worked, or chuckling as he recalled a joke told by his mate David Stedman, an officer's steward whose job it was to serve in the wardroom. At 6:10, orders came that all hands should be prepared to go to action stations within a quarter of an hour, so Joe passed the word to those nearby: young midshipman Archibald Moir, an officer cadet who was barely shaving and who'd only been on board a week; Ivan Barclay, the ship's doctor; and Stedman. If Joe and Stedman had any time for conversation it was likely to note that the usually dull run was about to get interesting. In a few minutes the alarm gong rang, and Joe and Stedman went their separate ways, Stedman remaining near the wardroom to hand up ammunition to the gunners on the after deck, Joe going forward to pass shells from the foremost store room.

On his way, Joe encountered Sub-Lieutenant Frederick Marsh, a young man his age from the Hackney area of London. It was a chilly morning, and Marsh had just sent one seaman to fetch his "British Warm," a woolen peacoat that was standard Navy issue. Now he asked Joe to get his binoculars from the bridge so he could better scrutinize the menace on the horizon. Joe went but quickly returned without the glasses, saying he couldn't get on the bridge. Marsh retrieved them himself without incident, passing a long line of men streaming to their stations, so Joe was either frightened and didn't go to the bridge or was turned back by the helmsman. He made it to his place in the bowels of the ship as the attack on the enemy began in earnest.

From the beginning they were doomed. Back at the after gun, Sub-Lieutenant Marsh oversaw the fixing of the sightsetter's voice-pipe, but no instructions came through it at first as to which ship the crew should aim at, or what the range was, and Sub-Lieutenant John Freeman had to send a man forward to get those answers and then bring back the reply. As officer of the after gun, Marsh shouted words of encouragement – "Go it!" and "Make it hot for them!" – but soon the Germans were answering their fire. The explosions were so loud that Marsh was deafened. Two of his men had been hit, and the sightsetter's right shoulder blown away. It was then that the captain appeared, giving orders and making signals with his arms to help Marsh understand him, but Marsh had no idea what he was saying.

Petty Officer Walter Webb, also at the after gun, heard the captain clearly. "God bless my little heart, lads, get her going, we're not done yet!" Theirs was the only gun still functioning, and they lobbed five more rounds at the enemy. But soon the after gun's sights were shot away and the training gear jammed, and Fox, given this news, ordered the confidential books destroyed and made the call "Every man for himself!" It was 7:15. Little more than an hour had passed since Bailey had first seen the flashing.

Within minutes, eight men gathered aft, strapping on lifebelts and struggling to loosen the Carley float from its berth. Because of their oilskins and lifebelts, they couldn't get at their knives to cut the ropes that held the Carley in place, and it was only when one of the men appeared with three butter knives from the pantry that they managed to free the thing that might just save them. They launched the float and jumped in, and right away began paddling with the Carley's short oars. The float was designed for only the most temporary refuge, with netting in the centre that formed a sort of basket for the men to stand in. They could hold on to the raft from outside as well, but either way, although they were afloat, they were also partly submerged in the frigid water. The enemy continued firing on *Mary Rose*, and the eight now moving away from her watched as some of their crewmates lowered the lifeboat they all called "Little Mary." Men began piling into the boat, but she was hit by a shell and disappeared in flame with her would-be passengers.

Where, in all of this, was Joe? In the foremost shell room, in the early minutes of the battle, he had slung forty or fifty rounds of ammunition before the lights went out and the guns stopped firing. There was a race to get through the narrow passageway and up out of the death trap the shell room might become. Clambering on deck he saw the crumpled forms of dead and wounded sailors, men he had known and lived with. Someone yelled at him to get a lifebelt, and he realized his shipmates were jumping into the water. He stripped off his oilskin and some of his clothes, thinking he'd swim better without them, and avoiding, perhaps, the brutal fact that the water was too cold for anyone to swim in for long. He was a poor swimmer, after all; he needed all the help he could get. To that end, there was a penny in his pocket. He patted it and looked overboard at the other men in the water – many dead, but some still swimming for their lives – and then he, too, plunged in.

The temperature of the North Sea in late October is just slightly above freezing, and if it occurred to Joe as the water closed around him that this was how Ernest and Lilian Carter had died when *Titanic* went down, he had little time for contemplation. Though it was early morning, beneath the surface of the water the light barely penetrated, and below him it was utterly, hopelessly black, as black as a grave. The bubbles caused by his thrashing muted the shouts of his fellow sailors and *Mary Rose*'s awful groan as her metal twisted, and the deck from which he'd so recently jumped appeared upside down in the water. It was difficult to know which way was up, and it surely seemed as if he was underwater for an incredible length of time before he suddenly surfaced, reflexively sucking in air like a hungry man swallows food. At the same time he inhaled a lungful of water thick with fuel oil, which seeped into his eyes and nose as well. He might have gone under again but for the luck of a bit of flotsam bumping against him. He grabbed onto it and kicked, feeling the water roll back from his shoulders like a reprieve. Somehow David Stedman appeared on the other side of this makeshift float, and the two remained there in the water for nearly fifteen minutes after *Mary Rose* sank. At such cold temperatures a man has difficulty moving his limbs after just ten minutes, so they were beyond lucky when their fellow sailors in the Carley spotted the two on their precarious raft and hauled them aboard.

Bailey, recounting his version of events some years later, said, "We were a good deal better off than it would seem, though, for the most of us were heavily dressed, and the animal heat of a man keeps him warm for a long time under oilskins and wool. The only ones that suffered much were a couple of lads who didn't have any more sense than to ditch most of their togs before they went over the side. They said it was so as not to be hampered in swimming – as if they expected to do the 'Australian crawl' to Norway or the Shetlands!" Cold or not, they were at least alive.

For all Bailey's bravado, things were not so wonderful in the Carley float. Shells burst in the water around them, and a depth charge that detonated on the sunken vessel was felt in the float, throwing the survivors violently against one another and sending a tingle through their bodies that was separate from the cold. There should have been provisions in the Carley, but there were none – no food, no flags, no flares – and now, with ten men aboard, they were submerged to their armpits in the heavy swell of the icy North Sea. The oil sat in a thick layer on the water and clung to their clothing. The smell of it was inescapable. Some of them coped better than others, given age and experience. Able Seaman William MacLeod, for instance, had "True Love for Maggie" tattooed on his arm and had been sailing the China Seas long before the war had started. Able Seaman Ernest Grummitt, stationed in the fore magazine near Joe, was twenty years Joe's senior; his days on ships had begun before Joe was born. Among the youngest and least experienced were the two plucked from the sea and almost left for dead.

After the German cruisers moved off, a great silence descended, and the men paddled as best they could with the tiny oars lashed to the float's webbing. They were eighty miles from Lerwick, one hundred from Norway, and the sea around them seemed larger than ever. Some of them must have known the terrible stories of men who'd been "saved" by Carleys, only to die of exposure with the buoyant device still dutifully carrying them along. The minutes became an hour, and finally they saw the trawler *Elise* slink past a mile out, looking for survivors. She moved toward them and away, tantalizingly close, but in spite of shouting and waving their arms, they failed to attract her attention. Soon they were alone again.

Around noon they saw several ships on fire, sinking slowly. But their spirits lifted when a lifeboat from the Norwegian ship *Silja* appeared, and the men in the Carley flagged her down by hoisting a black silk handkerchief on the end of a paddle. With just six men in the *Silja* lifeboat, there was plenty of room for Joe and the other *Mary Rose* survivors, and they climbed aboard, legs weak from the cold, and too overjoyed to be out of the Carley to feel exhausted. They were glad of the supplies, too, Bailey recalled: "biscuits and potted stuff – to say nothing of smokes." For the next two days, under sail and with the men taking turns rowing, they steered roughly east-southeast with the aid of a compass, although in the dark they were only able to read it by the light of matches that kept blowing out in the wind. Joe and Stedman began to get "a bit down-hearted and 'shivery' when the cold struck into the marrow of their bones," and Bailey had his shrapnel wound to contend with, so the men sang for comfort – popular songs and two or three hymns. "I don't just remember all that we did warble," Bailey recounted, "except, I'm glad to say, that 'Tipperary' wasn't on the programme."

Sometime after ten o'clock on the second night a pinprick of light was spotted on the horizon. They made for it, and at four o'clock in the morning put ashore at a lighthouse on the coast of Norway, thirty miles north of Bergen. The lighthouse keepers and their wives were roused from sleep and took the men in, warming them with blankets and dry clothing and feeding them. Berths were found for the exhausted sailors on the Norwegian steamer *Nordstjernen*, which then transported them to Bergen. By Monday, October 22, British newspapers were reporting on the ten men, saying they were "probably…the sole survivors of the crew of the *Mary Rose*." The men themselves, meanwhile, were transferred to the mail steamer *Louth* and headed for Aberdeen, Scotland, although that was not an easy passage. *Louth* was overcrowded, and in bad weather a number of the passengers were seasick. A few hours out of Bergen they encountered gale-force winds and had to anchor for the night. If, held there on the choppy sea, the men thought of their drowned shipmates and the gore they had witnessed during the attack, no clue of their despair remains. In a piece entitled "Brave Hearts on the Mary Rose," a *Daily Mail* reporter accompanying the *Louth* wrote that the boys "minded neither the black night of extinguished lights, the driving rain, nor the tumbled sea, but jested, laughed and even sang cheerily and undismayed."

Official word was slow to travel to the families of the affected men. When they arrived at Aberdeen they were cautioned "as to need for secrecy" and taken by train to Inverkeithing, except for Bailey, who was admitted to the Royal Aberdeen Infirmary. On October 26, on board HMS *Inflexible*, a court of inquiry was held, and Joe and the others were individually questioned about what had happened before, during and after the attack. They were quizzed about speeds, distances and number of rounds fired; about their own behaviour and their opinions of each other's behaviour. *At any time was there panic or disorganization? Did anyone go overboard before the call to abandon ship? Did the Mary Rose sink with her colours flying?* Freeman, questioned first and given the chance to stay and hear the others' testimony, declined: "I think the other witnesses would probably speak more freely if I were not present." But not a single man spoke poorly of his crewmates. Several said Bailey deserved special recognition for his "pluck and cheeriness" despite the agony he'd suffered from his wound while rowing to Norway.

With regard to the survivors' actions, the findings were favourable: "Everybody appears to have remained cool and collected and perfect discipline maintained under the most trying conditions of being under heavy fire from vastly superior forces." And yet there was this: while the members of the court of inquiry admired Captain Fox's gallantry, they were "strongly of the opinion that his decision was ill-advised." They claimed he should have known he would quickly be overpowered, leaving his convoy vulnerable, and if he had remained at long range, he might at least have lured the enemy away from the other ships. There was no mention that, in either scenario, men of the *Mary Rose* would be lost. "It is the cause of much regret to us to have to adversely criticise the judgement and action of such a gallant officer."

All of this had happened before a second telegram reached the Deverill household on November 3, 1917. It, too, was addressed to Mrs. M.A. Deverill, and apologized for "the distress which the receipt of the notification of your son's supposed death must have caused you." The error was "deeply regretted," the Admiralty assured Mary Anne, requesting that she "be so good as to return the communication in question…in the accompanying envelope, which need not be stamped." But of course Mary Anne could not do that. Instead Ethel must have complied with the request, for the original telegram has not survived. No doubt she and the rest of the family were more than willing to oblige the Admiralty, since the news that Joe was alive was a gift beyond measure.

Once the inquiry was over, the men went briefly to their depots and then were granted fourteen days' leave. Joe returned home, with the coin still in his pocket, and a cough that wouldn't go away. Though he was already sore with grief, it was only now that he finally learned of Mary Anne's death, devastating news indeed after all that had happened.

At the Goodwin he continued recuperating from the oily water he'd swallowed. His cough must have reminded him that he'd fared better than so many of his cohorts in the water, who'd not been able to escape the black liquid and died from swallowing fuel. For Joe there were also the extended effects of hypothermia from shivering in thin clothes for two days. He probably suffered from mental stress as well, brought on by painful recollections not divulged, and images that played in his mind no matter how hard he tried to banish them. During his convalescence he took up rug-hooking; the repetitive pulling of the wool strands through the heavy fabric and the pleasure of seeing a pattern eventually emerge were a balm to frayed nerves.

Certainly, for Joe and the nine other survivors, the joy of being alive was muted by loss. Of all the ships involved, *Mary Rose* had suffered the largest loss when the convoy was attacked, with eighty-six of her men perishing. Only a handful of bodies had been retrieved for burial in a Norwegian churchyard or brought to Lerwick and buried there; the rest remained in the sea, with the wrecked ships and the spent ammunition. Frederick Toms and John Bell, the two young men who'd joined the ship with Joe a year earlier, were dead, as were most of the men featured in the jokey photograph taken on *Mary Rose*'s deck. Survivors peer from the image too: Ernest Grummitt and William MacLeod with their pipes, Bailey with his mirthful expression, and Joe, sitting quietly at the edge of the frame. These men and the other six were burdened now with their memories of the event, and also with questions from relatives of the deceased, desperate for any clues about their last moments. Joe apparently took this duty to remember seriously and paid a visit to a dead friend's mother to relay what news he could of her sailor. But that is all that remains of the story: not who the man was, nor how the woman received Joe's words. Did he tell her, a mother who'd just lost her son, that he was a son who'd just lost his mother?

For some of the men's families this was not the first war death, nor the last: the parents of Engineer Lieutenant-Commander William Cleghorn had already lost two sons in France, and now William, too, was gone. He and his wife, Hilda, had been present when *Mary Rose* was launched in 1915, and he had since begun compiling a history of *Mary Rose* ships stretching back to the first one, sunk in a battle with the French in the 1540s. Hilda wrote to the survivors individually, hoping for details of William's last moments, and received long responses from Bailey and the two officers, Freeman and Marsh. If Joe was included in Hilda's queries, his response to her does not appear among the many papers she saved relating to the death of her husband.

Frederick Marsh's letter, sent from his parents' home in London that November, must have been somewhat disappointing, even though it was peppered with compliments. "In the Ward Room your husband was, to use his own words, 'a real social success'... It was unanimously agreed that without the 'Chief,' life on the *Mary Rose* would most certainly tend to be dull and gloomy. Of this, I myself am certain." But of the battle, Marsh would reveal little; he sounded instead like a spokesperson for the Admiralty, or a newspaper report trotting out a censored story. "I deeply regret to say that as we have been sworn to secrecy I cannot give you any details of the fight yet ... I can only say that from the beginning to the end, the story of the loss of the HMS *Mary Rose* is one of the usual British pluck, heroism, bravery and dogged determination to fight until the end." While the battle had been short, he assured her it had also been hard-fought "before 'the flower of all ships that ever sailed' quietly disappeared beneath the waves."

In a less guarded fashion, John Bailey wrote from the Royal Aberdeen Infirmary around the same time, thanking Hilda Cleghorn for "your kind parcel of cigs." He was still recovering from his shrapnel wound, and later the doctors would realize a piece of leather from his boot had been lodged inside his leg, inhibiting the healing process. He recounted the story of Cleghorn speaking briefly to him about the enemy ships, and how he'd watched him descend to the engine room, but added that he couldn't say exactly how he'd met his death or whether he had suffered. He only knew that they "were hopelessly out-gunned," and when the shell hit the turbines and stopped the ship, it must have killed all of the men below. It was the same shell, he wrote, that had wounded him and killed his mates at the torpedo tubes.

John Freeman, too, was more forthcoming than Marsh had been, but stressed in his letter from Devon that "you will quite understand, I am sure, when I ask you to keep it strictly private as you will see the Admiralty do not seem to wish it made public." He outlined his version of the events, including the awful moment when the lifeboat had shattered, filled with men. "I only wish I were able to tell you more, and to be able to give you some message from [your husband] to comfort you in your great distress." He added that he had already written to two other women and would gladly answer any other questions she had to the best of his ability. "I am leaving home on Saturday for Chatham Barracks. I do not know how long or what for, but I am certainly going to go sick if they try and send me to sea again just yet, as my nerves are considerably shaken and I cannot sleep, but I dream of this horrible massacre, for it was little else."

Joe and most of the other survivors were sent to Chatham Barracks at the same time, joining a mixed lot of sailors held in limbo there for one reason or another: some were between ships, others were resting or recuperating from illness, trauma or injury. Two months earlier, in September, the place of respite had been overflowing with sailors. Some had been bound for HMS *Vanguard* before she'd blown into tiny pieces; others had contracted spotted fever and had to be detained. The glass-roofed drill hall had been commandeered for the additional sailors, and the men were sleeping there in hammocks the night four Gotha bombers flew over Chatham in a moonlight raid. Although Zeppelins had attacked in the dark, this was the first time airplanes had made a nighttime attempt, and it had taken everyone by surprise. Two bombs landed in the drill hall, shattering its heavy glass roof and sending shards down upon the sleeping men. More than 130 sailors died in the carnage, and one seaman who'd been part of the rescue team later wrote, "It was a gruesome task. Everywhere we found bodies in a terribly mutilated condition. Some with arms and legs missing and some headless. The gathering up of dismembered limbs turned one sick…It was a terrible affair and the old sailors, who had been in several battles, said they would rather be in ten Jutlands or Heligolands than go through another raid such as this."

If any of the destruction was evident when Joe and the *Mary Rose* men arrived at the barracks, the news of why they'd been posted there soon overshadowed it. The men were to testify at a court martial further investigating *Mary Rose*'s response to the attack. Obviously the answers that had come from the inquiry only raised more questions.

On December 3, at ten o'clock in the morning, the proceedings began. The prosecutor, Commander Maxwell Anderson of HMS *President*, wanted the public excluded from the trial "in the interests of national safety," and although the demand was questioned in Parliament, permission was granted. Some of the most heartbreaking evidence came from Skipper William Wood of the trawler *Elise*, who described witnessing the attack and searching for survivors afterward. Joe and the others must have had the picture in their minds of *Elise* in the distance, coming so close but failing to spot them. Though he'd seen *Mary Rose* go down, Wood could find no trace of her or her men once the fighting was over. He and his crew picked up men from several of the ships, drifting in Carley floats and motor launches, and they towed two lifeboats behind them. When they could see no more boats or men floating in the water, they started for Lerwick, treating the wounded as best as possible en route. Despite their efforts, three of the men died on the journey.

The parsing of the day was thorough, though only Joe and six of his fellow survivors testified. The documents say that at the time of the hearing Marsh was ill, Bailey was still in hospital and Stedman had deserted – yet his absence must have been explained and forgiven, for his record places him on subsequent ships for the rest of the war. The seven were again called, sworn and cautioned, and asked to relay the events in detail. *What was the* Mary Rose *position relative to the convoy? Did the Captain ever discuss with you what he proposed to do in case of an attack? Was any attempt made to see if… men were wounded and could be got off the ship?* Witnesses from other ships were called as well, and asked pointed questions: *Is it usual for one of the destroyers to take station nine to ten miles ahead of the convoy at night?* This was a sore point with the board, who wrote that Fox should have kept *Mary Rose* within a mile of the convoy at all times and not been "practically out of touch." Though the survivors were found blameless, the court martial found what the inquiry had, that, once engaged by the enemy, Fox "should have shown more discretion" by keeping at long range when he realized he was outmatched.

Publicly, though, the Admiralty controlled the message, even censoring itself. A press release written as a sort of closure to the event bore the heroic title "The Last Flight of H.M. Torpedo Boat Destroyer 'Mary Rose,'" and included the passage "The Naval critics, with whose assistance we are wont to belittle the achievements of our Navy, will have doubtless much to say about this action. From the point of view of tactics, it lies open to unquestionable criticism." Thinking better of such an admission, the Admiralty quickly issued a retraction of that specific passage, saying it was "cancelled and should not be published."

Such directives were not unusual. They were a form of censorship known as D-notices, developed in 1912 by a committee comprised of the Admiralty, the War Office and media representatives to ensure that sensitive information remained secret. Anticipating the hostilities yet to come, the committee agreed that only matters relating to national security would be censored, yet it soon became apparent that such a term was open to interpretation. A D-notice had been issued restricting the press from reporting on the relationship between the Russian tsarina and the priest Rasputin, and a later one would forbid mention of rumours that the Prince of Wales was engaged to an Italian princess. For the most part the press respected the discretion requested of them, as did *Mary Rose's* survivors, especially in the months following the sinking. The silence frustrated the widows of the men who went down with the ship, and Eva Fox, wife of Lieutenant-Commander Charles Fox, was no different in that than Hilda Cleghorn, who had written to the survivors trying to find answers. On his daughter's behalf, Eva's father wrote directly to the Admiralty, asking for "any details of the action in which her husband was killed." A note in the file shows the request "might be acceded to, provided no details of importance are divulged." Eva approved of what she read. "Although a very sad loss to myself and his children," she wrote in thanks, "I am proud to think that my husband died so nobly serving his country."

Joe and the other survivors were soon reassigned, and in January 1918, the day before his twentieth birthday, Joe found himself back in the cold climes of Scotland. This time he was berthed on a hired drifter with a single gun, patrolling the water between Wick and Kinnaird Head, a little south of his previous posting at Scapa Flow. He was older now, and somewhat wiser for his experience on the *Mary Rose*. And he knew just how quickly a humdrum day or an ordinary night could turn into a harrowing situation. With that in mind he began to train himself to sleep standing up, wedging his small frame between two pipes near an exit, hoping for first chance up the ladder. And just in case, he was still in possession of his lucky penny.

More than 100 years after the sinking, Joe's lucky penny
remains in the possession of his great-grandson.

Doris's first passport no longer exists, but the photograph shows her in her good dress, hair curled for a special occasion. Prior to the Great War, British passports did not include photographs or even physical descriptions. Under the 1914 British Nationality and Status of Aliens Act, both were added. A passport consisted of a single sheet of paper folded into a cardboard cover and was valid for two years.

CHAPTER 13

Make Your Motto "Forward!" and Stick to It Like Glue

As the Americans stepped up their role in the war, the Russians exited. From the beginning the war hadn't gone well for Russia; her troops were ill-equipped and poorly trained, food was scarce in the cities, and in the first major battle against Germany, Russia's casualties had been almost three times greater than the enemy's. Instead of restoring a sense of national unity and proving to the world that Russia deserved respect, as the tsar had hoped, the war demonstrated the harshness and inequality of Russian society, and the general discontent of her citizens.

The war had been the tsar's undoing, too. When Nicholas came to the throne in 1894, Kaiser Wilhelm had noted in a speech that his cousin had taken on "truly one of the most burdensome inheritances upon which a prince can enter." Archibald Primrose, then British prime minister, had called Russia's monarchy "that awful Crown," and by now it had been altogether snatched away. Denied asylum in Britain, the tsar remained under house arrest with his family. The country was controlled by the Bolsheviks, who purported to represent Russia's working class. After the 1917 overthrow the world had spent months figuring out what these radical changes would mean for the war. Would Russia continue to fight next to her allies? Would the Bolsheviks make peace with Germany or change sides and fight alongside her? By the time the year was out, it was clear that the Russians had no intentions of re-entering the war, and in March 1918 the Bolsheviks signed a treaty with Germany, both sides declaring that they would "live henceforth in peace and amity with one another."

Under this new arrangement the Germans were feeling good about their chances in the west. Russia had ceded the Ukraine, Poland and

319

Finland, relinquished to Germany control of 90 percent of her coal mines and much of her industry, and paid for the release of war prisoners. The treaty also meant some fifty divisions of German soldiers had been freed up, and Germany flung everything she had into the western offensives. With German victories mounting, the British government raised the military age limit to fifty, and in France, British Field Marshal Douglas Haig issued a communiqué to his troops that newspapers referred to as his "clarion call." He acknowledged that "many among us are now tired," but that there was "no other course open to us but to fight it out…With our backs to the wall and believing in the justice of our cause each one of us must fight on to the end."

His call was directed to soldiers, but its message was widely circulated and taken to apply to all British people, military and civilian, and to all facets of their lives. Food rationing, at first voluntary and encouraged by kingly proclamations and mayoral speeches, had become compulsory in January. Households were matched with a butcher and a grocer, and purchases of sugar, meat, butter and milk were regulated with the use of coupon books. Magazines and newspapers offered cooking columns with tips for frugal meals, and published little reminders like "Save the wheat, and help the fleet." Rationing wasn't popular, and although even King George and Queen Mary had ration cards, not everyone was convinced things were fair. *Punch* ran a cartoon that showed a well-jowled couple in a chauffeur-driven, open-top car passing a food line. The car's windscreen holds a sign reading "Eat Less Bread," and the caption notes, with obvious sarcasm, "Doing Their Bit."

Ernie, by this time, was doing his bit as far as food production went. With their mother's death, Ernie and Doris had become more than a temporary problem. Ethel could fend for herself; her earnings had improved and, together with money Joe sent, allowed her to keep the flat in the Goodwin Buildings, with electoral roles listing Joe as an absent voter. Since neither Ethel nor Aunt Maggie could watch out for Doris and Ernie indefinitely, and Hanwell was to be avoided at all costs, Doris was returned to Harry's sisters, Maud and Nell, in Wimbledon. But they couldn't, or wouldn't, take both siblings. Instead, Ernie was sent to Laindon, Essex, where Harry's oldest sister, Ada, had moved, and not far from Canvey Island where the Deverills had holidayed in happier times before Harry's death. Ada and her husband now had a small farm called The Hermitage, with pigs and a pony. Did she offer to take Ernie in or was she compelled to? Whatever the answer, the arrangement had advantages for both: Ernie got a home and the chance to learn about the workings of a farm, and Ada gained another pair of hands to help with a heavy workload.

Small Ernie was a fish out of water in Laindon, a green place dotted with farms and hedgerows, and where the fields were covered in pale pink cuckoo flowers and dancing dog-daisies. Instead of the familiar city noises of traffic and too many people, there were the barnyard grunts and snuffles of livestock, and the solitary sound of your own footsteps on gravel paths. At night there was absolute quiet except for the chirp of crickets in the long grass outside the house, or the thrum of rain on the roof's wooden shingles. Ernie slept in an unheated room in the attic, where silverfish clung to the damp rafters, and although he shared the chores with a cousin, to Ernie fell the worst jobs, like mucking out the pigpen. In the eyes of a thirteen-year-old as fastidious as Ernie, farm life surely seemed a lot like a punishment.

He wasn't the only Londoner discovering the charms of rural life. With three million men away fighting, and women filling the jobs they'd previously held, it seemed only sensible to the men at the Board of Agriculture that women could also be encouraged to undertake agricultural work. Those farmers still on the land, though, were reluctant to accept female workers, expecting that they would not be capable of performing the physically demanding work, while women themselves, particularly rural women, saw farm labour as a step below even domestic service. Recruiters decided to target the urban middle class, and organizations such as the Women's Defense Relief Corps had some early success, advertising the work as a holiday for women to try their hand at haymaking, fruit picking and harvesting, while the Women's Farm and Garden Union offered free training on gardening and farming techniques.

By 1916, with food shortages an increasing problem, it became apparent that a more concerted effort would have to be put into recruiting female labour. Under the auspices of the newly created Department for

Food Production, the Women's Land Army was formed, and advertisements began to appear nudging women to their agricultural duty. "God Speed the Plough and the Woman Who Drives It," read the caption below one poster. It depicted a woman guiding a horse-drawn plough against a golden sunrise, as if the call were not just patriotic but divine. At a rally in London, crowds turned out to watch the spectacle of a parade of tractors driven by ladies. At another, women carried rakes, hoes and other farm implements, and banners fluttered, declaring "We Are All Fit" and "The Lasses Are Massing for the Spring Offensive." The women who volunteered for the Land Army were outfitted by the Department with high boots, a knee-length tunic, a felt hat with a round brim to keep the sun off fair skin, and breeches. The Land Army Handbook, issued to all members, felt it prudent to make this cautionary statement: "You are doing a man's work and so you're dressed rather like a man, but remember just because you wear a smock and breeches you should take care to behave like a British girl who expects chivalry and respect from everyone she meets." Although the papers claimed they looked "particularly well" in their mannish garb, not everyone was so admiring. In a village in Norfolk, locals threw stones at the arriving Land Army recruits because they disapproved of women wearing pants.

Laindon, too, had its Land Army girls. One girl assigned to milk and care for the cows at a dairy farm later recalled the early morning walk through the dark fields from the house where she was billeted. She munched bread and jam as she went, and eyed the bobbing glow of hurricane lamps as others also picked their way between shrubs and along mud paths to work. A day off was unheard of, but she and the rest of the Land Army girls were allowed to attend the Sunday service at St. Nicholas, the little church on the hill at the centre of the village. Tired from her early starts and the hard work, she often could not stay awake and was caught napping on several occasions. It's tempting to imagine Ernie there, seated in a pew with Auntie Ada's family, watching the girl doze through the sermon and later seeing her in the street, tipping his hat as any good Londoner would. Or maybe he stood behind her at the post office wicket, waiting his turn to mail a card home to Ethel. "Hoping you are quite well as it leaves myself at present. Have you heard from

Joe? Give my love to him, and to Doris when you see her." When he signed these cards he added a string of x's, counting them to be sure they could be divided equally amongst his siblings.

Like Ernie, the Land Army girls had been displaced by circumstances beyond their control. Although they were here in Laindon to do their bit for the war, they were likely no less lonely than Ernie and could attest to the truthfulness of the words spoken by the Minister of Agriculture, Rowland Prothero, in a speech in London: "It is hard work – fatiguing, back-aching, monotonous, dirty work in all sorts of weather...The accommodation is rough, and those who undertake it have to face physical discomforts...There is no romance in it; it is prose." That was true of Ernie's reality too. Ernie wasn't a shirker, but he was physically small and preferred wielding a paintbrush to lugging a slop bucket. He'd never known animals, and pigs were much larger and stronger close up than one would expect. There are hints that his relatives had little confidence in his abilities. With all he'd been through since the day he'd watched his father keel over while polishing his boots, Ernie hadn't quite come into his own. Despite growing up in some of the dirtiest areas of London, he'd always been meticulous, careful to wash his hands and keep his clothes clean, and a future among the pigpens of Aunt Ada's farm must have been hard to accept. Whether he, like the Land Army girls, found encouragement in the words of the appeal posters tacked to the walls behind postmasters' counters countrywide – "Make your motto 'Forward!' and stick to it like glue" – at the end of the day, curled in a blanket in his attic room, Ernie was miserable, just like Doris in Wimbledon.

Yet Laindon was a safer place to be than London when the so-called Spanish Lady came to call. A particularly virulent and deadly strain of influenza, the illness was labelled Spanish simply because neutral Spain reported her cases freely, while those countries still at war at first gave it little press. The outbreak almost certainly did not originate in Spain, but the name – Spanish flu or Spanish lady – stuck, and the illness gained yet more monikers. The Purple Death was one, on account of its victims developing heliotrope cyanosis and turning the shade of an amethyst as the person suffocated, choking on thick scarlet jelly that filled the lungs. Death came quickly. Dr. Roy Grist, a Glasgow physician, described the

CHAPTER 13

course of the flu in a letter to a colleague, saying that it started almost
benignly, with what appeared to be an ordinary case of *la grippe* – sore
throat, headache and fever. But then, patients "very rapidly develop
the most vicious type of pneumonia that has ever been seen…A few
hours later you can begin to see cyanosis extending from their ears and
spreading all over the face…It is only a matter of a few hours then until
death comes. It is horrible."

In Britain, the first recorded appearance of the illness was in Glasgow
in May 1918, and the sickness travelled south by June. Crowded London was hit hard. Its citizens and myriad wartime visitors were pressed
together on trams, in movie theatres, in workplaces and in overfull, sub-
standard housing, so it was inevitable that London and the bigger towns
and cities would bear the brunt. Hospitals were already overflowing
with war casualties, nurses and doctors were overworked, and, incred-
ibly, this particular virus preferred those in the prime of life to the very
young or the very old, so soldiers and sailors were easy targets, especially since they lived and worked in such close quarters. At first there was
uncertainty about what the illness actually was, with some newspapers
attributing it to "trench fever" brought back from the front, since it had
similar characteristics such as sudden fever, headache and sore muscles.
Others referred to it as a mystery disease, labelling it a plague or a form
of malaria. American rumours said it was some kind of germ warfare
started by German agents put ashore in U-boats, and *The Times* went so
far as to suggest that the disease was a new type of streptococcus stem-
ming from the German use of poison gas. With dark humour the *Edinburgh Evening News* dubbed London "the city of sneezes" and reported
that everyone seemed to be "carrying on a kind of sneezing competition
as to the number of times he or she can 'T-s-c-h' in the course of a day…
There is one strange coincidence, however, about this sneezing epidemic. It synchronizes with the outbreak of [ready-made] suits. Troubles
never come singly."

But the flu was no laughing matter. It carried its victims off almost
haphazardly, taking a half-dozen or more from a school, twice that
from the workhouse, an entire family elsewhere. Cinemas and pubs
closed their doors, and few shops other than druggists' had a lineup.

City streets were sprayed with disinfectant, and people tied handkerchiefs over mouths and noses to keep the flu at bay. Advertisers, seeing an opportunity to sell their products to a public hoping to avoid contracting the illness, climbed aboard the influenza cart. Everything from mints to beef teas was touted by their makers as having curative or preventative properties. Consuming Oxo Beef Cubes would "fortif[y] the system against influenza infection," while gargling a single tablespoon of Condy's Remedial Fluid mixed with water was billed as both a prevention and cure. The Dunlop Rubber Tyre Company placed ads that showed a man on a bicycle, and stretched rather far to make a link: "If the influenza fiend has had its grip on you, let your bicycle help you to throw it off. Get out into the fresh air whenever you can and ride gently along … at your own pace … And Dunlop tyres … mean no troublesome tyre worries to interfere with your bicycle cure."

Despite the dubious link, Ernie would have enjoyed the Dunlop tyre claim, and in Laindon he probably took every chance to follow the company's advice to ride. Ernie had been an avid roller-skater back in his old Marshalsea Road neighbourhood, so the move to a bicycle was a natural progression, and all his life he would love to cycle. A photo taken several years later attests to his comfort on two wheels. He slumps casually on the seat of a sturdy bicycle, one hand dangling at his side, the other resting on the handlebar. His right foot sits on the raised pedal, his pant leg tucked into a sock so as not to get caught in the chain; the other foot is planted on the ground, holding his balance. Dressed in a wool jacket, vest and tie, and with a flat cap shading his eyes from the slanting sun, he gazes steadily at the camera. In most other early photos of Ernie there is a Chaplinesque look about him – a thin-shouldered vulnerability that lifts off the paper – but in this single shot that quality is absent, replaced by a confident, relaxed demeanour.

In these early days, bicycle or no, Ernie was not content to be living in Laindon, just as Doris was not happy in Wimbledon. Despite all good intentions, the postcards Ernie and Doris received from the various family members clustered together back at the Goodwin Buildings only served to underscore the separation. And yet the children saved them, not as keepsakes of a sad time but as a reminder of the family they missed. *Fondest love from Auntie; With love from May; Heaps of love and kisses from Clara and Bert.* The fronts vary only slightly: cats and puppies for Ernie in Laindon; little girls and flowers for Doris in Wimbledon, sometimes with a rhyme. The backs contain barely more than a line and are as void of news as they are filled with x's. They give no insight as to how the senders spent their days, what was happening in their lives or what they knew of war. The cards Ethel sent offer nothing of her work as a factory girl at Cropper's box works – no comment that the bench-hands are almost all female; that they stand for most of the day pressing, folding, wrapping, tying; that they must wear their hair tied back lest it get caught in the machinery. There is no tidbit either of Clara and Bert's new baby daughter, Elsie, though that surely would have brought a smile. Nor is there word that Joe had begun corresponding with a Borough girl since he'd been home on leave, and they'd exchanged photographs. Grace Lett attended the Borough's Salvation Army meetings, though according to family stories she was no hallelujah lass in cape and poke bonnet, and she played the trombone rather than a tambourine. Like Joe's father, Harry, she broke a cardinal rule of the Salvation Army and smoked Player's cigarettes, and she liked gin and tonic more than was good for her. Perhaps romance was at play in the beginning, or maybe Joe had known Grace from childhood – she'd grown up in the Borough, the ninth of eleven children born to a "scavenger" and his wife who'd lived over on Sturge Street, just a few blocks from the Deverills' Red Cross Street home.

The photo Joe sent was inscribed simply "Best Wishes to Grace from Joe" and showed him and a friend posed together in their Navy uniforms. The friend perches on the edge of a brick wall prop, as tall seated as Joe is standing beside him. The man doesn't fit the description of any of the *Mary Rose* survivors, but the pose suggests he's a good pal: his arm rests with casual familiarity on Joe's shoulder, recalling the portrait of Harry and Joe on Joe's departure from childhood. The man wears a chain where Joe has a lanyard, signifying he's a bosun's mate, a step up the ladder from Joe. Still, Joe's boots are polished to a high shine and three chevrons are visible on his lower right sleeve. These Sea Service Chevrons were issued in May 1918 under Army Order #4: "His

Majesty the King has been graciously pleased to approve of the award of chevrons to denote service overseas undertaken since 4th August 1914." Sailors earned a red stripe if they'd been at sea on that date, and a blue one for each year thereafter, so Joe had so far received stripes for 1915, 1916 and 1917. Despite the more than three years of war the photographed friends have lived through, their expressions hold optimism and eagerness, as if they believe the worst is behind them. And for Joe, a happier path was already forming. When Grace returned a photograph, it showed her with a small, dark-eyed young woman named Nelly Baggett, a match for Joe if ever there was one.

Nelly lived in Lambeth, in the vicinity where the Roffs had grown up, and where Joe had lived briefly as a boy, before the move to Whitechapel. There were Evanses in her background, and later on, Joe and Nelly liked to think that somewhere in the distant past they'd come from the same Welsh stock. Nelly's father had been a fitter at the gasworks, but he was dead now, and her mother, Amy – like several of Joe's female relatives – was a charwoman, working at St. Thomas' Hospital, which these days had so many wounded soldiers in its care that the War Office had built temporary wards on its grounds. Nelly's mum saw the men come and go with what were often horribly disfiguring wounds. Surely she had wrenching thoughts of her own sons, all three of whom had enlisted. The youngest was a gunner who'd signed up in the spring of 1914, before the war had broken out, and served in France, Greece and Egypt. He'd been in and out of hospital several times, once for a mild case of shell shock, but he'd always pulled through. The middle boy, however, had recently died of wounds sustained at the Battle of Arras in France. Nelly's sister's husband was off fighting too, while his wife was at home with three girls to raise. So Nelly and her family knew war's harsh demands.

In every town, in every neighbourhood, death and injury had become regular news. If someone you loved hadn't died, then someone you knew had lost a loved one, which made it all too clear it could happen in any family at any time. The receipt of letters was brief comfort, for though the man had obviously been alive when he'd written, there was no telling what had become of him after the letter was sent. People shuddered to see the telegram delivery boys wheel up the street on their red bicycles and were relieved when they pedalled past without stopping. Some refused to open anything official. Even if they did, with no bodies returning home and many of the letters simply stating a man was missing, it was still possible to hold out hope. The Deverills' old Red Cross Street neighbour Lorenzo Bottone, nineteen-year-old son of the *ecco un poco* ice cream man, had apparently been killed in action in the Third Battle of Ypres, but the register recording money owed to soldiers who died in service adds one chilling detail to his story: "death presumed."

As summer approached, Doris received a postcard from Ethel that contained more than the usual x's and referred to Doris's impending move back to London. "Hoping you have heard from Beb. Joe and Ernie send their best love. See you soon." Doris's deep unhappiness in Wimbledon had finally been acknowledged, and Bebbie had offered to bring her back to Whitechapel, to live with her there. It wasn't an ideal situation, since Bebbie worked long hours at the cork factory, but at least Doris would be fed, clothed and sheltered, and living with someone she loved. Her departure was a load off the aunts, too. Nell Kraushaar was pregnant, and her husband, Percy, was fighting in France. She could only hope that he'd make it home again one day to meet his baby, but the reality that many fathers never did was hard to ignore. Maud's husband, Arthur Jordan, had also been called up, summoned from his desk at the Central Telegraph Office, but his work as a skilled telegraphist was still in high demand, and he was quickly transferred to Class W, reserved "for all those soldiers whose services are deemed to be more valuable to the country in civil rather than military employment." One never knew, though, when the powers that be might change their minds and decide that he, too, was needed as a soldier. The sisters relied on each other for support. Between them they had five children, and Doris was another mouth, another body and another concern when there were plenty already.

At Bebbie's, it was just the two of them in the small, familiar rooms at College Buildings, or walking hand in hand along Wentworth Street, where Doris had spent her first years. Although she was little when they'd left this area, she had often returned to it and knew the cry of the Jewish peddlers in Petticoat Lane and the pungent smell of Toynbee Hall's mossy bricks. She didn't remember her father, but she had seen him in pictures – the one that showed him with the tuba that towered over Ernie, and another of him in his caretaker's uniform, taken here at College Buildings, where he'd practised his music each night before bed. With time, her mother's image too would fade, and photographs like these would become treasure chests that could never be opened, no matter how much she longed for whatever was inside. The only blessing was that it was hard to miss what you couldn't remember.

Of course, Bebbie was a blessing too, and though she had no experience with the task, she did her best to be like a mother to Doris. Bebbie had lost her own mother at a young age, so she understood the pain Doris was feeling, though it wasn't discussed. True to the times, such emotion was not indulged or spoken of; in every quarter there was no end to the small- and large-scale suffering after four years of war – half a life for eight-year-old Doris. As the war chronicler Vera Brittain wrote to her soldier from her Camberwell nursing post, crying "must never be done, for there is so much both personal and impersonal to cry for here that one might weep forever and yet not shed enough tears to wash away the pitiableness of it all."

Pity was not a sentiment usually felt in relation to royalty, but these were unusual times. In July 1918 the Bolsheviks shot the tsar, his wife and their five children, as well as several servants and a doctor who'd been treating the tsar's hemophiliac son, Alexei. The awful details were not revealed for quite some time: that the deposed monarch, his family and servants had been awakened in the night and led to a small brick-walled room void of furniture in the house where they'd been held. Later accounts claim they did not know what was coming, and they stood calmly before their captors. The gunmen had been carefully selected ahead of time, and the leader took the first shot, hitting the tsar in the head and killing him instantly. Bayonets completed the job where the bullets did not, and then the corpses were piled into a truck and dumped in a mine shaft. The official story, released to the world in a newswire by the

Bolshevik government, reported that "a counter-revolutionary conspiracy" had been discovered, prompting the "shooting of the ex-tsar." No details were shared, and the wire promised reassuringly that "the wife and son of Nicholas Romanoff have been sent to a place of security," although of course that place was the bottom of a mine shaft, and they were dead, like the others. In his diary, King George didn't mention the efforts he'd made to prevent his cousin's asylum in Britain. "I hear from Russia that there is every probability that Alicky and the four daughters and little boy were murdered at the same time as Nicky. It's too horrible, and shows what fiends those Bolshevists are." In Germany, the Kaiser's bluff-and-bluster style was consistent. Writing after the war he claimed to have made efforts – unsuccessfully – to arrange for the family's release, and therefore "the blood of the unhappy Tsar is not at *my* door, not on *my* hands."

The world had grown weary of tragedy and seemed almost immune to news that would have shocked a scant four years earlier. Newspapers reported the murder of the tsar almost matter-of-factly, as if such an end to an outmoded, autocratic regime had been inevitable and predictable. One dismissed it as "a typical Bolshevist crime" and pointed out that "had he been wise enough and had a sufficiently strong will, Nicholas would have at once recognized the need for change," and revolution might have been averted. The *New York Times* ran the story of the tsar's murder on the front page, but it wasn't the lead article. Instead the headline proclaimed "All Germans Pushed Back Over the Marne; Allies Gain Three Miles South of Soisson." Nicholas II, tsar of Russia and "a man of almost shrinking shyness, yet remarkable for his dignity," went to his death unmourned by many.

In what was known as the *Kaiserschlacht*, or Kaiser's Battle, the Germans had made some progress on the Western Front in the spring and early summer of 1918. Weather had played a major role in their success, favouring them in May and June with stretches where "the sun was hot, and the roads were deep in dust, which rose like smoke under the feet of the marching troops." The Allies needed time to bring up reserves – both greenhorn Americans and past-their-prime Englishmen like Doris's

Uncle Percy, a middle-aged insurance man with little experience to prepare him for battle.

To keep the Germans from gaining any more ground, the Allies desired rain, the heavier the better and "the more mud the merrier." Philip Gibbs, a correspondent with the *New York Times*, wrote that "the days and nights were dry and mild; the ground firm; the roads good... [giving] the enemy all the advantage for his plans and organization of attack."

The Germans hoped the offensive being planned would finally end the war in their favour. Deciding that their best chance for victory was through Flanders, they launched a diversionary attack against the French in Reims, hoping to divide the enemy and draw the British down out of Belgium. But instead of a romp through French fields and an easy ford of the Marne River, they found themselves beaten back by an Allied army reinforced with a division of Americans still in possession of the vim and vigour that four years of war had wrung from their fellow soldiers. The Germans retreated, and this time the weather sided with the Allies. Heavy downpours forced the enemy to abandon both ammunition and equipment, and Gibbs wrote presciently of "heavy rain today in the north of France, and each drop of it will alter a little, perhaps, the history of this war. Let it rain."

The mud, rain, fog and swollen rivers that caused such havoc for the Germans in retreat also hampered the Allies' advances, prolonging what many on both sides expected was now inevitable. By August the weather had cleared, and men were fighting "stripped to the waist" beneath a hot sun. Canadian troops swung in with what Gibbs called "a brilliant piece of secret manoeuver," surprising the Germans and giving them a fierce fight in a place called Monchy Hill. They fought with "most dogged spirit" through the night, rushing machine-gun nests and eventually capturing 1,800 prisoners. They recaptured two wooded hills that the British troops had come to see as "green eyes staring down on our lines... and from which [had] come wicked machine gun fire when any of our troops moved in the open valley below." The success was uplifting, and gave momentum to the Allies. Gibbs called it a "vast tide of life moving very slowly but steadily," and reported that "[the Germans] no longer have even a dim hope of victory on this western front. All they hope for now is to defend themselves long enough to gain peace by negotiation."

That month, desertions by disgruntled German soldiers increased, and on a single day at Amiens, France, twelve thousand men surrendered to the Allies. Even without that staggering loss, morale was low and supplies were dwindling, and influenza had found many victims. It couldn't be long until the finish came.

By the end of September the German army's highest commanders assured the Kaiser that the war could not be won. Although the fighting continued, peace talks were underway, with one of the Allies' demands being that Kaiser Wilhelm abdicate. In every corner his support was plunging. By October his cherished navy rebelled when the admiral ordered one last battle to restore honour, "even if it should be a fight to the death." Unwilling to die for a lost cause, the men mutinied. By early November the unrest had leached into the naval base at Kiel and taken on a political tone that reflected the frustration of a war-ravaged empire. The bitterness travelled through cities and towns, quickly transforming from mutiny to widespread, unstoppable rebellion against the imperial government.

On November 9 the German chancellor officially declared that "the King and Kaiser has decided to renounce his throne." The decision had actually been made for him, and by the 10th, heeding the warning that his own troops might harm him, he began his journey toward the neutral Netherlands, never to return from a life in exile. One man who accompanied him wrote, "At every station thousands of people were gathered, greeting us with shouting, whistling, cursing. They threatened us, made signs of choking and hanging us, etc. In such manner was our poor Emperor received on Dutch soil." British papers revelled in the news that "Kaiser Bolts to Holland" and "Kaiser Signs [Abdication] 'With a Shiver.'" On the Mall in front of Buckingham Palace piles of stained and battle-marked German weapons appeared without explanation, their presence like a silent admission of defeat. Soon after, the papers printed the news everyone had been waiting for, the huge size of the type reflective of its importance: "Last Shot Fired" and "End of the Great War."

In London on Armistice Day, in spite of a grey rain, the rejoicings were profuse. Lloyd George opened the door of 10 Downing Street, his face "wreathed in smiles," and told the gathered throng that the war would be over at eleven o'clock that morning. There was cheering all around, and hats were thrown in jubilation over the garden wall. At Buckingham Palace, crowds came in waves all day, and people scaled the statue of Queen Victoria and sat in her white marble lap. Some were lucky enough to glimpse the king and queen when they appeared on the balcony. And even for those in the ordinary parts of the city – Ethel, May, Uncle Jack and Aunt Maggie in the Borough, Doris and Bebbie in Whitechapel – the sense of celebration was irrepressible. Church bells clanged and parades marched through the streets, and maroons were fired into the sky. Once the rockets had warned of terrifying air raids, but now they rang out like "a huge Cockney chuckle of delight." "Flags appeared on all sides with amazing rapidity," one paper reported. "They floated proudly over all public buildings, they appeared like magic from private houses, they were waved in the streets, worn (in miniature) in hats, pinned on coats, waved frantically on bus tops, lorries, charabancs, taxicabs, costers' carts, and on every description of vehicle that could pass through the surging, joyous multitudes that thronged the main arteries of London's traffic. And the cheering!...The heart of the great City was filled to overflowing."

To those who'd recently lost someone, the celebration seemed frenzied and almost manic, and the news bittersweet. Some cried instead of laughing, and others stonily watched the antics from wheelchairs, or with shattered or burned faces. Vera Brittain was cleaning bloody bowls when she heard the jubilation in the streets outside the London hospital where she was working. She continued to scrub and thought of the fiancé and brother and dear friends she'd lost. Later she'd write that the celebration had served as a realization that "the dead were dead and would never return." And the living – especially those of Ethel and Joe's age, caught between youth and adulthood when the war began – would have to find some way to carry the grief they'd ingested and go forward with that heavy load. Theirs was what Brittain called a "bankrupt, shattered generation...The best that we who were left could do was to refuse to forget, and to teach our successors what we remembered."

For many it was too much to ask, and silence was easier.

The logistics of bringing such large numbers back from so many different parts of the globe was a trial in itself, but over the next six months, those who'd served in their various ways began retracing their steps home. The time away had changed them, and their home world had altered too, and so began the laborious process of fitting pieces together again, whether broken lives or crumbled buildings. With the returning came keepsakes of war – diaries and poems written in mortal fear and carried through battlefields and trenches. Letters received from home and worn thin with rereading. Mementoes of inconceivable loss and suffering. Someone from the *Mary Rose* – one of the ten who survived, but no one knows who – kept a fragment of wood from the ship and delivered it to a dead stoker's wife. It couldn't come close to replacing the man or explaining the tragedy, but the gift was tenderly received and kept always. "Souvenirs" were brought home too: in the years to come, Joe's Nelly would reminisce that absolutely everyone pillaged, and only Joe, honest to the core, came back with nothing. Which wasn't quite true. He still had his penny, which he presented to Nelly. She traced it on paper and wrote inside the circle: "From Joe Deverill when he was saved."

Yet there were still hardships. It seemed especially cruel that though the brutality had ended, influenza went on killing, as if it was a poison seeping from the wounds of the world. One of its most exacting names was "war plague," since the illness was intrinsically linked, now and forever, with the years-long combat. The death toll kept climbing. Two of the men posted with Joe died within days of each other in December. Nelly's brother, who'd already been hospitalized for shell shock, was dangerously ill and eventually sent back to England in January, still suffering from pneumonia and then pleurisy months later.

In the north, the Navy remained cautious. Once the armistice had been called, the German High Seas Fleet had been directed under guard of the British, the sight of which none who had been there would forget. Both great fleets – 370 ships in all, with ninety thousand men aboard – rendezvoused in the North Sea, and the battleships of the Royal Navy manoeuvred into two long lines that stretched to the horizon. Not trusting the Germans, for no treaty had yet been signed, the British had guns at the ready and crews at action stations as the German ships slid single file into the gap and were escorted on to Scapa Flow. Once at their destination the German ships lay in neat rows, crewed by the same men who had mutinied at Kiel. Eventually most of these men were sent home and only skeleton crews remained to endure the cold Orkney winter, not allowed to go ashore or to visit other ships, and dependent on food supplies, cigarettes and alcohol sent twice a month from Germany. Nothing had yet been determined as to the fate of the ships, and so they sat, a bristling flotilla of angry grey metal. Two among them were *Brummer* and *Bremse*, the light cruisers that had attacked *Mary Rose* and her convoy in the North Sea.

Joe, who'd spent so much of his Navy career bobbing about the waters of Scapa Flow, was now plying the waters to the south, so was not present to see the Kaiser's pride brought low. But he was not a man to gloat. By now he'd been presented with his first good-conduct badge, awarded for consecutive character ratings of Very Good from the various captains he'd served under since becoming an Able Seaman. In the Ability column, though, his record shows he earned only a Satisfactory grade throughout the war, reflective perhaps of his youth, small stature and lack of ambition. Or maybe he couldn't thrive during war. Now that the fighting was over, his grade climbed to Superior and stayed there until the next world war, when it would dip again to Satisfactory. He was a plain, unremarkable man, happiest when the times matched his character.

But just when life showed the promise of becoming somewhat normal again, he learned of a new fracture in the family: Bebbie had decided to emigrate to Canada, and had received Uncle Jack and Aunt Maggie's blessings when she asked to take Doris with her. Although Joe, Ethel and Ernie understood the wisdom of a fresh start for Doris, the thought of the smallest sibling going so far away was hard to bear. Almost nine now, she had always been the bright spark, too young to be worn down

CHAPTER 13

for long by the family's misfortunes. War and illness had caused them to spend a lot of time apart, but they were still a unit, as the strings of x's on each of their letters and postcards would continue to attest. It was as if the x's signified a closeness that could not be articulated.

By the middle of June 1919, Doris had posed for her passport photo and packed her few possessions in a trunk alongside Bebbie's. Nestled among the skirts, blouses and stockings were the important things: for Doris, her mother's amethyst pendant and the postcards she'd received from Ethel and Ernie; for Bebbie, a faded photograph of a young man she never spoke of and the elegant funeral card for her mother. Bebbie's mother was also named Mary Ann; was it this old childhood ache that inspired her to care for Doris?

The adventure was enormous for both the girl and her guardian: at fifty-four, Bebbie was relatively old to be starting over in a new country, a spinster with a child in tow, and Doris was leaving all of her relatives here on *this* side of the water, and might never see them again. In preparation for their departure, Bebbie had resigned from her job at the cork factory, given notice at College Buildings where she'd lived since the days of Jack the Ripper, and withdrawn her savings, exchanging the money for forty dollars in Canadian funds, a figure that was jotted in the ship's ledger when she boarded. They had train tickets to Liverpool and passage paid on the *Metagama*, a liner built in 1914 for the Canadian Pacific Railway company, but which had been used throughout the war as a troopship. A photo taken in Montreal in 1915 shows the *Metagama* steaming out of port, her decks filled with dark-clad soldiers, women waving from the quay. There'd be no one to wave to Bebbie and Doris from the docks in Liverpool, but perhaps that was for the best. Good-byes at the train station were hard enough for those going as well as those staying behind.

As Doris sat with Bebbie in the idling train, who did she look out at to say her last farewell? Had Ernie made the trip from Laindon, brown from his work on Auntie Ada's farm? Ethel would have been there, thin and pale as always, with May beside her, smiling in an effort to make things easier for everyone. If Joe had been able to come, he would have stood waving in uniform, so mature now, though less than five feet tall. The whistle blew and the train pulled out of the station, and Doris's stomach whirled as that peculiar mix of sadness, fear and excitement grew.

Later, aboard the *Metagama*, she turned back to see England shrinking away behind her. Her entire life would be different now. The ship pushed south through the Irish Sea, passing the old Welsh homes of Benjamin and Margaret Jones, and soon the water stretched out on all sides of the *Metagama*, carrying Doris ever farther from all she'd known.

A week before the *Metagama* sailed, the Germans scuttled their fleet at Scapa Flow. For seven long months the ships had swung from moorings, interned under the watch of the British, waiting for the final peace terms to be decided. But in Paris, where the Peace Conference was being held, there was much arguing over not just the details of an agreement but also the wider question of how to create a perfect world where no one nation would have the upper hand over another. Nobody could agree on how such a utopia would come about, or what it would consist of, and the various players debated and deliberated and discussed, submitting proposals and counter-proposals that altered the map of the world many times over. Neither could the Allies come to a consensus on what should be done with Germany's fleet, with several countries wanting a share and all loath to bolster another's navy. The final version of the treaty was to contain a clause requiring the ships' surrender, and the German admiral in charge of the fleet at Scapa Flow, Ludwig von Reuter, wrote that such a move would be a "lasting disgrace." On a day that most of the British ships were out on exercise, von Reuter moved on a plan he'd made earlier and gave the signal to begin the scuttling. It travelled from ship to ship throughout the anchorage, and flood valves, seacocks, portholes and watertight doors were opened as the men slipped into lifeboats. Some vessels defiantly hoisted the prohibited black cross and eagle flag of the Imperial Navy, and within a few hours most of the German fleet was no more. At least one British admiral privately thought the seaport suicide "a real blessing," solving once and for all "the thorny question of the redistribution of these ships." One week later the Treaty of Versailles was signed, and the world, on paper at least, had found a precarious peace.

If the news reached the *Metagama*, it found her one day into her trans-Atlantic voyage. On board were just over 1,300 souls, of whom the majority were soldiers and their dependents. Men in uniform were not an unusual sight to Doris. For most of her life there'd been soldiers in the streets. But these ones spoke with a strange accent and were destined for places she'd never heard of, like Timmins, Swift Current and Murray Harbour. There were fifty-three children on board between the ages of one and twelve, and a photo taken in the cabin-class nursery shows a boy on a rocking horse, a child in a swing and two young girls reading beneath elephant-motif wallpaper. This room was off limits to steerage passengers like Doris, but she didn't feel well enough to venture there anyway. For much of the trip she was seasick, and she also fell down a flight of stairs, suffering a gash to her head. When she was up and about she might have met some of the other girls her age in third class – Siddie Wright, perhaps, en route to Windsor with her mother and two brothers, or Mary Pemberton, whose final destination was thousands of miles farther yet, all the way to Vancouver – but if so, they lost contact after they disembarked.

The voyage took nine days, and the *Metagama* arrived in Montreal on July 6, 1919. At seven in the morning, the ship's doctor and the immigration officials made their rounds, inspecting passengers' physical condition and perusing their documents. All but one were cleared to disembark. Doris and Bebbie had Canadian Pacific Railway tickets to take them the remainder of the distance to London, Ontario, where Bebbie's sister Frances would be waiting, but before they left Montreal Bebbie posted a card addressed to Joe, as head of the small Deverill family. It exists still, some one hundred years on. "Arrived quite safe at Montreal this morning at 6 o'clock ... Write you later on. With love from Bebbie."

PART THREE

The Forest City
1907–1934

Ingram-Cartwright Family Tree

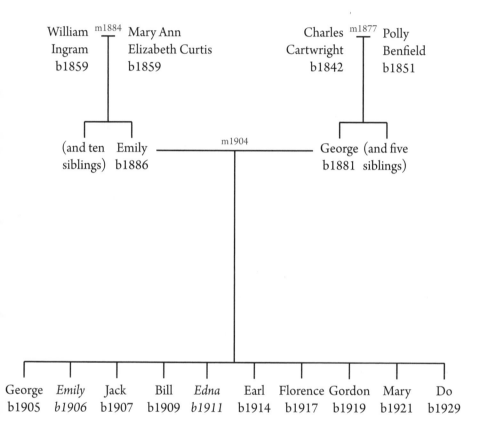

George
b1905

Emily
b1906

Jack
b1907

Bill
b1909

Edna
b1911

Earl
b1914

Florence
b1917

Gordon
b1919

Mary
b1921

Do
b1929

Italics denote infant and child deaths
b indicates born
m indicates marriage

George Cartwright's and Emily Ingram's engagement photos, circa 1904. George's fresh face reflects his kind-heartedness, while Emily's steeliness shows even here, in a photo taken to mark a happy time.

CHAPTER 14

My Own Darling Wiffie

In the early years of the twentieth century, London, England, was the largest city in the world, with some seven million residents. On the other side of the Atlantic, landlocked in the southern reaches of what had once been called Upper Canada, London, Ontario, was its strange little caricature, with just fifty thousand souls. Most of the roads were unpaved, and in heavy rain they turned to ankle-deep mud. While this newer London had streets with copycat names – York, Clarence, Kent, Wellington, Waterloo – woven into the mix were Tecumseh, Iroquois and Quebec. In England there'd been a River Thames, and here there was another, though a less fabled waterway than its namesake, with pebbled banks and mud hens roosting among the reeds.

Although early European settlement had stripped most of the forests and converted much of the area to farmland, by the 1870s people had started to realize the value of tree-lined streets and begun to replant, citing a tree's ability to "afford a cooling shade in the heat of summer and absorb much of the animal and deleterious vapours." Some fifteen thousand trees were planted along city streets and in the newly created Victoria Park, and prosecution was assured for any who harmed the young saplings. The result was a city-wide passion for trees that became a legacy, and London began to again deserve its nickname of the Forest City, bestowed decades before when it had been a small settlement cut out of a woodland of sugar maple, sassafras, black cherry and tall elm.

The oil fields in nearby Lambton County had contributed to the growth of London's prosperity in earlier times, as had the American Civil War, when the British thought it prudent to re-establish a soldiers' garrison within the city. Along the way other businesses cemented

London as an industry town: Labatt and Carling breweries, Hyman's Tannery, McClary's stove works and McCormick's biscuit company were prominent. The wealth they'd generated for their owners was apparent in the imposing stone mansions that dotted the city – Thomas McCormick's estate on Grand Avenue; Charles Hyman's whimsically named Idlewyld; turreted Buchan House, owned by Thomas Escott, who'd made a fortune in wholesale grocery. But the lucrative industrial core of London's business sector also meant that other streets were filled with the workers' clapboard houses. Backyards on King and Horton and surrounding streets were strung with laundry and held gardens that fed large families, and in the heat of the summer the grass grew long and insects buzzed between the potato drills.

Despite the city's plentiful homages to its namesake and the fact that the majority of its inhabitants had a family connection to Britain at some point in their pedigree, this London had not always welcomed newcomers with open arms. Prior to 1907, Englishmen had been given preference by Canadian employers, with some actively recruiting from British unions. Canadian Pacific Railway's Montreal car shops had favoured English metalworkers, and Penman's Knitting Mills in Paris, Ontario, had hired almost exclusively from the English Midlands, where hosiery firms flourished. When Eaton's Department Store in Toronto got into the garment manufacturing industry, it hired tailors and seamstresses away from English shops, and preferred salesgirls with British accents. The idea of a Canadian identity separate from the British was relatively immature, with most English-speaking Canadians feeling quite comfortable with their links to "Mother England." The English were family, after all, and weren't considered outsiders.

But in May 1907, when George Cartwright, a twenty-six-year-old stoker, arrived from Belvedere, Kent, on the outskirts of London, a recession had changed the employment landscape, and suddenly there were too few jobs and too many looking for work. The virulence previously directed toward Irish Catholics, Chinese and Italians now included the English – in particular the Cockney and the lower class deemed "the curse of the Empire" – and businesses posted signs that announced "No English Need Apply." On his travels through Canada, a reporter from *The Times* found that everywhere he went he heard the same complaints about the masses of Englishmen looking for work, especially "the degenerate Cockney": "the Englishman who succeeds is hardly ever a Londoner; the Englishman who fails completely is almost always a Londoner." One man he interviewed asked him, "Why do you send such wretched creatures to us? They can do no good here. I believe they are worse off in Canada than they were in England."

George Cartwright didn't fit the stereotype. When he couldn't get work as a stoker in London or Toronto or the surrounding towns, he hired himself out as a bricklayer, earning enough money that on the arrival in July of his young wife, Emily, and their two small children, also a George and an Emily, he marked the occasion by hiring a carriage with two white horses – "for luck" – to meet them at the train station. What a sight he must have been for Emily after her long journey: tall, slim and broad-shouldered; hazel eyes sparkling with a warmth that is evident in the photos of him through the years. She would have told him the frightful details of their crossing: a young French farmer had died on board and been buried at sea. And one day when she'd gone on deck to take some fresh air – she was pregnant with a third child and nauseous from the journey – the wind had blown so furiously that baby Emily had almost been torn from her arms. One of the deckhands had called to her, "Get back inside! It's too dangerous out here!" George, smiling, must have wrapped his arms around all of them and assured her that everything was fine now that the small family was together again.

The reunion was marred just two weeks later when their little girl succumbed to bronchial pneumonia. When Emily wrote home to Belvedere about the tragedy, her letter went to her sister Louie or one of her other siblings, since she'd become estranged from her parents. Although she and George had been childhood friends, and the Ingrams had known the Cartwrights most of their lives, Emily's parents, William and Elizabeth Ingram, had disapproved of the wedding and hadn't attended it or spoken to their daughter since, perhaps because when the couple married in 1904, nineteen-year-old Emily was three months pregnant. If that was the reason, it was sadly hypocritical since the genealogical paper trail reveals Emily's mother, too, had been a pregnant bride. Perhaps they were both strong personalities who couldn't figure out how to forgive. In a strange twist to the story, Emily's mother was pregnant while Emily was, and mother and daughter had children in the same year – the mother her last, the daughter her first. Someone, probably Louie, sent Emily a photograph of their mother with two-year-old Alice on her lap and wrote on the back "Dear old mum. I suppose you remember the day the wind blew and she lost her hat. That is Alice when she was a child." But Emily would never meet Alice or see any of her family again. It was a rift that was never healed.

After their marriage, George and Emily lived with the Cartwright family on Ashburnham Road in Belvedere, Kent. George's parents, Charles and Polly, had married nearly thirty years earlier at the thousand-year-old St. Dunstan and All Saints Church in Stepney before moving out of London's congestion to Belvedere, where Charles's uncle was the publican of the Belvedere Hotel. Charles worked there as a waiter for a while, but soon found employment as a labourer at Price's Oil Works, one of the many factories strung along the mud flats on the south bank of the Thames.

Slightly more comfortable than neighbouring Plumstead, Belvedere had its choice locations. Upper Belvedere, with its hills and parks and villas, was home to the affluent who commuted to London, while the lower town and its streets of two-storey workingmen's dwellings shared the marshes with the Crossness Sewage Works and heavy industry. Gypsies set up camp on the Belvedere Marsh each year, their painted caravans and circus-like tents parked in a tangle on the mud and surrounded by makeshift fences. The South Eastern and Chatham Railway threaded through the town next to the Lower Road, and on both sides of the tracks were factories such as Callender's Cable Works, makers of electric wire and cable; Vickers of machine gun fame; and Charles's employer, Price's Oil Works, manufacturers of "lubricators and burning oils." And burn they did. Newspapers frequently reported on fires at Price's. They were invariably spectacular episodes that drew huge crowds to the sight of billowing clouds of smoke and flaming oil spilling from pipes and cast iron vats. In the aftermath, it would have been

Charles's job, and that of his fellow labourers, to dig through the oily mess as Price's rebuilt on the five-acre Thames-side property.

Charles supplemented his wages with income from lodgers – first a doctor, then an engineer, then three men together, two coopers and a labourer. Eventually there were six children in the house as well, George's three sisters and two brothers, and though they moved several times over the years, the Cartwight family home was never any farther from the mud flats than the gentle rise of Ashburnham Road, where the row houses sloped ever so slightly uphill.

Similarly, Emily's parents, William and Elizabeth Ingram, had lived for years on Picardy Street, near the roundabout that featured an ornate, cupola-topped public toilet. Small stores with awnings to shade their windows fronted the street. A photo from the time shows a few strolling shoppers, while outside the cupolaed urinal, a donkey stands patiently. Other photos depict the slow pace of the town; this was a place where people knew your face if not your name, and passersby tipped their hats. The cream stone and brown brick of the Belvedere Hotel, where Charles Cartwright worked as a young single man, was on the corner of the street where the Ingrams lived, and the pub would probably have been the Ingrams' local were they inclined toward a pint.

William Ingram, like Charles Cartwright, was an import to Belvedere, though he'd come from much farther away. Born in Birmingham to a carpenter, he'd served a short stint as a private in the army but had become a stoker by the time he arrived in Belvedere, and although there's nothing definitive that places him precisely, in 1901 he is listed on the census as a "furnace stoker, oil works," so it's quite possible he was employed at Price's, like Charles. The stoker's job, whether on board a ship, on a train or in the bowels of a factory, was hot, dirty, backbreaking labour that involved shovelling coal into boilers to keep steam up in the engines that propelled the ship, drove the train or turned the cogs in the machinery on the shop floor. It was the stoker's responsibility to adjust the heat of the fires, shifting the coal and raking the beds to regulate the steam pressure. An overheated boiler could result in an explosion. It required some skill and some understanding of the boiler system, so a stoker was a step up from a general labourer in the hierarchy of menial jobs, and William Ingram may have believed he had reason to feel superior to Charles Cartwright.

William's wife, Elizabeth Curtis, the daughter and sister of dairy farmers, had been born in neighbouring Abbey Wood on a farm called High Grove. Her father had started out as a butcher and briefly tried his luck as a bailiff, but soon opted for the life of a dairyman, milking cows for a living. Unlike the dairymen of London's inner city, his was a simpler existence, his cows the healthier for it. George Duckworth, one of Charles Booth's investigators who'd reported on cowkeepers in Southwark, was well qualified to compare, and he noted that in picturesque Abbey Wood the "air was heavy with the scent of flowers." To the south were woodlands and rural lanes leading up into the hills of Bostall Heath. To the north was pastureland on the marshes beside the Thames. The place wasn't idyllic: trains were "infrequent and unpunctual," Duckworth reported, and the boom of guns being tested at the Woolwich Arsenal frequently broke the tranquility. But Elizabeth's father farmed here for forty years, and when he could do it no longer his sons took over.

To the west of Abbey Wood lay "happy Plumstead," as George Duckworth pegged it, "dull and ordinary outwardly, but…remarkable in many ways." Among these he counted the fact that the streets were quiet and tidy, at least until the children "tumble out of school and leave a litter of small paper bags which once held pennyworth of sweets or fruit." The roads also filled up at the dinner hour, when men filed out of the factories to go home for a meal. The town seemed asleep, Duckworth thought as he trudged the roads, though he knew that the women were at home but invisible from the street as they tended tiny garden plots in their backyards or hung laundry out of view of passersby. The difference, he wrote, was Saturday night when front doors opened and the streets woke up. On these nights, men sat on their front step to smoke their evening pipe, and anyone walking by the houses could hear laughter and chatter and "villainous strumming on cheap pianos." Plumstead, Duckworth observed, was a place of "newly married couples, young families, wives at home, daughters not yet grown up and expecting marriage and home life not factory work as a career, husbands and sons in full and steady work earning more money than they really know how to spend. Where in London is there another such place?"

In this Victorian utopia (if Duckworth's description is accurate), William Ingram and Elizabeth Curtis raised a family of eleven children, with daughter Emily being the second eldest. But sometime before Emily's New Year's Eve marriage to George Cartwright she fell out with her mother and moved in with her grandparents in Abbey Wood. "Quarrels with the Ingrams" is the vague explanation for the estrangement, but any detailed reason has not survived.

Before those disagreements arose, the Ingrams had known George's family well enough to feel some sympathy for the Cartwrights when things began to go badly for George's younger brother, Jack. As a child, Jack had had physical and mental difficulties, and when he was twelve their mother, Polly, took him to the East London Hospital for Children. The assessment was not hopeful. After the visit, the doctor wrote:

Dear Madam,

I wish it was in my power to give you a favourable opinion of your boy. But all along I have considered his case to be one of an incurable nature. It is almost certainly one of tumour of the cerebellum. Any attempt to remove the tumour is, in my opinion, too risky an operation to advise or sanction. I fear I cannot give any hope of the boy's sight improving, and any suggestion as to his earning his own living is an impracticable one.

Yours, J.A. Coutts.

And yet, Jack did earn money. On most days through his teen years he could be spotted on Belvedere's Lower Road, pushing his barrow made from an old Tate's sugar crate fitted with wheels. He hawked shrimps and oranges and sweets outside the factories, raising a hand to his father if he spotted him, and Charles would wave back, pausing to wipe the grime from his face and watching his son's lumbering teenage form head back the way he'd come. Depending on Jack's mood – it changed with the hour – he might stop at the Halfway House pub to chat with any who had a minute, and if he hadn't sold all his wares by then, he'd be able to unload them there. Balmy Jack, the locals called him, but it was affectionate. Everyone knew Balmy Jack Cartwright.

And so it went until Wednesday, February 11, 1903, when Jack was seventeen. The day began in a seemingly usual way, although Jack had vomited in the night and Polly had been cross with him for messing the bedding. He rose at half past six and got his mother some breakfast, then hung around the house until close to lunchtime, when he fetched his barrow, loaded his oranges and sweetmeats and set off, ostensibly for Callender's Cable Works, where on a regular day he'd push his wares among the men partaking of their midday smoke. But Jack never arrived at Callender's. He parked his handcart in the turning by the Halfway House pub, walked up the private crossing to the railway tracks and was hit by a train.

The inquest into Jack's death was held two days later at West Street School. The jury of sixteen men and the coroner called several witnesses, including Alfred Hills, a fishmonger who lived on Picardy Street near the Ingrams and knew Jack. He'd encountered him on the day he died and said the usually merry, whistling lad had been crying. He'd asked Jack what was the matter, and Jack replied that he'd been "queer all night," and that "Mother paid me for it." Hills told the jury that on occasion Jack had complained of being beaten, and that sometimes, when he was "funny," he'd talked about drowning himself.

Another witness, Frank Buck, a boy of seventeen who'd known Jack from their school days, made a more pointed claim to Jack's state of mind. He'd heard Jack talk about suicide many times, he said, fearing he was a burden on his mother since he couldn't get steady work. Frank said he had come across Jack some minutes after Hills left him, and he told the jury that Jack had asked him when the next train was due. Frank claimed Jack had said he was going to kill himself, but Frank hadn't believed him. "I told him I'd heard that tale before," Frank said – awkward words with Polly and Charles in the room.

More witnesses were called – a labourer, who related a simple exchange of greetings near the level crossing; a nearly deaf stoker, who struggled to hear the coroner's questions but assured the jury he'd seen nothing at the crossing; the engine driver, who said he'd not seen or felt anything, "even as small as a cat," between Erith and Belvedere, though he'd blown his whistle at every public crossing and had his man on the lookout according to regulations.

The guard of another passing train noticed the body lying face down in the permanent way and notified the signalman, who rushed to the site. One of Jack's legs was broken and his head was badly shattered, the brain protruding. His cap lay in the platelayer's footpath. An autopsy later concluded that Jack had not been run over by the train but, rather, struck by it, on the side of the head, as the engine passed. The examination also confirmed the diagnosis Dr. Coutts had made five years earlier: there was a large tumour on the left lobe of the cerebellum. The coroner believed the growth was likely to make the boy "excitable and uncertain in his movements."

Polly and Charles sat through the inquest, probably still in shock. Only Polly was questioned by the coroner, who asked if she'd ever beaten the boy. She replied no, and said that although she'd spoken to him sharply because he'd vomited on the bed, there'd been no disagreement between them that morning. She stated with some indignation that a rumour had been going around in the neighbourhood that she'd not been feeding Jack properly, but the coroner reassured her on that point: "The well-nourished state of the body proves the lack of foundation for any such statement."

If Polly felt vindicated by his support, she was disappointed by the verdict: "Suicide whilst suffering temporary mental derangement." She believed Jack's tumour had caused his actions, and that the tumour was the result of a blow to the head he'd received at school years before. When a reporter interviewed her after the inquest, she said that while Jack had been eccentric, he'd also been "perfectly harmless … and an exceptionally good boy." She'd been "overawed," she told the reporter, by the proceedings at the inquiry, and was sure that had she better represented herself and Jack, the verdict would have been different. On the very day of the accident, she said, Jack had contracted with a neighbour to dig a garden in exchange for a shilling or two, and with his earnings had planned to buy an incubator to hatch chickens and thereby make a fortune for the family. Such were his grandiose plans. They buried Jack a week to the day of his death in the Erith parish churchyard.

A year or so later, George and Emily posed for engagement photos. George's is a head and shoulders shot, faded at the edges, and he wears a sack coat, vest and tie over a tall stiff-collared shirt. The square jaw and honest gaze are Polly's, but the nose is Charles's. At twenty-three, George has yet to grow the signature moustaches that he will wear later in life and has the fresh and eager look of a young man ready to take a wife. Nineteen-year-old Emily is seated in her photograph, one elbow resting lightly on the upholstered arm of a chair. Her dress is dark lace and satin, and a gold chain hangs in loops from a cameo brooch pinned to the high, tight neck. She is looking off to the left of the photographer, her expression somewhat tender, and yet there is a steeliness in her eyes that suggests she is a woman of some rigidity. Whatever objections her parents had to her marriage to George – Emily's pregnancy, or rumours about Jack, and Polly's treatment of him – Emily had made her choice, and the two were married on the last day of the year, an ending, but also a beginning.

St. Nicholas Church had seen its share of beginnings and endings. It dated from the twelfth century, the footings hundreds of years before that, and it had been allowed to fall to ruin and been rebuilt many times over. In 1800, trees were growing in the aisles, but over the next century the building was repaired and renovated, and by the time George and Emily said their vows there it was a lovely mishmash of seventeenth-century red brick and stones of various hues – warm, honey-toned Bath stone, bluish-grey Kentish ragstone and soft white Portland. Most likely the entire Cartwright clan attended the ceremony: an older brother, three younger sisters and George's parents, Charles and Polly. The Ingram contingent was much smaller, though Emily's family was twice the size of George's. Emily's brother Will signed the register, as did her sister Louie, as much a spark as Emily herself. In a school photo taken when Emily and her sister were young, the two little girls are easy to pick out of the crowd of white pinafores and hair bows.

Both eye the camera with the same look of determination, their mouths set and chins jutting forward. These are girls not to be trifled with, their gazes tell you, and family lore recounts Emily as stubborn and Louie as outspoken; later in life she smoked a cigarette a day and rose at six o'clock each morning to polish her shoes.

The house on Ashburnham Road was full with the arrival of Emily. It was a terrace house, with a tiny garden out front and an expansive yard behind. All the others in the street were identical, attached one to the next in a long row, but they were also spacious and modern, with pretty bow windows. The Cartwrights' was on the corner, the last one at the top of the road. Its front door was on the side of the house away from the street, opening onto a gravel lane that hugged woodland tunnelled with footpaths. The woods belonged to the Royal Alfred Aged Merchant Seamen's Institution, a group dedicated to ensuring a home for old and destitute sailors. The jewel of the property was a grand manor set magnificently on a hilltop and surrounded by the woods that the Cartwrights' house abutted. The mansion had been renovated to house the old sailors in rooms reminiscent of ships' cabins; these were so much like the real thing that explorer Frederick Whymper claimed, "It requires only a very slight stretch of the imagination for [the sailor] ashore to indulge in the fond delusion that he is at sea again." The institute itself couldn't be seen from Ashburnham Road – instead the view was of thickly tangled greenery, including oak trees and Lebanon cedar, horse chestnuts and thick-leafed limes – but often the public were invited to celebrations on the grounds of the seafarers' home on the hill, and photos show large crowds enjoying bonfires, acrobat performances and cricket matches. George and Emily may have attended, following one of the many footpaths through the woods, petite Emily in a wide-brimmed hat to shield her reddish-blonde hair and fair skin from the sun, rangy George in a pork pie or a bowler, pants hanging from suspenders.

George and Emily didn't remain long in Belvedere. Living in such a small community meant encountering Emily's parents now and then, spotting one another on the street and ducking into the closest shop, or suddenly discovering a window display that was particularly interesting. If they showed up at the same celebration at the Aged Merchant

Seamen's Institution, one or the other might have made an excuse to go home early, or kept to a far area of the grounds. It can't have been easy or pleasant, so it's not surprising that before two years of married life had passed they were making plans to leave. They might have moved into London, where George had relatives, or to Birmingham, where Emily's father had come from. But all the talk in those days was of going to Canada. Newspapers wrote about the riches to be had there and ran notices headed "Canada! Canada! Canada! – Settlers intending to go out during the coming season should get their tickets…WITHOUT DELAY." When George and Emily chose London, Ontario, they mustn't have realized that a glut of English immigrants had already arrived there, and that things were not as rosy as they sounded in the papers.

A picture survives, taken to mark the occasion of Emily's emigration. George and Emily's two children are in the shot: George Jr. a toddler in a frilly white dress and stockings; baby Emily Louisa (after Emily and her closest sister Louie) in a white bonnet that almost obscures her face. George's father, Charles Cartwright, stands in front of a latticed fence. The thick vines curling through it are leafless, signifying that this photo was taken in early spring, perhaps just after George has sailed on the ss *Vancouver*. Charles's hair is thinning on top, his full beard white. He is of average height and build, and although he has been a labourer all his life, the work has not stooped him. He has a proud bearing and stands with shoulders square. He wears a black suit jacket and vest over a white shirt, and the glimmer of a pocket-watch chain is just visible. Polly, eleven years younger, sits in front of him, with Emily at her side and little George on her lap. Polly is portly, in a dark gown with lace at the throat. She is in her middle fifties, but her hair is still a glossy black. She wears it parted in the middle and drawn back in a style that is severe and unflattering for her round face and double chin. The smile she turns toward the photographer is sardonic, almost threatening, as if challenging her forebears to learn her story. Emily, in contrast to her mother-in-law, has her thick hair piled loosely on top of her head in the popular Gibson Girl style, and wears a pale skirt and blouse. Her gaze, though, is strangely similar to Polly's – her face tilted away from the camera but her eyes drawn to it, the wrinkled brow and half smile suggesting cynicism and a hardness that will stand her in good stead in the coming years. She will never see Polly and Charles again once she leaves England, and the baby in her lap will not survive.

With George and Emily's reunion in London, the children – little Canadians all – kept coming: Jack, named for George's unfortunate younger brother; Edna, who followed her sister to the grave on her own first birthday; Earl, given the middle name Ingram after Emily's estranged family; and also William Charles, or Bill, so fair among his dark-haired siblings that he was nicknamed Snowball.

With a growing brood to feed, George eventually got work in maintenance at the booming McCormick's biscuit company and was on staff when the factory was newly rebuilt in 1913 as a state-of-the-art facility, billed as one of the largest, most sanitary factories of its kind. It was undeniably impressive. Five storeys high, its white terracotta walls and tall windows gleamed, earning it the nickname of the Sunshine Palace. A postcard touting the opening called it "McCormick's new snow white sunshine biscuit and candy factory," and promised "hundreds of varieties of high class fancy sweet biscuits and candy." The workers wore white linen uniforms and caps to underscore the notion of cleanliness and hygiene, and when several hundred bakers and chocolate dippers and hard candy boilers and packers posed outside the "palace" for a photograph, the effect was dazzling. George, washing the windows and tinkering with the machinery, apparently enjoyed his job. A photo shows him in overalls at the factory's main entrance, gloved hands gripping a thick rope that extends up out of the frame. Above the image, someone has written "Who holds Mc's together? Pa!" One of the perks of working at McCormick's was the bags of broken cookie bits he could take home, delighting his expanding family, and Emily too, who'd begun to grow round with the birth of many children.

By 1914, George and Emily had moved from a house on Horton Street to one on Linwood farther north, but the new house wasn't much of an improvement. Thrift remained the order of the day in a world of outdoor toilets and a neighbourhood tap for water, yet even housewives like Emily could not resist trying newfangled toasters or some of the other technologies being touted round the city by door-to-door sales-men. A motorcar-sized replica of one of the new "hydro irons" made the rounds of London streets, promising a product "guaranteed for all time," and the sellers were so confident people would buy into electri-fied gadgets that they left small appliances at homes around the city free of charge for several months. At the end of the trial period, few were willing to give them back, having reaped the benefits of saved time and labour.

Things were also looking up in the area of public transit. A group called the Citizens' Sunday Car Committee, which had been lobbying for a decade to get the city to allow Sunday tram service, finally got its way, and trolleys began to roll on all seven days of the week. For those like the Cartwrights who couldn't afford a motor car, it was a great lib-erator. After church they could take a picnic to Springbank Park, a four-hundred-acre spread of rambling Thames-side paths and gardens that also had an amusement park complete with Ferris wheel, funhouse and roller coaster. As part of the city's early foray into the world of electrifi-cation, Springbank boasted electric lights, and the London Street Rail-way ran moonlight excursions to the park. On warm summer evenings, couples could be found strolling the pathways or dancing in the shelter of the pavilion to the strains of local orchestras. But George and Emi-ly had a house full of young children, and their evenings consisted of shared kitchen duties and then a lineup for the bath tub, with Emily checking for dirt behind the ears.

Even those dancing through the summer at Springbank or one of the other outdoor bandstands could not ignore the rumbling of war. It hovered like an impending thunderstorm on a hot night, invisible yet ominous and exciting. Early in August, as Britain waited for a response to its ultimatum from Germany, crowds gathered outside the office of the *London Free Press*, wondering if the Kaiser would back down and withdraw his troops from Belgium. Throughout the evening a copy boy appeared periodically in the window, pasting up handwritten notices of the latest developments. The final bulletin of the night was posted sometime close to midnight: "Great Britain declares war; God save the King!" Cheers rang out, and despite the fact it was midnight, an

impromptu parade wound its way through the streets. There was complete confidence in the outcome of any war, but few suspected that it
would go on and on, and that so many would perish.

A photograph shows the McCormick's cafeteria filled with soldiers, but George Cartwright was not one of them. There's no record
of his having enlisted, though the army took men between the ages of
eighteen and forty-five, and George, thirty-three in 1914, would have
qualified. But he was a married man with children to support, and that
demographic made up only 20 percent of the Canadian Expeditionary
Force in the Great War. In that first year a married man needed permission from his wife to volunteer, so maybe Emily didn't want him to go;
or maybe he himself chose to stay. In any case, George remained in the
employ of McCormick's, which had about eight hundred employees
and was working hard to keep them.

McCormick's had long been known as a comparatively good work
environment in this factory town, and now that it was a "sweets palace" it had a gymnasium for recreation and an attractive dining room
with decent, affordable food; the bill of fare included stewed prunes,
hot Oxo, meat pie and scalloped potatoes. But men in skilled positions
were going overseas, and there was new work to be had in munitions
jobs. The foundry E. Leonard & Sons, which made boilers and steam
engines for factories, now expanded to produce artillery shell bodies
as well, and the Empire [Brass] Manufacturing Company near McCormick's made the fuses to go inside them, as well as fittings for weapon-
ry. In response to the competition from other industries, McCormick's
hiked its pay rates to keep workers happy. So life continued somewhat
normally for George and Emily, if they could ignore the news from their
homeland and the fact that their families were entangled in the fighting
early on.

For the Ingrams, seeing brothers and brothers-in-law leave, knowing
they might never return, was especially hard, given that Emily's oldest
brother, Will, had died at the end of August, just after the war began.
The death wasn't war-related – he'd been at work for the flour mill, behind the wheel of a huge steam lorry laden with two tons of flour, when
he'd lost control of the vehicle, smashing into some shops on the High

Street and killing himself and three small children. Brother Fred was home only long enough to see Will buried and posthumously absolved at a coroner's inquest, and then he was shipped overseas, among the first to go because he was already a trained soldier. Emily's sister Louie – the one who, with Will, had stood by her at the wedding – had said goodbye to her husband, Bert Mantell, just days after war was declared. He sent frequent letters home to Louie as he moved from Woolwich to the Western Front. The notes opened with "My own darling wiffie" and closed with "Your loving hubby Bert," and were almost unfailingly cheerful and encouraging, except when he received news of Will's death. "But what a Hero," he wrote when he read of how Will had screamed for his delivery partner to jump from the lorry as soon as he'd realized the danger, and how he'd avoided others as he roared down the hill, shouting all the while for people to clear the road. When he'd crashed into the shops he may not even have seen the children, for it was the walls of the buildings tumbling down that killed them as they played in the passageway between the two stores. "Comfort his wife," wrote Bert, "... and if I get home I will work for you both." The letters came all through August, September and October, assuring Louie that he was "in the pink" and asking that she stay calm and not worry. "I'll come home in khaki when it's over." But Bert never returned. His last postcard, hastily scribbled and sent from Ham in the Somme Valley, was unusually brief: "I am all right up to now no time to write more." On October 22 he was killed in action, and Louie became a widow with three small children, sewing army shirts for a shilling a day. Just two days after Bert's death, his brother was also killed in France; by 1915, Fred Ingram was gone as well. Emily, far away in Canada, surely felt the losses too, each tragedy emphasizing her distance from family.

Though Emily and George were on the periphery of war's drama, reminders of it were close at hand. As headquarters for Canada's No. 1 Military District, comprising ten counties and responsible for the training and administration of the militia units within them, London was one of the Canadian Army's most important recruiting centres, and at Wolseley Barracks on Oxford Street, not far from the Cartwrights' Linwood address, there were sixteen thousand soldiers in training. The

green space at Carling Heights was now a tent city swarming with soldiers who sometimes marched through the streets singing, or wandered
through Smallman & Ingram's department store in their off-hours, flirt-
ing with the shop girls. Along with the munitions work underway at
E. Leonard & Sons and Empire Brass, Spramotor Company, a machine
shop on King Street, landed lucrative contracts to manufacture artillery
shells, and the place buzzed with activity. On the rear wall, visible from
the street with the shop doors open, hung a banner that read "To Kaiser
Bill, with compliments from the Spramotor Company."

At Western University, one of just five such schools in Ontario along
with McMaster, Toronto, Queen's and Ottawa, lecture halls emptied of
students – youth and intelligence being a target for army recruiters. And
the people of London, proud of the city's military roots, gave over their
young, believing, as did most in the early days of the war, that the fighting would be over by Christmas. Western's enrolment registers thinned
as students from arts, law and other faculties enlisted in what many saw
as a great adventure. Medical students also heeded the call, although
this caused some concern and prompted the *Western University Gazette*
to write that "the need for army surgeons is so great that those [medical
students] near the completion of their course are asked by the military
authorities to return to their schools and finish their studies." Another
writer echoed the cautionary note: "Nobody can foretell the length of
this war, and to empty our medical schools is to gamble on the chance
that the war will be over within a year." Whether or not eager recruits
acted on such advice and returned to school, certainly Western University continued to contribute significantly to the war effort. In 1916
the school raised and equipped No. 10 Canadian Stationary Hospital,
known as the Western University Hospital, a four-hundred-bed unit
staffed mainly by faculty and students of Western. At first based in Sea-
ford, England, its work in the field of blood transfusions was considered
pioneering – and prestigious for the university back home. The unit expanded and was eventually sent to Calais, France, where it occupied an
abandoned hospital and suffered through more than forty aerial bombing raids. The grimness of its mandate, handling not only flu and infection but also the horrors of war-inflicted injury, perhaps prompted the

staff to make room for merriment. A wartime photo exists of No. 10's Boomalackas, a comedy dance troupe named after a university chant; dressed up as Pierrot the clown, the privates and sergeants grin and tip their hats to the camera.

Despite the war, or because of it, McCormick's continued with the tradition of an annual picnic for employees and their families, and a picture taken at the event in 1916 shows three of the Cartwright boys – eleven-year-old George, eight-year-old Jack and seven-year-old Snowball Bill – sitting cross-legged on the grass, wearing summer suit jackets and straw boaters. Bill's hair can't be seen beneath the brim of the hat, but it remained Ingram blond in contrast to his older brothers, who'd inherited their father's dark colouring. Other photos taken at the picnic show lanky "Pa" falling at the finish line, legs constrained in a burlap potato sack, or hopping gleefully along with a partner in a three-legged race. There are many such pictures in the Cartwright family albums: George twisting to smile at the camera as he sits with his boys on a dock, fishing reel in hand; a group shot taken round a sandcastle at the beach in Port Stanley, George sitting in the water in a full-body bathing suit. Often Emily lurks in the background in these shots, woefully overdressed for the beach and with her purse dangling from her arm. Though not partaking in the fun, she grins broadly at her husband and children.

The images fit with stories that say the Cartwrights were a close and lively bunch. George was a joyful person, a model family man who adored his kids, who adored him in return. Emily was brusque by comparison, excessively tidy and efficient in domestic matters, and strict when it came to chores and responsibilities, but also given to hugging her children in frequent tight embraces, as if she understood the fragility of family all too well. She and George had not forgotten their old home, but they were content in their new one, and they entertained their children by chanting the train stops between Belvedere and London. Soon the children could name them too. "Not Wool-*wich*," corrected George. "Wool-*ich*. The w is silent." It was easy to remember, added Emily, because wool was itchy. The children would giggle. They liked to pronounce it wrong to see Pa's eyebrows furrow.

In season the boys toiled in the family's large garden, Bill's blond head shining among the foliage. He was industrious from a young age, and these duties were his first taste of hard work being satisfying. Sometimes at the end of the day George erected a tent so the brothers could camp out and listen to the crickets as they drifted off to sleep. Their jobs were hoeing and picking beetles off the potato plants, and looking for Emily's engagement ring when it disappeared into the dark soil. The ring never surfaced, but the garden grew, and with war shortages and the arrival of sister Florence in 1917, its yield was more important than ever. In 1918 the government established the Canada Food Board, mainly to increase food exports to Britain, and encouraged "war gardens" like the Cartwrights' in backyards all across the country. One Food Board poster called for "Soldiers of the Soil" and promised a national badge of honour for every boy who did his bit. Another cautioned that "Patriotic Canadians Will Not Hoard Food" and featured a guilty-looking couple in a darkened room, with bags labelled "hoarded flour" and "hoarded sugar" piled on the table between them. Through the window, the ominous silhouette of a police officer skulks by.

Though food wasn't officially rationed, the government urged restraint and produced pamphlets that spelled out "How to Live in Wartime," for it was not just food that came in short supply but coal, too, making winter nights longer and chillier than usual. At Christmastime, George hammered together a wagon as a present for Bill, a gift for which Emily found a practical use: with his brothers, Bill regularly hauled the little cart to McCormick's and raked through the ashes outside the factory's coal-powered generating station, collecting bits of the unburned fuel. The three took turns pulling the wagon the distance of a couple of miles – a long trudge with a heavy load. There were good pickings along the railway tracks, too. Chunks of coal sometimes fell from the tender cars, and now and then a sympathetic stoker tossed a shovelful over the side. Back at home the boys unloaded the precious coal and scrubbed the black dust out of the wagon so it was ready for its other incarnation as a delivery vehicle. Their mother had arranged for the Red Star News agent on Market Lane downtown to drop the daily newspapers at the Cartwright house, and each day Bill bundled them into his wagon, trekked over to the Wolseley Barracks on Oxford Street and hawked the papers to the soldiers at the camp.

As with so many children his age, he knew little of a world *not* at war, and the sight of men in smart uniforms on London's streets, of mounds of khaki wool for sale in department stores, of Victory Bonds posters urging "Faith in Canada," all were ordinary to him. Even breakfast cereals were entering the spirit of war. An ad promoting the corn flakes Bill loved showed that box of goodness with a band of armed soldiers in the background, under the heading "Undisputed Leadership." What that had to do with "the sweetness of the corn" the ad promised, Bill couldn't know, but nor would he have pondered it any more than he pondered the red tea kettle that had come with his mother from England and sat on the black stove day after day, whistling on command.

For Snowball Bill, nine years old in November 1918, the crowds that formed when the war ended must have brought back shadowy memories from almost half a lifetime before, when war had been declared. Thousands gathered in Victoria Park for a celebration that lasted days and unwittingly accelerated the spread of the influenza virus that had been swirling dangerously through the city since October. "London Cut Loose in Every Way Celebrating Allies' Glorious Victory," roared one headline. As in so many other places, Kaiser Wilhelm was burned in effigy, and people sang hymns as well as popular and patriotic songs. A huge bonfire was lit at the corner of Richmond and Dundas, and the Cartwrights were surely out in the street for the celebrations, Pa hoisting Earl on his shoulders, Emily carrying Florence in her arms, and all of them singing until their voices gave out.

Though George and Emily understood what had been lost over the last four years – and, more keenly, who – for the children the very notion of war faded as fall turned to winter and snowflakes twirled down upon the Forest City. George transformed the vegetable garden into a skating rink and, always game, played goalie while his children zipped around the ice wielding hockey sticks and wearing skates with screw-on blades. They wore sweaters Emily had knitted, and "Wool Itch" hats and scarves, and soon they were sweating from the exertion, the winter air reddening their cheeks. The neighbourhood kids were drawn into the fun as well, and after these wild games of shinny, Emily fed everyone carrot pudding made with Harry Horne's Double Cream Custard Powder, "the cream of them all." It was a proudly Canadian product, and she was a Canadian mother now, scouring the women's pages for recipes and household tips, or different ideas for homemade Christmas ornaments. This was the time of year when George made his trip into the woods for a tree that they decorated with ribbons, cranberry balls, paper chains, paper flowers and garlands made of dried fruit and popcorn. As always there was singing, and for supper a turkey courtesy of McCormick's, with hot gravy and mashed potatoes, and at the end of it all, Christmas pudding. The children didn't think about the fact that times were difficult financially, since the same was true for so many other families they knew, and they were always well fed and cared for. They took it in stride that they'd finish school at age twelve and head out to work to put money in the family pot.

By 1919, ten-year-old Bill had part-time work as a delivery boy for R.J. Young & Co., a men's clothing store on Dundas Street. A photograph from that time shows the shop windows full of straw hats and elegant suits and ties, and a satisfied customer emerging with a box under his arm. It was Bill's job to deliver such purchases when required, or to bring alterations back and forth between Young's and its master tailor, Gaetano Lombardo. Bill would pedal the lone family bicycle to Lombardo's tailor shop, and often music played by Lombardo's children poured from the windows even as the stitching was underway. Bill sometimes delivered to the Lombardo home, too, west of the Cartwrights' old place on Horton, and once, arriving at mealtime, he was invited in for dinner. Later, after the Lombardos had become famous, it was a thrill to recall that fact, but at the time the Lombardos seemed ordinary enough. Though they were Italian, they were in some ways a little like the Cartwrights – a newly Canadian family who loved treats from McCormick's, playing ball behind the Carling Brewery and swimming at one of the local watering holes in the Thames.

A generation earlier, Gaetano's wife's family, the Paladinos, had ended up in London by fluke when Carmelo Paladino, also a tailor, had been travelling from Lipari, Italy, to Buenos Aires and was forced to stop in New York because of a bad storm. A chance glimpse of an advertisement for a tailor brought the Paladinos north to Canada, where they did so well in business that they eventually called home for apprentices. Enter Gaetano Lombardo, a young man with a beautiful voice, who longed to leave tiny Lipari so that he could make more money and study his true passion, music. He married Paladino's daughter and ran his own thriving tailor's shop, but he also raised a bevy of children as his mini orchestra and was a tireless disciplinarian when it came to practice. The children practised at the tailor's shop before and after school. By 1919, Guy, Carmen and Lebert, still teenagers, were professional musicians, perfecting their "creamy sound" at venues in and around the city. But you could still hear music from Gaetano Lombardo's place of business as the younger children followed their father's regimen.

Though the Cartwrights were not on the road to musical fame and fortune, Emily, too, laid out a strict routine to ensure her children learned music. She and George didn't play an instrument, but all their children studied violin or piano or both. Some were more gifted than others. Jack could play perfectly by ear, which irritated his older brother, George. Friends waited outside, eager for playtime, peering through the windows to see when the boys would be finished. They snickered when Emily called from the kitchen, "George, you made a mistake. Play it again." Earl and Florence were young yet, but they'd have powerful voices in the years to come, and Earl had grand dreams of a career in opera; he kept framed pictures of opera stars on his wall. In his imaginings he'd be called Cartinelli rather than Cartwright – a Lombardo influence? – and audiences would swoon as they listened to him sing.

Bill had a humbler nature. He liked woodworking and soccer, things that were physical and hands-on. At Boyle Memorial he played on the school soccer team, and was the netminder the year they won the championship, but even that small claim to fame wasn't enough to warm him to school, and getting the strap once from the principal soured the whole experience. He had little interest in academics and never earned high marks in reading or spelling. He preferred helping Pa work around the house over reading a book, and he didn't grumble when Emily gave him errands to run on the bicycle. The bicycle was freedom, even if it was attached to chores, for he was the driver, deciding his route and navigating the obstacles. The way Bill saw it, life was simple: hard work brought just rewards and a satisfying sense of accomplishment. That was the way his father lived, and he didn't know a finer man than George Cartwright.

There are many photos of Bebbie and Doris during their early years in Canada. No one knows now who took those shots, but Doris's first Canadian friend, Emily Morley (right, in plaid dress), lived next door, and her father, also an emigrant from London, England, ran a photo supply shop.

Don't Forget to Remember

B ebbie and Doris's new world was neatly contained in the same small pocket of London East as the Cartwrights, where the vast buildings of McCormick's and the Kellogg Company dwarfed working-class homes on the surrounding streets. The earthy aroma of roasting grains competed with the smell of biscuits baking, but they were not the only factories around. There was the Jones box and label factory and the Ruggles truck factory and Hunt's flour mill and the furniture manufacturer, as well as countless hosiery mills with names like Holeproof and Supersilk that promised you would "end the mend" if you bought such superior products. Through the centre of this small, bustling neighbourhood ran a spur line from the Canadian Pacific Railway, branching off into Kellogg's, McCormick's and Empire Brass to aid in their cyclical states of shipping and receiving. London East was a hive of industry, if on a tinier scale than Doris and Bebbie had known in Whitechapel and the Borough, and the two newcomers were immersed in it from the time they arrived.

For the first few months they stayed with Bebbie's sister Frances in a small house on King Street, and Doris attended Pottersburg School. Just a single floor, with a side for the boys and a side for the girls, it was a modest structure compared with Charles Dickens back in the Borough. But now, as then, she loved school and made friends easily, and would have been happy to go seven days a week if not for the fact that she loved church, too. On Sundays, Frances's granddaughter Lilian, two years older than Doris, took her along to Egerton Street Gospel Hall, where the small congregation welcomed her like a daughter of their own. There was no official minister, just a series of lay preachers moved

to the task. The mission was "to provide a ministry that will be edifying to the children of God; to promote a fellowship that recognizes the
unity of the body of Christ; and to proclaim a gospel that will bring
salvation to the lost." They believed that the writings in the Bible were
infallible, and as with the Salvation Army, there was an evangelical focus
on being born again and on sharing the "good news" of Jesus's death and
resurrection to bring others into the realm. Doris learned songs like:

Down in the valleys of grief and despair,
Tell of the love of Jesus.
Say he is longing their sorrows to share,
Tell of the love of Jesus.
Tell of it, sing of it, ev'ry hour,
Tell of its sweetness and sing of its pow'r;
Oh, what a blessing to others you'll be
If you tell of the love of Jesus.

She became a regular Sunday school student, donning her knee socks
and her good dress and the hat Bebbie had bought her for Mary Anne's
funeral, and making the short walk with Lilian to the corner of Egerton and Florence streets, near the Western Fairgrounds. A photograph
shows her dressed in this Sunday best, standing on a street corner with
a bible in her hand. A girl and a boy appear blurry as they pass on either
side of her, but Doris pauses to pose for the camera, pleased to be captured this way.

In typical Gospel Hall style the church was plain, the interior of its
single storey painted beige and unadorned, so a contrast to the churches
Doris had known: towering Southwark Cathedral, ancient and grand;
St. George the Martyr with its four-faced clock and its Little Dorrit af-
filiation; and St. Jude's in Whitechapel, with its mosaic of Time, Death
and Judgment and the tiled Doulton fountain beneath it. Perhaps it reminded her more of a Salvation Army place of worship, humble in appearance and filled with music. Here, when she climbed the stairs and
opened the Hall's double doors, she entered a square room with pews
and a pulpit that stood on a platform. On the back wall, in large script,

were the words "We preach Christ crucified and risen again." Beneath the script sat the baptistery – an actual pool about four feet deep, since baptism at the Gospel Hall was by immersion and was not intended for babies but for people old enough to make a conscious choice about their faith. Here, too, was a message that resonated with worshipers: one side of the baptistery proclaimed "mighty to save"; the other, "able to keep."

Doris spent most of her time downstairs at the Sunday school, where she was put with a group of children her age. They sang songs and listened to Bible stories; sometimes there were competitions to see who could memorize certain verses, and the winner won books with a religious theme or some other edifying prize. Doris was thoroughly drawn in. The close-knit group made her feel not just safe but embraced, and the little chapel and the girls she befriended there – Ruth, Emily, Vera and Violet – became essential.

In many of the photos taken around the time she and Bebbie arrived, Doris is clearly happy, seemingly unperturbed by the shabbiness of her surroundings – peeling paint and patched clapboards, a crooked wooden doorstep and a yard of weeds and hard-packed dirt. Her hair is clipped somewhat unevenly just below her ears, and she wears the waistless dresses of the times, but she looks straight into the lens of the camera and beams. Here is home, the photos seem to say, suggestive of the resilience of youth, and in spite of the fact that "home" was a number of different addresses over the next few years.

Photographs of Bebbie are not so easy to read. Her clothing is plain and rumpled, and her hair is pinned loosely, giving her a slightly frazzled look. Although she is only in her mid-fifties, etched into her face are crow's-feet lines of age and worry, and her mouth has a perpetual droop that suggests she is not used to smiling. And yet there are several shots that imply a playfulness her looks belie. In one, she and a dog share a bench, and although she has her arm round the dog's shoulders as if he is a great friend, she pulls back from him as though to avoid a smelly lick. In another she wears a feather boa over a polka-dot dress – a most unlikely costume that must have been Doris's idea – and Doris stands beside her, eyes alight as she grins at the camera. That there are such candid shots, and so many of them, indicate changing times and an environment Doris and Bebbie find comfortable.

But there were challenges, too. Bebbie needed a job, and finding employment in the post-war world was difficult. Her application would have been one among many as war-weary veterans returned to find their old jobs no longer existed or hadn't been held for them. Many soldiers were unable to work in the professions they'd had before the war due to visible and invisible injuries. Post-traumatic stress – so-called shell shock – was often considered mere cowardice, or a lack of moral fibre, and men who suffered from it were frequently rejected for financial assistance. Still, Canada's assistance programs were more generous than those in most other countries, helping veterans acquire choice farmland, retraining the disabled, and offering the world's most substantial pension rates. Some returning soldiers saw the support as charity and refused help; those who were not so proud were aided by the London branch of the Soldiers' Aid Commission, whose task it was to coordinate the reintegration of soldiers into society. The Commission began by organizing reception parties when the trainloads of soldiers arrived in the city and distributing pamphlets with titles like "Back to Civvies" or "The Khaki Guide." Then it would arrange for retraining or help the men find jobs.

Despite this assistance, finding work with so much competition was daunting, and it was even more so for Bebbie, female, single, getting on in age and solely responsible for a young girl. Having family around was reassuring, but Frances and her husband, Tom, couldn't put Bebbie and Doris up forever, and the Sinclairs – Bebbie's niece's family – had ten people under one roof. Bebbie didn't expect charity. She knew that the rent would be paid and food would arrive on the table only by her own wits and effort, and she had been self-reliant and resolute since her early days as a single young woman in Whitechapel. Her years of experience in the male-dominated cork industry stood her in good stead, and against the odds she found work as a core maker at Empire Brass, which had so recently churned out munitions for the war.

The foundry job called for sharp eyesight, patience and attention to detail. If she wasn't particularly knowledgeable about metals and the principles of casting, she would have learned quickly as she worked over her bench, shaping the mixture of sand, clay and water into moulds of varying shapes and sizes. The shop was hot and noisy, the smell of molten brass singed her nostrils, and at the end of a long shift it surely felt good to stretch cramped muscles and rub tired eyes, to run a hand over the grey hairs come loose from their pins and step out into the fresh evening air. It wasn't a long walk home. Empire Brass sat on the north side of Dundas Street, just past the Ruggles truck plant and McCormick's. To reach Frances's house on King Street, with its backyard view of the smoke stacks at Kellogg's, Bebbie walked east past the cereal factory and the white walls of McCormick's, passing the Middlesex Mills hosiery company and turning right onto Eleanor, skirting Jones Boxes and Lithograph. It was a neighbourhood defined by its industry, and she and Doris came to know it quickly.

Soon she'd earned enough at her job that she and Doris rented a place of their own – first a little apartment on Queens and then a plain clapboard dwelling at 1068½ Dundas, even closer to Empire Brass. They could almost throw a stone and hit the pale brick wall of the building where Bebbie worked, and the storey-high sign advertising Empire's wares – brass fittings, wrought iron pipe – was clearly visible from the house. A block over, McCormick's gleamed in the sun.

Emily Morley, a church friend of Doris's, lived next door with her brother, Charlie, and their parents, John and Beatrice, who'd come from England in 1910, when Em was a baby. She was a year older than Doris, and in contrast to Doris, with her short bob, wore her hair in long ringlets, sometimes tied up with an enormous bow. Her father was a photographer and had a photo supply shop downtown, so maybe it was he who snapped the many backyard photos of Doris and Bebbie. Almost certainly he was behind the lens to capture an image of Doris and Em in swimsuits, Doris with a rubber cap hiding her hair, Em's locks falling freely over her shoulders. They stand knee-deep in rolling waves, and both girls are smiling, though Doris's is less broad and she eyes the water somewhat hesitantly. This is not the placid water of St. Julien's swimming hole on the Thames, so perhaps the Morleys have taken Doris along to Port Stanley for a day trip, and she can feel the pebbles disappear beneath her feet as Lake Erie swirls around her ankles. The Morleys often included Doris on such excursions, travelling south to Lake Erie or north to the Lake Huron holiday towns of Grand Bend or Ipperwash. In later years she'd recall how she loved these drives through the leafy countryside, Mr. and Mrs. Morley in the front seat, and Doris with Charlie, Em and their scruffy dog, Rex, in the back. To passersby they must have looked like a real family. Rex pushed his nose out to sniff the fresh air, and the children had to wrap their arms around him to keep him from jumping out to freedom.

Though Doris liked these adventures, even short trips away from Bebbie made her homesick. Once she was invited for a longer stay with another friend's family at a rented cottage near Springbank Park, and though she was only a few miles from London, she missed Bebbie terribly. Perhaps the experience brought back memories of being far from Mary Anne and her siblings in those last years of the war, when her mother was dying, and then of being sent to the aunts instead of Bebbie when she needed Bebbie's care more than ever. The homesickness was just like a physical ill, and great enough that the family drove her back to town by horse and buggy. The sound of the hooves clip-clopping homeward was a comfort as she drew closer to Bebbie.

The Morleys, though, were more familiar, and Doris was obviously at ease with them. Charlie and Em played mandolin duets for her, and Doris tried plucking the strings too. Sometimes Charlie got out his guitar, which looked enormous and somewhat comical against his slight frame. He was two years Doris's senior and gave her a butterfly brooch as a sign of his affection. He had what Doris called an "up-the-scale laugh," though maybe it was she who made him giddy and nervous.

Ten-year-old Doris was a striking girl by now, in spite of her lopped-off hairdos. She had large, wide-set eyes like her mother, and a warm, easy smile that conveyed her sense of humour. A casual shot shows her with Em before a backdrop of greenery, Doris in gingham and Em in plaid. Wearing mock-serious expressions, both girls crook one arm in the air and turn an ankle forward, posing as if they were Highland dancers. A third picture taken the same day includes Bebbie and Em's mother. The girls' shoes appear soiled, evidence of how they'd twirled in the dirt as they performed their dance. They stand close together, and Doris holds Em's shoulders as if introducing her. This is my friend, her gaze tells us. And Em is smiling.

Such a picture may well have been sent to Joe, Ethel and Ernie in England, and in return Doris received news that all was well in the Borough – that Ernie was working for Bean, Webley & Co. printers in Long Lane, and that Ethel had a job at Pascall's sweets factory. Not much had changed. They were still in the Goodwin Buildings with Uncle Jack and Aunt Maggie, so it was easy for Doris to imagine their days as they travelled through familiar surroundings – though as time went on she was less able to picture that damp brick and stone world. Joe, still an Able Seaman, was near Edinburgh at Port Edgar much of the time, close to the cemetery that held victims from the Battle of Jutland. His life, too, was moving forward from those difficult years. In August of 1920, he and Nelly Baggett, the girl to whom he'd presented his lucky penny, were married at St. George the Martyr Church, and Doris received a photograph that showed Joe in his naval uniform with Nelly at his side. There are flowers tucked into the knot at his neckerchief, and more flowers forming a garland around Nelly's head. The couple is surrounded by faces from Doris's past: little Elsie Morel, who was just a baby when Doris left England, and her dad Bert, the one-time munitions worker married to May's Aunt Clara, for whom Doris had been flower girl the year her mother got sick; tiny Uncle Jack stands in place of his long-dead brother Harry and looks as proud as a father; the chain-smoking Grace Lett – Nelly and Joe's matchmaker – is especially elegant in a dark, wide-brimmed hat trimmed with cherries; and Nelly's brother Albert, the gunner who'd come through shell shock and pneumonia, now looks like any ordinary brother dressed up for his sister's wedding.

With all the distractions of her new life, Doris missed home less than she might have, but surely the image of Joe on his wedding day felt bittersweet, as did the photograph, sent a year later, of his new baby girl, and the letters that came with their strings of x's, and the postcards that wished Doris "more of joy and less of strife." Sometimes there were presents, too. Aunt Maggie's daughter Clara sent a novel called *Into Stormy*

Waters, which seemed appropriate for a girl who'd crossed the sea on the *Metagama*. At heart, though, the book was more about God than adventure. The story followed the trials of a "little soldier of Christ" named Marjorie, who had what the author called merry, sparkling eyes, dancing footsteps, and a quick, fiery temper. Doris devoured such stories, which always took dark paths to happy endings and reminded the reader that you could be "poor in luxuries" but "rich in love."

Luxuries at 1068½ Dundas Street were still scant, but at some point Bebbie bought Doris an exquisite doll imported from Germany, where the tradition of bisque doll-making had flourished since the previous century. These dolls were prized for their high quality and their carefully painted, lifelike expressions, though during the war they had not been available to the enemy market. Doris's doll was brunette, like her, with tiny white teeth and blue glass eyes and eyebrows painted in a wispy, realistic fashion. She had long, composition limbs that bent at the elbows and knees, and her delicate hands could be turned this way and that at the wrists. Doris photographed her on a patch of grass beside the house, seated beside another doll – smaller and less of a beauty – and she must have loved her, for the doll remains, an antique now, wrapped in tissue in her original box, eyes fluttering open when she's lifted out.

The largest purchase was a piano Bebbie bought from the Pudney Brothers' music store at Dundas and Waterloo. The shop was a vibrant part of the London music scene, with musicians coming and going to buy instruments or sheet music for the latest "hot fox trots." One of the shop owners, Jack Pudney, had put together an orchestra with musicians who frequented his store, and together they played in London and the areas around. The arrangement worked well, for the shop promoted the orchestra, and the orchestra promoted the shop. An article announcing regular performances by Pudney and His Versatile Orchestra of Nine Musicians went on to remind readers that until fairly recently "piano music was heard only in the homes of the wealthy and musical artists." Pianos had been unaffordable for many, the article claimed, and there had been few assurances as to their quality. But all that had changed. "Today piano buying is safe, for promoting love for music among all classes of people and for providing a great stock of pianos that all classes

might select from." The piece encouraged shoppers to visit "the splendid music salon at 348 Dundas, just east of Waterloo Street."

Bebbie did, and purchased a large, square grand that took up plenty
of room in the small house. Doris began taking lessons from Miss
Elizabeth Holmes, a fifty-five-year-old spinster who taught in the par-
lour of her sister's house on Dundas Street, a few blocks from Doris's
home. Seated at the piano beneath the framed photographs of Holmes
relatives, her head bent in concentration, she would diligently stretch
her fingers this way and that before practising her scales, just as Miss
Holmes insisted, and now and again her teacher would remind her to
keep her back straight and to touch the keys lightly, but firmly. Doris's
enthusiasm meant she learned both notes and technique quickly, and
perhaps some of what she'd been shown by her Aunt Nell in Wimbledon came back to her. Walks home were pleasant, with the tunes she'd
learned repeating in her head. Some days it must have seemed that
music was everywhere, turned out as diligently as hosiery and biscuits.
If she passed Gaetano Lombardo's tailor shop, she might have heard
one of their regular practice numbers, "When You Wore a Tulip and I
Wore a Big Red Rose," and thought of Clara and Bert's wedding, and of
her mother in a straw hat with a wide dark ribbon.

Music *was* just about everywhere. As London and the rest of the
world put the war years behind them, people were eager to enjoy life,
and music was a big part of that pursuit. London had more than its share
of talented musicians, and on any given night the dance clubs and pavilions and concert halls were packed. Harry Wooster and his Orpheus
Orchestra played amongst the potted palms at Hyde Park, while the
Lombardos' band and Jack Pudney's orchestra crooned at the Winter
Gardens bandstand on Queens Avenue. The newspapers advertised
Après la Guerre dances and armistice specials, admonishing readers to
"follow the crowd," and venues like the beachfront London and Port
Stanley Pavilion that opened in the middle of the decade certainly had
plenty of room for merrymakers. The L & PS Pavilion, as it was called
before it became the Stork Club, had a 13,000-square-foot floating
dance floor, designed to withstand the burden of many feet while still
providing a "silken smooth" surface. Built at the water's edge in nearby

Port Stanley, the Pavilion offered so-called jitney dancing, as did most clubs of the day, where the price of admission only got you inside. If you wanted to dance, you bought tickets at five cents apiece, and rope boys herded people on and off the floor when a song finished. On hot summer nights at the L & PS Pavilion, the windows stood open to receive the breeze off the lake, and those needing a break from the fox trots and the waltzes could relax in wicker chairs beneath Chinese lanterns on the promenade.

The Winter Gardens in London wasn't nearly as fancy or as large as the Pavilion, but it drew crowds nonetheless. By day a row of automobiles for sale was lined up in front of the venue, under the simple sign "Used Cars," but by night they were cleared away to make room for dancers, and the place came alive with music. Bill Cartwright, with Grade 8 under his belt and retired from his short school career, got a job collecting tickets from patrons and saw first-hand the gleam of the brass instruments as they caught the light, and heard the mellow tones of the clarinets and saxophones. Radio and recording technologies were soon to change the music scene in London and beyond, but for the time being, in the early years of the 1920s, live performances were still the most common way to enjoy songs like "Carolina in the Morning," "Crazy Blues" and "Second Hand Rose," and Bill had his own particular window. On his way home after work, strolling along Queens Avenue in the glow of the street lamps, he whistled the tunes he'd heard or imagined himself as one of the dancers, guiding a fleet-footed partner across the smooth floors. For now, that girl was faceless, and nameless, and Bill, turning north toward home, couldn't know that she was only a few blocks away, curled up beside Bebbie on the sofa, her nose in a book.

They may have passed each other on the street now and then, not sensing the other's future significance, for Doris had several regular routes these days, walking to church and piano lessons, and also to school, which she now attended on Rectory Street. And she frequently walked to the doctor's office to pick up medicine for Bebbie, who had been diagnosed with heart disease and urged to rest and take better care of herself. That was a tall order for a single working woman with a child depending on her, but Doris resolved to ease the load for Bebbie as much as possible, running errands and doing chores at home, and being the best company she could be. Day by day, though, Bebbie looked older and more tired, just as Doris flourished. When word came that Ethel and Ernie wanted to move to Canada, there was joy at the news, but on Bebbie's part perhaps trepidation as well, at least until firm plans were laid. Who would pay their way, where would they live, could they find work and would it be down to her to support them until they did?

Not much is known of the particulars of the decision – who made it happen, or how it was done. One family story says that Ethel approached Aunt Maggie with her desire to leave England, and Aunt Maggie gave her approval but said she must take Ernie too. Others suggest the siblings emigrated as part of a Salvation Army scheme, and this may be true, since Joe and Nelly remained with the Army throughout their lives, and emigration assistance was still well underway. Perhaps they took advantage of the new Empire Settlement Act that came into effect in 1922 and sought to transplant farm labourers, juveniles and domestics. Imperialists in Britain's government were worried that Canada and her sister colonies were being increasingly influenced by other concerns – in Canada, by the French and the Americans – and it was thought prudent to "ensure that the fresh population required by the Dominions should as far as possible be British in sympathy, in spirit, and in origin." Assisted emigration would, it was believed, ensure a market for British goods overseas; from the Canadian government's perspective, it would fill an empty country with preferred immigrants whose values aligned with those of Britain. There was an urgency to the policies: America's labour markets, while restricting European migrants, were wide open to Canadians in 1921, and over the coming decade Canada would lose more than a million skilled and unskilled workers to its southern neighbour.

A variety of schemes were implemented under the Empire Settlement Act to encourage emigration from Britain to Canada, including reduced fares, agricultural training for those who promised to take up farm labour, and financial aid to families agreeing to buy farms. Females who opted for domestic service were assisted with the cost of transportation and guaranteed a standard wage, and British subjects in Canada could put forward friends and relatives for consideration as domestics or farm labourers. It was wrongly supposed that, in the case of females in particular, people would be happy for any paying work when faced with the alternative of unemployment. That may have been true to some degree, but women who had held well-paying jobs while men were away at war didn't want to return to a life of drudgery, whether in England or in Canada, despite the British Ministry of Labour's decree that "if there is not enough work to go round, ... women who have been accustomed to laundry work must go back to it."

None of the emigration schemes met with huge success. One plan to bring unemployed miners over to help harvest wheat saw more than 75 percent of them return home, while more than a third of the families who'd contracted to buy farms abandoned them and never repaid their loans. Of the million or so immigrants expected under the schemes only about 165,000 came, a disappointing response for both governments. And yet there were happy stories, like Ethel's and Ernie's. On their declaration forms they listed Uncle Jack as their nearest relative in England, with Ethel claiming she would be employed as a domestic at the home of one Alice Sinclair, Bebbie's niece, and Ernie recording that he would be working as a farmhand north of the city. In both cases their passage had been paid by their intended employers. When asked their purpose in going to Canada, Ethel and Ernie made the same reply in neatly formed script: "To make my home."

The *Minnedosa* sailed from Southampton on April 26, 1923, the day before Ethel's twenty-fourth birthday. Cousin May would later recall the day in a letter, writing: "We were all so sad when they went. My dad and I went to Southampton to see them off." And although Ethel felt equally bleak to be leaving May, otherwise she was content with her decision. Before they left the Borough she had her picture taken with Bert and Clara's little girl, Elsie, on the roof of the Goodwin Buildings. Ethel has her arm around Elsie, pulling her close, and Elsie's gaze is turned toward Ethel. But Ethel looks at the camera, and her smile – rarely seen in the family's photos – lights up her face. Despite her impending departure from home and family, this was unmistakably a happy occasion. The only thing missing was Joe, who was at sea and unable to attend his siblings' farewell, although he'd managed a quick visit days before. On the day prior to their sailing he wrote to them from HMS *Verdun*.

Dear Ethel & Ernie,

Just a few lines to let you know that I got back quite safe. I was very sorry I could not stop longer, so as to be able to come and see you off to the Boat, but still you must both cheer up and dont worry as you will be quite alright going across to your new Home. By the way, mind who you mix with on the boat, and what ever money you take with you never leave it laying about ... I dont say you will loose it, but it is always best to be on the right side.

Well dear Brother and Sister I hope you have a good trip across and I want you All (Ethel, Ernie, Doris) to remember that although the (Old Home) has broken up we are still Sisters and Brothers and I would like you to write and let me know how you get on, no doubt you think I will not trouble about you when you have gone, but I can assure you I will, as I felt very much upset when I had to say goodbye to you on Monday night not knowing when we should meet again, but still never mind I trust that I will see you All some day when you come over for a Holiday but still in the meantime be good and remember that I am always think-ing of you All.

When you get over the other side give my Best and Fondest Love to Dear Doris and tell her that I hope she will soon be com-ing over to see us, also give my best wishes to Miss Bedford and All. Well dears I think this is all I have to say at present so will close.

Please write so soon as you can as I shall be waiting anxiously to hear from you.

I remain,
Your Ever Loving Brother Joe

XXXXXXXXXXXXXXXXXXXXXXXXXXXXXXXXXXXXXXXXXXXXXXXXXXXXXXXXX

PS...Well Ethel and Ernie be good and don't forget to remember what I have said, because I promise you that I will not.

Cheerio and Bon Voyage

Though the parting was sad, the reunion on the other side was joyful, and made more poignant when the *Minnedosa* nearly collided with another ship. A bent and yellowed photograph with the date penciled on the back, taken on a crowded deck over the heads of passengers, shows another liner in cross-paths with the *Minnedosa*. The distance is scant, the two big ships dangerously close, and everyone on board appears to be watching the other boat slip past, churning grey water. For Ernie and Ethel the near miss had an eerie context: the Carters and their fate on the *Titanic* almost ten years earlier, and Joe nearly swallowed by the dark North Sea. But this time there was no disaster, and the *Minnedosa* continued safely on her way. The photograph was tucked away, the event all but forgotten in the days ahead, when other shots recorded the siblings' reunion. In one, Ethel stands in front of a leafy tree, hand on hip, wearing her usual shy smile. Doris, seated beside her, clasps her hands around her knees and squints into the sunlight. Despite the age difference – Ethel is twenty-four, Doris is almost thirteen – there is no mistaking them as sisters. Nineteen-year-old Ernie is pictured alone, wearing jacket, vest and tie, and holding his hat in his hand. He looks like a boy in a man's clothing, and quack grass rages behind him, shooting up against a wooden fence. In another shot, Doris links arms with Ernie, almost pulling him into the frame. His cap shades his face now, and he stands just a little taller than his diminutive sister.

Around the time of their arrival, the *London Free Press* reported on the number of young men coming to Canada as farmhands, and young women "flocking to Ontario" as domestics. One article claimed that Ontario was "sadly in need of both these kinds of workers," but Ernie was no farmer, as everyone already knew, and if Ethel had indeed come to Canada to work for Alice Sinclair, who likely couldn't afford to hire a helper, it's unclear why she began working for McCormick's soon after she arrived.

The problem of "the mateless woman in England and the lonely male emigrant on the other side of the world" might hold more answers. In August 1923 the *London Free Press* ran a story from Ottawa headlined "English Girl Seeks Canadian Husband: Sends Along Photo." She claimed to be tall, quiet and absolutely sincere, and wished to marry a straightforward, honest, Canadian man. "She says she knows many girls who came to Canada and seem happy in their Canadian homes. Mayor Plant intends to help her gratify her objective. Her photograph may be seen at his office any time." Ethel didn't have a mayor vetting potential marriage candidates, but right around this time – four months after her arrival – she married Alice Sinclair's son, Wilfred. Harry and Mary Anne's names are there on the marriage record, along with the details that Wilfred was a glass beveller and Ethel was a packer. Wilfred's father, George, and Bebbie signed as witnesses, and the ceremony took place at the Reorganized Church of Jesus Christ of Latter-Day Saints – so Ethel, too, was exploring religious options with an evangelical core.

Ernie took little interest in church matters, and he didn't last long on the farm – perhaps had never intended to. He soon left there to live with Bebbie and Doris in the house they'd moved into on Eva Street, still within the narrow rectangle east of the Western Fairgrounds. He got a job as a janitor at McCormick's, maybe because packer Ethel vouched for his pernickety tendencies, and he was apparently well liked and appreciated right from the start. "He cleaned like nobody's business," so the family story goes, and he had his own cubbyhole for his mops and buckets. His skills were so superior that in later years the managers at McCormick's occasionally whisked him home to do a bit of dusting or gardening. They only had to watch that he didn't get carried away in his enthusiasm and whitewash the patio. He must have loved the sunshine palace – white on the outside, white on the inside – and the fact that it was down to him to scrub it spotless. George Cartwright's family believed Pa held McCormick's together, but Ernie Deverill's knew that Ernie kept it gleaming.

Such a fellow was good to have at home, too. Though he didn't earn much, his contribution, both financially and domestically, was welcome. Like George Cartwright he brought home broken biscuits and candy, and in the mornings Bebbie and Doris could expect to wake up to a set table and hot tea, with toast at the ready. After breakfast was done, every last crumb was brushed away with quiet efficiency. And then Ernie was off to work, riding the bicycle his wages had bought him, and which allowed him to indulge his wanderlust in his off-hours. He rode even on snowy days, as photographs attest, circling wider and wider in his explorations of the Forest City and the countryside beyond, with the flaps of his hat pulled down to keep his ears warm.

These years were the beginning of Ernie's lifelong career at McCormick's. By then, George Cartwright had been with the factory for more than a decade, and as the maintenance man he knew Ernie, the custodian, but with hundreds of workers employed at the factory it's not unusual that their two families had never met, and wouldn't for some years to come.

By autumn of 1923, Doris Deverill was thriving on all fronts. She had two of her siblings with her again and had entered London Technical High School, where she continued to do well. A photograph shows her with five other girls, members of a baseball team, each clad in the sailor-style blouse that was the school uniform. Their bottom halves are covered by dark voluminous bloomers that end just above the knee, typical of girls' sports attire in that era. Doris stands at the centre, her church friend Ruth Rea, tall and slender, at the end, and all the girls wrap their arms around each other like champions, looking a little sweaty and dishevelled. In front of Doris, seated on the grass, a young girl holds the baseball in her hands, and the bat rests in her lap. She smiles ever so smugly, as if pleased with a win. Doris looks confident and determined in the shot, and in this way the image summarizes her time at high school.

The school's approach to learning had been designed a decade before by principal Herbert Benson Beal, who recognized that London's industrial and commercial sectors were booming, and that the city lacked skilled workers. He believed the standards at vocational schools could be improved, which would attract better students who could likewise be better trained. Such schools need not be "the natural dumping ground for all backward and defective children," but rather places

DON'T FORGET TO REMEMBER

where children – and adults – could learn and thrive. From the beginning there were night classes (Emily Cartwright took dressmaking, and Bill took woodworking), as well as the regular day school, where Doris was enrolled in Girls' Home Economics and Preparatory Courses. Photographs of the school's early years show students learning millinery, cooking and dressmaking. In the sewing studio a long table used for cutting fabric stands next to a couple of ironing boards and a small sink. In the centre of the room a number of girls sit in a row, heads bent over swatches of hand-stitching; beside them, fellow pupils sit at Singer sewing machines, feet diligently placed on treadles as they guide their garments beneath whirring needles. The girls wear their nautical blouses and seem absorbed in their work, adhering to a school rule that "Talking is not prohibited but a good worker, like a pair of shears, shuts up when she gets down to work."

In those first two years of high school, Doris scored well above average in almost every course, and saved her chatting, it seems, for after-school hours. She finished fourth in a class of twenty-seven students, earning bonus marks for excellent attendance, punctuality and good conduct. A note written at the bottom of her Grade 10 report card said "promoted."

But Bebbie was now dangerously ill. Her heart condition had deteriorated, and the doctor insisted she no longer work. Yet Ernie's income was too meagre to support the three of them. It must have seemed to Doris that her world was collapsing for a second time, bringing to mind the days in England when her mother had become too ill to keep her. Then, Bebbie had come to her rescue. But Bebbie couldn't fix things now.

Word of their predicament travelled through the neighbourhood, and the plant manager from Kellogg's soon knocked on the door, his message both a relief and a blow. He'd heard of their troubles, he said, and if Bebbie would consent to Doris leaving school, he could offer her a job at the cereal factory.

After he left, Bebbie and Doris talked it through at the kitchen table, both of them crying until their eyes were swollen and red. Doris loved school and wanted to finish. She'd miss the friends she'd made

there – the girls on the baseball team, her classmates in Home Economics. She might see them now and again outside of school, or at church,
but it wouldn't be the same. She'd hear their excited whispers about
the supposed ghost on the third floor – an apparition of an old woman
who was said to follow students in the hallway – and know *she'd* never
see it. The girls would chatter about things that had happened in class,
and Doris would know the teachers they'd mention – Miss Marshall
or Miss Maynard or short, red-haired Mr. Beal, the principal, habitually in tweed – but *she* would no longer factor in the stories, the events
would no longer be part of her own experience. There were other things
she'd have to give up: dance class, also shared with some of her school
friends, and the violin lessons she'd begun taking in a group class, learning to scratch out "Twinkle, Twinkle, Little Star" in a room above Sei-
gel's Shoe Store on Dundas Street.

It was a lot to forego, but without Bebbie's income they could not
go on, and for Doris, whose life might have been very different but for
the generosity of Bebbie, the choice was plain. There was nothing Doris
wouldn't do for Bebbie, and they both knew the job offer was a godsend.
On her last day of classes, Doris cried all the way home. In her fourteen
years, this was the happiest she'd ever been, and now that chapter of her
life had ended.

Doris and Bebbie, some time in the 1920s. The tall building in the background is likely part of the Kellogg's factory, which would come to play a huge role in Doris's life.

Doris with beau Fred Stephenson, bright, handsome and university-bound.
Bill Cartwright on Florence Street, relishing his role as family chauffeur.

CHAPTER 16

In the Sweet By and By

Had he known Doris Deverill, Bill Cartwright, with his great aversion to school, would have been baffled by her dismay about leaving. For several years now he had been gathering experience in the working world, with his paper routes and his ticket-taking stints at the Winter Gardens. He'd expanded his parcel-boy work to include Rowland Hill Shoes and W.G. Young Jewellers, and occasionally worked part-time at McCormick's, too, where his father still did the night shift. He and Ernie might have parked their bicycles side by side, or wheeled past each other on their rides through the city.

The money Bill earned continued to go into the family pot. There were seven Cartwright children now, and their house was full and noisy. London, too, expanded, and the rural character of streets like Linwood, on the edge of the city, gradually disappeared with the installation of sewage systems and water mains. The work went on even in the winter months, when a trench in which to lay the pipes was dug down the middle of Linwood Street. After dark, logs were placed in the channel and set afire to keep the ground from freezing so the work could continue by day.

Bill was fascinated by the project. At night, with the orange light flickering on his ceiling, he'd creep out of bed and peek through the curtains at the watchman tending the burn. He would have liked to join him and ask questions of the man, but knew better than to ask permission. Sleep was precious in a household as large and busy as theirs, and even more so with Bill's youngest sister, Mary, needing special care. She'd been tiny and weak from the beginning; indeed, she had almost died before anyone knew what was wrong. When the doctor had diagnosed her condition as rickets, he prescribed sunlight, but warned that it was probably too late to expect her to survive. The pain in her back, pelvis and legs must have been excruciating, and hard for Emily, too, who could do little but watch her child suffer. Medical discoveries about vitamin D and rickets would come very soon, but the crucial link had not yet been made, and Emily always believed that if not for a chance encounter she had when strolling Mary along Oxford Street, her daughter probably would have died. Peeking in at the girl and discussing her ailments, the woman Emily met urged her to go up the street to a small dairy farm that had a "special cow" whose milk could make Mary well again. Desperate, Emily seized the advice, and every day Bill or one of his brothers walked to the farm for milk for their little sister. Whether from the milk's calcium, "Dr. Sun's" vitamin D, or both, she slowly grew well and became a happy, ordinary girl whose favourite pastime was playing house and copying Emily's approach to domestic chores. In the Linwood backyard, Bill made her a tent out of potato sacks so she could sweep the "floor" with her child-sized broom. And the entire family felt a surge of pride when, at age four, she sang "All Things Bright and Beautiful" for the congregation at their new place of worship, Church of the Resurrection.

They were proud, too, of the church itself, and had joined with others in the neighbourhood to build it. Pa had helped install electric lights, and Bill, though just fifteen, had made the hymn boards, planing and sanding and admiring the grain. A petition to the Anglican Lord Bishop of Huron for the dedication of the church was submitted, signed by the ten families who had worked so hard to make it happen, among them Alf and Ethel Ellis, friends of George and Emily. Alf was a carpenter, and his name was at the top of the list of petitioners, penned with a bold stroke beneath the typewritten request. "This building … we now certify to be ready for use, [and we] do humbly pray your Lordship to dedicate the same." In January 1925, on the first Sunday after Epiphany, the small congregation had the inaugural service in the humble structure they'd built. The ceiling was low and the windows were plain – no magnificent stained glass panels here – but despite this simplicity it was gratifying to see the place finally come together from nothing.

From the outset the Cartwrights were dedicated members. Most of the family can be found in a formal photograph of the church choir, heavy curtains forming a backdrop, while a more casual shot shows Emily in a choir gown and cap, an open hymn book clutched in her hands. She's standing outside at the house on Linwood Street, posing in front of the blackened boards of an old shed with three horseshoes nailed above the window for luck. The expression she turns to the camera is solemn above double chins. She, like her husband and children, took church commitments seriously, so she must have been pleased when George the younger received accolades from the church wardens for the printing of addresses that were presented to the Bishop, and then too when Pa was given a letter of appreciation for the hard work he put into the Sunday school's Christmas entertainment. "You must have been pretty well tired out by the time you got home," wrote the minister. "This is but a part of the splendid service that you are always so ready [to] render to the Church, and I do want you to know how much I value the co-operation which you continually give to the work of the parish."

It was in the years following this that Bill grew fond of the Ellises' daughter, Dorothy. At first it must have been just a friendship, blossoming naturally when they saw each other on Sundays or at youth events organized by the church. But Bill was growing up. In 1926, when he was seventeen, he landed his first full-time job, in the dye house at Penman's Knitting Mills, which had opened a London factory a few years earlier. He was soon promoted to man the Ludwig fully fashioned knitting machine, which could knit twelve stockings at a time – an important evolution since stockings were big business in the 1920s, with hemlines on the rise. Once they'd been worn to keep a woman's legs warm under her floor-length skirts and petticoats, but now they were visible, and a highly fashionable accessory. They came in nude, peach, gray, gun metal, black and blonde, in "top-to-toe silk" or "durable lustrous rayon." There were checkers and stripes and polka dots, and special sizes for the short and stout or long and lanky.

Dorothy Ellis was between those extremes. Pictures from the late 1920s show her and Bill posing as a couple, bespectacled Dorothy perched atop a picnic table with her arm around Bill's shoulders and her feet resting on the bench he's seated on. Her hair is styled in a curly bob, and she wears a fur boa and a knee-length skirt, showing off her hose. Bill looks delighted by her company, and Emily (says the family story) heartily approved of the match, knowing Dorothy came from a "nice family." She had grandparents back in Bognor, Sussex, and Dorothy had visited them there in 1924. It didn't hurt Emily's opinion of the Ellises that their ancestral hometown was frequented by the upper classes who visited for its healthy air, or that Queen Victoria had reportedly loved the place, calling it "dear little Bognor." Emily's view was reinforced when King George granted Bognor permission to add the term *Regis* (meaning "of the king") to its name, an honour bestowed because the king had lived at the seaside town while recuperating from lung surgery. Further cementing Emily's estimation of Dorothy as a perfect girl for Bill was the fact that Alf Ellis, Dorothy's father, was a warden of their new church, and a Mason.

The busyness of the times, and maybe a hint of keeping-up-with-the-Ellises, prompted George to buy a car, as so many other families were doing. Perhaps he chose his maroon Chrysler 72 from the lineup of used vehicles for sale outside the Winter Gardens, with Bill along to offer his thoughts. It was the first in a series of Cartwright family cars that weren't entirely dependable, though ads claimed the 72 outdistanced all rivals, and that until you drove it you couldn't possibly imagine the feeling of it flashing from five to twenty-five miles an hour in a span of just seven seconds. Roomy, fast and handsome, the Chrysler 72 was said to "cradle...you softly over cobblestones and rutted dirt," and offered a smooth and luxurious ride beyond description. After the purchase, several members of the Cartwright clan posed for pictures inside and outside the car, or seated in a row along the running board. In one image George roosts there, dressed in suit and tie and fedora, hands folded in his lap as if to calm himself, face beaming with pride and excitement. But if he imagined himself zipping to church and lodge meetings with quiet efficiency, his dream didn't unfold as planned. When he tried to manoeuvre the car into the shed, he gave it a bit too much gas and crashed straight through the tin wall into the yard beyond. From then on he was too nervous to drive and took up the role of polisher instead, and the responsibility of family chauffeur fell to an eager Bill, who was relaxed and comfortable behind the wheel. Never mind that the vehicle frequently broke down, and leaked when it rained, causing George to joke that "you need rubber pants to drive that car." Bill loved the Chrysler for the same reason he'd loved his bicycle – but even more: because of the potential for double dates with Dorothy Ellis and a friend and his gal.

Family obligations came first, of course, and Bill would have chauffeured the Cartwrights to the annual McCormick's picnic the year a panoramic photo captured the event. The Cartwrights usually won the prize for the largest number of family members attending. This year, Bill, Earl and their father stand at the back of the crowd, Bill and George similarly posed with their arms crossed over their chest. Florence, Gordon and Mary – the latest addition – can be found hunkered down in front with others of their young age. Almost everyone wears a hat, and among the wash of felt fedoras, straw boaters and flat caps, on the far right of the crowd, is Ernie Deverill. A careful scan of the skull-hugging cloche hats finds Doris, too, and her friend Ruth Rea, just rows away from the Cartwright men, though they're not yet acquainted. Conspicuous by her absence is Emily. If this photo was taken in 1929, a forty-three-year-old heavily pregnant Emily was most likely at home, enjoying the quiet and resting her swollen feet.

In the fall, when she gave birth to this last child, she left it to her oldest boys to name the baby. Bill picked Dorothy for Dorothy Ellis, and Jack picked Marguerite for his own current flame. The eldest, George Jr., an avid reader, chose Dorraine for a book character with whom he'd become smitten. They were all indulged, but Dorraine Dorothy Marguerite was simply called "Do," a short, easy name for the tenth child to be born to George and Emily Cartwright.

If later she often spoke of her sadness at leaving school for work, Doris had nothing bad to say of her years at Kellogg's. The smell inside the factory was much like the smell that enveloped the neighbourhood, but stronger – a sweet and earthy fragrance of grains roasting. Just recently the entire plant had been re-equipped with automatic machinery, so the noise from the various contraptions was constant. It was a large, modern space where some five hundred motors hummed at once, and electric ovens toasted the corn flakes until they were light and crispy. Only the bran was still dried using steam. When the raw product arrived by train, it was sweetened in huge vats in the juice room, then poured onto a conveyor belt and moved through the dryer. Boxes were printed and folded and glued on the bottom, and the waxed paper bags were tucked inside; these were sent like ducks in a row with their mouths open along another conveyor belt for filling. The full boxes travelled on to the inspector and the weigher, who removed every tenth box from the belt and set it on a scale to ensure it held the amount W.K. Kellogg had promised. There were sample boxes too, holding just one ounce of cereal. Even these bore the maker's name, and reminded consumers that "the original has this signature," which guaranteed the contents. If all was as it should be, the boxes continued on their travels to be sealed and, finally, shipped out.

Kellogg's by now was a highly successful company, pushing its products with grand claims as to their wide-ranging health benefits. Ads for a new cereal, Shredded Krumbles, showed a young woman clutching a basketball or swinging a tennis racket, and labelled Krumbles "the real energy food." Mineral salts "hidden away" in the bran helped strengthen muscles and bone and rebuilt "weary nerve cells." You could "help yourself to health" just by eating Kellogg's Corn Flakes, and Kellogg's All-Bran was "a staunch ally of modern medicine." If Doris believed the company's boasts about All-Bran's powers, she surely hoped the cereal would cure Bebbie's ailments too. An advertisement featured sketches of two women the same age, one looking fresh and youthful, the other drab and worn out. The ad claimed the dreaded affliction of constipation could sap your energy and give you wrinkles, pimples, gray hair, headaches, bad breath and stomach problems, not to mention its ability to fog your brain, weaken your overall system "AND LEAD TO OVER 40 OTHER SERIOUS DISEASES!" There were enticements for little ones, too: if you mailed in your box top with a dime, you got a *Funny Jungleland Moving Pictures* book in return. The books were massively popular, a forerunner to the prizes that eventually came inside the cereal boxes. Each page bore pictures of animals divided into three pieces so kids could flip the pages and put the head of an elephant with the body of a lion and the legs of a giraffe, and so on. Later editions featured ads masking as children's rhymes:

> *Sing from daylight until night,*
> *Sing from dark until it's light.*
> *Kellogg's Corn Flakes every morn,*
> *It's the sweet heart of the corn.*

Doris lived just a block from the factory and was less punctual than she'd been at school, but whenever her workmates spotted her running with seconds to spare, they'd punch her time card for her, to make sure she wasn't counted as late. The other girls teased her for her short stature – she wasn't much over five feet tall – and on the days she got there in good time they offered to lift her up so she could punch her own time card, or to help her see out the windows in the packing room where they assembled, filled and inspected the cereal boxes all day, every day. The workers alternated on the seven-to-three shift and the three-to-eleven, which meant a walk home in darkness, "by the light of the silvery moon," as the song said. The job was monotonous, but the people were not. Doris knew many of the employees beforehand: several of Bebbie's relatives, from the family that Ethel had married into; the plant manager who'd hired her; and the janitor Frank Price, a tall skinny Englishman she saw every week at church with his tiny wife, the aptly named Minnie, who was round-faced and motherly, given to affectionate squeezes. Doris thought their story terribly romantic. Engaged back in Warrington, Lancashire, Frank had come ahead to Canada, and when he'd earned enough he had paid the passage of his bride-to-be. She sailed over on the *Metagama*, as Doris had, and on her immigration form under "destined to" she wrote "Frank Price...to whom I am to be married on arrival." And that's just what happened. Frank took a train to Quebec City to meet Minnie's ship, and the two were wed at the Immigration Building there and boarded the train home as husband and wife.

There were plenty of other familiar faces at work, girls Doris's age or a little older, and an easy camaraderie arose as they gossiped about the young men working the bran dryer or the glue station – which ones were handsome, and which ones less so because they knew it. One of these friends was Georgie Hogg, who'd go on to earn the daunting title of inspector at the factory, but for now was just one of the girls. In photos taken at Georgie's family's farm in Thamesford, just east of London, Doris sports a battered straw hat and baggy overlong pants, and smiles as she clowns with Georgie, her sister Mina and a friend, Anna Doan. There's a shot of Doris on a horse with her friends alongside, and one snapped in front of a barn, the girls' hats perched at goofy angles. In another, Doris swings from a beam, her legs clamped over Anna's shoulders, while the next shows Doris on hands and knees, plump Anna straddling her back. Doris has labelled the picture "fooling around," and in every shot taken that day the girls are laughing.

Doris's photo albums hold many pictures of friends, young women beaming from faded prints, and certainly in the wider world there was much for girls like them to celebrate. They were the beneficiaries of decades of campaigning and activism by people such as the Pankhursts, whose family had fractured over the cause of women's suffrage, and Emily Davison, who'd died so publicly for it when she was trampled beneath the king's horse. Canada, too, had its champions for the rights of women, and although the country was quicker than most to enfranchise its female citizens and bring change to a federal elections act which decreed that "no woman, idiot, lunatic or criminal shall vote," there was still much denied them. While women might cast a ballot for their choice of Member of Parliament, and even become one themselves, they could not be appointed to the Senate, whose members must be "qualified persons." Women, it was argued by the government of the day, were most decidedly neither qualified nor persons.

Several strong-minded women took umbrage with that and challenged the government's position in the Supreme Court. Nellie McClung was one of them, "as vivid as a tiger lily at a funeral," according to *Canada Monthly* magazine, published in London by the Western Canadian Immigration Association. A teacher and novelist who once raised eyebrows when she organized a football team for girls, McClung had been born near Chatsworth, Ontario, some ways north of London in Grey County. She had a fine sense of humour and a gift for persuasive oratory, and in Manitoba she went head-to-head with the Conservative premier of the day, Sir Rodmond Roblin, who claimed in honeyed tones that "Nice women don't want the vote." McClung was having none of that. "Have we not brains to think? Hands to work? Hearts to feel? And lives to live? Do we not bear our part in citizenship? Do we not help build the Empire? Give us our due!"

But Nellie McClung and the other women who'd petitioned the Supreme Court – Emily Murphy, Irene Parlby, Louise McKinney and Henrietta Edwards – were shocked when the court upheld the government's position that women might be "persons in matters of pains and penalties, but…not…in matters of rights and privileges." Refusing to give up, they appealed to what was in 1929 Canada's highest court, the Privy Council of Great Britain, and at last won the day. Whether or not Doris and her friends knew of the "Persons Case," as it had come to be known, or understood what these women had achieved on their behalf, they would certainly have agreed with the Privy Council's ruling that "the exclusion of women from all public offices is a relic of days more barbarous than ours… And to those who would ask why the word 'persons' should include females, the obvious answer is 'Why should it not?'"

Doris's life must have felt rich at this time, with work and play co-existing. She was busy at church, too, teaching some of the Sunday school classes and showing the younger girls crafts, or helping in the kitchen at special events, brewing tea and coffee and assembling dainty sandwiches. Once a year on Dominion Day the Gospel Hall congregation went en masse to Springbank Park, blankets and picnic hampers in tow, and someone arranged for a photographer to take a panoramic shot of the group, the camera poised above the crowd so the faces in the photo are upturned, as if to heaven itself. Frank and Minnie Price are there, Frank's height and long face singling him out, Minnie blending in but recognizable by her smile. A curly-topped Rea boy can be spotted, one of twin brothers of Doris's friend Ruth, whose father John was a lay preacher. Doris stands out from the rest, her hair full and dark and wavy, wearing a ruffled dress and smiling up at the photographer with an easy confidence.

To Bebbie – so much older than her sixty-four years now, and increasingly unwell – Doris must have seemed the picture of vitality when she rushed in from work one Tuesday in July 1929, just two days after her nineteenth birthday. She was working the three-to-eleven shift and had come home for a quick bite to eat. They were living in a simple white house of two storeys now, just the right size for the two of them with Ernie. It was their fifth place together since they'd arrived in Canada ten years earlier, and they'd come almost full circle, to 1063 King Street, a few doors away from where they'd begun at Bebbie's sister's place.

Only Doris and Bebbie were dining that night; Ernie was at McCormick's, scrubbing and sweeping with gusto. They sat down together at the table, but they had barely begun their meal when Bebbie wheezed and clutched her chest, grabbing as if trying to pull something out of herself. A strange gurgling sound came from her throat, and her eyes bulged with pain, or with fear. She fell to the floor and went silent. Doris stood up and her chair slammed backward. She crouched beside Bebbie but had no idea how to help, so she ran to the door and screamed for the nearest neighbour. It was too late. Bebbie's heart had stopped, and she was gone.

Doris didn't remember her father's death the way Ernie did – how Harry had collapsed in the act of polishing his boots, alive one minute, dead the next. His body had lain in the cramped quarters of their College Buildings flat in the days and nights preceding the funeral, but she had no recollection of her mother dressing him in his Salvation Army uniform in preparation for the burial, and no memory of tears, whether falling silently or coming in a torrent. She didn't know who'd cradled her in that time of grief – she was just a toddler – but it might as easily have been Bebbie as her mother.

Nor had she first-hand experience of Mary Anne's death five years later, far away at Cane Hill, though by then Doris was old enough to recall. Her mother had died out of sight – an inmate at a lunatic asylum – so the only reality of the event for Doris was a plain coffin lowered into a common grave amid the grandiose tombstones of Nunhead Cemetery. Bebbie had held her hand that day and looked out for her ever since.

This loss was different from the ones Doris had suffered in the past, for Bebbie had been a balm for those wounds, and finally, in a way, a mother, too. She had been a part of Doris's life for longer than Mary Anne had, and the two of them had ventured far together, overseas and around and around the streets of London East. July withered while Doris and Ernie leaned on each other in their grief. Ethel stepped forward as the informant for the death registration, naming herself Bebbie's niece in the absence of a more accurate term. She was married to Bebbie's sister's grandson, but her connection to Bebbie had been formed long before that. Notices in the newspaper called her "niece," too, and referred to Bebbie's "two adopted children, Miss Doris Deverill and Ernest Deverill." With Bebbie's sister's family, the siblings greeted the friends and neighbours who came to the house on King Street to pay their respects. The funeral was held there too, presided over by John Rea. The unassuming house filled with people and flowers, and afterward Ernie and Doris placed a "card of thanks" in the announcements column "for the kindness and sympathy shown them in their recent sad bereavement." When Bebbie was laid to rest, it was easy to choose the epitaph, and seemed fitting to use the name Doris had bestowed on her back in Whitechapel: "Bebbie … Safe in the arms of Jesus."

In the patriarchal 1920s, no one thought Doris should continue to struggle along without a parental figure, even though she was nineteen. Small Ernie, twenty-five now, had always been under someone's wing and emanated boyishness, though he could probably care for himself much better than people realized. Though they could have lived alone, and had been paying the rent and bills for years, the Gospel Hall community enfolded them like orphaned children, and Minnie and Frank Price offered a place in their home on Florence Street, a block from the chapel. As before, they didn't travel far, but very little of their own could be brought into the bungalow. Bebbie's piano – a true old Victorian lady with heavy curved legs and claw feet – was a massive square grand, and there was no room for it at the Prices'. Most of the other furniture also had to be sold, which was just as well, for any money made from the items would help pay for Bebbie's plot at Mount Pleasant Cemetery and the marker that bore her name. Only the essentials came with them, and the keepsakes small enough to tuck away in a drawer. Doris still had the few things of her mother's that she'd brought from England, and now she added Bebbie's small collection of jewellery to the group: a ring, a brooch and a locket, all made of brass. She had Bebbie's prayer book, too, a gift from her confirmation in Whitechapel in 1889, that frightening year after the string of famed murders began, and there was the funeral card for Bebbie's mother, saved since 1877.

Doris ached with her loss but found solace reading Bebbie's prayer book. She called up the songs she sang at church to set her back on course; so many of the hymns were about death and the peace that awaits us "in the sweet by and by." Her faith was a gift, for in her mind there was no question (and no point questioning) that Bebbie had gone to a better place – had "pass[ed] through the portals of the unending day" – and that Doris would join her when her own time came.

There was plenty to keep her mind and hands occupied as she and Ernie settled in with the Prices. Ernie once again found himself in a room in the attic, but this time there were no silverfish, no damp mould and no farm chores, and both brother and sister felt welcome. Doris shared her tiny space next to the dining room with June, the Prices' little girl, and helped Minnie – whom she called Mrs. Price – with the household chores, polishing the wooden buffet, dusting the oval portrait of a soldierly Frank – Mr. Price – that hung in the living room near the front door. The formal use of titles, Mr. and Mrs., was a sign not only of the times, but of the situation. Doris and Ernie weren't children, after all, yet they were wards, a responsibility the Prices had undertaken out of kindness and a generosity of spirit. Though the Deverills and the Prices grew fond of one another, there was no replacing Bebbie, but neither was there a need to.

And so the months passed, and the Prices' house on Florence Street came to feel enough like a home. Doris wouldn't stay forever, but for now it suited. And there were already hints of change in the future, for as her circle of friends expanded, inevitably it began to include young men – some from work, some from the youth group at church. Frank Price was in charge of the teenagers from the Gospel Hall, supervising when they went on hikes and picnics or swimming at one of the local watering holes. Doris wasn't much of a swimmer, but she could paddle around well enough to enjoy herself with the others. The black pages of her album contain photos of those days: of wet-haired swimmers straddling a fallen tree, or picnickers round a small cooking fire, a young man in a tie and rolled-up shirt sleeves handling the fry pans. Beneath one picture Doris has written "end of a great day." Her sentiments were the same after a young man named Stan Pittaway asked her on her first date. He worked at the CNR car shops and wanted to bring her along on an employee excursion to Niagara Falls. It was the first time she saw that natural wonder, though she was equally impressed by the fancy restaurant at which they ate, complete with white tablecloths and finger bowls.

Stan wasn't the man for Doris, though. That honour soon went to Fred Stephenson, a small, slender fellow with a thin face and tidy hair who appears in a staff photograph taken outside the Kellogg factory's main door, beneath the "Visitors Welcome" sign. Doris is there too, seated in front with a string of young women, each clad in her wrap-around smock and white cap. Three rows of men stand behind them, some in suits, some in overalls and coveralls, and above them the square panes in the huge factory windows are visible. Doris somehow manages to look stylish in her frumpy uniform, and she links arms with the girls on either side of her. Under her cap there may well be a Marcel wave, and under her smock a pretty dress either sewn at home or saved for. She loved fashion – T-bar shoes and cloche hats and loose shimmery dresses – and had a natural flair. Fred Stephenson, by contrast, appears exceedingly plain.

His stint at Kellogg's was a summer job. He was a year younger than Doris and had just finished high school, and the money he made as a gluer went toward his tuition at the University of Western. It was probably at Kellogg's that Fred and Doris met, for their circles didn't otherwise overlap. Fred lived south of her and past the Grand Trunk Railway, where Egerton met Hamilton Road. He attended Egerton Street Baptist Church and had been a student at Sir Adam Beck Collegiate. He almost disappears into the class picture from his fourth year there, last man on the end of the back row. His cohort, by its own reckoning, was "good looking" but not very remarkable. The school journal, *The Lantern*, noted that "if we should suddenly drop out of existence the only noticeable difference would be the empty seats in the south west corner of the auditorium each morning, and the absence of visitors to the lower forms." In contrast, the graduating fifth years claimed that "none [could] dispute their position as the best, most brilliant, most brainy and ideally model pupils within the hallowed precincts of these most venerable halls." Fred was one of twenty-four students on the staff of *The Lantern*, so perhaps he had contributed to the tongue–in-cheek sparring of the classes, or suggested the eye-rolling editor's note at the end of the fifth years' passage: "Ye Gods!"

Few were spared *The Lantern*'s teasing. One whole section of the journal was dedicated to poking fun at students and was a great read, since it named names and exaggerated people's foibles. Albert Bartley, a fifth year with a finger in every piece of the school pie, but whose particular passions were the debating and oratory clubs, was roasted with a dig at his gift of the gab: "Now, I'd like to say something before I begin my speech." Another exchange insulted Larry Taylor and went like this:

F. Styles – "*What shall we do tonight?*"
L. Taylor – "*Let's think –* "
F. Styles – "*Naw, let's do something you can do too.*"

Nor did Fred Stephenson escape unscathed, the entry seeming to suggest he was overly literal and fond of the necktie.

Fred Stephenson – "*I want to see what you have in ties, please.*"
Clerk – "*Yes, sir, now here's one that's very much worn.*"
Fred – "*Oh, I've got plenty of worn ones at home. I want a new one.*"

Most photos of Fred do show him in collar and tie, as if the apparel was part of his physical self. The knot of a tie peeps out from his overcoat in a shot taken with his friend George Dean, whose family had owned a dairy in Fred's Egerton Street neighbourhood, south of where Doris lived. There's snow on the ground, and the two friends pose in front of a car with a cloth top and spoked wheels. Both young men wear gloves, but George's coat falls open to reveal a vest and bow tie, and he sports a puffy wool cap on his head. Fred wears his coat well-buttoned, and a businesslike fedora shades his eyes. Behind these natty dressers and their wheels is a rickety shed with a birdhouse nailed to its peak. It must be Doris behind the camera, causing the cautious smile Fred allows, and the tilt of his head. Maybe Anna Doan is beside her, for George Dean was her beau, and the four of them fell into a routine of gathering at the Stephensons' house on Saturday nights, playing board games and listening to the *Lucky Strike Radio Hour*, which spun the latest dance tunes. Between numbers the announcer sang the praises of Lucky Strike cigarettes, which were toasted according to an "extra secret process" that expelled nasty irritants and ensured a rich but mellow flavour. "Sit out a dance," the announcer suggested, and "reach for a Lucky."

Listening to radio music at the Stephensons' house was one of Doris's favourite pastimes, and not just because she was falling in love with Fred. The music made her miss Bebbie's square grand just as she missed Bebbie herself. Although she played the piano at church now and again, it wasn't the same as having a piano at home, where you could play when the mood struck and for as long as you liked, and sing along in your warbliest voice. She'd been putting money aside with the intention of buying a piano someday, and Fred's father, John, who worked as an engineer for the piano manufacturer Sherlock-Manning, might have advised her. Sherlock-Manning made sturdily built mid-quality pianos, and if they couldn't challenge the distinctive sound of a Heintzman, Doris could be assured that Canadian pianos generally were of such superior manufacture that there was little demand for imports except of the most prestigious makers, such as Steinway of New York. Soon a slender upright Sherlock-Manning on small cast iron wheels found space in a corner of the Prices' living room.

Fred was an only child, but he had friends and relatives up and down Egerton Street and in the immediate neighbourhood. He lived with his parents, John and Pearl, next door to his maternal grandparents, James and Louisa McDonald, who rented out the upstairs apartment in their yellow brick house. His mother's cousin Harry Cave, a recent graduate of Western's medical school, was the current tenant. Farther along the street an uncle ran a small grocery store beside his house. The family ties were solid and real, which was the usual way when mothers and fathers didn't die before their time.

Things were progressing nicely for Fred and Doris, and it seemed obvious what would follow. They exchanged gifts at Christmas, and Doris pasted the card that accompanied his into her scrapbook. The drawing on it showed a wheeling bluebird, the symbol of happiness. In a photograph taken on a steep, grassy slope, the couple perches on a boulder, each with an arm around the other. Smiling broadly, Doris looks radiant; a poster girl for the times. Her waved hair frames her delicate face, and a pearl necklace rests against the simple dark dress that matches her hat. She's wearing T-bar shoes and pale stockings, and tilts her head toward Fred's, almost but not quite touching. Fred looks unusually relaxed. He's tie-less for once, with his shirt sleeves rolled to the elbows. His hair is still precisely combed and parted, and his smile restrained, but less so than in other photographs, and a genuine happiness lights up his eyes.

By this time he was a freshman in the University of Western's business administration program, caught up in campus life, which was so different from the factory environment of Kellogg's. Before the first month of school was up, the business students were treated to a lecture by Denton Massey, agricultural entrepreneur and renowned preacher, who held his listeners spellbound even though he admitted "there is no thrill to a potato and no sex appeal in wheat." He told the young executives-to-be that there were five principles to which they must adhere – ambition, ability, loyalty, patience and honesty – and that the last was especially essential to anyone determined to make his mark. "Do not hitch your wagon to a star, but to the moon," he advised. "It's the closest, and you're much more likely to succeed." The future looked rich with possibility, not just for Fred, but for Doris by proxy. While he studied, she remained at Kellogg's, topping up boxes of Shredded Krumbles and oven-popped Rice Krispies.

Bill Cartwright was at Kellogg's too, having left Penman's and secured a full-time job there a couple of weeks before his twentieth birthday. Like the others, he alternated between day and night shifts, and when he worked late he would watch out the window and wave when he saw his lanky father trudging along the railroad tracks toward McCormick's. Bill had started off in the juice room, adding sweetness to the grains, but he was working the bran dryer the first time he noticed Doris Deverill. For Bill it was an unforgettable moment, the kind that got crooned about by the Lombardos and the Pudneys and on the *Lucky Strike Radio Hour*. Dorothy Ellis had moved on from Bill; she was studying nursing and had hooked up with a University of Western medical student whom she would eventually marry. But if Bill's heart was shattered, spotting Doris on the packing line – even in her Kellogg's cap and dowdy smock – was a potent fix. It's easy to imagine his skin reddening under his fair hair, and his friend Curly teasing him incessantly about the girl with the gorgeous grey eyes.

He introduced himself and struck up a friendship, but it was far less than Bill wished it would be, for he'd begun sending her anonymous cards signed with a mysterious "?" Several bore romantic images of bewigged lords on bended knee to pomaded ladies, and others professed in verse what Bill hadn't yet said aloud: "Today I am thinking about you, thinking of how you smile. Thinking that life is sweeter because of your cheer each mile." One cartoon card showed a gent at a gas station, wearing a fedora and wide-leg striped suit. His car had a heart-shaped rear window and a licence plate that read "Feb. 14," and the pipe-smoking attendant stood with hose at the ready. "1 Gal is all I want," the text proclaimed, "and you can GAS who that GAL is." Did Doris guess the sender was Bill? She saved the cards in her scrapbook, along with a postcard she received from him when he visited some Cartwright relatives who'd settled in Toledo, Ohio.

Dear Doris,

We got hear at 9 o'clock on saterday and went to sand lake. on sunday went in swimming. This is the picture of a school that my cusin Jack is going to.

by for now.
Bill

Sweet as Bill was, Doris's thoughts were elsewhere. In the spring of 1931, in the latter half of his freshman year at Western, Fred began experiencing strange and worrisome symptoms – headaches, vision and hearing problems, loss of balance, even seizures and facial paralysis. Maybe his mother went right away to her cousin Harry with her concerns, and Harry put them in touch with Dr. Stuart Fisher, a neurologist and lecturer at the university. Fisher had served as a doctor in France during the war and then back at home for a time at a psychiatric hospital that treated "mental and nervous casualties" of the war. He'd done his training at Western but had studied further in England, where he'd worked with the famed doctor Frederick Walker Mott, known for his theories of hereditary insanity in female cases like Ellen Roff's and Mary Anne Deverill's. For Doris, though, the clearest links to those days were Fred's symptoms and the unfathomable diagnosis of a brain tumour. If she recalled her mother's headaches and strange behaviour as the cancer had spread to her brain, she'd have seen the similarities with Fred and suspected the worst.

Although he stuck out the school year and even commenced working again at Kellogg's that summer, he was soon confined to bed. Doris was likely at the Stephensons' as often as possible in those difficult days, reading to Fred or just sitting quietly with him, the hours so different from those they'd spent with their friends, playing board games and listening to music that coloured the world breezy and hopeful. Maybe, when Fred dozed, she sipped tea at the kitchen table with Pearl and hoped her presence was comforting, if nothing else.

At the end of August Dr. Fisher arranged for Fred's admission to the university hospital in Rochester, New York. Neurosurgery was relatively new, and in 1931 there were only twenty-nine neurological surgeons at work in the entire field throughout the United States. One of the most prominent, Dr. William Van Wagenen, worked out of Rochester and may have been the doctor who operated on Fred that summer, then sent him home to Fisher's care, incised and bandaged. But all was not well. The *Western University Gazette* piece written about Fred that autumn says that he rallied for a while after the surgery, but in the end "death intervened," and he died at home two weeks after his twentieth birthday.

Six friends acted as pallbearers, one of them George Dean, who stands beside Fred in the photo that includes the birdhouse. Presumably Anna Doan attended the funeral too, and for the two of them and Doris it must have been piercing, for some time to come, to hear the songs they used to laugh away to at the Stephensons' kitchen table, singing along. "Happy Days" those had been. Fred's death, so soon after Bebbie's, was Doris's fourth monumental loss, and once again her path in life shifted.

As was her way, Emily Cartwright sits fully dressed on the beach while the rest of her family soaks in a sunny day at Port Stanley in the early 1930s. Front, from left: Gordon, Do, Jack, Mary, Pa George, Bill beside Pa, Earl in front of Bill, and George Jr.; Florence stands at the back behind her parents, whose differing natures were surprisingly well-matched.

CHAPTER 17

A Cosy Nest

N ews from England was less frequent now. The grand dame of the family, Aunt Maggie, had become an old lady. She was bothered by rheumatism and had left her cleaning job at the Borough Polytechnic a few years earlier, with assistance from a "compassionate fund" due to her long years of service. Clara's Elsie – the one who'd posed with Ethel on the rooftop of the Goodwin – was a teenager now, and a help to her gran and then her mother when her father, Bert, the wartime munitions man, died unexpectedly of complications from pneumonia at the age of just thirty-nine years. May, Doris's wonderfully chatty cousin, had kept up her friendship with Ethel by way of letters, and sometimes wrote to Doris, too, promising, "I haven't forgotten you," and sending photographs of herself at Richmond Park, wearing just the style of clothes Doris favoured at the time, and showing the same large, wide-set eyes, passed down from their mothers' line. She'd married a Borough man in 1927 and borne two children, and was still living in the area of Marshalsea Road, where family roots were long and entwined. "[But] these days are so different," she mused. "Families split up more…It's not like it was when we all lived near to each other." Her father, Jack, Doris's uncle, was one such wanderer, at least in an emotional sense. He'd lived on the periphery of May's life since the death of her mother when she was a child, never quite able to pull his load, or not feeling he was required to, given Maggie's capable presence. Even May's children called him Uncle Jack instead of Grandpa. In a photo May sent after her son was born, May and Jack sit beside each other on a low stone wall, alike in their smallness and neither smiling. Baby Cyril is resting in May's lap, but his head is craned toward his grandfather, as if he's curious about who this wiry, suited man could be.

Joe occasionally corresponded too, with apologies: "I am afraid that letter writing isn't one of my good points," he often began, and yet the notes that followed were always charming and peppered with spelling mistakes and the sort of ordinary news that illuminates a person's own particular world. He wrote of the marvellous singing at Salvation Army events he and Nelly attended, and asked of the seeds he'd sent, "Did the loopins take?" He and Nelly had a second daughter now, and enjoyed simple pleasures: "We were not sorry to see the end of winter…We thought we had lost our hydrangeas, but no, they are really lovely this year, a mixture of Pink and Blue blooms. You can guess how proud Nelly is of them."

There was some contact with Harry's sisters as well, so Doris knew that Auntie Ada was still at The Hermitage with her ponies and pigs, and aunts Nell and Maud remained in Wimbledon. But Mary Anne's sister Jennie Vanson and her girls were fading from Doris's story, and if you'd asked her about the notorious Ellen Evans/Roff/Humphreys, who'd been an inmate of one form or another since before Doris's birth, she wouldn't have known who you were talking about. Or if she did, she never spoke of her. Ellen was still at Newington Workhouse, though nowadays workhouses were officially called Public Assistance Institutions, and inmates were called residents. And yet the stigma remained as certainly as the dark, damp buildings themselves. Ellen would be at Newington until her death in the 1940s at the age of seventy-five. Others had forgotten her too, for apart from the single record of potter Fred's visit to her at Stone Asylum in 1903, there is no mention of anyone writing or coming to see her, and her death certificate reads "widow of ____ Roff, occupation unknown."

Doris knew little of her family's history – less as the years rolled on and memory thinned – and her accent no longer gave obvious clues to where she'd come from. A hint of the Cockney emerged here and there in her speech, but for the most part she sounded, and felt, Canadian. The big trees and the small city suited her, and though some of her most profound heartbreaks had occurred here, *this* London was home.

For Bill, it always had been. There were few streets in the city he hadn't traversed, either by bicycle or car, and these days he had an enthusiastic passenger in his youngest sister, Do, who stood behind the driver's seat, peering over his shoulder and urging him on. "Go faster, Bill! Pass 'em!" He taught her the names of the cars on the road, and she called them out as she spotted them. When Bill was at work, Do's scooter had to suffice, and she raced it up and down the street, wearing out the heel of her right shoe to Emily's chagrin.

Bill was still at Kellogg's, and especially happy for the job now that the Great Depression was in full swing. It was estimated that some 30 percent of Canadians were out of work, and over the first half of that harsh decade thousands wrote to the prime minister to express anger or despair, or even to ask for money to buy groceries or a winter coat. Richard Bedford Bennett was a wealthy Conservative who had promised to end unemployment when he was elected in 1930, but that proved more challenging than he'd anticipated, and the economic crisis ballooned. One woman from a town north of London wrote to him on behalf of her destitute neighbours, who had newborn triplets and a lot of bad luck. "The parents are English," the woman added, "but a very fine type, not the kind with the hand out for help." When Bennett responded, tragedy had already occurred: "Dear Mr. and Mrs. Samuels, I am enclosing herewith a $20 bill, which I trust may be of some little service to you during the Christmas season. I learned the other day that one of the triplet boys had passed away and I extend to you my sincerest sympathy." The letters show that Bennett's response was not unusual for him – he frequently took pity on the individual and sent money for a mortgage payment, or for a boy's wagon, or for "underware for my husband from the Eaton catalog." But the problem was deeper than a millionaire's pockets. "Dear Sir," one young man wrote,

I am just writing a few lines to you to see what can be done for us young men of Canada. We are the growing generation of Canada, but with no hopes of a future. Please tell me why is it a single man always gets a refusal when he looks for a job. A married man gets work, & if he does not get work, he gets relief. Yesterday I got a glimpse of a lot of the unemployed. It just made me feel down-hearted…I say again whats to be done for us single men? do we have to starve? or do we have to go round with our faces full of shame, to beg at the doors of the well to do citizen. I suppose you will say the married men must come first; I certainly agree with you there. But have you a word or two to cheer us single men up a bit?

In the early part of this decade of unemployment and hardship, Bill was laid off from Kellogg's, and though it was only because machinery was being repaired, he must have worried, given the economic climate, that he wouldn't be asked back. In the interim he was lucky enough to be hired on at McCormick's, taking stock, until Kellogg's was ready to have him again. In retrospect he needn't have fretted. While its main competitor, Post, cut expenses and slowed down on advertising – the typical response of businesses during hard times – Kellogg's did the opposite. Its advertising budget doubled and now included radio as well. The fabled Rice Krispies characters, Snap, Crackle and Pop, were born in this era and depicted as tiny gnomes gathered around a musical cereal bowl, singing into a radio microphone and wielding a banjo-spoon. The risk paid off. While its competitors hid in the shadows of financial gloom, Kellogg's claimed the spotlight, and its profits soared even as the Depression intensified.

Back at the cereal factory, Bill had the pleasure of glimpsing Doris now and again during the workday and feeling his heart do cartwheels. He hadn't given up on her and continued to send cards signed "?" – finally adding his name in tiny letters, hidden on the back inside page. At last he plucked up his courage, bolstered by bringing a buddy along, and knocked on her door. He was both relieved and nervous when she herself answered, and, cheeks turning red, he blurted, "Would you like to come for a ride?"

Doris looked past him to the car parked in the driveway, polished to a shine, and then to his friend Curly who stood grinning beside him. Bill couldn't know it, but the Prices were not at home to give their permission, and even if they had been, she wouldn't have gone driving alone with two boys. She said no, but smiled before she closed the door. Bill, backing out of the driveway, realized his heart was still thumping wildly, and despite being rebuffed, he felt inexplicably joyful.

Before long he approached her again, this time suggesting a double date with another friend and his girl. The friend had a car with a rumble seat, which was a fair-weather contraption as there was no roof over that seat, but the day was fine for the eighteen-mile trip to St. Thomas, halfway to Port Stanley on Lake Erie. Bill and Doris sat shoulder to shoulder in the narrow rumble, Bill's smile wide, no doubt, and a touch of sunburn on his forehead. Doris might have tied a scarf over her hair to keep the wind from whipping the kinks of her marcel wave into a snarl. Sitting so close to this jovial new friend, she must have been tempted to compare him with staid Fred, a well-educated young man who'd been described in the *Western Gazette* as having a "very kindly and quiet disposition." Bill had an easy laugh and a booming voice, and was an exceptionally poor speller. He was round and strong while Fred had been slight and fine-boned. But it was early for comparisons. At St. Thomas they had ice cream at a diner called Diana Sweets and then made the drive back to London with the sun sinking in the evening sky. Did they know that they were falling in love? Such intimate details were not passed down, but an image of them persists in the mind's eye: Bill waving from his friend's car, and Doris smiling as she closes the door behind her. She hums as she walks to her little bedroom off the Prices' kitchen, and looking at herself in the mirror as she unties her scarf sees high colour and bright eyes. The lightness in her chest is a sure sign of happiness.

It went on from there. Doris's scrapbook filled up with Bill's cards, and he began to call her Dory, which no one else had ever done. She found herself seated at boisterous Cartwright family dinners, swinging a bat at backyard baseball games, and riding around town with Bill and their tiny chaperone Do, who looked astonishingly like her brother and seemed to know even more than he did about cars. Do was someone you wanted on side, Doris sensed, and brought her an offering of a stuffed bear within their first few meetings. Do adored the bear, which came with her on the car trips and on her scoots – "*bbbrrrrrmmmmm!*" – around the corner to purchase a five-cent ice cream cone. She was less certain about the pretty girl her brother seemed so attached to, but was willing to give her a chance – which was more than could be said for Emily.

In Doris, Emily Cartwright sensed that "vapour of the slum" that some believed clung to people born in unfortunate places and raised in unfortunate situations. She thought of Doris as a little orphan girl who was not nearly good enough for her Bill. She didn't approve of the Gospel Hall either, which in her mind wasn't a real church and therefore not an appropriate place to worship God. A typical overprotective mother, she was also the product of a country and a time that had struggled with burgeoning benevolence, and where divides between race and religion and class had been more clearly defined. She wanted the best match for Bill and for all her children, and in her mind, Doris Deverill, hailing from Whitechapel and the Borough and still with a hint of the Cockney about her, wasn't that. For Doris, Emily's frostiness was bearable because George was warm and welcoming, and Bill and his siblings were loud enough to drown out any barbs that tried to repeat in Doris's mind.

For the most part she was dazzled by this family. Even back in England, when her mother was still alive, her own family gatherings had never had so many players – nor so much musical accompaniment – and so to Doris the most ordinary Cartwright occasion seemed like a party. If Bill's sister Florence was home, she was often singing, with a rich contralto voice that had benefitted from rigorous training. She was serious about becoming a professional singer. Emily and George couldn't afford the lessons she wanted, but diligent Florence discovered that the Metropolitan United Church paid for their soloists' lessons, so she left the family church and began attending that one instead. Emily could be consoled by the fact that at least it was a *real* church – if not Anglican – with a rather magnificent bell tower, and room for fourteen hundred worshipers to sit and listen to her eldest girl's robust voice.

Earl was still crooning too, and had grown as handsome as a movie star – fair like Emily, but angular like George. He liked to sit on the fence in the backyard and strum his guitar like a lone cowboy, but he also loved opera and had a collection of records that got played on the gramophone in the Cartwright living room, as well as a fat book about opera stars that Do liked to look at with fingers grubby from her latest treat. "You have to wash your hands first," he insisted, holding the tome behind his back until she scrubbed up. She'd have muscled in in front of whoever was washing dishes, because at this house there were always great trays of them after each meal. But the chore schedule was strictly adhered to, to ensure that everything got done: on Saturdays someone swept and washed the kitchen floor, the dining room floor, and the basement stairs, and someone else helped with laundry and ironing, feeding the sheets and the tablecloths through the large roller of the ironer to remove every wrinkle. Special care had to be taken to dust in the grooves of the carved legs of the dining room table, and to wipe the smudges from the windowpanes, signs that Do had wandered past with sticky hands. If Doris mused that Ernie's talents could be put to good use at the Cartwright house, she was likely impressed at how smoothly things ran anyway, and what a happy place it was given that so many personalities resided under one roof.

Soon she was invited along on their excursions outside town, and in pictures she can be seen posing as if already a member of the family – the Cartwrights and Doris in identical black swimsuits rented from a beachside pavilion, the group lined up on a log at the water's edge or crowded around an umbrella at Port Stanley, Earl with his ukulele. Mackie's restaurant, famous for its orangeade and French fries, is visible behind them. The background remained Emily's usual spot too, as she sweats in hat, dress, stockings and sand-filled shoes.

McCormick's picnics often happened in Port Stanley as well, the employees and their families filling the specially rented railway cars that transported them from London, bypassing the usual stops at places like Yarmouth Station and Kettle Creek Ravine, and depositing them at the very foot of the bluffs at Port Stanley. With both Bill's dad and Ernie working for the company, Doris now had all the more reason to attend, arm in arm with boyfriend and brother. The group of Doris, Ernie and the Cartwrights trekked the short distance from the train depot to the incline railway, picnic basket swinging, tartan wool blankets tucked under arms. The incline cars held fifty or so riders, and with hundreds eager to enjoy the fun, a long line formed for the trip to the picnic grounds at the top of the steep hill. A bell rang to signal a full car, and the vessel began its upward haul, passing its returning sister at the halfway point. Despite the wait, the ride was a highlight of the day, and in full sun the view from the cars out over the sandy beach and sparkling expanse of Lake Erie was magnificent.

Back at work, the boys at Kellogg's soon stopped inviting Doris to wiener roasts or out for a soda. There was no turning her head. Bill and Doris had become a couple, and the evidence was apparent when Bill gave her a friendship ring for Christmas in 1932, set with a sapphire stone with a tiny diamond in the centre. More telling yet was Bill's participation in the Gospel Hall's youth group; photos record him relaxed and happy among Doris and her friends, the images labelled "Young People's hike up Highbury" and "Y.P. trip to Strathroy." Bill had moved into Doris's world and was comfortable with the change.

It was inevitable – even more now than with Fred – that the friendship would transform, and that a question would be asked and answered. Doris was playing the piano in the Prices' living room when Bill came to the door. She let him in, and almost immediately he handed her a package. Inside was a second ring: a white gold band with a large centre-set diamond and forget-me-nots engraved on each side. The Prices were sitting right there, looking on, and Doris was a little embarrassed by their presence, and by Bill grinning at her, waiting for an answer. But he need not have wondered: of course it was yes.

Together they went to show Emily the ring, both of them hoping she would offer congratulations. Instead she raised her eyebrows as she looked at Doris's slender hand. "Aren't you a lucky girl to get two diamonds in one year!" If Emily thought back to her own parents when she and George had decided to marry, and how they had more or less disowned her, the memory didn't quell her disapproval of Bill's choice, or even keep her from expressing it. For Emily, the rift with her own parents could never be healed; both were dead now and had never met or acknowledged their grandchildren.

Bill was crushed by his mother's disapproval, but the planning began even with that dark cloud. The betrothed couple was photographed at University Hill, sitting on the grass and holding hands, and though Doris wears a hat and a corsage and Bill is in suit and tie, this is a less formal engagement portrait than those fashionable in their parents' time. Doris still had the picture of Mary Anne at about her age, newly engaged to oil and colourman Harry, with shiny buttons running up her fitted dress, and her hand resting on a pile of books so as to show off her ring. What would Mary Anne and Harry have made of Bill?

The roles Doris's parents or even Bebbie would have played in this exciting time were necessarily doled out to others, and a notice in the paper read "Mr. E. Deverill announces the engagement of his sister, Doris Deverill, to William C. Cartwright, son of Mr. and Mrs. George Cartwright. The wedding to take place Sept. 22." Minnie Price hosted a shower at the Gospel Hall, and, a week before the wedding, a trousseau tea, which was traditionally the job of a mother who invited friends and family to view the items the bride had bought, made, or received as gifts for her new life as a married woman. Fancy sandwiches and cakes were served to the guests, and tea was poured from a silver teapot, and later it was all described in the women's pages of the newspaper: "Mrs. Frank Price entertained on Thursday evening at her home on Florence Street, at a trousseau reception for Miss Doris Deverill...The bride-elect received in a gown of Nile green georgette with corsage of sweet peas and maidenhair fern, assisted by Mrs. Price who received in a gown of brown georgette. Many beautiful gifts were displayed. Little June Price was the door attendant."

Doris asked Ruth Rea to be her maid of honour and chose a pink satin dress to suit Ruth's long, thin frame, with a fashionable beret and elegant black suede slippers that would ensure minimal towering over the bride. She herself would wear a floor-length plain gown with two rows of ruffles on the shoulders above the short sleeves, and elbow-length white gloves. Her friend Bella offered "something borrowed" that proved the perfect accent to the gown's simplicity: her own veil of white tulle with delicately embroidered edges. It would be a small wedding party, with Bill's oldest brother, George, as best man, and together the couple decided that Do, cute as she was, could not be trusted to behave in the role of flower girl, but that if it wasn't her, it shouldn't be anyone else either. Do was more enamored with marbles than romance anyway, and had a colourful collection that she toted around in a sock.

The ceremony was to be held at the Gospel Hall, but even if Emily had warmed to Doris, this last detail was one she couldn't bear. Powerless to do much about it, at the last minute she told Bill she wouldn't attend his wedding. That she simply couldn't, because of where it was being held, and the fact their own dear minister would not be officiating. Do, overhearing and finding the drama somewhat thrilling, stated that she wouldn't go either. And all the while, as Doris was fussing with the orange blossoms that crowned her bridal veil and pinning the boutonniere to nervous Ernie's lapel, Bill implored Emily. She wouldn't be moved. Eventually his father took him aside and told him to go to the church. "Don't worry," he added in his calm, quiet way. "She'll be there."

The flowers of late summer, early autumn, graced the little chapel – chrysanthemums and tall sturdy gladioli, as well as huge dahlias offered from a neighbour's garden. Trailing ferns and ribbons, Doris's own bouquet shook a little as she and Ernie walked down the aisle toward Bill. Ethel stood near the front of the church with her husband and small children and Bebbie's relatives, wearing a large corsage that marked her special place as sister of the bride. All the Cartwrights were present, and Bill must have exhaled with relief to see feisty Do and his disgruntled mother standing in that long row of familiar faces, while his beautiful bride walked slowly toward him. Once they had spoken their vows, Florence sang "Because," a song that promised "a wider world of hope and joy," and her big voice filling the small church captured his elation thoroughly.

There were less perfect moments. As the wedding party and the guests spilled out onto Egerton Street, Em, the girl who'd been Doris's first friend in Canada, rushed up to offer her congratulations. She grabbed the lovely borrowed veil in both hands and pulled, ripping the tulle with its fancy trim. "That means good luck!" she exclaimed, but Doris was sick at the thought of it being damaged. And then there was her new mother-in-law. In almost all the photographs of that day, Doris wears her easy, genuine smile. One slightly blurred shot captures carefree laughter. But another shows her with Bill and his parents. The men each stand on the outside, and the women are pressed together in the centre, ever so slightly tilting away from one another. Doris's smile is strained, and Bill's hand holds her elbow, like a reminder of support: we're in this together, 'til death do us part.

After the wedding the newlyweds set off on their honeymoon in the Chrysler 72. It was the beginning of a week-long trip to sites not far from home, the kind of excursion that had become popular in recent years. Official government maps came with a lengthy boast about the highways of Ontario. "Perhaps it is not generally known that the Highway from Windsor to the Quebec border, via London has all been paved and that a person can travel over 500 miles of pavement without a detour…Ontario's highways are alluring and attractive and…the picture just ahead is always worthwhile." They travelled east toward Lake Ontario, passing farmer's fields and villages. Summer crops had long been harvested, and the trees had only just begun to show glimmers of their fall splendour. Trees were the first thing Doris had loved about Canada when she'd come as a young girl, and for all the road trips of her future, with Bill at the wheel, she'd be happy to gaze out the window watching them go by. This was only the first of many such trips, but also singular. When night fell, the full moon was so bright they could have turned their headlights off and had no trouble seeing the ribbon of road.

They spent their first night in Hamilton at the Royal Connaught, feeling rather posh when the hotel doorman took their keys to park their car. Ever practical, Bill cautioned him to turn off the gas tank, since the Chrysler was not only a sieve in the rain but leaked gas too. Rather than spend a lazy Sunday morning at the hotel, they were up early and drove into Toronto to attend a service at the newly opened People's Church, where evangelical sermons were delivered to capacity crowds, accompanied by music from a 135-member choir and a forty-piece orchestra. Pastor Oswald Smith was a zealous crusader; like the Salvation Army's William Booth, he wrote books and hymns, published a magazine, travelled on missionary work and was always evangelizing, in person and on the radio. He'd made himself and his church famous, so for Doris and Bill the chance to visit and hear him speak was surely thrilling.

With the pastor's inspiring words lingering, the honeymooners continued to Niagara Falls and snapped a few pictures, though none so dramatic as those others had captured months earlier, in February, when the American falls had frozen over. "Jack Frost silences Niagara," one paper exclaimed, running a photo of impressive mounds of ice and the river reduced to "scarcely a trickle." Such an event was rare, and was surely hard to imagine for those visiting in September, when Doris and Bill did, eager for the sight of a river that was anything but silent roaring over the precipice, creating a perpetual mist and impromptu rainbows.

Soon they were back at home. Bill was due on the nightshift at Kellogg's and wasn't taking any chances with Suzy LeBeau, the shift supervisor, whom everyone agreed could "scare the daylights out of you." Like most married women of her day, Doris had quit work to begin her role as a wife and homemaker, retiring her packing-line smock for a flowered apron, and she was busy setting up house in the apartment she and Bill had rented – the upstairs rooms at Fred Stephenson's grandparents' place next door to his mom and dad. When Doris thought of Fred in those days it must have been with tenderness, and surely Fred's family felt a similar affection for Doris, welcoming her and her new husband into a space they might once have hoped she'd share with Fred. It was obvious she was happy, and that Bill adored her – his Dory. She pasted snapshots of the apartment into her photo album, showing a lush Boston fern by the window, fringed pedestal lamps, and pictures hanging. Doris's Sherlock-Manning piano rests against one wall, a silver-faced clock in a smooth wooden case gracing its top. Arranged round the room are a couch and doily-covered chairs, the furniture tucked so closely together you could almost reach out a foot and touch the piano from the couch, or join hands from chair to chair. Vying with the piano for pride of place is the polished wooden cabinet of a Sparton radio, with a picture of Ernie sitting on top of it. The photos suggest a happy home, or as Doris herself wrote under one of them, "A Cosy Nest."

At home alone on a Friday night, the curtains pulled and the lamps turned low, the radio crooned smooth songs with lyrics for lovers:

"Moonglow" by Benny Goodman, or Guy Lombardo's "The Sweet-est Music This Side of Heaven," tunes perfect for newlyweds drifting through the fog of romance. Bill and Doris were smitten enough to em-brace such sentimental ballads, but the real beauty of their story lay in its ordinary rather than its heavenly proportions, in the small moments still ahead of them, and the daily ways that would form the tapestry of a strong, enduring marriage.

When Doris considered how much her life had changed since she'd gone from London to London, it was likely without nostalgia. Her thoughts were of the present now, with Bill, and of their future togeth-er, though all the while her past grew longer, and little reminders of it stayed with her, such as the photo of Harry in front of the Whitechapel flat, his hand on a lattice gate, Mary Anne smiling from an ivy-framed window. Or the one of Benjamin and Margaret Jones relaxing in old age on Red Cross Street, Benjamin holding a cat on his lap while cows moo in the distance. Margaret eyes the camera in this photograph, but hard as she looks she will never see Doris, her great-granddaughter, though it will be Doris who keeps the picture safe for a lifetime and passes it on to another generation.

So just as the beginning of this story could not be a beginning, so the end is no end. The family saga cycles on from here, veering and darting wherever it goes, always changing. And like a tree it grows new shoots that in turn grow more, the leaves unfurling for their time in the sun, then curling and dropping. Each new life that enters the story will be part of someone else's past and a source of the questions: who am I, where did I come from, how did I get here from there?

Doris and Bill at Lake Erie's Rondeau Park in 1933,
the summer of the year before they married.

D oris and Bill were married for nearly sixty-five years, and raised four children in a little house on Florence Street, paid for outright after a few years of saving early on. Right away, Ernie came to live with them. The Prices' family was growing, and although he might have afforded a little place of his own with his salary from McCormick's, Doris worried that he'd be lonely. The uncertainty they'd grown up with – together and then not, shunted from relative to relative – probably fuelled her concern. Bill, coming from such a close-knit, strong family himself, commiserated, and with a heart as big as his voice told Ernie, "You'll always have a home with us."

And so he remained a regular fixture, year in, year out, his plaid slippers tucked beneath his narrow bed, his suspenders hung on a hook behind the door. He paid board and the telephone bill, helped with the cooking and cleaning, and contributed to the purchase of Bill's shiny automobile, parking his green bicycle alongside it and taking care not to scratch the paint. Ernie never learned to drive but that didn't deter his travels, whether by bicycle to Toronto and back, sleeping by the side of the road, or by train to Detroit and a baseball game, or to Atlantic City where he'd eventually take his nieces and nephews to stroll the boardwalk and eat hot dogs and candy floss. He was also their babysitter when the need arose, and his nieces recount the times he'd pause at their bedroom door, hearing them awake and giggling. "Are you girls asleep yet?" he'd ask, peeking into the room. "Yes," they'd reply, though of course how could they be, if they were answering? But Ernie would say "Okay" and close the door, and the girls would shrivel again with shared laughter. He was like a second dad, and if his idiosyncrasies sometimes annoyed Bill and Doris – he painted when the notion took him: red and green on the patio stones, orange and yellow on the metal lawn chairs, battleship grey on everything else – they never considered revoking their promise to share their home.

They grew old together as a threesome, Bill and Ernie going bald while Doris's dark hair turned grey. Ernie hung on to his Cockney accent and the sayings that had long since fallen out of use back home: "pip, pip, cheerio." His suspenders and his cap remained part of his regular attire, so that even when he'd been in Canada for longer than he'd ever lived in England, he seemed transplanted, and a contrast to his larger, louder brother-in-law. But he and Bill shared a quirky sense of humour. A photo shows them wearing polka-dot ties and women's wigs, clowning for the camera. Ernie's hand rests on Bill's shoulder, and their faces contort with the comedy of the moment. Other photos capture an unsteady Doris on roller skates, her smile wide as her youngest son holds her up, and Doris and Bill on a bicycle built for two, since she could never balance without him. There are many such pictures documenting these lives, tracing not only the happy moments but also the gradual effects of time: the widening waistlines, the sagging skin, the fading vitality.

The idea that time was passing spurred first Ethel and Ernie and later Doris and Bill to travel back to England in the 1960s to visit Joe. Aunt Maggie and Uncle Jack had long since passed away, as had their father's sisters, Ada and Nell and Maud, who'd looked after Doris and Ernie briefly in those dark months during the war that bracketed their mother's death. Decades had gone by since any of the siblings had seen their brother Joe. And although letters had been mailed back and forth sharing news, words were a poor substitute for the sight of one another, and the feel of a hug after so many years. Doris had been nine when she'd left England, Ethel and Ernie twenty-four and nineteen. Joe had been a fresh-faced sailor, taking on the role of patriarch when he reminded them that "although the (Old Home) has broken up, we are still Brothers and Sisters." Now Joe was retired, and shared with his grandchildren his claim to fame of having been batman to no less a personality than Lord Louis Mountbatten, uncle of the queen's husband. Joe was well-suited for the job, quietly efficient but not servile. Typical of many in their senior years, he didn't talk much about his youth but spent time puttering in the garden, or in his armchair chuckling over Beano comics and smoking fragrant Boar's Head tobacco. Did he and Ernie laugh to see one as bald as the other, and to note that the little brother, while still short, had grown taller than the big one? Did Joe and Ethel, so close in age, speak of old times, or did they leave that sadness unmentioned? Could he see the child he'd known in the middle-aged woman Doris had become, and did he smile to hear Bill call her Dory, the two of them so obviously a match? Doris was photographed standing on a rain-soaked sidewalk in the Borough, Marshalsea Road a wash of grey walls and dark pavement behind her. She smiles, and although the intent of the picture is obvious – here is Doris, back home again – she is very plainly a visitor. In another photo taken to mark the trip, Joe and Doris stand together in Joe's tiny garden, a profusion of pink hydrangeas behind them. Doris is dressed as for a special day, wearing a navy outfit with a gold maple leaf brooch, and Joe, too, is turned out in good clothes. The camera catches Doris's smile but Joe's expression is somewhat reserved, and there are dark shadows beneath his eyes. The visits came none too soon.

Of the four of them, Ethel died first, on a cold February day not long after her visit to England. She was a widow by this time – in fact her husband had died just before she arrived home from that trip – and since then she'd been living with her daughter and her young family. She and the daughter had been on their way home from shopping, had stepped off the bus and begun the short walk to their door. Ethel could only manage a few steps at a time and had to keep stopping, and her daughter would bend and ask if she was okay. Before they reached the door, Ethel collapsed, and when help arrived it made no difference. She died at Victoria Hospital, just sixty-six years old. Joe wrote, "I still can't grasp the fact that Ethel has passed on…I am consoled by the fact that she enjoyed her stay here, and I received a very cheerful letter only a couple of days before she died."

A little over a year later, Joe met a similar, sudden end. He was feeling unwell and had gone to see his doctor, who was also a friend from the Navy. When he collapsed in the office, his friend was unable to revive him.

Ernie lived on, cooking minty peas and Yorkshire puddings that sometimes failed to rise, and growing so beloved by Doris and Bill's grandchildren that his eventual death in the late 1970s – like his siblings before him, of heart trouble – was a loss for three generations. And it was only then – when Bill was already retired from Kellogg's and he and Doris had been married for nearly fifty years – that they found themselves alone again.

One spring when Doris was eighty-five, she and Bill were kneeling in the garden, planting flowers, when she felt sudden, severe pain in her waist and ribs. She went inside and rested but the pain continued intermittently for days. The doctor advised Tylenol, but soon she was worse and so exhausted that the simplest tasks around the house were too much. Tests confirmed cancer, virulent and incurable, and though the diagnosis was devastating, her worries were more for others than herself. How would Bill fare without her? And would the children and grandchildren stay close in her absence? She worried especially for the ones who'd left the church and had no faith to bolster them, and Bill shared that dismay. A nurse showed him how to administer morphine. Every day he cared for her at home, trying to adjust to the strange reality that she would die before he did. It was not how he'd expected things to be, and there was nothing he could do about the fact that she grew smaller as the illness took over, spine crumbling little by little.

In the fall of 1997 their youngest son, Jeff, finished building a house along the banks of St. Mary's River near Sault Ste. Marie, and Doris longed to see it. With the blessing of her doctor, her children Jean and Bill Jr. took their parents north in a large rented van with reclining seats and room for the oxygen tanks in the back. The six-hour drive through northern Michigan took thirteen hours because of road construction delays, and although Doris must have suffered on the trip, the trees were stunning at that time of year, their leaves turning varying shades of orange, gold and crimson. All through their childhoods, her children had laughed at how she'd marvel at the trees. Now the display was like a gift just for her – as were the days at Jeff's, full of music and singing and gorgeous views through the many long windows of his home. Bill and

Doris slept in a bed together for the first time in months, for at home she could no longer manage the four steps up to the bedroom, and the narrow bed in Ernie's old room at the foot of the stairs was too small to hold both of them.

Back in London, the morphine barely masked Doris's pain, and the hum of the oxygen machine was constant. By Christmas she was in bed most of the time, with Bill in an easy chair his son had brought in so he could sit comfortably beside her. They had Christmas dinner that way, with daughter Jean perched on a chair in the doorway, plate in her lap. Over the next couple of weeks Doris spoke less, and her face assumed the disconnected expression people have when they're dying. One night early in January 1998, Bill said goodnight to her and went upstairs to their bedroom, and she remained below with Jean, who woke at every sound she made, sensing the end was close. Twice Doris rose and Jean helped her to the bathroom, but a third time she simply slid out of bed and lay on the floor. Light as she was, Jean couldn't lift her, and she phoned Bill Jr. to come and help. Bill slept through all of it in the room above. Jean called the nurse as well, but when she arrived and examined Doris, she said there were no broken bones and that Doris might linger for hours or days this way. She assured them that they were doing everything they could by keeping her as comfortable as possible. "She's just dying," she told them. Bill Jr. went back home to get some rest, and Jean lay on the bed with her mother, sometimes singing, sometimes talking quietly. Doris slept for most of those hours, but two or three times she sat straight up and looked around, not saying a word. Jean calmed her and urged her to lie down again.

At the end of that long night Jean heard Bill coming down the stairs and went into the hallway to meet him. "She's going, Dad," she told him, and he entered the room and sat in the chair beside his wife, putting his hand on her arm. He leaned forward and kissed her, and within moments she took a single gasping breath and then stopped breathing. Bill put his hand on her neck and said to Jean, "She's gone."

Later, Jean told her sister, "It was as if she had waited for him to come and say goodbye."

Doris's funeral was hard for Bill, and for the first time in his adult life he seemed vulnerable. His hair looked whiter, and his usually big voice shook, but he turned to one of his grandchildren and said with a raw fierceness that was grief and love entwined, "She was the most beautiful girl I ever knew." In a way she remained with him, and each night he kissed her picture and said aloud "Goodnight, Dory," as he climbed into bed alone. As so often happens, his own decline accelerated after her death, and the years he had left were few and somewhat shapeless without her, though sparked, now and then, by his large and loving family and a lifelong habit of being happy.

He and Doris had both been healthy and vibrant into deep old age, thanks to good luck and clean living. They'd share a burger when they ate fast food, and they never indulged in alcohol, except occasionally, after a heavy meal, to sip crème de menthe at the suggestion of their daughter Marilyn, who told them it might be good for their digestion – and secretly thought they might find it fun, too. And so the changes that age and illness bring came relatively suddenly for her and then him, and a year after Doris's death, debilitated by arthritis in his knees and shoulders, and slowed by grief, Bill was not well enough to live at home anymore. At first he balked at the idea of moving and declared that the only way he was leaving was feet first, but soon he admitted he didn't like being on his own at night, and he was afraid of falling with no one there to help him. And home wasn't the same without "that great lady," as he would sometimes call Doris in his fond rememberings. As Jean and Bill Jr. got him ready to go to the nursing home that last day, he paused in the doorway of the house he and Doris had shared for so many years, turned back to the inner rooms and called out "Goodbye, old house!" As he shuffled outside, a long-time neighbour stood in her picture window, crying and waving. The car backed out of the driveway, and Bill – the passenger now – was escorted away.

The staff at the nursing home called him Wild Bill, though really he was anything but. He did get regular visitors, and parties in the party room, complete with hats and noisemakers and booming Cartwright voices and offspring thundering out songs on the piano. Old friends from Kellogg's visited too, and on these special occasions Bill wore a crisp white shirt, a wide striped tie and a navy blazer that brightened his blue eyes, still shining in the face that had so aged around them. These were the Sunday clothes that had served as his Gospel Hall attire and gave him a manly, dignified air. Once he was picked up in a taxi that could accommodate the wheelchair he now needed and was brought to a pool party at his son's place, and he sat basking in the sunshine, watching his daughters and sons and their daughters and sons, and so on. It was a lovely day, but you could see in his eyes how it tired him. His hands shook, and his voice had lost its richness. But he brightened when he talked about Doris. He believed – as she had – that they would meet again, and he was biding his time.

Only in his last months, at ninety-three, did he begin to have trouble remembering. He said to Jean, "I know you're my daughter, but I can't remember your name." He couldn't feed himself anymore, and she and her brother and a granddaughter would take turns visiting to spoon in pureed meals. It wasn't long before he didn't eat anything at all. On a Saturday in late November the home called to say they'd moved him into palliative care, and he didn't have much time left. Jean went to be with him, as she'd been with Doris – which Jean said afterward was not just a help for her own grief, but a privilege too. Bill Jr. came as well, with his wife and daughter, and Do and Mary; Bill's little sisters were old ladies now, remnants of the Cartwright clan that had won prizes for largest group at the McCormick's picnics.

They'd been sitting with him for a while, in quiet company, and it was snowing heavily outside. Shortly before midnight they decided they should go before the weather worsened, and return in the morning. Jean leaned over and told him "We're going home now, Dad," and they stood and began to put on their coats. It was then that he made the same gasping breath that Doris had – once and then twice, and then silence, as the snow kept on falling.

꩜ ꩜ ꩜

For the genealogy enthusiast, the gathering of names and dates and facts is addicting, each search brand new and exciting. Once, would-be family historians sat in darkened rooms, threading rolls of microfilm onto metal spools and endlessly scrolling, jotting their findings into notebooks, thankful that the Mormon church saw it as a mandate to collect the kind of information connecting the living to the dead. Today, most people do their research at home on a computer, and genealogy has become big business. But no matter how the information is acquired, ultimately what most are seeking is their family story. A book is the pinnacle of that effort, a chance to analyze and interpret all the facts and clues and ultimately bring our ancestors to life.

When we wrote our previous family memoir, *The Occupied Garden*, we had no need for the genealogical tools of birth and death registers, census records or electoral rolls. Our story was set in relatively recent times – living memory for many of our family members. With *The Cowkeeper's Wish* we wanted to tell an older story, and most of those who'd lived it were long gone. So we began just as genealogists do: taking what we thought we knew (names, dates and places), then adding the anecdotes (the lore and the gossip) and searching out tangibles that might help us prove or disprove or discover (letters, photographs, keepsakes). Using the clues we found, we delved further, sometimes uncovering an important piece of our story. For example, the lore that our great-great-grandmother Mary Evans was called Lazy Mary on account of her husband always tying her boots, coupled with Mary's seeming disappearance from the census records after his demise, and the fact of the family's poverty, led us to search the Poor Law records to see if she might have ended up in the workhouse. Eventually we did find her there, a "pauper charwoman of Red X Street" residing at the Mint Street workhouse.

To tell a good family story there must be context, and there are many small bits of information that can be used to add colour and drama to the fabric of the tale. A census or marriage record often provides a person's occupation, so a bit of digging to find out exactly what a "moulder at Doulton Works" might have done and where he might have done it will bring some interesting information to light, especially if he dies of an illness so closely tied to his work, as did our Fred Roff.

Newspapers often yield great surprises; we found cowkeeper Benjamin Jones there, with his watery milk, running into trouble with the nuisance inspector. And while a search through newspapers of the day may not reward the genealogist with such specific mention of their ancestor, it could include a story about an incident at the factory he worked at – a strike, a bombing, a closure – and through that article the searcher can imagine the impact of the event on their protagonist. When Jack the Ripper began his murderous spree in Whitechapel, our Bebbie was a young woman living alone in the very area where he committed the deeds. A chilling connection, but of perhaps greater interest was the link that surfaced between our Vansons and the daughter of one of the murdered women. A good researcher, ever alert for clues, always notes the witnesses on marriage records, and we were curious when we noticed that one of the names on the Vansons' entry matched that of the daughter of a Ripper victim, identified in an account of the inquest into the death. A bit of cross-referencing and some further digging confirmed that indeed they were one and the same, a salacious little detail to add to our tale.

Pulling the focus further back and overlaying family events with the history of the time provides even greater perspective, and when personal information is unavailable from your family, other people's accounts of an historic event can enrich your own story. Our mother had passed down the tidbit that her Uncle Joe had been one of only a handful of survivors when the *Mary Rose* sank off the coast of Norway in World War I. A visit to the National Archives in London rewarded us with the ship's logs and a transcript of the inquest into the sinking – even our great-uncle's own few words – but additional sleuthing turned up crew photos and letters and descendants of other survivors who had information they generously shared.

For us, the authors, this collaboration has come to an end, but the story we've told has not and likely never will. We present it as just another snapshot in a collection – a group photo to which our narrative has added the colour.

ACKNOWLEDGEMENTS AND NOTES ON SOURCES

Our gratitude to the many who helped us in all sorts of ways, starting with our great-aunts Do and Mary Cartwright, and Bill and
Doris's children: Marilyn Charbonneau, Jean Gillman, Bill Cartwright,
and Jeff Cartwright. Thanks to our sister Heidi den Hartog, chief re-
search assistant, and our many cousins, for sharing their memories of
our grandparents. We're also grateful to other relatives and friends in
North America for their various contributions: Jim den Hartog and
Helen den Dekker, David Judd, Mary Lou Rigg-Kolano, Roger Hughes,
Julie Trimingham, Phil Dwyer, Janice Merrill, Thomas Balne, Gene
Kasaboski, and Jeff Winch. And to those in England for adding pieces
to our puzzle: Audrey Cook, Margaret Rawles, Bubblie Grubb, Hilary
Leamon, Susan Searle, Trevor Torkington, Kenneth Chamberlain, and
Sally Compobassi. To Pam Buttrey, author of *Cane Hill Hospital: The
Tower on the Hill*, David Payne at Southwark Cathedral, Chris Bennett
at the Croydon Local Studies Library, and Victoria Sloyan at London
South Bank University Archives. Thanks, too, to our many HMS *Mary
Rose* connections, including Joe Woodman, Carl Lewis, Peter Sketch-
ley, Sue Shpeley, Colin Morris, Madeleine Bone, and the intrepid Sue
Church. We're also grateful to Derek Fairbridge, and to Audrey McClel-
lan for her eagle eye, to the folks at Douglas & McIntyre, the Transatlan-
tic Literary Agency and the Canada Council.
     The following resources were essential to our research:

Ancestry.ca
Bexley Local Studies and Archive Centre
British Newspaper Archive, britishnewspaperarchive.co.uk

Casebook: Jack the Ripper, casebook.org
Charles Booth archive, London School of Economics Library
Charles Booth's London, booth.lse.ac.uk
Croydon Local Studies Library
D.B. Weldon Library, Western University
Imperial War Museum
Internet Archive, archive.org
Ivey Family London Room, London Public Library
    (London, ON)
Lives of the First World War, livesofthefirstworldwar.org
London Metropolitan Archives
National Archives, UK
Salvation Army International Heritage Centre
Southwark Local History Library
St. Bartholomew's Hospital Archives and Museum
Tower Hamlets Local History Library and Archives
Wellcome Library, wellcomelibrary.org

NOTES

Part 1

Chapter 1

22   **black holes**: John Hollingshead, *Ragged London* (London: Smith, Elder, 1861).

23   **poor ground** to **Christian sepulture**: Mrs. Basil Holmes, *The London Burial Grounds: Notes on Their History from Earliest Times to the Present Day* (New York: Macmillan, 1896).

24   **foul and filthy state**: "Convictions under the New Nuisances Removal Act," *Morning Post*, 26 September 1855.

24   **thoroughly ignorant**: *Report of the Medical Officer of Health for Southwark* (London: Vestry of St. George the Martyr, 1863), Wellcome Library.

24   **Sure I am**: *Report of the Medical Officer of Health for Southwark* (London: Vestry of St. George the Martyr, 1857), Wellcome Library.

25   **the cow with the iron tail**: John S. Farmer and W.E. Henley, *Slang and Its Analogues Past and Present*, vol. 2, *C to Fizzle* (London, 1891).

25   **highly artificial**: *Report of the Medical Officer of Health for Southwark* (London: Vestry of St. George the Martyr, 1866), Wellcome Library.

25   **mischievous state**: "The Vestry of St. George the Martyr," in *The Lancet Sanitary Commission on Workhouse Infirmaries* (London: The Lancet Office, 1866).

27   **as vile**: A. Welby Pugin, "The Present State of Ecclesiastical Architecture," *Dublin Review*, February 1842.

27   **free seats**: Mann, Horace. *Census of Great Britain, 1851: Religious Worship in England and Wales* (London: George Routledge, 1854).

27   **Here in Great Britain**: Edward Miall, *The British Churches in Relation to the British People* (London: Arthur Hall, Virtue, 1849).

29   **Flagrant**: "Flagrant Milk Adulteration," in *The Sanitary Record: A Journal of Public Health* (London: Smith, Elder, 1877).

29   **The defendant**: "The Police Courts," *London Daily News*, 4 July 1877.

30   **removable evil**: F.A. Rollo Russell, *London Fogs* (London: Edward Stanford, 1880).

31   **a terrible crash**: "Chronicle," *The Graphic*, 30 July 1870.

31   **Were the church thrown open**: "St Saviour's, Southwark," *Morning Post*, 22 July 1880.

32   **nothing original**: Augustus Hare, *Walks in London* (London: Daldy, Isbister, 1878).

32   **painful journey**: George Sims, *How the Poor Live* (London: Chatto and Windus, Piccadilly, 1889).

36   **a humble heroine**: "A Humble Heroine," *Reynolds's Weekly Newspaper*, 10 May 1885.

36   **Such a woman**: "Special Notes," *Reynolds's Weekly Newspaper*, 26 April 1885.

37   **The story I'm**: Mrs. Clement Nugent Jackson, *Gordon League Ballads* (London: Skeffington and Son, 1903).

37   **crushing sorrow…so willing**: "Her Majesty's Busy Life," *Penny Illustrated*, 20 June 1887.

37   **beings**: "The Classes, the Masses, and the Glasses," *Nineteenth Century: A Monthly Review*, December 1886.

37   **in different tones**: "The Royal College of Music," *Gloucester Journal*, 12 May 1883.

38   **perfectly disgraceful**: "Housing of the Working Classes," *Hansard's Parliamentary Debates*, 22 February 1884.

38   **Willy** and a **large family dinner**: Queen Victoria's journal, 22 June 1887, quoted in "A History of Jubilees" at www.royal.uk/history-jubilees.

39   **or rather, perhaps**: Charles Booth, *Life and Labour of the People in London*, 2nd series, *Industry* (London: Macmillan, 1903).

Chapter 2

44 **razzle-dazzle**: "The Cross Bones Burial Ground and the Razzle Dazzle," *Reynolds's Weekly*, 3 January 1892.
45 **That is no answer**: "A Workhouse Scandal," *Gloucestershire Citizen*, 15 November 1888.
47 **one of the most dreadful**: "The Murder in Whitechapel," *The Times*, 10 August 1888, viewable online at Casebook.org.
47 **bound to come**: Henrietta Barnett, *Canon Barnett: His Life, Work and Friends*, vol. 2 (London: John Murray, 1918).
47 **double event**: "A Mysterious Postcard," *North London News*, 6 October 1888.
49 **All right, old cock**: "The East-End Murders," *Lloyd's Weekly Newspaper*, 14 October 1888.
49 **otherwise Conway, otherwise Kelly**: "The East-End Murders," *Morning Post*, 4 October 1888.
49 **Were your addresses**: "The London Tragedies: Mitre Square Inquest," *Daily Telegraph*, 12 October 1888, viewable online at Casebook.org.
50 **weary of a vagabond life**: "The Burglary at Mrs. Lambert's Shop," *Hereford Times*, 13 December 1856.
50 **This was the first job**: "The Burglary at Mrs. Lambert's Shop," *Hereford Times*, 18 October 1856.
52 **more and more versed in sin**: Olive Nassau-Senior, "Mrs. Senior's Report," in *Boarding-Out and the Pauper Schools* (London: Henry S. King, 1875).
52 **gutter to poor rates**: "Entertainment to the Hanwell School Children," *London City Press*, 29 January 1870.
52 **It is from no want of kindness**: Southwark Apprenticeship Papers, 1875–1876, London, England, Poor Law and Board of Guardians Records, London Metropolitan Archives (LMA).
53 **George William Rapley**: "Long-Lost Relatives," *Lloyd's Weekly Newspaper*, 30 June 1889.
53 **James Boneer**: "Long-Lost Relatives," *Lloyd's Weekly Newspaper*, 26 May 1895.
53 **Matthew (Henry)**: "Long-Lost Relatives," *Lloyd's Weekly Newspaper*, 24 September 1893.
54 **the duty of the enumerator**: "The Census for 1891," *Oxford Journal*, 4 April 1891.
55 **The healing gift** to **Transplant**: Hill, Octavia, *Homes of the London Poor* (London: Macmillan, 1875).
57 **reasonable rents**: "Provision of Dwellings for the Working Classes," *55th Report from the Ecclesiastical Commissioners for England* (London, 1903).
57 **so dark**: "Interview with Miss Sheepshanks," George H. Duckworth's Notebook, District 31, June 1899, Charles Booth's London, London School of Economics (LSE) Library.
58 **They prowl about**: "The Bandit Gangs of London," *Pall Mall Gazette*, 13 October 1888.
58 **savage assault**: "Police Intelligence – Southwark," *Morning Post*, 28 July 1884.
59 **a discordant row**: "The Salvation Army," *Hull Daily Mail*, 15 November 1897.
59 **great annoyance**: B.G. Morley, *A History of Newington Lodge, 1849–1969* (London: Borough of Southwark Welfare Department, 1969).
60 **He has no right**: William Booth, "A Merry Christmas," *Salvation Soldiery* (London: International Headquarters, 1890).
60 **beating a drum**: From an article in *Bethnal Green Eastern Post*, November 1882, quoted in Robert Sandall, *The History of the Salvation Army*, vol. 2 (London: Thomas Nelson and Sons, 1947).
60 **the skeletons did**: From an article in *War Cry*, quoted in "The Skeleton Army in Potton," on the Bedfordshire Archives and Records Services website, bedsarchives.bedford.gov.uk.
60 **ordinary working**: William Booth, "How I Founded the Salvation Army," *Vancouver Daily World*, 1 October 1907.
61 **promoted to glory**: "The Funeral of Mrs. Booth," *Reynolds's Weekly*, 19 October 1890.
61 **a bird's-eye** to **if you put**: William Booth, *In Darkest England and the Way Out* (London: Funk and Wagnalls, 1890).
63 **behind a curtain**: Charles Booth, *Labour and Life of the People*, vol. 1, *East London* (London: Williams and Norgate, 1889).
63 **one middle-aged woman** to **a set of courts**: "Walk with H. Barton," George H. Duckworth's Notebook, District 31, May 1899, Charles Booth's London, LSE Library.
63 **vicious** to **fairly comfortable**: Charles Booth, *Labour and Life of the People*, vol. 1, *East London*.
64 **I certainly think**: Charles Booth, *Labour and Life of the People*, vol. 1, *East London*.

Chapter 3

68 **He'd bought a bed**: Joseph Tabrar, "He's Going to Marry Mary Ann" (1885).
68 **the pearl of kindness**: William Booth, "Every-Day Religion," *War Cry*, 22 September 1900.
68 **that heroic maid**: "Alice Ayres," *The Spectator*, 9 June 1888.
70 **a very rough lot**: "Interview with Reverend W.A. Morris, St Ann's Vicarage, South Lambeth Road, nd.," Notebook B92, Charles Booth's London, LSE Library.
71 **Potter's dust**: Jack London, *The People of the Abyss* (London: Macmillan, 1903).
72 **with drunken wives**: "Interview with H. Wyborn, Superintendent of the M or Southwark Division," George H. Duckworth's Notebook, District 31, March 1900, Charles Booth's London, LSE Library.
72 **I am a man**: Trial of Robert Plampton, 28 January 1884 (ref. no. t18840128-301), on the Proceedings of the Old Bailey website, www.oldbaileyonline.org.

72 **sincerely attached**: "Poor Law – Irremovability – Pauper Lunatic – Deserted Wife," *Magistrates' Cases Relating to Poor Law* (London: Stevens and Sons, 1906).

73 **constantly associating** and **visibly pregnant**: "Irremovability and Deserted Married Woman," *The Poor Law Officers' Journal*, April 1905. Included with Ellen's file at London, England, Poor Law and Board of Guardian Records, 1430–1930, LMA.

74 **pickles**: Charles Booth, *Life and Labour of the People in London*, 2nd series, *Industry* (London: Macmillan, 1903).

74 **Among grocers**: Charles Booth, *Life and Labour of the People in London*, 2nd series, *Industry*.

74 **a magnificent spectacle** to **abominable**: "The Prince of Wales in Southwark," *London Evening Standard*, 17 February 1897.

75 **It is an open secret**: "Notes – Mainly Personal," *Dundee Evening Telegraph*, 23 February 1897.

76 **a grave and gross**: "The St. George's Workhouse Inquiry," *British Medical Journal*, 21 September 1895.

79 **Flags and banners**: "South of the Thames," *Morning Post*, 23 June 1897.

79 **thin-faced and undersized**: "A Real Jubilee Eviction," *London Daily News*, 10 June 1897.

80 **A never-to-be**: *The Letters of Queen Victoria*, 3rd series, vol. 3, *1896–1901* (London: John Murray, 1932).

81 **By the time [the hill]**: Edward Balne, *Autobiography of an Ex-Workhouse and Poor Law School Boy*, 1972, Burnett Archive of Working Class Autobiographies, Brunel University, London.

81 **Sadness was in the air** and **forlorn**: Charlie Chaplin, *My Autobiography* (London: The Bodley Head, 1964).

82 **old clothes hawker**: Lunatic Reception Orders, Southwark, 1893, London, England, Poor Law and Board of Guardian Records, 1430–1930, LMA.

83 **desperado** and **The spectacle**: Charlie Chaplin, *My Autobiography*.

83 **the first heavy** to **Woe betide**: Edward Balne, *Autobiography of an Ex-Workhouse and Poor Law School Boy*.

84 **The word fascinated** and **Her presence**: Charlie Chaplin, *My Autobiography*.

85 **laxity of attention**: "Strange Death of a Girl," *Leigh Chronicle and Weekly Advertiser*, 8 December 1899.

85 **a pauper palace** to **For twenty-four years**: "Reports on the Hygienic Condition and Administration of Metropolitan District and Separate Schools," *British Medical Journal*, 13 March 1897.

85 **outings in the pure air**: Reports of the Medical Officer, Minutes of the Board, Central London School District, 18 July 1885, CLSD/011, LMA.

85 **If you take the case**: "Reports on the Hygienic Condition …," *British Medical Journal*, 13 March 1897.

87 **If you put your finger**: George Carpenter, *Chavasse's Advice to a Mother* (New York: George Routledge and Sons, 1898).

88 **dark, unfurnished**: Quoted in "A History of the Evelina" on the Historic Hospital Admission Records Project website (hharp.org).

89 **play a considerable part**: *Report of the Medical Officer of Health for Southwark* (London: Vestry of St. George the Martyr, 1896), Wellcome Library.

89 **The churches**: William Booth, "The General's New Year's Address," *War Cry*, 17 January 1883.

90 **maximum of health**: "Notes and Comments," *South London Press*, 3 November 1900.

90 **I would not like**: "Proposed Female Inspector," *Dundee Evening Post*, 6 June 1901.

91 **drastic purgatives**: George Carpenter, *Chavasse's Advice to a Mother*.

Chapter 4

95 **General J.F. Maurice**: "General J.F. Maurice on National Health," *Edinburgh Evening News*, 24 October 1902.

95 **the first element**: Arnold White, *Efficiency and Empire* (London: Methuen, 1901).

96 **a white veil**: "The Death of the Queen," *Gloucester Citizen*, 24 January 1901.

96 **The last moments**: Frederick Ponsonby, *Recollections of Three Reigns* (London: Eyre and Spottiswoode, 1951).

96 **She was so little**: Michael Balfour, *The Kaiser and His Times* (Boston: Houghton, Mifflin, 1964).

96 **I am afraid**: *The Letters of Queen Victoria*, 3rd series, vol. 3, *1896–1901* (London: John Murray, 1932).

97 **a powerful and potential**: "The Procession," *Western Gazette*, 8 February 1901.

97 **All those in Germany**: "Nipped in the Bud by the King," *Hull Daily Mail*, 6 February 1901.

97 **the grey mare**: "Counting Heads," *Burnley Express*, 16 March 1901.

98 **Hardly a week**: Article in *The Telegraph*, 12 October 1900, Southwark Local History Library and Archives.

98 **are to food**: Laura Nettleton Brown, *Scientific Living for Prolonging the Term of Human Life* (London: L.N. Fowler, 1909).

98 **Gelati, ecco un poco**: "Hokey Pokey of Yesterday," *Dundee Courier*, 7 June 1935.

100 **decimated by disease**: "A remarkable report …," *London Evening Standard*, 19 January 1894.

100 **a shocking state** to **as stunted**: "The 'Insanitary Area' in the Borough," *London Evening Standard*, 20 January 1894.

101 **It is essentially a playground**: George H. Duckworth's Notebook, District 31, March 1902, Charles Booth's London, LSE Library.

101 **drawing apples**: Alexander Paterson, *Across the Bridges* (London: Edward Arnold, 1915).

101 **human rabbit warren**: Charles Morley, *Studies in Board Schools* (London: Smith, Elder, 1897).

102   **I have allotted off a window**: London County Council, Education Officer's Department: Division 8, Lant Street School, 16 May 1902, LCC/DIV08/LAT, LMA.

102   **softens the manners** and **the three R's**: Charles Morley, *Studies in Board Schools.*

102–104   **The girls of Lant** to **the Borough boys'**: "A Master's Story," *London Daily News*, 1 February 1897.

105   **something in the blood**: "Interview with Mr. Bain, Headmaster of the Webber Road Board School," Notebook B/273, March 1899, Charles Booth's London, LSE Library.

105   **very sorry**: "London Labour Movements," *Reynolds's Weekly*, 19 June 1892.

106   **Somehow women**: "Interview with the Reverend C. Donaldson, Vicar of St. Mary's, Hackney, Wick," George H. Duckworth's Notebook, Police District 13, September 1897, Charles Booth's London, LSE Library.

106   **they don't do more**: "Interview with Sub-Divisional Inspector George Weidner," George H. Duckworth's Notebook, District 3, 28 October 1898, Charles Booth's London, LSE Library.

106   **The jam girls**: "Interview with H. Wyborn, Superintendent of the M or Southwark Division," George H. Duckworth's Notebook, District 31, March 1900, Charles Booth's London, LSE Library.

107   **vapour of the slum**: Alexander Paterson, *Across the Bridges.*

107   **Cold meat**: Norman Douglas, *London Street Games* (London: St. Catherine Press, 1916).

108   **Report re Wandering Lunatic**: City of London, Orders of Removal, Lunatic Admissions 1903–04, London, England, Poor Law and Board of Guardians Records, LMA.

108   **She is at the present**: City of London Mental Hospital [later Stone House Hospital], Patient Records, Female Casebooks, Casebook 14, 1902–1904, CLA/001/B/01/014, LMA.

108   **That there is an excess**: George H. Savage, *Insanity and Allied Neuroses* (London: Cassell, 1901).

109   **fairly good** to **Very agitated**: City of London Mental Hospital [later Stone House Hospital], Patient Records, Female Casebooks, Casebook 14, 1902–1904, CLA/001/B/01/014, LMA.

109   **an unnatural, inborn**: Selden Haines Talcott, *Mental Diseases and Their Modern Treatment* (New York: Boericke and Runyon, 1901).

110   **Dear Sir** and **Dearest Victor**: City of London Mental Hospital [later Stone House Hospital], Patient Records, Female Casebooks, Casebook 14, 1902–1904, CLA/001/B/01/014, LMA.

110–111   **diligent enquiry** to **Ellen Evans, properly Roff**: City of London, Orders of Removal, Lunatic Admissions 1903–1904, London, England, Poor Law and Board of Guardians Records, LMA.

112   **a landscape**: Isaac Ray, "Observations on the Principal Hospitals for the Insane," *American Journal of Insanity*, April 1846.

113   **It is by domestic**: J. Mortimer Granville, *The Care and Cure of the Insane* (London: Hardwicke and Bogue, 1877).

113   **Giant Despair**: Selden Haines Talcott, *Mental Diseases and Their Modern Treatment.*

113–115   **foolish jealousies** to **Weary of earth**: City of London Mental Hospital [later Stone House Hospital], Patient Records, Female Casebooks, Casebook 14, 1902–1904, CLA/001/B/01/014, LMA.

Chapter 5

117   **a choice-looking ruffian**: "Notes of a visit to the Salvation Army Elevator," Notebook B/283, 16 February 1900, Charles Booth's London, LSE Library.

118   **much more ignorant**: "Interview with Ensign H. Salter, officer in charge of the Borough corps of the Salvation Army," Notebook B/274, 13 March 1900, Charles Booth's London, LSE Library.

118–119   **devoted** to **God bless**: *The Bandsman and Songster*, 1907–1909, PER/3, Salvation Army International Heritage Centre.

119   **On a Saturday night**: "Bandsmen's Stories," *War Cry*, 25 December 1910.

121   **The old merchant**: H.G. Wells, *Tono-Bungay* (London: Macmillan, 1909).

122   **The fairly comfortable have left**: Charles Booth, *Life and Labour of the People in London*, 3rd series, *Religious Influences* (London: Macmillan, 1902).

122   **the outside peace**: *The Daily Graphic*, 1890, quoted on the Victorian Dictionary website, www.victorianlondon.org/entertainment/vauxhallpark.htm.

123   **The cornet**: *The Bandsman and Songster*, 1907–1909, PER/3, Salvation Army International Heritage Centre.

123   **improving wonderfully**: *The Local Officer*, 1897–1908, PER/12, Salvation Army International Heritage Centre.

123   **the best colour**: *The Bandsman and Songster*, 1907–1909, PER/3, Salvation Army International Heritage Centre.

124   **skillfully** and **The war**: William Booth, *Salvation Army Music* (London: Salvation Army Book Department, 1900).

124   **Every convert**: *The Local Officer*, 1897–1908, PER/12, Salvation Army International Heritage Centre.

125   **stifles the mind**: Arthur Symons, *A Book of Aspects* (London: 1909).

125–126   **plasticity** to **A good many children**: *Report of the Interdepartmental Committee on Physical Deterioration* (London: 1904).

127   **The rats**: Henrietta Barnett, *Canon Barnett: His Life, Work and Friends*, vol. 1 (London: John Murray, 1918).

128–130   **Round about** to **pauper funeral**: Maud Pember Reeves, *Round About a Pound a Week* (London: G. Bell and Sons, 1913).

131   **married women in London**: Clementina Black, *Married Women's Work* (London: G. Bell and Sons, 1915).

131   **raise the dignity**: "Lord Rosebery on the Dignity of Manual Labour," *Daily Telegraph and Courier*, 1 October 1892.

131   **of the most moderate character**: "Borough-road Polytechnic," *Morning Post*, 23 September 1892.

132   **by the kindness**: "Bright and Brief," *Western Times*, 25 April 1902.

133   **I don't care**: "Life in the Workhouse," *Reynolds's Newspaper*, 8 April 1900.

133   **Easy the descent**: Charles Booth, *Labour and Life of the People*, vol. 1, *East London* (London: Williams and Norgate, 1889).

133   **I have just been shown**: Homerton Workhouse: Book for Surprise Visits by the Guardians, 1900–1908, CBG/340, LMA.

134   **the only reason given**: "Occasional Notes," *Pall Mall Gazette*, 21 March 1879.

134   **octogenarian pedestrian**: "The Octogenarian Pedestrian," *Dundee Evening Telegraph*, 26 July 1904.

Chapter 6

137   **earnest and conscientious exertions**: Freedom admissions papers, 26 September 1905, COL/CHD/FR/02, LMA.

137   **no man of feeling** and **staggered**: "The General Honored," *War Cry*, 25 September 1905.

138   **like a pacific Caesar**: *Daily Express* quoted in "The King in Paris," *The Cornishman*, 7 May 1903.

138   **Edward the Encircler**: Wilhelm II, *The Kaiser's Memoirs* (New York/London: Harper and Brothers Publishers, 1922).

139   **the dear old City**: William Le Queux, *London: The Invasion of 1910* (London: Eveleigh Nash, 1906).

140   **strong and dignified**: "The Kaiser and the Anglo-German Friendship Committee," *The Advocate of Peace*, December 1907.

140   **a sincere pleasure to the Queen and myself**: "The Kaiser: State Banquet at Windsor," *Exeter and Plymouth Gazette*, 13 November 1907.

141   **an excellent way**: "Our Domestic Circle," *Manchester Courier*, 4 December 1908.

141   **rock with laughter**: F. Anstey, "London Music Halls," *Harper's New Monthly Magazine*, January 1891.

142   **completely lost to view**: Maud Pember Reeves, *Round About a Pound a Week* (London: G. Bell and Sons, 1913).

142–143   **foreign land** to **one sees the proprietor**: George R. Sims, "Off the Track in London: In Alien Land," *The Strand Magazine*, April 1904.

144   **Great improvement**: George H. Duckworth's Notebook, Police and Publican Districts 7, 8 and 9, 1898, Booth/B/351, Charles Booth's London, LSE Library.

144   **One sharp turn**: George R. Sims, "Off the Track in London: In Alien Land."

144–145   **because they have** to **Dear Sir**: *Report of the Royal Commission on Alien Immigration, with minutes of evidence and appendix* (London: Printed for HM Stationery Office, Wyman and Sons, 1903).

146   **to learn as much** to **worst parish**: Henrietta Barnett, *Canon Barnett: His Life, Work and Friends*, vol. 1 (London: John Murray, 1918).

147   **When a Christian**: *Report of the Royal Commission on Alien Immigration.*

147   **the Jewish question** to **The Christian would**: Ernest Carter, "Notes on the Jewish Question in Whitechapel," *Economic Review*, January 1901.

148   **I hold a parson's work**: Edward Mack and W.H.G. Armytage, *Thomas Hughes: The Life of the Author of Tom Brown's Schooldays* (London: Ernest Benn, 1952).

148   **the dirty**: Rosa Waugh Hobhouse, *Mary Hughes: Her Life for the Dispossessed* (London: Salisbury Square, 1949).

149   **We Hughes**: John Rennie, "A Friend of All in Need," *East End Life Newspaper*, 19 May 2014.

149   **in service lies greatness**: Muriel Lester, *It Occurred to Me* (London: Harper and Brothers, 1937).

149   **shabby and sometimes verminous**: Howard Spring, "Faithful Lives," *Quaker Faith and Practice*, 1949.

149   **was always telling us**: Rosa Waugh Hobhouse, *Mary Hughes: Her Life for the Dispossessed.*

149   **Suppose I keep**: Sydney W. Hart, "The Carters of Whitechapel," *Hackney Gazette*, 21 May 1963.

150   **a welter of rags**: Jack London, *The People of the Abyss* (London: Macmillan, 1903).

151   **a mixture of good**: George H. Duckworth's Notebook, Police and Publican Districts 7, 8 and 9, 1898, Booth/B/351, Charles Booth's London, LSE Library.

151   **Jews' pokers**: Jerry White, *The Rothschild Buildings* (London: Pimlico, 1980).

152   **a thoroughly vicious**: George H. Duckworth's Notebook, Police and Publican Districts 7, 8 and 9, 1898, Booth/B/351, Charles Booth's London, LSE Library.

152   **memory uncertain**: City of London Mental Hospital [later Stone House Hospital], Patient Records, Female Casebooks, Casebook 14, 1902–1904. CLA/001/B/01/014, LMA.

153   **It is for sweated work** and **Did you hear that**: "Women's Sunday," *Hull Daily Mail*, 24 June 1908.

153   **What's the old man doing?**: "In Hyde Park," *Western Times*, 23 June 1908.

153   **whether they be with us**: "No Vote, No Census," *Votes for Women*, 23 March 1911.

154   **cosy**: "Cosy Corners for Married Couples," *British Journal of Nursing*, 20 December 1902.

155   **I've found my destiny!**: "Peeps into the Past," *War Cry*, 25 February 1961.

155   **He was the finest-looking**: Harold Begbie, *Life of William Booth* (London: Macmillan, 1920).

155   **in the hope**: Henrietta Barnett, *Canon Barnett: His Life, Work and Friends*, vol. 1.
155   **The secret of cold**: William Booth, "Good Singing," *The Christian Mission Magazine*, August 1877.
156   **We dares not**: Richard Little Purdy and Michael Millgate, eds., *The Collected Letters of Thomas Hardy* (Oxford: Clarendon Press, 1980).
157   **the steady stream**: Karl Baedeker, *London and Its Environs* (London: Dulau, 1908).
157   **lined green** and **The music was much appreciated**: *The Bandsman, Songster and Local Officer*, 1910–1924, PER/3, Salvation Army International Heritage Centre.
159   **Death of His Majesty**: London County Council, Education Officer's Department: Division 8, Lant Street School, May 1910, LCC/DIV08/LAT, LMA.
159   **with a softness**: "Funeral Probably May 20," *New York Times*, 8 May 1910.

Chapter 7

164–165   **remarkably lively** to **Perhaps you may hear of two**: Article by George R. Sims aka Dagonet, for *Sunday Referee*, 1888, viewable online at Casebook.org.
166   **his curiosity was greater**: "The Passing of an Institution," *Gloucester Citizen*, 6 September 1922.
166   **These cuffs**: Article by George R. Sims aka Dagonet, for *Sunday Referee*, 1888, viewable online at Casebook.org.
166   **on the steady side**: "Interview with William Arthurson: cork sorter and notcher," 24 October 1894, Notebook B/82, Charles Booth's London, LSE Library.
167   **empty brown** to **sometimes the tramps**: Henrietta Barnett. *Canon Barnett: His Life, Work and Friends*, vol. 1 (London: John Murray, 1918).
168   **four-penny bits**: Jerry White, *The Rothschild Buildings* (London: Pimlico, 1980).
169   **my whole being**: Joseph Malaby Dent, *The Memoirs of J.M. Dent: 1849–1926* (London: J.M. Dent and Sons, 1928).
169   **top-hatty**: Alan Crawford, *C.R. Ashbee: Architect, Designer and Romantic Socialist* (New Haven, CT: Yale University Press, 2005).
169   **developing the high**: Henrietta and Samuel Barnett, *Practicable Socialism: Essays on Social Reform* (London: Longmans, Green, 1895).
170   **"A Life in Buildings"** to **Cheapness**: A Lady Resident, "A Life in Buildings," in *Life and Labour of the People in London*, 1st Series, Poverty (London: Macmillan, 1904).
171   **If you have water**: *Royal Commission on Housing of the Working Classes* (London: Eyre and Spottiswoode, 1885).
171   **In the great buildings**: *Royal Commission on Alien Immigration* (London: Printed for HM Stationery Office, Wyman and Sons, 1903).
172   **shuffling** and **As a rule**: "Suffrage Raiders," *The Times*, 19 November 1910.
173   **the weakest portion**: E. Sylvia Pankhurst, *The Suffragette Movement: An Intimate Account of Persons and Ideals* (London: Longmans, Green, 1931).
174   **improved**: City of London Mental Hospital [later Stone House Hospital], Patient Records, Female Casebooks, Casebook 14, 1902–1904, CLA/001/B/01/014, LMA.
175   **An army of women**: "No Vote, No Census," *Votes for Women*, 24 March 1911.
175   **the daughter of a sister**: Constance Lytton, South St. Pancras, London, 1911 England Census, The National Archives (TNA).
175   **Decline to give**: James S. Brown, South St. Pancras, London, 1911 England Census, TNA.
175   **apply Common Row**: Emily Wilding Davison, St. Margaret and St. John, London, 1911 England Census, TNA.
176   **we amused ourselves**: Emmeline Pankhurst, *My Own Story* (London: Eveleigh Nash, 1914).
176   **open your eyes**: "Census Humours," *Sheffield Daily Telegraph*, 3 April 1911.
176   **a delightful**: "The Florence Nightingale Memorial," *Votes for Women*, 7 April 1911.
178   **the most curious place**: "The Most Curious Place in England," *Royal Magazine*, May–October 1899.
178   **the most primitive corner**: "A Quaint Island near London," *Portsmouth Evening News*, 17 May 1901.
179   **pale-faced boys**: "Country Holiday Homes," *Sunday at Home* (Religious Tract Society), 1887.
181   **Prettily laid out**: Karl Baedeker, *London and Its Environs* (London: Dulau, 1908).
181   **On this lawn**: J.H. Rosney, "Socialism in London," *Harper's New Monthly Magazine*, vol. 76, 1888.
182   **There were no fireplaces**: Jerry White, *The Rothschild Buildings*.
182   **dust distributor**: Henrietta Barnett, *Canon Barnett: His Life, Work and Friends*, vol. 1.
183   **the number of foreign**: Inspector's Report, Whitechapel Commercial Street Council School, January 1910, ED 21/12130, TNA.
183–184   **necessitous** to **there are not many**: Report of the Medical Officer of Health for the London County Council, 1910, Wellcome Library.
186   **foreign children**: Inspector's Report, Whitechapel Commercial Street Council School, January 1910, ED 21/12130, TNA.

Chapter 8

189 **suicide**: "Deaths from Heat," *Aberdeen Journal*, 7 July 1911.
190 **No Work, No Rent**: "London Strike Ended," *Aberdeen Journal*, 12 August 1911.
190 **We are not white slaves**: "15,000 Women Out," *London Daily News*, 14 August 1911.
190 **drawn in to the staunch**: "Women Strikers of Bermondsey," *Morning Post*, 19 September 1911.
190 **no cane to adopting the methods**: "Fall in and Follow Us," *Dundee Evening Telegraph*, 13 September 1911.
191 **Never such a crowd**: *Daily News* quoted in "Coronation of George V," *The Cornishman*, 29 June 1911.
192 **with its pomp**: "Suffragette March," *Aberdeen Press and Journal*, 19 June 1911.
192 **England – Restive**: "England – Restive," *Hull Daily Mail*, 3 January 1912.
194 **Bandsman Deverill**: "Easter in Heaven," *War Cry*, 6 April 1912.
196 **the drudge of the family**: May Craske, "Girl Life in the Slum," *Economic Review*, April 1908.
197 **unsurpassed in cuisine**: "Shipping," *Yorkshire Post and Leeds Intelligencer*, 21 March 1912.
197 **shoveling out paupers**: "Colonisation and Emigration," *The Graphic*, 21 March 1891.
197 **Englishmen need not apply**: "Prospects in USA and Canada," *Hull Daily Mail*, 16 March 1912.
197 **cheerful reading to a few**: "Our London Letter," *Tamworth Herald*, 21 December 1901.
198 **William Lickfold**: Letter from the East End Emigration Fund found in Canadian Passenger Lists, March 1910, from Library and Archives Canada.
198 **the little families**: Rosa Waugh Hobhouse, *Mary Hughes: Her Life for the Dispossessed* (London: Salisbury Square 1949).
200 **It is useless**: George Behe, *On Board RMS* Titanic: *Memories of the Maiden Voyage* (Gloucestershire: The History Press, 2012).
200 **realized something**: Lawrence Beesley, *The Loss of the ss* Titanic (Boston: Houghton Mifflin, 1912).
201 **chummed to that awful**: George Behe, *On Board RMS* Titanic.
202 **thin, stooping to confidence all felt**: Lawrence Beesley, *The Loss of the ss* Titanic.
203 **quite by chance**: George Behe, *On Board RMS* Titanic.
203 **appeared out**: Josephine Robertha Watt, article in the Jefferson High School newspaper, 1917, quoted on the Encyclopedia Titanica website (www.encyclopedia-titanica.org/titanic-survivor/bertha-watt.html).
204–205 **a more than usually to a sea of faces**: Beesley, Lawrence, *The Loss of the ss* Titanic.
206 **heaps died**: George Behe, *On Board RMS* Titanic.
206 **Male, estimated age**: RMS Titanic Resource Guide at the Nova Scotia Archives website (novascotia.ca/archives/titanic).
206 **While [these details]**: Lawrence Beesley, *The Loss of the ss* Titanic.
206–207 **between the first shock and keen-eyed**: Obituary, *The Times*, 20 April 1912.
207 **just the one**: Obituary, *Oxford Magazine*, May 1912.
207 **in death to extraordinary beauties**: "St. Jude's: Memorials to the Rev. E.C. and Mrs. Carter," *East London Observer*, 28 December 1912.
208 **long and painful**: "Death of Canon Barnett," *Gloucester Journal*, 21 June 1913.
208 **To reply to so many**: Henrietta Barnett, *Canon Barnett: His Life, Work and Friends*, vol. 2 (London: John Murray, 1918).
208 **lady's good works and The General**: "Our London Letter," *Gloucester Citizen*, 22 August 1912.
209 **the irreparable loss**: Queen Alexandra, quoted in George S. Railton, *General Booth* (London: The Salvation Army Book Department, 1912).
209 **City men to With love**: "General Booth's Funeral," *Hull Daily Mail*, 29 August 1912.

Part 2

Chapter 9

213 **she threw herself**: Emmeline Pankhurst, *My Own Story* (London: Eveleigh Nash, 1914).
214 **a person unworthy**: Hate mail to Emily Wilding Davison from an Englishman, included in the Emily Wilding Davison Centenary Exhibit, LSE Digital Library (digital.library.lse.ac.uk/exhibitions/emily-wilding-davison-centenary).
214 **the price of liberty**: Emily Davison, "The Price of Liberty," *Votes for Women*, 5 June 1914.
216 **With commendable**: "Little Kirkcaldy Girl Knocked Down," *Dundee Courier*, 9 May 1914.
217 **in a low to The head mistress**: London County Council, Education Officer's Department, Inspectors Reports: Lant Street School, 1894, LCC/EO/PS/12/C/031, LMA.
218 **I regret very much**: London County Council, Education Officer's Department: Division 8, Lant Street School, 22 March 1907, LCC/DIV08/LAT, LMA.
219 **A few minutes**: Charles Booth, *Life and Labour of the People in London*, 2nd series, *Industry* (London: Macmillan, 1903).
219 **to acquaint**: Richard Mudie-Smith, comp., *Handbook of the Daily News Sweated Industries' Exhibition* (London: May 1906).

NOTES

219 **Boxes enter**: Thomas Holmes, "The Boxmakers," in *Handbook of the Daily News Sweated Industries' Exhibition*, compiled by Richard Mudie-Smith (London: May 1906).
220 **The temptation**: Clementina Black, *Sweated Industry and the Minimum Wage* (London: Duckworth, 1907).
220 **and it is commonplace**: Clementina Black, *Married Women's Work* (London: G. Bell and Sons, 1915).
221 **new expenses**: Philip Snowden, *The Living Wage* (London: Hodder and Stoughton, 1913).
222 **She was sent here**: Stephen M. Weissman, *Chaplin: A Life* (New York: Arcade Publishing, 2011).
222 **She is very strange**: Lunatic Reception Orders, Lambeth, 1904–1905, London, England, Poor Law and Board of Guardian Records, 1430–1930, LMA.
222 **almost unbearable to it was without enthusiasm**: Charlie Chaplin, *My Autobiography* (London: The Bodley Head, 1964).
224 **a threat that goes on**: H.G. Wells, *Mr. Britling Sees It Through* (New York: Macmillan, 1916).
224 **World Wide War to for the first time**: "World Wide War," *Western Times*, 6 August 1914.
225 **War to the appearance of the German fleet**: Headline and article in *Manchester Courier*, 5 August 1914.
226 **Are *you* reading to stupendous drama**: Advertisements in *Western Gazette*, 2 October 1914.
226 **The great war**: Herbert Wrigley Wilson, *The Great War: The Standard History of the All-Europe Conflict* (London: Amalgamated Press, 1914).
226 **I can see them again**: "The British Force," *Sheffield Evening Telegraph*, 18 August 1914.
227 **Song of the Moment**: "Tipperary: Song of the Moment," *Hull Daily Mail*, 20 August 1914.
227 **Marching Anthem**: "It's A Long, Long Way to Tipperary," *Warwick and Warwickshire Advertiser*, 20 March 1915.
227 **They will wear**: "War News in Brief," *Essex Newsman*, 22 August 1914.
227 **With the exception**: "Lightning Soap," *Essex County Chronicle*, 28 August 1914.
227 **Those who intended**: "Arthur Wood and Sons," *Surrey Mirror*, 1 September 1914.
227 **everywhere women will have to**: "The Task Before Women," *Votes for Women*, 7 August 1914.
228 **the army of charwomen to therefore in her hour**: Clementina Black, *Married Women's Work*.
229 **seized with giddiness**: Article in *South London Press*, 17 October 1914.
229 **The world loses more**: Henrietta Barnett, *Canon Barnett: His Life, Work and Friends*, vol. 1 (London: John Murray, 1918).
229 **a feeling of utter**: Charles Booth, *Old Age Pensions and the Aged Poor: A Proposal* (London: Macmillan, 1906).
230 **not being likely**: Charles Roff, First World War Service Records, WO 363, TNA.
230 **petticoats for all**: "Petti-coats for Able-Bodied Youths," *Western Gazette*, 4 September 1914.
230 **Oyez! Oyez**: "Oyez, Oyez, Oyez!" *Western Gazette*, 4 September 1914.
231 **storm of noise**: Llewelyn Wyn Griffith, *Up to Mametz and Beyond* (Yorkshire: Pen and Sword Military, 1931).
231 **It did not move**: R.H. Tawney, "The Attack," *Westminster Gazette*, August 1916.
231 **a diabolical and sustained crescendo**: Henri Barbusse, trans William Fitzwater Wray, *Under Fire: The Story of a Squad* (London: J.M. Dent and Sons, 1917).
231 **a symphony**: R.H. Tawyney, "The Attack."
232 **every boy**: *The Navy List* (London: J.J. Keliher, 1915).
232 **the Women of Britain**: "To the Women of Britain," Poster No. 55, Parliamentary Recruiting Committee (London: Romwell Press, 1915), Art.IWM PST 4884, Imperial War Museum (IWM).
232 **Do you realise**: Poster accompanying the article "Why Aren't You in Khaki?" *Daily Mail*, 27 February 2014.
232–233 **of robust frame to a band of black crepe**: *The Navy List*.
235 **Directions for Knitting**: John Paton, Son and Company, "Directions for Knitting Soldiers' and Sailors' Comforts" (Glasgow: Maclare, Macdonald, 1914).
236 **of unusual shape and We knitted in theatres**: Constance Peel, *How We Lived Then: 1914–1918, A Sketch of Social and Domestic Life in England During the War* (London: The Bodley Head, 1929).
236 **anyone lending the book**: Olive Whiting, *Khaki Knitting Book* (New York: Allies Special Aid, 1917).
236 **Socks**: Jessie Pope, *Jessie Pope's War Poems* (London: Grant Richards, 1914).
237 **we have blown up**: "Two Bombs for Chancellor," *Birmingham Daily Gazette*, 20 February 1913.
237 **he is always betraying us**: "Bomb Outrage," *Manchester Courier*, 21 February 1913.
237 **Once They Were**: "The Ablest Woman, the Ablest Man in England," *Los Angeles Herald*, 19 November 1915.
237 **So grave**: "The Women's Great Procession," *Daily Mirror*, 12 July 1915.
237 **one of the most successful**: "What a Ripping Speech, Daddy," *Western Daily Press*, 19 July 1915.
238 **Shells made by a wife**: "Women and the War," *Western Gazette*, 23 July 1915.
238 **The women of this**: "Without the Help of Women Victory Tarries," *Dundee Courier*, 19 July 1915.
238 **no person shall**: "At the Court at Buckingham Palace," *Supplement to The London Gazette*, 1 September 1914.
239 **There isn't a big Power**: H.G. Wells, *The War in the Air* (London: George Bell and Sons, 1908).
239 **not yet convinced**: "The First German Air Raids of England," in *The Times History of the War*, vol. 7 (London: The Times, 1916).
240 **It is far better**: "It is far better," Publicity Department, Central London Recruiting Depot, Whitehall, 1914–1916, Art.IWM PST 12052, IWM.

442

240 **any hostile**: "The First German Air Raids of England," *The Times History of the War*, vol. 7.
240 **the heart of the city**: "The Zeppelin Raid," *Western Gazette*, 4 June 1915.
241 **take shelter**: "Public Warning," Official Aircraft Warning Poster, 1915, Art.IWM PST 2785, IWM.
241 **as not only**: Alfred Rawlinson, *The Defence of London 1915–1918* (London: Andrew Melrose, 1923).
242 **We don't want**: Paul A. Rubens, "Your King and Country Want You" (London: Chappell Music, 1914).
243 **brilliantly** and **Traffic**: "The First German Air Raids of England," *The Times History of the War*, vol. 7.
244–245 **I feel quite confident** and **fell close together**: Alfred Rawlinson, *The Defence of London*.
245 **working class property**: "The Zeppelin Raid," *Newcastle Journal*, 18 October 1915.
246 **The youngest was dead**: Henry Keatley Moore and William Berwick Sayers, *Croydon and the Great War* (Croydon: Corporation of Croydon and Central Public Library, 1920).
246–247 **I was shivering** to **all was dark**: "Impressions of the airship raids over London on 8 September and 13 October 1915, as recorded the next day by boys of Princeton Street, Elementary School, Holborn," digitized letters, Add. MS 39257-39258, British Library.
248 **Look at William**: E.V. Lucas and Geo. Morrow, *Swollen Headed William (After the German!)* (London: Methuen, 1915).
249 **to induce** and **If this effort**: "Lord Derby Makes a Direct Appeal," *Dundee Courier*, 22 October 1915.
249 **If the man**: André Chevrillon, *England and the War* (New York: Doubleday, Page, 1917).
250 **Lor', how I wish**: "The Conscript," *Aberdeen Weekly Journal*, 19 November 1915.

Chapter 10

254 **Sure a little bit of wastage**: "Scapa Flow. A Hymn of Hate," *The Orcadian*, 5 December 1918. Quoted in C.W. Burrows, *Scapa and a Camera* (London: Country Life, 1921).
254 **What we have to do** and **After the most terrible**: "Turning the Balance!" *Daily Mail*, 5 June 1916.
255 **after relating our losses**: "Sharply Criticise British Excuses," *Harrisburg Telegraph*, 3 June 1916.
255 **The records give**: Rudyard Kipling, "Echoes of Jutland Battle," *Western Daily Press*, 19 October 1916.
255 **One comprehends**: Rudyard Kipling, "Destroyers in Jutland Fight," *Leeds Mercury*, 19 October 1916.
256 **Daddy**: "Daddy, what did *you* do in the Great War?" Poster No. 79, Parliamentary Recruiting Committee (London: Johnson, Riddle, 1915), Art.IWM PST 0311, IWM.
256 **How will you fare**: Harold Begbie, "Fall In," September 1914, Art.IWM PST 12115, IWM.
257 **shirkers**: "Tribunal at Work," *Burnley Express and Advertiser*, 17 May 1916.
257 **slackers** and **hiding behind**: "Slackers and 'Slackers,'" *North-Eastern Daily Gazette*, 19 June 1916.
258 **two Zepps an' a cloud**: "War Parlance," *The Tatler*, 17 March 1915.
258 **poisonous** and **a suitable costume**: "The Girls on Munitions," *Yorkshire Evening Post*, 16 September 1916.
258 **Bill and Dan**: "Drama of a Gas Factory," 5 August 1919, Clipping from unidentified newspaper in Southwark Local History Library.
258 **Quiet for the Wounded**: "The Medical Services on the Home Front," September 1914, Q 53311, IWM.
258 **poisonous** and **a suitable costume**: "The Girls on Munitions," *Yorkshire Evening Post*, 16 September 1916.
260 **scientific preparations**: "The 'Food' That Everybody Is Talking About," *Derby Daily Telegraph*, 28 July 1917.
260 **Anxiety for relatives**: "War-Strain," *Yorkshire Evening Post*, 4 April 1916.
260 **All Munition Badges**: "All Munition Badges to be Returned – Drastic Government Action," *Aberdeen Evening Express*, 20 December 1916.
261 **When You Wore**: Jack Mahoney and Percy Wenrich, "When You Wore a Tulip and I Wore a Big Red Rose" (New York: Leo Feist, 1914).
261 **Alleged** to **to daughter**: Admissions and Applications, Newington Institution, December 1916 to January 1917, SOBG 11-4, LMA.
262 **the flower**: Battle Honours Plaque for HMS Mary Rose, Photograph Q 58500, IWM.
263 **mail runs**: Lewis R. Freeman, "Against Odds," in *Sea Hounds* (New York: Dodd, Mead, 1919).
263 **Passed derelict**: Ship's Logs: *Mary Rose*, 14 January 1917, ADM 53/48832, TNA.
264 **I am still shaking**: Georgina Lee, *Home Fires Burning: The Great War Diaries of Georgina Lee* (Stroud: Sutton Publishing, 2006).
264 **the whole heavens**: Graham Hill and Howard Bloch, *The Silvertown Explosion: London 1917* (Stroud: Tempus Publishing, 2003).
265 **Here, too, hot**: "Neighbourly Hospitality," *War Cry*, 27 January 1917.
265 **a huge workshop**: "Lord Mayor and Birmingham's Efforts," *Birmingham Daily Post*, 21 December 1915.
266 **and getting** to **The heroism**: L.K. Yates, *The Woman's Part: A Record of Munitions Work* (New York: George H. Doran Company, 1918).
267 **winning** and **It is realized**: "Lloyd George's Winning Way," *Dundee Courier*, 8 December 1916.
267 **The New Conductor**: Leonard Raven-Hill, "The New Conductor," *Punch Magazine*, 20 December 1916.
267 **keen and zealous** to **Very able**: Royal Navy Officers 1899–1919, ADM 196/143, TNA.
269 **fresh impressions**: R.G.R. Evans, *Keeping the Seas* (New York: Frederick Warne, 1920).
270 **something of the**: E. Keble Chatterton, *Q-Ships and Their Story* (London: Sidgwick and Jackson, 1922).
270 **Stopped**: Ship's Logs: *Mary Rose*, 1 May 1917, ADM 53/48834, TNA.
271 **it was a favourite**: E. Keble Chatterton, *Q-Ships and Their Story*.

271 **Picked up**: Ship's Logs: *Mary Rose*, 1 May 1917, ADM 53/48834, TNA.
271 **a graveyard**: Charles Minor Blackford, *Torpedoboat Sailor* (Annapolis, MD: United States Naval Institute, 1968).
272–273 **At Sea to the authorities**: Joseph Taussig, *The Queenstown Patrol, 1917: The Diary of Commander Joseph Knefler Taussig, US Navy* (Newport, RI: Naval War College Press, 1996).
273–274 **like beavers to Surely we had seen**: J.K. Taussig, "Destroyer Experiences During the Great War," *United States Naval Proceedings*, January 1923.
275 **it seemed that the vessel**: J.K. Taussig, "Destroyer Experiences During the Great War."
275 **We learned to understand**: "Romantic Re-union," *Hull Daily Mail*, 19 November 1929.
275 **he saw us waking**: Ernst Hashagen, *U-boats Westward!* (New York: G.P. Putnam's Sons, 1931).
276 **Do you mean**: J.K. Taussig, "Destroyer Experiences During the Great War."
276 **the film sensation**: "The Inner Circle," *Sunday Post*, 20 May 1917.
277 **11:15 pm**: Ship's Logs: *Mary Rose*, July 1917, ADM 53/48835, TNA.

Chapter 11

281 **a great State Hospital**: "The Hospital World," *British Journal of Nursing*, 30 August 1913.
282 **in a dying condition**: Lambeth Guardians Minute Book, 1917, LABG-1, LMA.
282 **I personally examined**: Examination Book, Lambeth Infirmary, LABG-5, LMA.
283 **moving picture comedian**: World War 1 Draft Cards: Charlie Chaplin, National Archives at Atlanta.
283 **struggling young nondescript to It was a depressing day**: Charlie Chaplin, *My Autobiography* (London: The Bodley Head, 1964).
284 **peculiar and stupid**: Walter William Sutton, First World War Service Records, WO 363, TNA.
284 **little to say**: George John Lammie, First World War Service Records, WO 363, TNA.
284 **antiquated terms**: Maurice Craig, *Psychological Medicine* (London: J and A Churchill, 1917).
285 **The patient is unable to able to appreciate**: J.M. Moody, "The New County Asylum," presented to the Court of Quarter Sessions in 1883 and quoted on the Cult of Cane Hill website (http://www.simoncornwell.com/urbex/projects/ch/doc/moody1.htm).
285 **strong clothing**: "Notes and News," *Journal of Mental Science*, 33 (April 1887).
285 **How will this**: "Obituary: Sir Frederick Needham," *British Medical Journal*, 20 September 1924.
286 **with energy to the patients throughout**: Cane Hill – signed minutes, 1916–1918, LCC/MIN/889, LMA.
287 **Let's put the doctor**: "Unconsidered Trifles," *Hastings and St. Leonards Observer*, 11 July 1903.
288 **workhouse child and It is absolutely**: Central London District Schools, Hanwell, 1901 England Census, TNA.
288 **the Assistant Matron**: Cane Hill – signed minutes, 1916–1918, LCC/MIN/889, LMA.
289 **impressive noise to with perfect clearness**: H.A. Jones, *The War in the Air: Being the Story of the Part Played in the Great War by the Royal Air Force*, vol. 5 (Oxford: Clarendon Press, 1935).
289 **I thought I was being buried**: "Daylight Murder," *Western Daily Press*, 16 June 1917.
290 **the children behaved**: London County Council, Education Officer's Department: Division 8, Charles Dickens School, 13 June 1917, LCC/DIV08/CHA/LB/002, LMA.
290 **During danger**: "To Protect the Children," *Flight: First Aero Weekly in the World*, 12 July 1917.
290 **theatres and thinking of them**: "Funeral of the Children Killed by Bombs," *Yorkshire Evening Post*, 20 June 1917.
291 **Nicky**: Angus Holden, *Four Generations of Our Royal Family* (London: George Allen and Unwin, 1937).
291 **a continental name**: "Anti-German Riots in London," *Leeds Mercury*, 9 July 1917.
291 **WE ARE RUSSIANS**: Joanna Bourke, "Another Battle Front," *Guardian*, 11 November 2008.
292 **relinquishing the use**: "The House of Windsor," *Globe*, 17 July 1917.
292 **Made in Germany**: Leonard Raven-Hill, "Made in Germany," *Punch Magazine*, 27 June 1917.
292 **I, Albert Henry Crawshaw**: "Change of Surname," *London Gazette*, 28 February 1919.
292 **He began to**: Charles Frederick William Fray, First World War Service Records, WO 363, TNA.
293 **confusional insanity**: "Schedules of Forms of Insanity," Commissioners in Lunacy, 1907, Health Archives and Records Group.
293 **organic dementia**: Maurice Craig, *Psychological Medicine*.
293 **things did not fit**: D. Maxwell Ross, "Notes on the Case of a Cyst," *British Journal of Psychiatry*, April 1917.
293 **act[ed] like a charm**: Henry J. Berkley, *A Treatise on Mental Diseases* (London: Henry Kimpton, 1901).
294 **In some cases the amnesia to our nervous system**: Maurice Craig. *Psychological Medicine*.
294 **hereditary insanity and one cannot**: "Hereditary Insanity," *Luton Times and Advertiser*, 27 May 1910.
296 **Then everyone quickened**: H.K. Moore and W.B. Sayers, *Croydon and the Great War* (Croydon: Corporation of Croydon and Central Public Library, 1920).
296 **in a few moments magnificent**: Alfred Rawlinson, *The Defence of London 1915–1918* (London: Andrew Melrose, 1923).
297 **no shelter is bomb proof**: Air raid notice from undated clipping, Southwark Local History Library and Archives.
297 **tube camps**: *Daily Mail* clipping in WW1 diary of Lydia Peile, private papers of Mrs. L. Peile, 1916–1917, Documents.2589, IWM.

Chapter 12

302   **salvo answering**: Lewis R. Freeman, "Against Odds," in *Sea Hounds* (New York: Dodd, Mead, 1919).
302   **I think it's a submarine**: Loss of HMS Mary Rose, October 1917, ADM 137/3692, TNA.
304   **Stick it**: Lewis R. Freeman, "Against Odds."
304   **German Fast**: "German Fast Raiders' Criminal Inhumanity," *Yorkshire Evening Post*, 20 October 1917.
304   **Crews Left**: "Crews Left to Drown," *Birmingham Daily Mail*, 20 October 1917.
304   **no effort**: "North Sea Scrap," *Nottingham Evening Post*, 20 October 1917.
304   **It is regretted**: "Crews Left to Drown," *Birmingham Daily Mail*, 20 October 1917.
306   **Go it!**: Loss of HMS Mary Rose, October 1917, ADM 137/3692, TNA.
306   **God bless** and **Every man**: Loss of HMS Mary Rose, October 1917, ADM 137/3692, TNA.
306   **Little Mary**: Private Papers of Engineer Lieutenant-Commander W.H. Cleghorn, RN, Document 753, IWM.
308   **We were a good deal**: Lewis R. Freeman, "Against Odds."
308   **True love**: William MacLeod, Royal Navy Registers of Seamen's Services, ADM/188/374/213752, TNA.
309   **biscuits** to **I don't just**: Lewis R. Freeman, "Against Odds."
309   **probably...the sole**: "Where is the British Fleet?" *Birmingham Daily Mail*, 22 October 1917.
310   **Brave Hearts**: "Brave Hearts on the Mary Rose," *Daily Mail/Yorkshire Evening Post*, 25 October 1917.
310   **as to need for secrecy**: Loss of HMS Mary Rose, October 1917, ADM 137/3692, TNA.
310   **At any time** to **It is the cause**: Loss of HMS Mary Rose, October 1917, ADM 137/3692, TNA.
312–313   **In the Ward Room** to **you will quite understand**: Private Papers of Engineer Lieutenant-Commander W.H. Cleghorn, RN, Document 753, IWM.
314   **It was a gruesome**: R. Bedwell, *The Chatham Air Raid: Events of Monday, 3rd September, 1917*, Drill Hall Library, Chatham.
314   **in the interests**: "Destroyers Lost in North Sea," House of Commons Debate, vol. 99, col. 1991, 28 November 1917.
315–316   **What was the *Mary*** to **I am proud**: Loss of HMS Mary Rose and HMS Strongbow, October 1917 to February 1918, ADM 137/3723, TNA.

Chapter 13

319   **truly one** and **that awful Crown**: "The Late Tsar Nicholas," *Aberdeen Daily Journal*, 22 July 1918.
319   **live henceforth**: "Treaty of Brest-Litovsk," 3 March 1918, on the Avalon Project website (http://avalon.law.yale.edu/20th_century/brest.asp).
320   **clarion call**: "The Nation at War," *Gloucestershire Chronicle*, 20 April 1918.
320   **many among us**: "Our Backs to the Wall," *Surrey Mirror*, 19 April 1918.
320   **Save the wheat**: "Save the Wheat and Help the Fleet," Ministry of Food, 1917 (London: Hazel Watson and Viney), Art.IWM PST 4470, IWM.
320   **Eat Less Bread**: "Doing Their Bit," *Punch Magazine*, 26 September 1917.
322   **God Speed the Plough**: "National Service," Women's Land Army, 1917 (London: David Allen and Sons), Art.IWM PST 5996, IWM.
322   **We Are All Fit**: "The Women's Army," *Manchester Evening News*, 13 May 1918.
322   **You are doing a man's work**: *Women's Land Army LAAS Handbook* (c 1917), quoted at womenslandarmy.co.uk.
322   **particularly well**: "The Women's Army," *Manchester Evening News*, 13 May 1918.
323   **It is hard work**: Barbara McLaren, *Women of the War* (London: Hodder and Stoughton, 1917).
323   **Make your motto**: "A Land Woman's Appeal to All Women in the Land," recruiting poster from c 1917, at womenslandarmy.co.uk.
324   **very rapidly**: N.R. Grist, "Pandemic Influenza 1918," *British Medical Journal*, 22 December 1979.
324   **trench fever**: "House and Home," *Hull Daily Mail*, 27 June 1918.
324   **the city of sneezes**: "City of Sneezes," *Edinburgh Evening News*, 22 June 1918.
325   **fortif[y] the system**: "Oxo," *Liverpool Daily Post*, 31 October 1918.
325   **If the influenza fiend**: "Let Your Bicycle Help You Recuperate," *People's Journal*, 17 August 1918.
326   **scavenger**: John Lett, St. George the Martyr, Southwark, 1901 England Census, TNA.
326–327   **His Majesty**: "What's That on His Sleeve? An Overseas Service Chevron," on the Long, Long Trail website (http://www.longlongtrail.co.uk/soldiers/how-to-research-a-soldier/tips-for-interpreting-photographs-of-men-in-uniform).
328   **death presumed**: Lorenzo Bottone, UK Army, Registers of Soldiers' Effects, 16 August 1917, National Army Museum.
328   **for all those soldiers**: "British Army Reserves and Reservists," on the Long, Long Trail website (http://www.longlongtrail.co.uk/soldiers/a-soldiers-life-1914-1918/enlisting-into-the-army/british-army-reserves-and-reservists/).
329   **must never be done**: Vera Brittain, *A Testament of Youth* (London: Victor Gollancz, 1933).
329   **a counter-revolutionary**: "Ex-Czar of Russia Killed by Order of Ural Soviet," *New York Times*, 20 July 1918.

NOTES

330   **I hear from Russia** and **the blood**: Miranda Carter, *George, Nicholas and Wilhelm: Three Royal Cousins and the Road to World War I* (New York: Alfred A. Knopf, 2010).
330   **a typical Bolshevist**: "The Late Tsar Nicholas," *Aberdeen Daily Journal*, 22 July 1918.
330   **All Germans Pushed**: "All Germans Pushed Back Over the Marne," *New York Times*, 20 July 1918.
330   **a man of almost**: "The Late Tsar Nicholas," *Aberdeen Daily Journal*, 22 July 1918.
330–331   **the sun was hot** to **stripped to the waist**: Robert Ward, "Weather Controls over the Fighting during the Summer of 1918," *Scientific Monthly*, October 1918.
331   **a brilliant** to **All they hope for**: Philip Gibbs, "Breaking the Hindenburg Line: An Eye-Witness Statement Issued August 7th," in *Source Records of the Great War*, vol. 6, *1918* ([New York]: National Alumni, 1923).
332   **even if it should**: Arthur J. Marder, *From the Dreadnought to Scapa Flow*, vol. 5, *Victory and Aftermath* (London: Oxford University Press, 1970).
332   **the King and Kaiser**: "Germany Declares Herself a Republic: Proclamation of November 9th," in *Source Records of the Great War*, vol. 6, *1918* ([New York]: National Alumni, 1923).
332   **At every station**: "Germany Declares Herself a Republic: Count Detlef von Moltke," in *Source Records of the Great War*, vol. 6, *1918* ([New York]: National Alumni, 1923).
332   **Kaiser Bolts**: "Kaiser Bolts to Holland," *Birmingham Mail*, 11 November 1918.
332   **Kaiser Signs**: "Kaiser Signs 'With a Shiver,'" *Lancashire Evening Post*, 11 November 1918.
332   **Last Shot**: "Last Shot Fired at 11 a.m. Today," *Nottingham Evening Post*, 11 November 1918.
332   **End of the Great War**: "End of the Great War," *Lincolnshire Echo*, 11 November 1918.
333   **wreathed in smiles**: "London's Rejoicings," *Manchester Evening News*, 11 November 1918.
333   **a huge Cockney chuckle**: "Celebrating Armistice Day," *Hull Daily Mail*, 12 November 1918.
333   **Flags appeared**: "How London Celebrated Great Day of Victory," *Daily Mirror*, 12 November 1918.
333   **the dead were dead**: Vera Brittain, *A Testament of Youth*.
334   **war plague**: "Notes on the Day," *Devon and Exeter Gazette*, 26 October 1918.
337   **lasting disgrace** and **a real blessing**: Arthur J. Marder, *From the Dreadnought to Scapa Flow*, vol. 5, *Victory and Aftermath*.

Part 3

Chapter 14

343   **afford a cooling**: Pat Morden, "London Has Special Claim to 'Forest City,'" *London Free Press*, 25 June 2011.
344–345   **the curse of the Empire** to **Why do you send**: "An Indictment of the Londoner," *Yorkshire Post and Leeds Intelligencer*, 7 December 1908.
348   **air was heavy** to **newly married**: George H. Duckworth's Notebook, Police District 48, 1900, B/376, Charles Booth's London, LSE Library.
350–351   **queer all night** to **Suicide**: "Boy's Suicide on the Railway at Belvedere," *Erith Times*, 20 February 1903.
351   **perfectly harmless** to **overawed**: "Interview with the Boy's Mother," *Erith Times*, 20 February 1903.
353   **It requires only**: Frederick Whymper, *The Sea: Its Stirring Story of Adventure, Peril and Heroism* (London: Cassels, Petter, Galpin, 1877).
354   **Canada! Canada!**: Advertisement in *Gloucestershire Echo*, 18 February 1907.
358   **My own darling wiffie**: Herbert Thomas Mantell, postcards from August to October 1914, No. 2003-12-21, National Army Museum.
359   **the need for army surgeons** and **Nobody can foretell**: Articles in *Western University Gazette*, November 1915.
361   **Soldiers of the Soil**: "SOS," Canada Food Board poster (Toronto: Harris Lithograph, 1914–1918).
361   **Patriotic Canadians**: "Are You Breaking the Law?" Canada Food Board poster (Hamilton, ON: Howell Lithograph, 1914–1918).
361   **How to Live**: "How to Live in Wartime," pamphlet (Ottawa: National Service Board, 1917).
362   **London Cut Loose**: "London's Day of Thanksgiving and Rejoicing Greatest in Its History," *The London Advertiser*, 12 November 1918.
364   **creamy sound**: "Carmen Lombardo Dead at 67," *New York Times*, 18 April 1971.

Chapter 15

368   **to provide a ministry**: "Egerton Street Gospel Hall," *The Orb* (London Bible Institute), 1943.
368   **Down in the valleys**: James Rowe and Daniel B. Towner, "Tell of the Love of Jesus," in *Hymns That Help in Sunday Schools, Young People's Societies, and Other Church Services* (New York: Lorenz Publishing, 1903).
370   **Back to Civvies** and **The Khaki Guide**: Mentioned in *This Hour of Trial and Sorrow: The Great War Letters of the Leonard Family* (London, ON: University of Western Ontario, 2016).
374   **little soldier** to **rich in love**: Mrs. Henry Clarke, *Into Stormy Waters* (London: Sunday School Union, 1901).
375   **hot fox trots** to **follow the crowd**: Items in the Jack Pudney section on the Big Band Sounds of London Ontario website (http://londonbigbands.ca/pudneyjack.htm).

446

375   **silken smooth**: Frank and Nancy Prothero, *How Sweet It Was: Fifty Years at the Stork Club* (Port Stanley, ON: Nan-Sea Publications, 1979).

377   **ensure**: "Overseas Settlement Committee," *Labour Gazette* (Department of Labour Canada), June 1924.

378   **if there is not enough work**: "Unemployed Women," *The Scotsman*, 10 March 1919.

380   **flocking to Ontario**: "Many Domestics Arriving," *London Free Press*, 24 August 1923.

380–381   **sadly** and **the mateless**: "Subsidies and the British Immigrant," *London Free Press*, 30 August 1923.

381   **She says she knows**: "English Girl Seeks Canadian Husband," *London Free Press*, 29 August 1923.

382   **the natural dumping ground**: Rebecca Coulter and Ivor Goodson, *Rethinking Vocationalism: Whose Work/Life Is It?* (Toronto: James Lorimer, 1993).

383   **Talking is not**: *MemoraBealia: 75th Anniversary Edition* (London, ON: H.B. Beal Secondary School, 1987).

Chapter 16

388   **This building…we now certify**: Family Collection.

390   **dear little Bognor**: "A Short History of Bognor-Regis," on the Bognor Regis website (bognor-regis.org/History/index.html).

390   **cradle…you softly**: "The Illustrious New Chrysler 72," *National Geographic*, October 1927.

392   **the real energy** to **weary nerve cells**: "Kellogg's Shredded Krumbles," *The Delineator*, June 1920.

392   **help yourself to health**: "Help Yourself to Health," in *Boys' Life* (Boy Scouts of America), June 1929.

392   **a staunch ally**: 1920s ad depicted in Michael Pollan, *The Omnivore's Dilemma: The Secrets Behind What You Eat* (New York: Dial Books, 2009).

392   **AND LEAD TO**: 1920s ad quoted in James C. Worton, *Inner Hygiene: Constipation and the Pursuit of Health in Modern Society* (New York: Oxford University Press, 2000).

393   **Sing from daylight**: *Kellogg's Funny Jungleland Moving Pictures* (W.K. Kellogg, 1909).

394   **no woman, idiot**: Nellie L. McClung, *In Times Like These* (Toronto: McLeod and Allen, 1915).

394   **qualified persons**: Section 24 of the British North America Act 1867.

394   **as vivid as a tiger**: Natalie Symmes, "Nellie McClung of the West," *Canada Monthly*, February 1915.

395   **Nice women**: Nellie McClung, *The Stream Runs Fast: My Own Story* (Toronto: Thomas Allen, 1945).

395   **Have we not brains**: "Roblin Refuses Suffrage," *Grain Growers' Guide*, 4 February 1914.

395   **persons in matters**: Nellie McClung, *The Stream Runs Fast*.

395   **the exclusion of women**: *The Canadian Encyclopedia* (2006), s.v. "Persons Case."

397   **two adopted children**: "Death of Mrs. Martha Bedford," *London Free Press*, 31 July 1929.

397   **card of thanks**: "Bedford," *London Free Press*, 2 August 1929.

398   **in the sweet by and by**: Sanford F. Bennett and Joseph P. Webster, "In the Sweet By and By" (Boston: Oliver Ditson, 1868).

398   **pass[ed] through the portals**: John R. Clements, and Edward M. Fuller, "When I Pass Through the Portals," in *Gospel Hymn Book: A Collection of New and Standard Hymns* (New York: Lorenz Publishing, 1903).

400   **good looking** to **I want a new one**: "Skoolnuze," *The Lantern* (Sir Adam Beck Collegiate), 1929.

401   **sit out a dance**: *Lucky Strike Radio Hour*, 17 September 1931, script in the John J. Raskob Papers, Hagley Digital Archive (http://digital.hagley.org/raskob-1385).

402   **there is no thrill**: "Business Students Hear Mr. Massey," *University of Western Ontario Gazette*, 18 December 1930.

404   **mental and nervous casualties**: Chip Martin, "A History of Healing," *London Free Press*, 27 May 2013.

405   **death intervened**: "Fred Stephenson Called by Death," *University of Western Ontario Gazette*, 15 October 1931.

Chapter 17

409   **The parents are English** to **Dear Sir**: Michael Bliss and Linda M. Grayson, *The Wretched of Canada: Letters of R.B. Bennett* (Toronto: University of Toronto Press, 1971).

411   **very kindly and quiet**: "Fred Stephenson Called By Death," *University of Western Ontario Gazette*, 15 October 1931.

412   **vapour of the slum**: Alexander Paterson, *Across the Bridges* (London: Edward Arnold, 1915).

415   **Mr. E. Deverill**: "World of Women," *London Free Press*, 4 September 1934.

415   **Mrs. Frank Price**: "World of Women," *London Free Press*, 22 September 1934.

416   **a wider world**: Guy d'Hardelot and Edward Teschemacher, "Because" (London: Chappell, 1902).

417   **Perhaps it is not generally**: "The Highways of Ontario," on an Ontario Road Map, Department of Public Highways (1930).

418   **Jack Frost**: "Jack Frost Silences Niagara," *Sheffield Independent*, 10 March 1934.